"Literary magazines may have been dubbed 'little magazines' from the start, but there is nothing small about the ambition and scope of this eclectic volume of essays by scholars, writers, and editors that spans 150 years ... [This] book is both a history and a how-to that illuminates the influence, delights, problems, and engaging idiosyncrasies of these important magazines in American literary culture."

—*Publishers Weekly*

"This tastefully produced work celebrates the energetic spirit of those who persevere in chasing—and making—'an object filled with objects' amid a variety of obstacles."

—*ForeWord Reviews*

"In what is both a historical overview and an encyclopedia of literary magazine publication, editor Travis Kurowski's compilation most certainly should be regarded as *the resource* on the subject."

—*Portland Book Review*

"The history of the American literary magazine will not only interest upper-level English students, but all those yearning for a deeper understanding of the American Dream. Travis Kurowski collects historical and contemporary pieces of the literary conversation, from Ezra Pound to T.C. Boyle, and puts a definitive stamp on what exactly the American literary magazine is and where it will go. ... Travis Kurowski's work succeeds in bringing the past, the present, and the future of the literary magazine together in such a manner in which readers and writers alike will remember the purpose of all of this in the first place."

—*The Summerset Review*

PAPER DREAMS

PAPER ★ DREAMS

WRITERS AND EDITORS
on the
AMERICAN
LITERARY MAGAZINE

Compiled and edited by
Travis Kurowski

ISBN-13: 978-0-984-04057-5
ISBN-10: 0-984-04057-9

Page composition by David McNamara
Cover design by Jamie Keenan

First published in the United States by Atticus Books

ATTICUS
BOOKS

Madison, NJ
atticusbooks.net

Distributed by Itasca Books
5120 Cedar Lake Road
Minneapolis, Minnesota 55416
(952) 345-4488 / (800) 901-3480
orders@itascabooks.com

ACKNOWLEDGMENTS

I need to thank Gary Percesepe, Frederick Barthelme, and Rie Fortenberry, without whom this book would not have happened. Thanks also to York College of Pennsylvania for the generous support during the compilation and production of the book. And, of course, thanks to Atticus Books publisher Dan Cafaro for believing in the project and supporting literary magazines. Finally, an unending thanks to my wife, Sarah, and my daughters, Ella and Zoe, who put up with my obsessions.

Permissions

TABLE OF CONTENTS

III. AFTER MODERNISM

IV. PRESENT & FUTURE

DEDICATION

This book is dedicated to the memories of Charles Newman (1938–2006), Ted Solotaroff (1928–2008), Curt Johnson (1928–2008), Joseph F. McCrindle (1923–2008), Ben Sonnenberg (1936–2010), Jeanne Leiby (1964–2011), and Barney Rossett (1922–2012)—people who worked tirelessly and beautifully in the production of literature and literary magazines. Each passed away during the conception and production of this book.

LITERARY MAGAZINES, BY BILLY COLLINS (2010)

I don't know about you
but I go right for the poems

flipping past the stories and the essays

not interested in discovering how much time
someone wasted on
the lost cinema of the Netherlands

not wanting to get roped into a drama—
a couple of characters riding
a slow camel across the desert of a plot.

I want to go in and down.
I want to fly into myself,
a curious bird who wore away its beak
pecking on the door of the women's prison.

And even if the poems are bad,
which they often are,
and they get no farther than the barn out back
with grandfather's overalls on a hook

I can always find an image
to plunge into, a couple of lines
that I can pass through like a wall of air.

This morning on the little dock
at the edge of the breezy lake,
I saw nothing new for an hour or so—

then a redwing blackbird
appeared on a thin reed
a few feet away from where I sat,
hung on sideways, swaying,
then cried out and sped off in the air,

and that, gentle subscribers,
was more than enough for me.

THE PARIS REVIEW

$12.00   161 $16 IN CANADA

OBJECTS FILLED WITH OBJECTS

by Travis Kurowski

Literature is a conversation, claims poet and editor G. C. Waldrep, and so, too, is this book. Paul Bixler chatting with Felix Pollack about the literary magazine after World War II. Rick Moody swapping stories with Laura van den Berg about editors. Abby Ann Arthur Johnson and Gorham Munson disagreeing over which 1920s magazines were most significant. Some of these interactions were deliberate (such as Jayne Marek critiquing Ezra Pound's ideas about modernism), but most of them are a necessary by-product of passionate and intellectual involvement in the same mode of literary production—the American literary magazine—and are made manifest by these texts now sharing space within the covers of this book.

This book is a set of primary and secondary documents spanning the history of the American literary magazine, at the same time both the backbone and the outer rings of American literature. The book began as a special 2008 issue of Frederick Barthelme's *Mississippi Review* about the 100th anniversary of the contemporary literary magazine, that was guest-edited by Gary Percesepe and myself. Our centenary timeline came, in part, from Steve Evans's 2006 article in *The Modern Review*:

> If we take Ford Madox Ford's *The English Review* as a plausible first instance of 'the little magazine' that we've since come to know, then we'll be marking the centenary of this peculiar cultural form in 2008, just the blink of an eye from now in literary time. Much about literary life has altered since 1908. . . But what of the means by which those works were first delivered? the stages onto which those manifestos stormed? the form underlying all those

fine (and thus bitterly insisted upon) distinctions as to policy, aim, and audience? Is the little magazine itself just a vestige of the heroic early days of the modernist project... a convention grown as stale in the digital age as the sonnet had in Williams's?

The year 1908 was, of course, an arbitrary date. Rick, Gary, and I knew that any kind of "lit mag birth year" couldn't be pinned down. It might just as easily have been 1912, with the first issue of Harriet Monroe's *Poetry* magazine, or as far back as 1840, with Emerson's transcendentalist magazine *The Dial*. As with the invention of cinema or the automobile, the literary magazine was not born at any particular time or place, but gradually emerged in fits and starts, thanks to the inventiveness of those working within the field and the demands of literary expression. But we felt it was an important subject, and knew that it had been some time since anyone had examined the history all at once. *TriQuarterly* and Pushcart Press put out a book on the topic in 1978, and *The Missouri Review* did an issue about literary magazines in 1983. But there had been nothing comprehensive since. In 2008, Evans's essay had given us a reason to go ahead with it.

Contributors rallied around the concept, and the magazine basically sold out soon after it was published. But I still felt that there was more to be said. Working on that issue of *MR* demonstrated to me (1) how few comprehensive resources were out there about the literary magazine and (2) how little most of us—myself included—knew about this foundational part of American literary history.

In order to examine the subject of literary magazines, one must face a simple but daunting question: what *is* a literary magazine? They are perhaps easily defined as periodicals focused on publishing literature—a definition that works fine on a broad scale, but falls short when magazines are looked at individually. For example, *The Southern Review* seems to have little in common with the more stylized *Esopus*, any issue of which looks more like an exhibition from Williamsburg's Pierogi Gallery smashed between two paper covers than it does anything from a magazine rack.

The word 'magazine' is a direct descendent of the Arab-French word *magasin*, meaning "store house." This makes not only etymological sense but also common usage sense, as magazines are paper rooms—and, increasingly, electronic rooms—within which writing and images are stored for public consumption. Following this line of thought, literary magazines are store houses of the literary bent, and so differentiating from other magazines largely in content and design (furniture and décor) rather than kind (type of structure). And by literary bent, I mean focusing on *how* the writing is written as much as on *what* the writing is about. This is not to say such things are not a concern at *Sports Illustrated* or *Vogue*, but if they are of a concern there, it is to a much lesser extent.

Literary magazines, unlike most magazines published today, are not general interest magazines, but focused instead towards a particular niche reader market: those readers interested in literary writing and conversations about such writing. Every magazine attracts a community of readers who share certain ideas, even if only about the possibility of exploring it through language. In the case of a political magazine, such communities are perhaps more evident; one only need imagine a community of readers of the liberal magazine *The Nation* standing alongside readers of the conservative *National Review* to get a clear picture of this. But any reading experience is an act of community building, even if the majority of the communities are imagined. I would argue that magazine readers create imagined communities in the same sense Benedict Anderson used the phrase to describe nation building through the dissemination of language via print culture in his book *Imagined Communities*. Here is Anderson's description of early newspapers' influence in the development of national identities:

> We know that particular morning and evening editions
> will overwhelmingly be consumed between this hour and
> that, only on this day, not that . . . The significance of
> this mass ceremony—Hegel observed that newspapers
> serve modern man as a substitute for morning prayers—is
> paradoxical. It is performed in silent privacy, in the lair
> of the skull. Yet each communicant is well aware that the
> ceremony he performs is being replicated simultaneously
> by thousands (or millions) of others of whose existence he
> is confident, yet of whose identity he has not the slightest
> notion.

Literary magazines, though not as homogenized as large circulation newspapers, have this in common with them: each creates its own community of readers. This, I believe, is one of the main reasons modernist literary magazines were so popular. In the midst of such overwhelming societal changes—sociological, industrial, political, and aesthetic—these magazines gave people a tie-in to an imagined community of readers. They fostered a sense of belonging and purpose in addition to the individual literary offering they presented the reader.

And these communities were no less real for their being imagined. Literary communities such as those created by readers of *Poetry* or *The Masses* for—respectively—Imagist or socialist readers were no more fictitious to the reader than Google headquarters is to the average Internet user. Here is an example of the reality of such literary communities in a 1966 remembrance of *The Masses* (1912–1918):

NOVEMBER 2007

POETRY

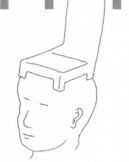

$3.75 USA
$5.00 CAN
£3.00 UK

The absurdity of defining magazines as "big" or "little" in terms of their circulation becomes obvious when we look back to the periodicals of an earlier generation. So-called "big" magazines like the *World's Work* and the *Woman's Home Companion*, great when the century was young, have vanished without a trace or a tear, while their tiny sisters like *Poetry* and the *Little Review* (the latter for many years now extinct) continue to engage our attention. But of all the "little magazines" which still exercise an influence, few compare with the legendary old *Masses*, the Greenwich Village literary and political journal which flourished briefly in the early 1900s. Although its circulation was never large, it was very big indeed in importance and excitement, and it rang bells worth hearing today.

Maybe—and I am speculating here—literary magazines, due to their subject matter and even the smallness of their production, create a somehow more significant and longer lasting community than larger circulation magazines and newspapers, something "big in importance and excitement."

But the communities literary magazines create do not define them. I personally find most useful the definition of *Esopus*'s own founding editor Todd Lippy, who claimed that "[t]he magazine is an object filled with objects"—to which I would then add: the literary magazine is a literary object filled with literary objects. And leave it at that. But that is likely not specific enough for some, and understandably so. Therefore I offer up the following (though I prefer the preceding): A literary magazine is a text object intended to be published at some regularity under the same name and primarily focused on the distribution of literary text, though often also interested in popular culture, politics, and art.

Now if someone could just come up with an agreed upon definition of "literary" we would be all set.

However these magazines are defined, the history of the American literary magazine runs hand-in-hand with the history of American literature. As Ezra Pound wrote in 1930, "The work of writers who have emerged in or via such magazines outweighs in permanent value the work of the writers who have not emerged in this manner. The history of contemporary letters has, to a very manifest extent, been written in such magazines."

Though the literary magazine form reaches at least as far back as Pierre Bayle's *Nouvelles de la République des Lettres* from late seventeenth century France, literary magazines are more of a twentieth century phenomena, serving as a voice for the century's literary movements and nurturing nearly all of the century's most prominent writers. And if current trends in publishing continue, the 21st century will witness further growth of literary magazines, as computers and easy access to the Internet make it easier for amateurs and professionals in the field to more rapidly begin new literary magazines online and off.

In 1978, Michael Anania estimated approximately 1,500 literary magazines were then in existence, up from the six hundred published between the years 1912 and 1946. Three decades later, the numbers have doubled, with (according to Dutrope.com) close to three thousand such magazines operating in 2012. We are living in a literary magazine renaissance, a popular interest in periodically published literary and artistic works such as has not been seen since the modernist literary magazine explosion, if even then.

I was twenty-three years old when I picked up my first literary magazine. The year was 2002. I had recently begun a longstanding habit in college at Southern Oregon University, wandering the second floor of the library alone, touching the books, looking at the titles, every so often picking one up and paging through it. I would spend hours in the afternoon between the shelves of books waiting for something to catch my interest—*A Mathematician's Apology, The Banquet Years, A History of Cosmology.* I did this mostly between classes or after lunch. I had friends, even the occasional girlfriend. And I was busy. Every semester I overloaded my school schedule, built sets for the theater major, and worked about twenty hours a week bartending in town. Nevertheless there I was in the library, for all intents and purposes, wasting my time.

My wife told me she did the same thing in college in Mississippi, and many writers have described similar experiences to me from their own lives. There is to me an almost sensual pleasure to be found in all that text, maybe due to the implied promise that interesting things will be found. There was an electric feeling being around all that language and whenever I make it to bookstores these days, I find that there still is.

One afternoon towards the end of my junior year, I ended up over by the periodicals—a small section in the library over by the inter-library loan desk and flanked by a couple of couches and chairs. I randomly picked up the Spring 2002 issue of *The Paris Review* off the rack. I suppose it wasn't completely random. Craig Wright, my fiction writing teacher, had often mentioned the names of these magazines in class: *Ploughshares, Shenandoah, Mississippi Review.* Yet he had never given us more than their names. So what more did this thing matter to me than, say, *A History of Cosmology*? I opened it and began reading the first story, Jim Shepard's "Climb Aboard the Mighty Flea." In a sense, I never stopped reading it.

The contents of this book begin in the pre-origins of the literary magazine and provide some broad theoretical and historical discussion of what the American literary periodical might be. The following sections offer up perspectives from literary magazine history, eventually working their way up to the present day, and on into speculations about the future of such publications. This is all followed by contemporary writers such as T. C. Boyle and Lucy Ives giving their opinions about the contemporary literary magazine. Finally, the appendix materials in the back offer additional information and resources, such as a detailed timeline of literary magazine history and some information for writers and teachers.

The groundwork for my own ideas about literary magazines came from the very texts and writers that follow. This is, I truly feel, a collection of the best that has been thought and said on the subject. To say more myself would be merely to copy my own teachers. It is better they spoke for themselves.

Note: As much as possible, the following texts were left in their original states regarding any errors, such as with spelling and grammar. For our understanding of the history of the American literary magazine, it is overall the accurate representation of the documents themselves which is of greatest importance.

REASONS FOR CREATING A NEW LITERARY MAGAZINE

by Jill Allyn Rosser (2008)

There probably hasn't been a new one created in the past six-and-a-half days.

You genuinely enjoy asking businesses, institutions, and individuals for money they probably won't give you.

There are serious, good, seriously good writers whose work is being completely ignored, and you are so nuttily optimistic as to believe that literate people are going to read them in your new Yet Another Literary Magazine when they already have piles and unread piles of them preventing easy relocation from, and/or navigation through, their domicile.

You believe even your less-than-literary friends will set aside *Time, People,* and *Self* to read your YALM.

Whole floors in university libraries devoted to computer banks and skyrocketing Google stock during a time of recession have not convinced you that paper texts are slipping into any-day-now desuetude.

It thrills you to think that a friend while traveling in Peru might accidentally leave your YALM on a windy day on a bench very close to a splashing fountain in a plaza, where some bilingual Peruvian will pick up your YALM to protect it from the windborne droplets and recognize the brilliance of one of the writers you have discovered and begin the translation chain that will ultimately lead to that worthy author's Nobel.

You don't believe for a second that no one will see let alone read your YALM unless you procure an impossibly bountiful promotional budget.

You are the sort of person who spends all day on an outdoor ice sculpture when the next day's weather forecast calls for seventy-degree sunshine. You were the one I saw standing rapt before the giant cow sculpted out of butter at the Ohio State Fair. You probably plant flowers each year that the local deer eat before they can bloom.

You know better than anyone else what is good and what isn't good literature.

You love shuffling paper and thinking up new unsuccessful ways to say no without hurting anyone's feelings.

You don't believe that writers will send you their least exciting work on the reasonable assumption that no one will get around to reading this brand-new YALM anyway.

You wouldn't mind losing dear friends whose work you feel you must reject because you don't think it is their "most exciting" work.

You begin many of your sentences with I, and in order to eliminate this locutionary tic you adopt we, meaning you and the assistant editors you will probably steamroll with your smarter opinions.

Your recycling pile just isn't big enough.

There are mediocre writers whose work is being hyper-praised, and you want to crowd them out with pages and pages of work by very good writers.

You believe that the cream rises to the top, that the corrupt power of networking is hogwash, or if it isn't that you can reverse or undermine it. You believe that people will not really expect you to return "favors" if they have published your work in the past.

You want to solicit Great Writer X at a time when GWX is in a forlorn slump of irrelevancy and hasn't written a thing in months. Whose writing then mysteriously starts up again, like the Tin Man getting a squirt of oil, only this would be a Tin Man with a heart and the new writing would be gloriously unrusty and powerful and poignant and you would be the first mortal to read it.

Being the youngest sibling, you have always liked the idea of being called a "Senior" or "In-Chief" or "Executive" something-or-other. If you have a Ph.D. in literature you probably use "Dr." as your title when buying air tickets online.

You remember a moment of euphoria when, leafing through some little outdated YALM picked up for a quarter at a book sale, you found a poem that was absolutely magnificent by someone who was so unknown his own brother never heard of him.

You remember that moment and some of the many moments of disappointed leafing, too.

You want to give someone, once and for all, the experience of leafing that ceases to be leafing by the second page, that becomes stop-what-you're-doing absorption all the way through, even if it means not preparing for class on the day you're being evaluated for tenure.

You want to be Sylvia Beach to James Joyce, Ezra Pound to T. S. Eliot, John Wayne's stuntman, Garbo's make-up artist, the bread unacknowledged binding the BLT.

You love messing with manila folders, paper clips and rubber bands. You love piling work on people who are incredibly busy and who are not being paid for what you must ask them to do. You secretly adore pointing out basic errors to writers who should know better and who will dislike you more for each reminder and think of you thereafter as a grammatical prig.

You want to be the one who knows, the one who always knew and will always know, and you want everyone finally to know it.

You will allow your arrogance as an editor to exceed your arrogance as a writer, because your efforts in the former capacity are just about as altruistic as it gets—more purely motivated than translation, than gardening, than parenting.

You want to hand some writer that heart-cartwheel moment of a first acceptance. Ever. And maybe of a second and third.

Unless that writer starts to overuse phrases like "heart-cartwheel."

I. ORIGINS

The exact origins of the American literary magazine—like that of nearly all the arts—cannot be pinned down, but they begin in such events as early Roman newspapers and the Gutenberg printing press. But the literary periodical itself is largely agreed to have an origin in the French periodical *Nouvelles de la république des lettres*, quickly followed by similar publications interested in literature on the European continent (many in Germany), and only later in America. These early publications, though focused on literature as subject, were not focused on the publishing of literature itself. Regarding English-language periodicals, the origin point of periodicals publishing literature primarily begin with the Pre-Raphaelite publication, *The Germ* (1850). In America, its origins can be found in Ralph Waldo Emerson's *The Dial*, though magazines had been in the country since before its birth.

Pages from *Nouvelles de la République des Lettres*

by Pierre Bayle (1687)

The following are facsimile reproductions of the first pages from the May 1687 issue of the French literary periodical, *Nouvelles de la République des Lettres* (1684–1718), edited and largely written by Pierre Bayle—an early model for the contemporary literary magazine. In 1978, historian and former *Southern Review* editor Lewis Simpson wrote of *Nouvelles* and literary magazines in general:

> Today when we pick up, say, a forty-five-year-old number of an American literary quarterly (often a hybrid form, a mingling of the critical quarterly and the general literary magazine, containing not only essays and reviews, but stories and poems), we may find in it a poem, a story, or an essay that we have long regarded as speaking with its own luminous autonomy. We are slightly shocked to see it in a magazine. Marked by periodicity, it seems to be the aspect of mortality . . . Nothing is so old as yesterday's news, and that includes the literary news. Many of us have probably not heard of the journal or the editor, but the archetypal literary periodical is Pierre Bayle's *Nouvelles de la République des Lettres.*

NOUVELLES
DE LA
REPUBLIQUE
DES
LETTRES.
Mois de Mai 1687.

A AMSTERDAM,
Chez HENRY DESBORDES, dans
le Kalver-Straat, prés le Dam.

M. DC. LXXXVII.
Avec Privilége des Etats de Holl. & Weftf.

Avis au Lecteur.

L'avis qu'on a donné, que le Sieur B. ne fait ni ne lit les Nouvelles de la République des Lettres, doit être censé subsister pendant qu'on n'avertira pas du contraire.

NOUVELLES
DE LA
REPUBLIQUE
DES LETTRES.

Mois de Mai 1687.

ARTICLE I.

*Lettre de Monsieur van Dale à un de ses
amis, au sujet du livre des Oracles des
Payens, composé par l'Auteur des Dialogues des Morts.*

MONSIEUR,

J'Ai lû, avec bien du plaisir l'His-
toire des Oracles faite par un Auteur François, où je suis copié fi-
délement. J'approuve la liberté qu'il
s'est donnée, de tourner ce que j'a-
vois avancé dans mes deux dissertations sur ce sujet, au génie de sa Nation.

Celui de nos peuples est un peu dif-
X   ferent :

To Popularise Literature in the States: An Excerpt from *The Magazine in America*

by Algernon de Vivier Tassin (1916)

In January, 1741, three days apart and in the small city of Philadelphia, were published the first two magazines of this country. These facts themselves make one suspect cut-throat work. It is perhaps significant that the stormy and colourful career of the magazine in America began with a royal row.

One was published by Andrew Bradford, the other by Benjamin Franklin. Their appearance had been preceded by the usual announcements in the newspapers and by a very unusual altercation. For Franklin claimed that the idea and the plans of the magazine had been stolen from him. [John] Webbe, who had announced Bradford's, admitted that Franklin had told him of the project but said this did not restrain him from publishing one himself without Mr. Franklin's leave. During the quarrel both Franklin and Bradford accused each other of using their position of Post Master to foster their private ends. Only three numbers appeared of Bradford's magazine, the *American or a Monthly View*; and only six numbers of Franklin's, the *General Magazine or Historical Chronicle*. Franklin in his first number ridiculed his competitor's; but he seems not to have been proud of his own, as no mention of it occurs in his autobiography.

Between this and the end of the century there were at least forty-five magazines started. Besides those addressed to a more general audience, they included a musical magazine, a military, a German religious, and a children's magazine. Thus, the sparsely settled new States were decidedly over-exploited. When in 1787, Mathew Carey requested advice about founding the *American Museum* Jeremy Belknap wrote him from Boston: "Several attempts have been made within my memory both here and at the Southward to establish such a repository of literature, but after a year or two they have uniformly failed. To what other causes the failure may be ascribed I will not say, but this appears to me to be one, viz: the too frequent publication of them. We are fond of imitating our European Brethren in their monthly productions without considering the difference between our Circumstances and theirs. Such a country as this is not yet arrived at such a pass of improvement to keep up one or two monthly vehicles of importance." However barren were some departments of literature in the early days, then, magazines indicated at the outset their eternal disposition to multiply faster than the traffic will stand.

From a very early date editors had been keenly conscious of the need for variety. *The New England Magazine*, 1758, price eight pence a number of sixty pages, gave in an advertisement this description of its contents:

CONTAINING AND TO CONTAIN:

Old-fashioned writings and Select Essays,
Queer Notions, Useful Hints, Extracts from Plays;
Relations Wonderful and Psalm and Song,
Good Sense, Wit, Humour, Morals, all ding dong;
Poems and Speeches, Politicks, and News,
What Some will like and other Some refuse;
Births, Deaths, and Dreams, and Apparitions, Too;
With some Thing suited to each different Geu (gout?)
To Humour Him, and Her, and Me, and You.

The editor of the *Massachusetts Magazine* was constantly adding new departments, but insisted that all its contributions should be of a popular nature. "It has been hinted by some well-wishers that deeper researches into the arcana of science, more especially the abstruser parts of philosophy and the mathematics, would give the magazine a celebrity with the learned. In reply we beg leave to remark that the British *Universal Magazine* was materially injured by an adherence to this plan; and America presents a more recent instance of a magazine supported by a host of scholars which literally sunk beneath the impending weight of technical terms and the pressure of amplified definitions." If they had not hitherto consulted the desires of the fair sex sufficiently or gratified the delicacy of their taste, they trusted to compensate for their negligence in the future; and they hoped at the same time that the scientifick sons of Providence and the accomplished seniors of Yale would deposit their respective offerings at the shrine of Fame; and it could be seen that the proceedings of Congress and the Commonwealth had been detailed with all the amplitude which prescribed limits would allow. The *Nightingale* was establishing a department of Criticism which would give candid and impartial accounts of all American publications. "The food which the editors served up has been found to be disagreeable to some fastidious palates and inadequate to supply the cravings of some insatiable stomachs. Yet they do not conceive their dishes to be filled with the mere whipt-syllabub of learning and the flummery of the muses. The most hungry might have found a solid beef stake of science to feast upon, and they are sure the pepper of criticism and satire have been given in abundance sufficient to prevent a nausea. Good humour has always smiled at their table, and variety has garnished the viands." Indeed, when one considers the exceedingly heavy fare offered almost without exception by the books and pamphlets of the day, the magazines should have afforded a delightful treat. Political and religious controversies were sedulously avoided by most. All of them had their regular light essayists of the Bickerstaff lineage — the Gleaner, the Drone, the Babbler, the Trifler, the Scribbler, Philobiblicus. The poetry sometimes constituted a fourth or a sixth of the issue, and with a recklessness which would turn the modern editor pale was collected in a department at the end of each number. The chief function of poetry as a filler-up of chinks left between more solid prose had not yet evolved. Every magazine had its Pegasus, its Cabinet of Apollo, its Seat of the Muses, its Parnassiad; even the most prosaic had its Poetical Essays or its Poetical Provision. Nor was the poetry all of the lofty variety of "An Elegant Ode on the Mechanism of Man"; there were lines "To a Lady on Striking a Fly with Her Fan," or to "The Fly On Being Let into a Lady's Chamber"; and there was much narrative verse, serious or jocose. Even the *Boston Magazine*, 1784, six of the twelve original members of which became the parents of the Massachusetts Historical Society by virtue of their design to publish a Gazeteer of the State giving a sketch of every town in the commonwealth, announced that though it would rather be too grave than too sprightly and though it hoped it would never be trifling or superficial or ludicrous, it would apply itself to the publication of everything that is curious and entertaining.

All the editors, too, were alive to the desirableness of embellishing their magazines with "elegant copperplates." A frequent announcement runs, "As soon as a number of Subscribers equal to the expence of this magazine are procured, every number shall then be ornamented with some pleasing representation." These were very expensive, and in days when there were very few advertisements (indeed, almost none at all in the monthlies, except on the cover pages) they were a decided consideration. Yet at a time when into the average household never entered a picture of any sort, they must have given great delight. The first volume of the *Boston Magazine* contained twenty-seven illustrations; its plan was two engravings and a piece of music to each number. The *Massachusetts Magazine* tried for a time the experiment of furnishing eight additional pages of letter press in lieu of copper plate engravings, "but the admirers of this polite art earnestly called for their reassumption." Thus in addition to popularising literature, the early magazines were popularising art also.

The prospectus of the *New York Instructor*, 1755, might well have served for most.

> The design of this paper is to communicate to the Publick *Select Pieces* on the *Social Duties*, and such historical or Speculative *Remarks* as may be thought useful to be collected from the best English writers; which if read either in a Morning at *Tea*, or after *Dinner* by the Younger Sort, cannot fail of leaving a good effect upon the mind, as well as improving them in their Reading and Morals. If any *Getlemen of Taste* will please to recommend any particular *Pieces*, all due Regard shall be paid to them in their Turn. And these collected into One or more *Volumes* will be worth preserving, especially to those who cannot readily come at the Originals. Occasional *News* will sometimes be added likewise. N.B. No *Controversy* of any kind will have Admittance. To be continued Weekly (if suitable Encouragement). Price, Two Coppers. Whoever pleases to preserve these Papers entire and will return them to the *Printer* at the end of the year shall have a Copper a Piece for each.

Alas for the thrifty who saved their papers! It is thought that only ten numbers were published.

Almost as frustrated as their appeal for subscriptions was their demand for original pieces. The second volume of the *Massachusetts Magazine* laments the want of more originality. "Indulge us to observe that men of learning in this country are not always blest with leisure. Yet the *Massachusetts Magazine* can compare in point of originality with its American brethren and transatlantic cousins. There is no work of this kind in any quarter of the globe which is totally original. A correspondence has been established in Europe, and an agreeable interchange of literary good offices promises to be a happy result." The second volume of the *Boston Magazine* confesses that it began with high hopes of originality, the first volume indeed having a third of its pieces original. But the second volume has been compelled to publish many extracts, which will, however, increase learning, improve the morals, and mend the heart. The editor is particularly obliged to the sons of Harvard for their productions and he shall always be happy to have it in his power to announce to the public the effusions of their pens. *The American Moral and Sentimental*, New York, 1797, printed for the editor next door to the Tea-Water pump, was a type of a great many magazines which did not essay the struggle for originality. This publication, as perhaps might be gathered from its name, reeks with edification. The *Philadelphia Magazine and Review*, 1799, thought that the desire for originality had wrecked many ventures. "We are led to believe that they failed for some other cause than the want of discernment or liberality in those to whom the editor looked for support. For one publication of ours we receive at least five hundred from Great Britain . . . yet we shall always be glad to print any original verse or prose or agreeable talk." Mathew Carey designed the *American Museum* in 1787 to fill a new niche. "Having long observed in the various papers printed on this continent a vast number of excellent and invaluable productions, I have frequently regretted that the perishable nature of the vehicles -which contained them entailed oblivion on them after a very confined period of usefulness and circulation. The respectable character who now fills the presidential chair of this commonwealth having expressed the same sentiment a few months since, I conceived that a publication designed to preserve the most valuable could not fail to be highly useful and consequently among an enlightened people to meet with encouragement." He contemplated also a re-publication of many of the best pamphlets prior to and during the war, with occasional selections from European prints. But even this lofty design had room for pieces of a more popular kind, though, with the exception of some of the verse, none were for entertainment merely. In the announcement for volume two he said: "So far was public opinion against it and so very confined were the expectations formed of a work which professed to be void of originality and to be in some measure only a handmaiden to the newspapers, that at the appearance of the first number there were not twenty subscribers."

The editors all felt that their mission was to educate the people. "M" is writing to a magazine and accounts for the defective literature of his native country by the scarcity of books.

> There is hardly a library in the United States, public or private, which would enable a man to be thoroughly learned in any one language. The public library of Philadelphia is a respectable one for its age and will probably in time exhibit a very large collection. The same may be said of the library belonging to the University of Cambridge in Massachusetts. If I mistake not, however, they are both very defective, and the latter particularly so, in modern publications. Nor are the deficiencies of our public libraries by any means supplied by private collections, or by the enterprise and literary character of booksellers. There is hardly a greater desideratum in the United States than a bookseller who to a large capital in business would unite a taste for literature, a zeal to promote it, and a disposition to make the public as early as possible acquainted with every new publication of value that is made either in Europe or America. As it is, we seldom see a European publication here, unless it be of a peculiarly popular cast or unless it

be sent for by a gentleman who has heard of its character. Thus you see, Mr. Editor, I view everything of this kind with cordial satisfaction and cannot help flattering myself that the establishment of your magazine will materially subserve the interest of letters and science in America.

The tenor of another letter is the same.

It is with pleasure we observe the numerous literary institutions in these States, happily calculated to disseminate a knowledge of the Arts and Sciences. But very few of our Youth can be educated in these seminaries, and though good policy may forbid that any considerable number of them should receive a collegiate education, it may, notwithstanding, be of essential service to the community that our young men in general who shall devote themselves to commerce and to mechanical and agricultural employment should possess considerable degrees of literature. A deficiency of learning hath often been very sensibly regretted by many worthy characters in these States when elevated to public and important offices; and frequently ignorance hath not only exposed them to ridicule but been injurious to the interests of the public. We mention particularly a circumstance that exposed a very popular patriot in London a few years past, to contempt and occasioned him to become a subject of ridicule in the public papers of the metropolis. In an oration he made at Guildhall, instead of speaking in the superlative degree, which he wished to have done, through ignorance he made use of the double comparative — *more better.*

This last appeared in the *Christian's, Scholar's and Farmer's Magazine,* published By a Number of Gentlemen in Elizabethtown, New Jersey. The title is a delightful illustration of that breadth of aim which most of our early magazines exhibited. It was the design of this performance to promote religion, to diffuse knowledge, and to aid the Husbandman in his very necessary and important toil. The full title of the *Massachusetts Magazine* was Monthly Museum of Knowledge and Rational Entertainment — Containing Poetry, Musick, Biography, History, Physics, Geography, Morality, Criticism, Philosophy, Mathematicks, Agriculture, Architecture, Chemistry, Novels, Tales, Romances, Translations, News, Marriages and Deaths, Meteorological Observations, etc., etc. But the desire to cover as wide a ground and to give as much as possible for the money is perhaps illustrated best by Mathew Carey's announcement that he had procured a set of smaller types (his type, like that of all the magazines, was already maddeningly minute) better calculated for the purpose of his magazine; as they would comprise one-third more matter than the former in the same number of pages!

"In America," ran the announcement of the *Philadelphia Monthly Magazine*, "periodical publications may properly be termed the literature of the people. The state of manufactures, agriculture, arts may as yet be deemed in their infancy, and in them new discoveries and improvements are daily making. We solicit the aid of our readers that these may become known. Medical Facts and observations. Law Cases and Decisions, together with the miscellaneous material which usually adorns a magazine we intend to publish. Magazine poetry has usually been considered as synonymous with the most trivial and imperfect attempts at verse-writing [in 1798!], but no piece will be admitted which cannot lay claim to true genius and poetic merit. Review of new publications will proceed generally by extracts."

It is possible that each new editor, even with before him examples of constant failure, hoped to make some money (if he did, he spent it at once on enlargement), and certainly he expected to pay expenses. But chiefly he thought of himself as a torch-bearer. To popularise literature in the States, where few books of literature were read and almost none were published; to disseminate news of improved ways of doing things among people who would never hear of them otherwise — this was their high calling. Making all allowance for their stately and diplomatic periods, it animates every line of their announcements.

Influence, Commerce, and the Little Magazine

by Eric Staley (1983)

Toward the end of the nineteenth century two very different and unrelated phenomena were occurring which gave birth to the generations of literary magazines that we have come to know today. The first phenomenon was quite literary. Simply put, the country had finally come to accept and identify its American authors, to recognize an American voice in letters, and to develop a taste for it. The short story came into its own as a "form," not simply as a tale that had been shortened for the magazine, but as an independent art form with its own internal rules and life. Consequently, practitioners such as Bret Harte, Mark Twain, Ambrose Bierce, and, later, Stephen Crane had an opportunity to satisfy a literary appetite left wanting by the deaths of poets such as Whittier, Lowell, Holmes, and Whitman, who had already helped establish an American poetry by the early 1890s. Earlier on, good writing, the creative essay, *belles lettres*, had been the desirable end of a serious magazine editor's search for contents, and by the 1860s the profession of magazinist was generally recognized as a possible, though in most cases meager, living.

The second phenomenon was anything but literary. The major east coast businesses and the advertising agencies that represented them began in the late 1870s and 1880s to alter their marketing strategies from local to national. The principal early vehicle for advertising had been the newspaper; it now became as much the general magazines which, taken as a whole, were reaching millions of readers all over the country each month. Greater populations, completion of westward expansion, a generally higher level of literacy, increased leisure time, all contributed to the interest and popularity of magazines, swelling their individual circulations to 300,000 or considerably better in many cases, and providing a new and expanding market for products and services. It did not take Edison's new light bulb long to shine over the advertiser's head and signify a new marketing strategy and the commercialization of American magazines. The first phenomenon had to do with taste and cultural identity and a new popularity for literature; the second provided large amounts of money to build magazine industries for those magazines with the broadest appeal and largest circulations.

The study of American magazine history dates from 1741 when Benjamin Franklin and Andrew Bradford published the first real magazines in this country. They were called, respectively, *General Magazine* and *American Magazine*, and they appeared three days apart—Bradford's first, much to Franklin's chagrin. All of the early general magazines carried some literature—usually pirated British works—while specializing in Addisonian essays about American politics, social customs, and national goals.

Magazines oriented toward literature arrived by the early 1800s, when *Salmagundi* came in on the tide and, like many others to follow, rode the crest for a short while, had its brilliant moment, and then became part of literary history. In this period of less than half a century there came to be more editors than poets and more magazines than the imagination could fathom. Monthlies and quarterlies broke upon the literary shores of America and returned to the sea of words only to be replaced by others. Dozens of magazines surfaced yearly, and a dozen more went under.

Salmagundi; or the Whim-Whams and Opinions of Launcelot Langstaff, Esq. was established by its "upstart" editors, William and Washington Irving and James Kirk Paulding in 1807. It was 1815 for the *North American Review*, 1819 for *Red Book*, 1824 for *Atlantic Magazine*, 1828 for the *Southern Review*, and 1840 for *The Dial*—all of which had little to do with the magazines of the twentieth century bearing the same names, save their shared interest in the literature of their times and an editorial dedication that sometimes defied reason. Of these magazines, only *Southern Review* and *North American Review* show a sense of series, of continuation, over both centuries. That their magazines' names had already been used may not even have been known to the founders of some of the later versions. In the case of *Salmagundi*, for instance, both Robert Boyers of the recent version and the Irving brothers of the original selected the same title, though the Irvings worked in the comic and satiric tradition while Boyers was attracted to a more serious cultural/political persuasion. What was important to both, however, was that salmagundi referred to a salad or stew, and that suggested to the Irvings and Boyers a "miscellaneous phenomenon," a metaphor that served them both well.

Salmagundi. Such could be the generic label, perhaps of most literary magazines, at least the ones we have come to call eclectic in the current sense. All manner of things from political opinion, to literary criticism, to original writing in all genres, spiced with cultural diatribe, aesthetic polemics, and editors' bile have found their way into this stew which cooks in thousands of basements and universities throughout the country. The word "magazine" derives from the Arab-French *magasin*, meaning store-house. Yet all magazines cannot be called that. Throughout their history synonyms have been popular in titles such as miscellany, museum, review; or, nearly, lyceum, album, or medley—names found in the scratch of the editor's head to suggest contents for all manner of tastes, from all manner of places.

On every magazine editor's wall should hang a plaque, perhaps hand-set from the California Job Case in Goudy Old Style, run on a Chandler-Price letterpress, and printed on Cambric Laid, bearing this verse from an 1828 issue of the *Cincinnati Literary Gazette*:

> This is the Age of Magazines—
>   Even skeptics must confess it:
> Where is the town of much renown
>   That has not one to bless it?
>
> *Museums, Mirrors, Monthlies*—strike
>   Our view in crowds and dozens:
> And so much do they look alike
>   We see they all are cousins.
> Their phizzes seem so thin and wan,
>   So hopeless their conditions
> They all must go to shades below
>   In spite of their physicians.

When I teach American magazine history as a course for English and journalism majors, an interesting response to literary magazines is evident. Although we spend two weeks on literary magazines and the class has a lot of hands-on experience with them from the many examples I bring to class, most of the students do poorly on parts of the examinations that test their knowledge of these magazines. Earlier in the semester they have handled and studied *New Yorker*, *Esquire*, the *New Republic*, *Smart Set*, the early *Vanity Fair*, and a host of other "slick," polished, high circulation and high profile magazines that carry excellent writing in many forms. These have made their impression, and although the time spent on literary magazines is an intense unit, the students seem prone to relegate them to a lesser degree of importance; they seem less likely to remember that the *Little Review* was the first to publish *Ulysses* than that E. Simms Campbell, a Harlem cartoonist, developed the character Esky as the symbol of identity for the early *Esquire*. It is not only the physical appearance of the slicks, but also the selection of contents and the editorial catholicity of taste that is behind this attraction. It is a catholicity usually not found in literary magazines.

Not that literary magazines *should* have such a broad range of contents.

All magazine editors seek influence and healthy circulations, but the best the literary magazine can hope to achieve is influence *out of proportion* to circulation. This is achieved in a number of ways. Magazines like *American Poetry Review*, *Poetry*, and *Field* reach this goal by being extremely selective in their type of contents—in this case, poetry, and prose about poetry—while *Georgia Review*, *Antaeus*, and *Ploughshares*, for instance, carry an array of *belles lettres* which display an identifiable and even idiosyncratic editorial policy. Their circulations range from about 1,500 to 26,000 (according to the *International Directory of Little Magazines and Small Presses*), but they definitely tend toward the lower of the two figures with an average circulation of perhaps 3,000. Yet their titles are as close to household names as we will find among literary magazines, and they are recognized immediately by everyone in the literary community, a population in excess of 26,000. Their actual range of influence may well be several factors beyond their number of paying readers. The price of influence without high circulation is expensive, however, and may threaten a magazine's existence.

In 1788 Noah Webster wrote in his *American Magazine*, "The expectation of failure is connected with the very name of magazine." Editors inherit from their predecessors the constant awareness of potential collapse. Magazines are subject to the tastes of their time, and their longevity is often determined by how quickly they can adjust to changes in taste or how readily they can abandon a formula that is not saleable to the degree necessary for survival. Most modern literary magazines, for example, proudly refuse to adjust to one well demonstrated marketing fact—that literature alone is not appealing to broad audiences. Insofar as the market goes, literary concerns are the most dangerous of the many possibilities. *The Atlantic* learned this lesson in the 1890s when its circulation dropped from over 40,000 to about 7,000 under the "literary" editorship of Horace Elisha Scudder. When Walter Hines Page took over in 1898 he changed the course of the magazine in one year by re-introducing social and political commentary and controversy, a policy that continued under his successor, Bliss Perry. It was not until Ellery Sedgwick bought the magazine in 1909—its circulation up to 15,000 but still limping—that the new formula was really applied successfully. Sedgwick's formula—"to innoculate the few who influence the many"—has since that time stood the magazine in good stead.

Literature as a flavoring in a magazine's stew has always been like a popular exotic spice—a little has enhanced the flavor; a lot has made its consumers few. The small and independent literary magazines and the university reviews which specialize in the publication of fine literature usually operate in more red ink than all the black they print. The independents are often subsidized by the salaries of owners/editors earned at other work; the universities frequently, but not always, absorb the deficits of their magazine's budget year. An end to this support is predictable, even in the best of times, and a magazine may last two to ten years, sometimes longer, before demise for most is inevitable. The long-term survivors almost always owe their survival to trustees, together with substantial subscription bases and sound reputations, or, very occasionally, to a well planned combination of subscriptions, market sales, and advertising. Clearly, what is most important and what keeps literary magazines struggling along and reproducing is not the economics of the venture, but the service they perform for literature and for the small, but important, audience they reach.

It is the nature of this audience that makes the difference. The literary magazines, the opinion magazines, and those of culture and the arts are read by people who themselves exert influence on what the whole population will have available to read, the direction in which government and political/social thought will evolve, and the degree to which our history will be preserved. Literary editors are sometimes fond of identifying their contents and their audiences as mainstream, but this is simply not the case. Mainstream audiences read *Reader's Digest* and watch television, and are more likely to have heard of Jacqueline Susann and Harold Robbins than Ann Beattie or Raymond Carver.

It is a literary editor's mistake to offer a bland assortment of contents in an attempt to appeal to the many—a mistake based on a misunderstanding of audience and mission. A literary magazine must not be reluctant, or fearful, to take risks, to *depart* from the mainstream. Without that willingness, no influence is acquired, and few subscriptions are generated.

The single element of success for all magazines, whether they last three years or three hundred, has always been a clear and distinguishable editorial policy. Regardless of the nature of their contents, magazines must not only identify their audiences and shape policy accordingly, they must also act with a visionary understanding of their own importance to present and future readerships and, in so doing, help to shape the very audience they wish to reach. The original *Salmagundi* was of a type, yet distinct. George Graham made a success of *Graham's Magazine* (1840–1860) by blending the proper number of editorials with excellent illustrations and the best literary writers around, including Bryant, Cooper, Longfellow, Lowell and Holmes. Graham was a public relations man with an ability to create a magazine that would appeal to a large number of people; he also knew his own limitations and chose E. A. Poe as literary editor for the early years and gave him decisive powers on literary contents. Most importantly, however, he was one of the first magazine publishers to pay his writers handsomely, and he had the acuteness to decide, when *Godey's Lady's Book* cut out new territory for women readers, that his magazine should follow. Thus, *Graham's*, along with *Godey's*, was able to establish an unprecedented circulation of at least 40,000 by the beginning of the Civil War.

Large circulation is hardly the only register of lasting importance, however. The same sense of editorial policy and demand for the finest contents governed the operations of the first *Dial* (1840–44). Under the guiding hands of Margaret Fuller for half its short life and Ralph Waldo Emerson for the other half, in four years a publication was created which stands today as the most studied of all American literary magazines. Yet, during its own time it never achieved a circulation above 300 and was a joke to the editors of other magazines. However, its authors were members of the Transcendental Club, and the editorial policy this group gave to the magazine was singular and of historic moment.

Other success stories can be found among the humor or comic magazines. Although their lives were never long, nor their circulations large, they identified an element in American letters that would later come to full blossom in the writings of Samuel Clemens. Such early ventures as *Salmagundi* (1807–08) and *Judy* (1846–47, an American version of *Punch*) led to later and longer lasting efforts in the 1860s and 70s with magazines like *Mrs Grundy*, *Punchinello*, *Keepapitchinin*, and *Puck*, when American humorous writing reached a level of popular commerce. The editors of all these magazines shared a common interest in levity and satire, sought the best writers in this genre, and successfully achieved audiences during their own time and an important niche in magazine history. The first *Vanity Fair* (1859–63) was to some extent a humor magazine, and the contemporary *National Lampoon* is a classic in the genre.

Of course, there are other factors that make success a little easier, and money is chief among them. In 1741 when Andrew Bradford began his *American Magazine*, and Ben Franklin its only rival *General Magazine*, it did not cost much to publish and circulate a magazine, especially for men who both were printers and Postmasters. To them, the activity was something of a luxury hobby. These first American magazines were circulated locally (Philadelphia) and reached the couple of hundred people the two men knew, spreading to a few hundred more by word of mouth. Even later, in the early nineteenth century, circulations of a couple of thousand—certainly less than 10,000—were considered very good and could be achieved by family and friends selling subscriptions door-to-door and establishing "home clubs" for groups of readers who could buy the magazine at discount subscription prices. But when Graham and Louis Godey came along with the money to risk at a time when the country was expanding and there were mail routes to reach beyond the local, the economics of magazine publishing changed. The best of authors, the most beautifully engraved illustrations, quality paper, marketing, contents to appeal to many—all cost money, but they also bought the highest circulations up to the Civil War. From this point on, magazines that wanted to compete with the likes of *Graham's* and *Godey's* had to be born with silver fonts in their presses.

It was start-up money alone that got *Graham's*, *Godey's*, *Scribner's*, *Atlantic*, and the various Harper brothers' magazines under way, certainly not advertising dollars, which at this time were negligible. Advertising has been around since the first magazines; Franklin's *General Magazine* carried an ad in 1741 in the form of a printed notice for a ferry traveling from Annapolis to Williamsburg. It was not until the later 1880s and the early 1890s, however, that advertising truly became an important ingredient to a magazine's commercial success.

Harper's, *Atlantic*, and *The Nation* all resisted advertisements beyond their own publications and concerns at the end of the nineteenth century, but eventually they yielded, to varying extents, and survival became more and more dependent on their ability to attract advertising revenue to pay the production costs for 40,000 to 500,000 copies of their magazines. The problem was compounded when many of the highest circulation magazines—*Ladies' Home Journal*, *Saturday Evening Post*, *Collier's*, and *Munsey's*, for example—dropped their per-copy charge to five or ten cents from more than twice that. At the turn of the century, the advertising revenue of *Ladies' Home Journal* led the field, bringing in between $500,000 and $750,000 a year, clearly enabling the magazine to recover its production costs through advertising revenue. The magazine could have been given away and, at a nickel a copy, almost was. The other magazines were forced to drop their per-copy charge in order to compete, and they began to accept more advertising in order to stay profitable. To this day, only *Playboy* has always made a profit on both its advertising and copy-sales revenues.

Advertising became so essential that publishers were tempted to lie about their circulations, and the subject was a touchy one. George Rowell, one of the first heads of an advertising agency, was once chased out of Fletcher Harper's office for merely requesting circulation figures for *Harper's* advertisers, and Rowell lost a $20,000 account for asking. It was not until 1914 that the Audit Bureau of Circulations (known as the ABC in the trade) was founded to legitimize and require publishers' circulation reports. But in spite of the importance it has come to have, advertising comes only after there is money and circulation to attract it. The money that was made before national magazine advertising was possible was made from subscribers, pure and simple.

Today when a major magazine is begun that intends to serve a large audience—take, for example, *Vanity Fair*—publishers talk about millions of dollars start-up funds. These are dollars out front to support the magazine's first year at a minimum, and they are risked. Down the line, another $100,000 will be spent here and there on subscription drives, demographic studies, format experiments, and whatever is necessary to make the magazine more appealing to more people. Advertising is a given today if a high circulation magazine wants to survive, and it must be sold in advance on the basis of "dummy" issues and market studies that accurately predict circulation figures. The ads in the first issue of *Vanity Fair* were lavish, full color, multi-page affairs in some cases, that clearly offset production costs. Advertising played a role in the beginning budget of *Vanity Fair*, but not in the beginning budgets of magazines a hundred years ago. And the more literary magazines tended to continue doing without national marketing strategies the longest.

Before national magazine advertising became so important to the economics of publishing, the distinctions between literary magazines and general magazines were less evident. *Southern Literary Messenger*, for instance, was a literary magazine (as its name implied) as well as a general interest magazine. Even *Godey's* and *Graham's*, which were clearly aimed at popular audiences, carried the literary work of the same best writers of their time as the more class-conscious and self-styled literary magazines such as *Harper's* and the *Atlantic*. That *Godey's* and *Graham's* also carried popular sentimental romances and adventure stories not to be found in many other literary magazines, only broadened their audience and caused more than a little jealousy. After national advertising began, jealousy had to be forgotten, some conforming had to take place, and advertising had to be courted. Or, one could become a literary magazine in the twentieth-century sense and search for support of another kind—from an institution, from the wealthy, from a group of trustees, or out of one's own pocket. Enter the modern age with which we are familiar.

It is quite conceivable to me that a literary magazine like *Georgia Review*, for instance, could become more commercial if it chose to. The range of its contents approximate those of, say, the *Atlantic*, and certainly the quality of writing in its pages and its reputation as a quality magazine could rival any of the slicker and more commercial magazines. *The Georgia Review* and others like it are, however, within a tradition that historically shuns such commercialization, partly as a response to audience demand and partly because of an inability of early literary magazines to attract the advertising necessary for commercialization. Today, the latter factor is more a habit of mind than a fact. Advertising for other publications, for presses, writing programs, writing conferences, editorial services, word-processing equipment, and for a whole range of other products and services now available commercially to the writing community and backed by budgets that do, in fact, itemize for advertising—such opportunities could be drawn upon more systematically to commercialize more the major literary magazines. But the literary magazine's sense of identity and historical inheritance rules against this choice, at least for now.

Unfortunately, along with the literary editor's decision not to become commercial by accepting and attracting product advertising, came the germ of a predilection against self-advertising as well. Distrust of marketing in general has become endemic among literary publishers today, and all too many editors are content to reach small coterie audiences rather than to expand their sphere of influence. The best of our contemporary literary magazines, especially those with a broad base of creative contents and *belles lettres*, if given $10,000 purely for marketing and competent publicists to spend it, should be able to raise their circulations by several thousand in a year. In most cases, the funds for marketing are not there. However, so very little literary magazine marketing is apparent, even within the limitations of small budgets, that if significant marketing funds were made available it is not clear that editors would choose or know how to apply those funds. Instead of a publishing and editing environment in which literary magazines can preserve the integrity and pride their twentieth-century predecessors began with, we have unimaginative editing and marketing that does not dare to be successful. Existing outside the competitive marketplace has its advantages for literature, but it also can needlessly limit the circulation literature can expect.

If the awareness of potential magazine failure was a reality that lent a certain *élan* to the magazine of a hundred years ago, especially to literary magazines like the *Dial*, it has in this century become a more damaging reality that is often embraced as a cult of failure that is a self-fulfilling prophecy. Noah Webster strove against such an attitude when he spoke of the "expectation of failure," but now that expectation is at best met with complacency and at worst embraced as a heroic self-sacrifice to the great god, Letters. In spirit, our present literary magazines are more like the *Dial* than *Graham's*—content to live with small circulations, to avoid the appearance of commercialism, to ignore marketing, and to allow history the privilege of judging final worth. In fact, however, only a few of these magazines attempt to set out in new directions or to truly reveal an editorial task and policy and, in so doing, elevate their editors from amateurs to professionals. Without that editorial vision, survival, and certainly independence, are unlikely, and the cult of failure comes on like a magazine moral majority—the losers of the game who claim superiority because of their loss. The last shall be first. But the last, in this case, is full of look-alikes and read-alikes with few features to distinguish one from the other.

We are discussing here a situation that has arisen in the last forty years or so of American magazine history, and it cannot be easily categorized and understood. I have suggested how that situation has come about, some of the history leading up to it, and some of the ramifications following. It is very difficult to determine how well today's literary magazines achieve influence out of proportion to circulation and what their future will be, and it is equally difficult to assess the demands that commercialism and marketing will levy against literary magazines as outside funding from university, federal, and private sources dry up. We can only dig into the historical soil from which literary magazines have sprung, examine their physical, cultural, and economic roots, and state a few maxims as the lessons of magazine history:

—A small circulation may mean little beyond difficulties in financial operations if influence is present.

—Imitation alone is failure.

—Mainstream is constantly created anew and may not constitute a desirable literature or audience.

—Commercialism is a question of degree, not kind.

—Editorial distinction and vision are necessary to lasting success on any level.

—No risk, no gain.

—Failure is guaranteed to those who place value upon it.

II. THE MODERNIST LITTLE MAGAZINE

It is largely understood that the contemporary literary magazine has its origins in literary modernism, with such publications as *The English Review* (in the U.K.), *Poetry*, and *Little Review*. These "little magazines" changed the way readers read and writers wrote, heralding a new direction for literature and its publication in the United States. Moreover, scholars such as Mark Morrison and Robert Scholes have demonstrated that literary modernism owes a large thanks to these publications, as they were some of the few locations where experimental writers and artists could find support for their work, promotion of that work, and where they could learn and meet fellow artists, forming the literary and artistic community that made up a significant part of the influence and electricity of early twentieth century modernism.

Excerpt from *The Awakening Twenties: "Dial" and "Little Review"*

by Gorham Munson (1985)

In 1920 the Washington Square Bookshop was already living on its original reputation as a launching-pad for flights into the theater, little magazines, and book publishing . . .

In what a high-pitched anticipatory mood we ducked into this book shop once or twice a week to see what was new on its magazine rack. Here were the publications of the new movements in American art and thought and literature. Here were the reviews that were stimulating the young. Here were the magazines we wanted to write for . . .

Dial

In 1919 the *Dial* was a fortnightly edited by Robert Morss Lovett. Clarence Britten was the editor who made the assignments, a brisk, bright man whose untimely death was a distinct loss to liberal journalism. There were rumors that summer of impending changes at the *Dial*, and by December an announcement told of a change so great that the *Dial* would virtually be a new magazine when next it appeared on the rack of the Washington Square Book Shop.

In the 1950s E. E. Cummings noted this transformation, or rather metamorphosis. "Through Harvard I met Scofield Thayer; and at Harvard, Sibley Watson—two men who subsequently transformed a do-gooding periodical called *The Dial* into a first rate magazine of the fine arts; and together fought the eternal battle of selfhood against mobism; the immortal battle of beauty against ugliness." It was unfair to call the old *Dial*, founded at Chicago in 1880 by Francis F. Browne and moved to New York in 1918 by his successor,

Martyn Johnson, "a do-gooding periodical." The old *Dial* correctly called itself a fortnightly journal of "Criticism and Discussion of Literature and the Arts." Its editors in 1918 were not professional "do-gooders," but were of the new breed of intellectuals—Clarence Britten, George Donlin, Harold Stearns, and Scofield Thayer; and a supplementary group—John Dewey, Thorstein Veblen, and Helen Marot. But Cummings' comment stirs memory of the ubiquity of Harvard men in the American resurgence, as the years from 1912 to 1918—from the founding of *Poetry* in Chicago to the moving of the *Dial* from Chicago to New York—have been named by Richard Chase.

Walter Lippmann on the New Republic and John Reed on the *Masses* had come from Harvard at about the same time; Van Wyck Brooks on the *Seven Arts* had preceded them by a year or so. T. S. Eliot had been graduated from Harvard in 1909 and had emigrated to England. Harold Stearns had grubbed his way through Harvard a few years after Eliot and had been taken on the *Dial* by Martyn Johnson. If a Harvard graduate, fresh from courses by Santayana and Babbitt, Briggs and Copland, had real talent and wanted to enter on a literary career, he found Harvard friends and connections already established in strategic editorial positions and sometimes received help from them, but only if deserving, in getting their careers launched. So it was with Scofield Thayer of the class of 1913.

Born in 1888, Thayer was the only son of a man who had made a fortune in textiles at Worcester, Massachusetts. He had received an excellent education—at Milton Academy where T. S. Eliot was a sixth-former when he entered, in Europe where he was accompanied by a tutor, at Harvard where he was an editor of the *Harvard Monthly* and from which he was graduated cum laude in 1913, and finally at Magdalen College, Oxford, for study in the classics and philosophy. The war disrupted his postgraduate studies, and he returned to the United States and began his career as patron of artists and writers. He sent money to James Joyce in Zurich when Joyce was in dire need of a thousand dollars. In the winter of 1917/18 he bought stock in the *Dial* and lent money, intended as a gift, to it. Fortunately for the welfare of the arts in America, Thayer was exempted from military service and left free to develop his interest in the *Dial*.

When I first heard of Scofield Thayer, he was living at one of the choicest places in the Village—on the top floor of the Benedick (now occupied by New York University) on the east side of Washington Square. It was said that his bookshelves were stacked with first editions and rare books and his walls decorated with Aubrey Beardsley drawings. A fine view of the whole of Washington Square, then still Henry Jamesian in character, could be had from a high, narrow windowseat.

My impression of Scofield Thayer on the one occasion I met him—at tea in John Cowper Powys' rooms—was that of a literary dandy. He dressed with studied taste. This impression of dandyism one also receives from the

Adolph Dehn caricature of Thayer in dressing-gown, quill pen in hand, which was reproduced in the *Dial* for June, 1926, and captioned "Le Byron de nos jours." And the E. E. Cummings caricature, *S. T. at the Dial*, reproduced in Nicolas Joost's *Scofield Thayer and the Dial* (1964)—suggests a Parisian dandy of the brothers Goncourt time.

Thayer was "slender of build, swift of movement, always strikingly pale," noted Alyse Gregory in her reminiscences of the American resurgence and the early *Dial* years. He had "coal-black hair, black eyes veiled and flashing, and lips that curved like those of Lord Byron." Alyse Gregory said that he seemed to many "the embodiment of the aesthete with over-refined tastes and sensibilities" but this she felt was far from the case. "He was ice on the surface and molten lava underneath," she declared, and added that "his mind was inflammable and satirical, and it was at the same time sober and sad." This is helpful in dispelling any notion that Thayer was a butterfly but gives no clue to the mental disaster that was to overwhelm him in the later Twenties.

It will be recalled that Scofield Thayer was an admirer of Randolph Bourne, the emergent leader of the young intellectuals. Thayer bought stock in the *Dial* mainly because Bourne was an unofficial contributing editor. Both men believed that the young intelligentsia was crucial to the perpetuation of ideals through art and literature. Both were convinced that "the world will never understand our spirit except in terms of art. When shall we learn that 'culture,' like the kingdom of heaven, lies within us, in the heart of our national soul?" Thus was Thayer guided toward that serious aesthetic role, with its touchstone of intensity, which he was to act superbly as editor of the new *Dial*, from 1920 to 1925.

Thayer associated with himself on the old *Dial* another wealthy young man from Harvard—James Sibley Watson, Jr., of Rochester, New York. Watson came on as president of the Dial Publishing Company. Thayer was secretary treasurer. When the final agreement was made on November 15, 1919, for the two Harvard aesthetes to take control of the *Dial*, Watson retained the title of president and Thayer took the title of editor. But President Watson, who was taking a degree in medicine (radiology) at New York University, was a very important editorial associate as well. He was, in fact, more avant-garde in taste than Thayer.

The magazine Thayer and Watson acquired late in 1919 was a fortnightly with a circulation of about ten thousand. They changed it into a monthly magazine of the arts, international in scope and aesthetic in outlook, that was to affect us like an entirely new publication when the January, 1920, number appeared on the rack of the Washington Square Book Shop. It had a new format, designed by Bruce Rogers; and it was new in impact. There had never been anything like it in the history of American magazines. The impact of this January, 1920, number was chiefly made by the opening contributions: a Gaston Lachaise frontispiece, "An Autobiographic Chapter" by Randolph Bourne, and seven poems and four line drawings by the Harvard poet and artist E. E. Cummings.

In an unfinished novel, Bourne had written about a six-year-old boy named Gilbert, essentially himself, and had depicted the child's expanding life and his going to school. Any unpublished fragment by Bourne was eagerly read in 1920, but the most exciting writer in this first number was E. E. Cummings. The typography of his poems was revolutionary but, as we soon perceived, not arbitrary. His lyricism had a freshness that we tried to describe by saying that it was of the time of Queen Elizabeth. "O Distinct / Lady of my unkempt adoration"—this gave the thrilling note of the new lyrist.

To the next number of the *Dial* Cummings contributed an essay on the sculpture of Gaston Lachaise that reinforced the impact of the frontispiece of the January number. Lachaise, Cummings said, is "inherently naif, fearlessly intelligent, utterly sincere." Casting aside moderation, he praised him for what he called the negating of OF with IS. Accompanying this essay were drawings by Lachaise and two photographs of his sculpture. One reader of the *Dial* who was powerfully affected by the work of Lachaise was Hart Crane who later became a worshipful friend of Gaston and Madame Lachaise.

With this second number Gilbert Seldes was appointed an associate editor (later changed to managing editor). Another Harvard man, Seldes was to add brilliance to the *Dial* in its Theatre Chronicle and its book review section, and to participate in its editorial attitudes and practice.

The *Dial* was an education in the arts for an advanced public that had been forming during the resurgence and emerged after the war. The *Dial*'s circulation at the end of the first year of Thayer's editorship numbered about six thousand. By the end of 1922 it had reached nearly fourteen thousand. It was an expensive undertaking for Thayer and Watson. The deficit at the end of the first year was about $100,000.

But the greatest service of the *Dial* to American culture was its impact upon American writers. It conducted to them new impulses of modern arts and letters that instigated their own creative efforts. What made the *Dial* thrilling was its discovery of the best new writers coming out of undergraduate literary magazines like the *Harvard Monthly* and the short-lived *Sanscullotte* at Ohio State University where Ludwig Lewisohn taught; out of the American Ambulance Service in France and Italy; and out of postwar Greenwich Village.

The great discovery of the *Dial*, next to Cummings, was Kenneth Burke, whose short story "Mrs. Maecenas" came out in March. "Mrs. Maecenas" told of the hunt for a genius in the student body carried on by a college president's widow and how she placed her hopes on seventeen-year-old Siegfried and urged him on to "experience," and in the end reacted in distaste to the pimples on his adolescent chin. It was an elaborate and artificial tale with fine conversational gambits and clever quotations from Siegfried's writings. Its ivory tower ambience enchanted two young writers, Hart Crane and me, who were cover-to-cover readers of the *Dial*—notes on contributors, briefer mentions, advertisements and all—who compared notes with each other after every issue of the *Dial* for several years. We forthwith decided to wager on the rise of Kenneth Burke to literary leadership in our generation, "this youngest generation" as it was soon to be dubbed.

In April, Kenneth Burke reviewed the autobiographical fiction of John Cournos and exclaimed: "Heaven alone knows what is to become of the novel"—a cry that was to be repeated and amplified with the publication of *Ulysses*. In July, Burke had another story, an artificial, very literary thing called "The Soul of Kajn Tafha," which did not in the least shake the Crane-Munson estimate of Burke's promise, even though it had a kind of artificiality Burke would soon outgrow.

Crane and I also noted the reviews of Malcolm Cowley in February and April, but they had little impact on us. Cowley's effect on "this youngest generation" was to come two years later. Impact, however, was definitely what Cummings' review of *Poems* by T. S. Eliot had in the June number. Cummings called the slim volume "an accurate and uncorpulent collection of instupidities" and spoke in a phrase I long remembered of "the positive and deep beauty of his skilful and immediate violins." Cummings declared, "Before an Eliot we become alive or intense as we become intense or alive before a Cezanne or a Lachaise," and he summed up the volume as "an extraordinarily tight orchestration of the shapes of sound."

In that same June number there was an essay that intoxicated Crane and excited me, and had a lasting effect on both of us. This was "Some Remarks on Rimbaud as Magician" by W. C. Blum (Sibley Watson). There have been many essays and translations of Rimbaud since Dr. Watson's—translations by W. C. Blum of *A Season in Hell* and *Illuminations* followed in the July and August numbers—but Watson's pioneer efforts to introduce Rimbaud to American writers and readers have not been superseded as were Pound's notes in the *Little Review*. Rimbaud, Blum (Watson) stated, wished to be "a true wizard of dreams consciously working changes in his receptive apparatus, trying to regain and perfect that omnipotence of thought which Freud attributes to the savages." This staggered Crane's imagination, and he became completely intoxicated when Blum quoted Rimbaud's famous declaration: "I say it is necessary to be a *seer*, to make oneself a SEER! The poet makes himself a seer by a long, immense, and reasoned *derangement of all the senses* . . . For he reaches the *unknown!*"

W. C. Blum followed up his introduction of Rimbaud with a review of P. D. Ouspensky's *Tertium Organum* (September, 1920), which also made a powerful impression on Crane and me, though neither of us went to Ous-pensky's pages at once. "What [Ouspensky] has accomplished," said Blum, "is an artistic synthesis of certain liberating implications of the new math-ematics with the very old affirmations of the mystics." Blum summed up *Tertium Organum* as "a rather strong statement in favour of freedom."

The *Dial* set a high standard in book reviewing and didn't miss noticing any important book either. An interesting example of its alertness was its review (October, 1920) of a new revolutionary economic text. Both the *New Republic* and the *Nation* had overlooked it, and the *Freeman* had merely listed it as a book received. But the *Dial* described this new analysis of financial economics—*Economic Democracy* by C. H. Douglas—and promptly assigned it to an important reviewer. Ordway Tead noted that a new outlook on the confusing problem of finance and credit was required. Although he failed to grasp the constructive part of Douglas' book, he did imply that *Economic Democracy* should be required reading for open-minded students of postwar economic problems.

I have been noting the formative impact the *Dial* had on two of its young readers, one of whom was a poet of genius. But both of us were representa-tive of the oncoming "men of the Twenties." Now I should stress the truly catholic education the *Dial* gave to public taste.

What rich fare the *Dial* spread before its enthusiastic readers all during 1920. Provocative of future controversy were two chapters from Brooks's *The Ordeal of Mark Twain*, a pioneering literary application of psychoanalysis that *then* seemed brilliant. Memorable too was Sherwood Anderson's short story "The Triumph of the Egg," perhaps his best. Ezra Pound was repre-sented by "Fourth Canto" and "Hugh Selwyn Mauberly"; Marianne Moore by two poems. And then there was a series of notebook jottings, "Dust for Sparrows" by Remy de Gourmont, an idol of Kenneth Burke and other youthful aesthetes. In the October number appeared "The Approach to M. Marcel Proust" by Richard Aldington and "Saint-Loup: A Portrait" by Mar-cel Proust; and in November, T. S. Eliot offered "The Possibility of a Poetic Drama." That number also carried ten poems by William Butler Yeats. And there was a charming serial of literary reminiscences by Ford Madox Hueffer.

It should be possible to understand now why it is said that the *Dial* provided a higher education in the arts and letters of the twentieth century. But often, I must repeat, it was education with impact, as was true of the se-rial publication of "Belphegor: An Essay on the Aesthetic of Contemporary French Society" by Julien Benda. This essay was a forerunner of the attacks on romanticism that would be unloosed at the end of the Twenties by the New Humanists. Benda declared in italics that "*modern French society requires of art that they make it experience emotions and sensations and no longer expects to realize from works of art any kind of intellectual pleasure.*" He vigorously at-tacked Bergson and "the purely emotional conception of art." His was a salutary influence on some of us young romantics who would later become more classical in taste.

We, the younger writers, knew the *Dial* was a great magazine while it was happening. We concurred at once with the judgment of the English editor A. R. Orage, which the *Dial* quoted in its house advertising: "Perhaps the most fully realized of all the promising literary magazines now current in the world. It is in all probability considerably in advance of the American reading public for whom it is intended, but it is all the better on that account. Culture is always being called upon to sacrifice popularity, and, usually, even its existence, in the interests of civilization."

Malcolm Cowley recalled that "for the young American writer, it was marvelous to have a magazine that would publish his best work, and pay him for it." But the last word on the *Dial* was spoken by one who helped it to achieve the editorial brilliance of its five years under the active editorship of Scofield Thayer. "The Dial made a noise in the world," wrote Gilbert Seldes. "It directly affected the artistic life of a generation, and indirectly the life of our whole time."

LITTLE REVIEW

Of the little magazines displayed on the rack of the Washington Square Book Shop in this pivotal year of 1920, the most famous and the best was *Little Review*. Ranged beside it were *Pagan*, *Quill*, *Plowshare*, *Modern School*, *S4N*, and *Contact*; but *Little Review* was easily the front runner of these small, unsubsidized, uncommercial, avant-garde publications. It had, in fact, gained a big head start in its Chicago period, 1914–1917.

The founder had been Margaret Anderson, a young woman of beauty and vivacity who had rebelled against family life in Columbus, Indiana, and escaped to Chicago. At Columbus, Margaret Anderson, just out of Western College for Women, though not a graduate, wrote: "I had a green room overlooking lilac bushes, yellow roses and oak trees. Every day I shut myself in, planning how to escape mediocrity (not the lilacs and roses but the vapidities that went on in their hearing)." And escape she did—to Chicago.

In Chicago, Margaret Anderson did miscellaneous book reviewing for a religious weekly and for Francis Hackett on the Chicago *Evening Post*. Then she got a very minor editorial job on the old *Dial* and also did some clerking in Browne's Book Store, which Frank Lloyd Wright had designed. On the *Dial* she was "initiated into the secrets of the printing room—composition (monotype and linotype), proofreading, make-up. This practical knowledge was indispensable when I began the *Little Review*." Floyd Dell succeeded Francis Hackett at the *Chicago Evening Post*. Margaret Anderson reviewed books for Dell and went to a sort of salon his first wife, Margery Currey, created.

These soirees at the Dells were golden in Harry Hansen's memory when he wrote his sketches of Chicago literary life in *Mid-West Portraits* (1923). He recalls the talkers—Sherwood Anderson with his drawl; Theodore Dreiser always folding and unfolding a handkerchief; John Cowper Powys, rhapsodic on great writers; Arthur Davison Ficke from Dell's home city of Davenport, Iowa; Maxwell Bodenheim with his snarl; Edgar Lee Masters who looked like Thackeray; Carl Sandburg, newspaperman and poet, and many many others. Of this circle Margaret Anderson has written: "Floyd Dell and I talked of Pater and of living like the hard gem-like flame....I liked Sherwood—because he, too, was a talker of a highly special type.... Sherwood and Floyd would talk to chairs if they had no other audience . . . But Dreiser had no more wit than a cow."

The Dell circle was Margaret Anderson's preparation for founding a little magazine in 1914. As she tells it in *My Thirty Years' War*: "If had a magazine I could spend my time filling it up with the best conversation the world has to offer." That was Margaret Anderson's editorial platform and policy, her editorial standard and goal. She aspired to be the mistress of a salon-in-print, and it was a man from the Dell salon—a certain Dewitt whom she called "Dick"—who gave her part of his salary each payday to start her magazine-salon.

Members of the Dell circle were often represented in the early numbers of the *Little Review*. Sherwood Anderson wrote about "The New Note"; Vachel Lindsay contributed a poem, "How a Little Girl Danced," inspired by Lucy Bates; George Burman Foster wrote a series of articles on Nietzsche; Arthur Davison Ficke contributed poems on Japanese prints; Margery Currey reviewed Ellen Key; Llewellyn Jones wrote on Bergson; notes on John Cowper Powys' lectures appeared. It all had the flavor of a soiree at the Dells. Of herself at this time, Margaret Anderson recalled that she "spoke only in gasps, gaps and gestures," and her editorials were like that—excited and breathless.

Then Emma Goldman came to Chicago. Margaret Anderson heard her lecture and had just time to turn anarchist before the third number of the *Little Review* closed. This conversation cost "Dick's" support but Eunice Tietjens gave a diamond ring, Frank Lloyd Wright gave a hundred dollars, others chipped in, and the *Little Review* precariously continued. "I became increasingly anarchistic," Margaret Anderson has told us. "Anarchism was the ideal expression for my ideas of freedom and justice.... I decided that I would make my life a crusade against inhumanity." But in a year or so her highly personal enthusiasm for Emma Goldman cooled and a new stimulus, a Chicago art student out of the Midwest, walked into the *Little Review* salon-in-print—Jane Heap.

"There is no one in the modern world whose conversation I haven't sampled, I believe, except Picasso's," said Margaret Anderson. "So I can't say it isn't better than Jane Heap's. But I doubt it in spite of his reputation. I felt in 1916 and feel today that Jane Heap is the world's best talker."

Jane Heap (who signed her editorials "jh") became an associate editor under the singular title of "Advisory Board" (singular because there were no others on the board), and from then on: "Jane and I began talking. We talked for days, months, years . . . We formed a consolidation that was to make us much loved and even more loathed."

In 1917 the *Little Review* salon moved from Chicago to New York, and there Margaret Anderson "found the same difference between the quality of talk in Chicago and New York (in Chicago's favor) that I found later between that of New York and Paris (in New York's favor)." A snobbish "motto" appeared on the front cover—Making No Compromise with the Public Taste—which flaunted the feeling of superiority and exclusiveness of the salon-between-covers. But with the appointment of Ezra Pound to the post of foreign editor, the *Little Review* began to lose some of the random improvisation that a salon mistress encourages and to achieve more coherence as a magazine. Margaret Anderson had corresponded with Pound who was an exile in London, and "when he wrote suggesting that *The Little Review* employ his talents as foreign editor we hailed the occasion."

When we recall the major writers Pound brought into the *Little Review*, we see that Margaret Anderson and Jane Heap could hardly fail to make history in "little magazine" publishing. First, there was T. S. Eliot represented by a cerebral fiction, "Eeldrop and Appleplex." Pound himself was a regular contributor: "A Study in French Poets," "The Chinese Written Character" (mostly by Fenollosa), "De Gourmont: A Distinction," and other critical forays. Pound also sent over frequent contributions by Wyndham Lewis, poems by William Butler Yeats, prose by Ford Madox Hueffer. He edited a whole number devoted to Henry James. But the greatest catch he made for the *Little Review*, the leviathan of letters he hooked, was James Joyce. Serial publication of *Ulysses* started in 1918 and in the pivotal year of 1920 came the famous Gerty McDowell episode, after which Margaret Anderson and Jane Heap were haled into court.

But by January, 1920, when the younger patrons of the Washington Square Book Shop searched the magazine rack with the keenest expectancy for the new issue of the *Little Review*, Pound's name had gone from the masthead. The January, 1920, issue carried an un-Poundian debate over the "Art of Madness" between Evelyn Scott and jh. As a mad personality, the Baroness Else von Freytag-Loringhoven had captivated Margaret Anderson and Jane Heap. But the young poet Hart Crane who lived in the same building above the *Little Review* hid in a doorway when he saw the baroness coming down the street, preceded by three dogs, her arms clanking with cheap bracelets, two tea-balls bouncing on her bosom, and long-handled spoons affixed to her black velvet tam-o'shanter.

The baroness was, in fact, regarded even by sympathetic subscribers as a *Little Review* aberration, a "crush" of its editors, and their rave notes on her art fell on deaf minds. It had been very different when Margaret Anderson and jh had raved about Mary Garden. Carl Van Vechten had bought one hundred copies of the *Little Review* to distribute the "rave" to friends. But this infatuation with the baroness' poems was adjudged by us otherwise devoted readers to be an extremely silly sentimentality.

The *Little Review* in 1920 carried only two or three pages of advertising in an issue, but a full-page advertisement of Crane's Mary Garden Chocolates excites interest long after this candy has disappeared into oblivion. This advertisement was secured by Hart Crane from his father, a prosperous candy manufacturer in Cleveland. The layout consisted simply of a picture of the opera singer and a box of candy and an endorsement—"Your chocolates are the finest I have ever tasted anywhere in the World"—over Mary Garden's signature. One may suspect that Hart Crane had something to do with the naming of the chocolates and the endorsement, as well as with the placement of the advertisement in a medium that gave a print order of only four thousand copies.

But it was Joyce's *Ulysses* that issue after issue made the *Little Review* preeminent in the avant-garde arena. A naturalistic short story writer named Israel Solon often spoke out in the *Little Review* salon in a department reserved for "the reader-critic," and Solon spoke for most of the writers who followed the *Little Review* when he declared (January, 1920) that "James Joyce is beyond doubt the most sensitive stylist writing in English. There is enough skill and matter in a single episode of *Ulysses* to equip a regiment of novelists .... He gives me more than I can ever carry away." Such was the effect of Joyce on those who were serious about experimental writing, and one ventures to say that they all read the *Little Review*.

The magazine, however, had other readers who were disgusted by experimental virtuosity. Wrote one of them to Margaret Anderson after reading Leopold Bloom's musings about Gerty McDowell: "I think this is the most damnable slush and filth that ever polluted paper in print." Margaret Anderson sat up all night to answer this letter—"such was my hurt for Joyce, my own hurt." She said that she regarded Joyce's *Ulysses* as "the high watermark of the literature of today" and fired back: "He is not writing for you. He is writing for himself and for the people who care to find out how life has offended and hurt him." For once Margaret Anderson's repartee was weak, and it was to be weak again when she commented explosively on her approaching day in court by publishing *Ulysses*.

More than once the Post Office had confiscated copies of the *Little Review* containing installments of *Ulysses*. A new attack came in the fall of 1920 when John S. Sumner, secretary of the Society for the Suppression of Vice, moved against the editor for publishing the Gerty McDowell episode.

He served papers on the Washington Square Book Shop for selling the offending number, and Miss Anderson and Miss Heap sought the help of John Quinn, art patron and militant lawyer, to defend the case. Quinn appears to have considered it a lost cause from the start, but he was a friend of Joyce and Pound and a financial backer of the *Little Review* (to the extent of $1,600), and he armed himself to fight the dragon of Comstockery. Powerful Anthony Comstock had died in 1915 and his successor, Sumner, was not as fanatical; but the dragon was still formidable and usually victorious over artists. The artists, as a matter of fact, did not know how to combat the dragon.

You have no sense, Quinn told the editors of the *Little Review*, and exacted a pledge that they would not open their mouths when they came before the three judges. This was wise, for Margaret Anderson was bursting with a "defense" that was nothing but a defiance of the sort that many Americans were then showing against Prohibition. "I am not in the defy business but in the law business," Quinn reminded her.

Margaret Anderson's defense was a haughty attack upon the stupid law and the stupid public. It brought out all her snobbery. The artist was superior to the public and had no responsibility to the public. Her attack was all founded on the fancied superiority of one psychological type over other types and on ignorance of inspired common sense applied to the question of censorship. But we were all unsophisticated in those days on a question that had been argued by Plato and Hobbes, Milton and Mill; and the defiant emotionalism of the *Little Review* constituted our stand, too, against Comstockery.

At the trial Quinn put on three witnesses—John Cowper Powys, who denied that *Ulysses* was capable of corrupting the minds of young girls; Philip Moeller, who offered a psychoanalytical apologia for *Ulysses*; and Scofield Thayer, who admitted under examination that he would have taken legal advice before publishing *Ulysses* and then wouldn't have published. Quinn got his three clients off with the minimum fine of one hundred dollars.

It was reserved for Judge John M. Woolsey in 1933 to rise to the historic occasion and hand down a classic decision on the charge of pornography brought against Joyce. In 1920 Margaret Anderson simply could not rise to the occasion. It was perhaps enough that she had recognized the genius of Joyce; she should not have been expected to found a criticism of Joyce as well. She set out to fill her magazine with "the best conversation in the world," and she succeeded by inviting the very best into her magazine-salon. She shall be known to the literary historian as an editor of genius when it came to picking the best writers of her time.

SMALL MAGAZINES

by Ezra Pound (1931)

I.

The earlier history—I might almost call it the pre-history of the small magazines in America—has been ably and conscientiously presented by Dr. Rene Taupin in his *L'Influence du Symbolisme Francais sur la Poesie Americaine* (Paris: Champion, 1930); and I may there leave it for specialists.

The active phase of the small magazine in America begins with the founding of Miss Monroe's magazine, *Poetry*, in Chicago in 1911. The significance of the small magazine has, obviously, nothing to do with format. The significance of any work of art or literature is a root significance that goes down into its original motivation. When this motivation is merely a desire for money or publicity, or when this motivation is in great part such a desire for money directly or for publicity as a means indirectly of getting money, there occurs a pervasive monotony in the product corresponding to the underlying monotony in the motivation.

The public runs hither and thither with transitory pleasures and underlying dissatisfactions; the specialists say: "This isn't literature." And a deal of vain discussion ensues.

The monotony in the product arises from the monotony in the motivation.

During the ten or twenty years preceding 1912 the then-called "better magazines" had failed lamentably and even offensively to maintain intellectual life. They are supposed to have been "good" during some anterior period. Henry Adams and Henry James were not, at the starts of their respective careers, excluded; but when we reach our own day, we find that Adams and James had a contempt for American editorial opinion in no way less scalding than—let us say—Mr. Maxwell Bodenheim's, though their expression of it was rarer and suaver.

The elder magazines, the *Atlantic*, *Harper's*, *Scribner's*, *Century*, had even in their original titles more or less and in varying degrees abjured the pretentions of the London "Reviews," i.e., to serious and consecutive criticism of literature. They had grown increasingly somnolent, reminiscences of General Grant being about their maximum effort toward contemporaneity. About the beginning of this century there was a new and livelier current in the trade. The methods of Armour's meat business were introduced into distribution. A commercial talent blossomed in the great firm of Condé Nast. A bright young man observed a leakage in efficiency. The advertising men had to collect such ads as the contents could attract. In the new system the contents were selected rigorously on the basis of how much expensive advertising they would carry. Hence the sameness in impression given by successive numbers of these bright and snappy periodicals. I mean to say that each of these publications expresses, fundamentally, one idea and one only. The thinking man can learn from them one thing only; when he has learned that, he thirsts for further and more diversified knowledge.

It is also to be observed that people who would not be taken in by a free advertising circular are delighted to pay five cents for a mass of printed paper that costs twenty cents to produce. The principle of this had been duly formulated by the late Mr. Barnum.

These things—if the reader will permit me to allow him to take a few intervening steps for himself—these things ultimately leave a vacuum. They leave a need for intellectual communication unconditioned by considerations as to whether a given idea or a given trend in art will "git ads" from the leading corset companies. Or, in the milder zone, whether it happens to agree with what Aunt Hannah had heard from her uncle, and which would therefore "please" or, in the magistral words of one of the editors of the *Atlantic*, be "familiar to our readers."

II.

In 1911 Miss Monroe and her backers recognized that verse, to be of any intellectual value, could not be selected merely on the basis of its immediate earning capacity. This idea was not new, but it was not at that moment functioning vigorously in other editorial offices.

I don't know of any other constructive idea that is directly traceable to the Chicago office.

Irritated by the faults of work published in the opening numbers, I compiled a list of the more glaring. This was intended to be used as part of the magazine's rejection slip. I also, for the sake of convenience and to avoid useless discussion of the phrase "good poetry," put a label on a complex of three ideas or principles.

These things appeared in *Poetry* as a manifesto and as "Don'ts of an Imagist."

They were not a complete *ars poetica*. They were of necessity platitudinous. Any science has to start with platitudes (shortest distance between two points, etc.). Dr. Taupin has done me the honor to state that if these propositions were platitudinous, they were, at any rate, a handy summary of the best Latin culture and of common sense about writing.

Poetry provided a place where the tennis about these ideas could be played. Miss Monroe never pretended to adopt either a contemporary, European, or international criterion. Certain principles that Europe had accepted for eighty years have never penetrated her sanctum. It is possible that recognition of these ideas would have prematurely extinguished her magazine. On the other hand, she may never have grasped these ideas. She has repeatedly protected her readers; i.e., she has assumed that the intelligence of her readers is so far below that of the authors whom she has printed that the readers are at certain points not permitted to read and to judge for themselves what the writers believe.

We Europeans consider this an insult to the reader; and "we" (the author of these presents), as an American, consider it a pessimistic lack of confidence in our compatriots.

Miss Monroe has occasionally mutilated a work by excisions and has occasionally failed to see the unity of a longer work and given it in fragments.

Nevertheless, she has done valuable service by reason of the purity of her intentions. She meant to provide a place where unknown poets could be printed; she has done so. Where new ideas and forms could be tried, she has done so. She has provided a meal ticket when the meal ticket was badly needed.

She has printed on her own motion Mr. Lindsay's "General Booth Enters Heaven."

She has printed, after six months argument with me, Mr. Frost.

She printed (after Marion Reedy had with great difficulty persuaded him to write Spoon River) some poems by E. L. Masters.

She printed, after six months argument with me, Mr. T. S. Eliot's *Prufrock*.

She printed me a year or so after Mr. Mencken had done so.

She printed without protest the early work of "H. D." and of Aldington; work by Yeats, F. M. Hueffer (Ford).

She also mutilated my "Homage to Sextus Propertius" at a time when I had to take what I could get, and long after I had ceased to regard *Poetry* or its opinion as having any weight or bearing or as being the possible implement or organ for expressing any definite thought.

The *Review* served as a forum from 1912 to 1914, perhaps to 1917. It served, and probably still serves, as a meal ticket; and among its now unknown writers there may be some who will emerge as formed literati.

III.

The term "art movement" usually refers to something immobile. It refers to a point or an intersection or a declaration of conclusions arrived at. When the real movement or ascent has occurred, such a declaration is made, and things remain at that point or recede.

A movement for the purgation of poetic writing occurred from 1908 till 1914. Later Mr. Eliot added certain complexities.

The principles of purgation declared in the DONT'S were, in varying degree, applied to western United States subject matter by various authors. Of the authors who refused to recognize them, Vachel Lindsay alone remains known. He had got hold of another essential; and by reason of it survives, more or less. Poetry should be speakable or singable, as Mr. Lindsay ceaseth not to declare. Mr. Lindsay's limitations can be observed by the reader for himself.

Miss Monroe's sympathies were obviously with Mr. Lindsay; with Mr. Masters, who declined; and with Mr. Sandburg, who increased, who cut the bunk out of his writing in measure as Mr. Masters inserted it in his.

Poetry continues as a very meritorious trade journal. It was not open to general ideas. It persists by reason of having limited itself to poetry. The action of literature in prose and in ideas was continued in the *Egoist*. The history of these free non-commercial reviews can be most briefly told by a list of their contents.

Poetry had printed the authors I have mentioned, and the others found in its indexes. *The Egoist* took on what the *New Age* would not print. The *New Age* was a durable London weekly devoted to guild socialism but allotting a few pages of each issue to art and letters regardless of their economic bearing and indifferent to their capacity to please the British *universitaire* taste.

The *Egoist* serialized Joyce's *Portrait of the Artist*; and Wyndham Lewis' *Tarr*. It printed more information about French and other Continental writers than other British reviews would carry. The term "Little Magazines" might seem to exclude the *English Review* as it was in 1908 and 1909 to 1910. It had the format of an old established review. It professed vainly to take its place with other permanent periodicals. It failed into obscure glory. It committed the error of not dying in its own name. It was denatured and voided of significance. Nevertheless, it might be taken as paradigm. It was, under Ford Madox Hueffer (Ford), the most brilliant piece of editing I have known. In its first year and a half it printed not only the work of Hardy,

Swinburne, Henry James, Anatole France, various other monuments, various other writers of extensive reputation (Wells, Galsworthy, Bennett, etc.), but it also printed the work of, I think, all the first-rate and second-rate (as distinct from third-, fourth-, and fifth-rate) writers then in London: Wyndham Lewis, D. H. Lawrence (his earliest printed work), myself, Cannan, Walpole, etc. Eliot had not then reached London. Joyce's *Dubliners* was not then written, or at any rate the manuscripts were not submitted.

After Mr. Hueffer was given the gate, Mr. Willard Huntingdon Wright (at, I believe, Mr. Mencken's suggestion) tried to transform the *Smart Set* and to create an American equivalent to Hueffer's English review.

He knocked his circulation from 70,000 to 40,000 in, if I remember rightly, the first six months. He then told the objecting proprietors that the gulf which separated them was vast and impassable, and handed in his resignation. Thus ended the quixotic attempt to turn a successful periodical into an intellectual organ. He had managed to print a few of the stories from *Dubliners* and a few of D. H. Lawrence's best. Either he or Mencken reprinted a good deal of my *Ripostes* from the London edition. He had tried to buy up all the best stuff then on the London market. I received the impression that he rather expected to find Mr. Thomas Hardy sitting behind a ticket window passing out manuscripts at so much "per thousand." But it was a gallant effort and shows that intellectual hunger and the attempt to provide for it are not the exclusive property of the tattered eccentric.

Mr. Mencken solved his own problem in the *American Mercury*. I leave this subject to the tender mercies of the younger generation of critics. The *Mercury* has been hermetically sealed against almost all writing which seems to me to have any permanent interest or value, but that does not necessarily imply that it is either otiose or void of utility.

IV.

The origins of the small review are lost in obscurity. Rossetti and Swinburne contributed to a *Westminster Quarterly* that rose and faded, etc. The *English Review* in 1908 had, I presume, Continental inspiration. The editor wanted to do in England something comparable to what he saw done in France. *The Egoist*, at least the literary segment, wanted to carry on without capital what the *English Review* had done by squandering its fiscal resources. The original intentions of those who start papers are not always salient in their history. The *Egoist* started as a woman's rights paper; the *Little Review* started apparently as a reaction against the excessive modernism of Miss Monroe's *Poetry*. Mr. Ficke in its pages set out to prove that the sonnet was "Gawd's owne city." Some years later (i.e., in, I think, 1916) Miss Anderson printed a number with half the pages blank and the threat to print the next number wholly blank if she couldn't find something fit to put in it.

This date coincided with several events, notably a disturbed condition in Europe. Mr. Lewis had brought out one *Blast* in July, 1914. One more number appeared in 1915. Due to lack of English competition there was no trouble about sending manuscripts to the United States.

From 1917 to 1919 the *Little Review* printed all that Mr. Wyndham Lewis produced; it printed nearly all that either Mr. Eliot or I produced. It wrote itself almost immediately into the history of European letters by publishing the opening chapters of *Ulysses*. It printed work by Yeats, Lady Gregory, John Rodker.

So far as one could gather, it was regarded as wildly erratic and unbalanced. Mr. Ben Hecht protested. He told me the editors were ignorant; that I had no conception of the depth, height, and extensiveness of their ignorance. He said that it was complete and all embracing, and that I was making these people a clearing house for European literature and thereby effecting a crime.

The triviality and frivolity of the *Little Review* will be instantly apparent to anyone who will take the trouble to open my *Instigations*, which is largely reprinted from the *Review's* pages. From the districts west of New York Miss Anderson received the manuscripts of Mr. Sherwood Anderson, Mr. Maxwell Bodenheim, Mr. Hecht, aforementioned.

The law under which the *Review* was suppressed may be read by any member of the public who will take the trouble to do so. It is reprinted in my *Instigations*. Most readers will not take the trouble to read it. They can also find a reference to it in Mr. Cummings' play *Him*.

After its suppression as a monthly the *Little Review* re-emerged as a "more or less" *Quarterly*. It gave the first adequate publication of photos of Brancusi's sculpture. It printed Mr. Hemingway and Mr. Cocteau in translation. I had a hand in preparing several of these quarterly issues but was finally ejected for frivolity. Mr. Hilaire Hiler and I shared the editorial disapproval.

As far as possible, I am trying to confine this article to statement of the positive achievement of various impractical publications and to avoid personal anecdote save where such anecdote is necessary to clear understanding of what happened or how it was possible.

The agreement on which I had taken the foreign editorship of the *Little Review* had been that I was to choose half the contents; that John Quinn was to provide $750 annually for two years for foreign editor's salary and payment of foreign contributors; and that the American editors were to provide for the printing and distribution. After a few months of the new program (Lewis, Eliot, Joyce, and myself, with promise of a few older and established writers) the American editors prevailed on Quinn to prevail on himself and his friends to provide $5,000 for production expenses. This was done without my knowledge. Quinn was soon dissatisfied with the New York management. I have no wish to register an unasked opinion as to the relative causes of irritation. Quinn urged me with no inconsiderable violence to emerge from the partnership, and a few years later arranged that I take on a sort of informal foreign function for the *Dial*.

In 1916, or the end of 1915, Thayer had been in England and had been on the point of contributing a small sum toward the starting of an independent review under the direction of myself and Eliot. For reasons unknown to me he left the country without further reference to the matter or to his promise or offer. Thayer's and my point of view seldom coincided. The *Dial* stated that it could not expect to be my spiritual home, and requested me to collect manuscripts from a number of European authors, essentially the *Little Review* list with George Moore and Alice Meynell added, plus certain foreign writers with "names"—Anatole France, etc.

As nearly as I can now discern, the *Dial* wanted to be in America what the *Mercure* had been in France. It was, however, more retroactive than the *Mercure* had been in its better days. It cannot be said that my early relations with the *Dial* were in any way comfortable. During its ten years of existence the *Dial* obviously paid a considerable sum of money to authors and was to that extent useful in so far as these authors were meritorious and, during that period, needy. The reader must judge for himself whether the *Dial* in ten years had more effect on American literary life than the *Little Review* during its two years of most active existence, or than the *Little Review* as monthly and later as quarterly.

I retain the view that Thayer could have had more fun for his money, for a great deal less money, if he had gone on with the earlier scheme; but perhaps it was not the sort of fun he was looking for. There may have been advantages in having a review that looked sober and authoritative. There may have been advantages in being able to buy the work of any author one chose and to refuse Arnold Bennet. I retain the opinion that if the *Dial*, when it had got round to printing L. Aragon as early as 1921, had crammed the manuscripts I collected into six issues instead of dragging them through twenty-four, it would have provided a greater liveliness. I am not sure that the *Dial* would like to see itself listed among little reviews. It had the merit of selecting its manuscripts, if not with unmixed motive, at least with some motive other than expediency.

It stood for what I consider at least one false idea, namely, that criticism is as important as original writing.

It is, curiously enough, not so important that an editorial policy should be right as that it should succeed in expressing and giving clear definition to a policy or set of ideas. A review is not a human being saving its soul, but a species of food to be eaten. Healthy reaction, constructive reaction, can start from a wrong idea clearly defined, whereas mere muddle effects nothing whatever.

Poetry had begun with a pure heart. It had had one clear enunciation of views as to style or to good writing.

The *Little Review* had had the pure heart *à outrance*. Its editors never accepted a manuscript save because they thought it interesting, and their review remains the most effective of any we have yet had.

The *Dial* has, however, left its imprint. I believe that criticism is now more thorough and less sloppy than it was ten years ago. I am not sure that the *Dial* ever profited greatly by its idea. It seems to me that this newer sobriety in criticism has begun to show only during the last few years. And it must be recognized that the *Dial* was not the only periodical working to this end.

I cannot say that the ideas Mr. Eliot has selected to have discussed in his *Criterion* have been unfailingly lively. Many of them seem to me to be unworthy of any human attention whatsoever, and he persists in printing one or two scribblers who are beneath all possible biological contempt. Nevertheless, he has induced a care in the use of critical terms that was absent during the antecedent period of critical or reviewatorial slop. The gulf, for example, between the expression of a theological opinion by Mr. Chesterton and by Mr. Eliot is a gulf great and impassable.

If the *Criterion* is not strictly a magazine "in the United States," it emerged definitely from American racial sources; and the story of American letters cannot be told without mention of it (or of the *Egoist* and, in less degree, the *New Age*).

The *Little Review* during its most brilliant years had been, among other things, trying to "civilize America," i.e., to introduce international standards of criticism. *Poetry*, as I have tried to indicate, had refused to make this attempt, and still refuses to do so. A man who asks favors for his work because it is written in some particular place appears to me to be not patriotic but merely pusillanimous.

The *Criterion* has tried to extend this program and to introduce international critical standards in England—a far more difficult task, a task almost hopelessly quixotic.

You cannot, however, divide literary history on a merely geographic basis. In 1910 or 1912 France was immeasurably ahead of us in poetry and, save for Henry James, in prose.

With the exhaustion of France and with the introduction of international standards we arrived by 1920–25, to the present, at a new condition of things. An American book is now quite often as good as a French book or a European book. American books do not circulate freely in Europe because an American book is seldom worth four or five European books. It has cost four or five times as much. This problem of international communication is a matter of publisher's economics, not of intellectual standards.

V.

As I see it, "we" in 1910 wanted to set up civilization in America. By 1920 one wanted to preserve the vestiges or start a new one anywhere that one could. Against the non-experimental caution of *Dial* and *Criterion*, the *transatlantic review* was founded in Paris, Ford Madox Ford as editor, Quinn as sustaining member. It printed work by Hemingway, Robert McAlmon, and Cummings. Cummings was already established, via, I think, *S4N* and the *Dial*.

S4N had attempted to establish a critical group in New England—Fitts, Munson, and, I think, Winter. I have up to now failed to discover any active fecund principle in the work of this group; but they, as I see it, were working with pure intention.

It was reported in Paris that the *transatlantic* ceased because the payment never came for copies "sold" in America. At any rate, it ceased and *transition* reigned in its stead.

This paper has published the later Joyce and his epigons. It has provided space for experiment. One should dissociate the ideas of experiment and of significant achievement.

Honest literary experiment, however inclusive, however dismally it fail, is of infinitely more value to the intellectual life of a nation than exploitation (however glittering) of mental mush and otiose habit.

The stutterings of a Stein are more productive of thought than the highly paid copy of some of Mr. Lorimer's *deorlings*.

The best criticism of Miss Stein known to me has been unconsciously recorded in another "fugitive" publication, namely, Mr. Walsh's *This Quarter*.

In a list of notes on contributors we find that Miss Stein took "postgrad" work in psychology at Johns Hopkins, giving special attention to "fatigue and unconscious responses."

As for the abuse of the stream of consciousness theories in writing, once it has been asserted that this stream is conglomerate, a mixture of impressions, of half-ideas, intersections, emergencies, etc., and once this is recognized, we return mentally enriched very probably; but nevertheless we return to the value of arrangements, to the value of clear definitions, to the value of design in composition.

The stream of consciousness in *Ulysses* is as different from any stream of consciousness that has actually occurred as is a plot of Racine's. It is equally a composition and a condensation. After the principle of "conscious flow" has been manifested, the relative value of presentations of such imagined streams will depend, as writing in the past has depended, on the richness of the content and on the author's skill in arranging it. There is no formula that can, by merely getting itself adopted, enable a man to exceed his own capacity.

of traditional notions of the wholeness of individual character . . . [In modernism] all realities [had] become subjective fictions."[6] Reflecting on these momentous changes, modernist writers and artists attempted to express the flux of reality by dispensing with conventional modes of depiction and by experimenting instead with abrupt and unusual juxtapositions, sensory immediacy, linguistic play, and combinations of prosaic subject matter with idiosyncratic and esoteric allusions, all of which radically challenged aesthetic conventions.

Not surprisingly, the many aspects of modernist development have given rise to an impressive—and confusing—range of interpretations. Standard histories of modernism, particularly those predicated upon New Criticism, are currently being revised, although for the most part scholars still orient their studies toward literacy and critical works written by men. Such an approach may express itself in the form of theoretical positions that do not include attention to women's history, or in a "humanism" that claims to include women's history and feminist theory but that in fact subsumes them, once again, into a presumably "universal" position.

In one discussion, for instance, historian Albert Gelpi finds that modernism, like the Enlightenment and Romanticism, was a response to "the rising sense of threat and confusion at every level of life in the West, religious and psychological, philosophic and political: a sense of crisis."[7] This crisis developed from the decay of the Romantic notion of "the individual's intrinsic capacity to perceive and participate in the organic interrelatedness of all forms of natural life and . . . to intuit [through the imagination] the metaphysical reality from which that natural harmony proceeds" (3). Gelpi believes this decay turned into a skeptical modernism, of which the salient characteristics were "complexity and abstraction, sophisticated technical invention and spatialized form, the conception of the artist as at once supremely self-conscious and supremely impersonal" (5). The dualism of such paradoxical constructions reinscribes a good many of the qualities it seems to

---

[6] Malcolm Bradbury and James McFarlane, eds., *Modernism: 1890–1930* (Harmondsworth: Penguin, 1976) 27.

[7] *A Coherent Splendor: The American Poetic Renaissance, 1910–1950* (Cambridge: Cambridge UP, 1987) 3. Albert Gelpi's book includes only one woman, Hilda Doolittle, as a major figure. While Gelpi claims he will "call attention, from time to time, to the ways in which elitist, individualist assumptions about gender, race, and class limit and even distort the work under discussion," his discussion is still predicated upon "what the poetry *does* rather than what it does not do" (6)—which means that the book necessarily privileges the white male purview underlying the bulk of the writing, responds to men's work in great part, and marginalizes "gender, race, and class" in a convenient phrase that gives just a nod to three factors that in actual life enormously shape writers' experiences and expressions.

question, most obviously in the familiar notion that modernist dissonances expressing "crisis" necessarily undergirded a drive toward an encompassing consonance. It is also apparent that this sort of critical language itself reflects the values of a masculinist viewpoint that reinforces hierarchy.

Another way in which dualism tends to be reinscribed in conservative literary histories concerns the "break with the past" that many critics see as essential to the modernist agenda, as if the artistic expressions of the twentieth century were an abrupt and complete change from earlier traditions. In discerning and interpreting such a break, Michael Levenson decides, for instance, that the emphasis he sees on "two-ness" in the pronouncements of Eliot, Pound, Ford, and Hulme indicates a desire for "thorough historical discontinuity" (ix), which would obviously invest these men's works with pivotal significance in the development of modern thought. One kind of radical discontinuity, however, is absent from Levenson's own "genealogy" of modernism; this book, too, concentrates on the work of a few—mostly very familiar—male writers, despite its overt language of reproduction that might at least suggest the presence of women. Of course no single book can do justice to the huge range of writers and artists who might be included in a discussion of modernism, but it is particularly ironic, given Levenson's refusal even to acknowledge the influence of such women as Dorothy Richardson, Gertrude Stein, and H.D., that he writes, "Part of the difficulty of modernism is that it has suppressed its origins" (xi). Indeed.

The problems occasioned by ignoring or suppressing women's contributions must be taken seriously, since the effects infiltrate every aspect of history-making and canonization. One instance of such a "filtering" effect, as Shari Benstock terms it in *Women of the Left Bank* (27), can be found in the language of the following scenario from Hoffman, Allen, and Ulrich's *The Little Magazine: A History and a Bibliography*, in which the authors note that little reviews often served as the key to recognition for beginning or experimental writers:

> One may speak casually of an Ernest Hemingway's receiving his first half-dozen publications in little magazines and thereby gaining a reputation . . . But let us be more specific. Hemingway publishes his first story in *The Double Dealer* in 1922. Assume that the editor and a few other people read this story and liked it. These people talk enthusiastically of the story and perhaps twice as many read the next Hemingway offering. Soon many admirers are talking—a snowball is rolling in the advance guard. A half-dozen little magazines are printing Hemingway stories and he has several thousand readers. An obscure, noncommercial press in Paris publishes his first thin volume, *Three Stories and Ten Poems*. The snowball rolls into Scribner's office. Finally

in 1926 comes *The Sun Also Rises*. A writer has been started on the road to success—by the little magazines and their readers. [14]

One might well add, "and by their editors and sponsors." If the appearance of *Three Stories and Ten Poems* in 1923 helped Hemingway's "snowball" to gain crucial momentum (or at least to bring him to Contact Editions' affiliation with Three Mountains Press, which printed his *In Our Time* a year later), then thanks in good measure can be laid not only at publisher Robert McAlmon's door but also at the door of his wife, Bryher, whose funds and connections helped provide for the success of Contact Editions.[8] After two brief publications in *The Double Dealer*, Hemingway's next appearances were in *Poetry*, with poems and bits of literary gossip that were to become characteristic, and in the *Little Review*, with six stories that later appeared in *In Our Time* and the poem "They All Made Peace—What Is Peace?"[9] Clearly, the discernment of the women who edited little magazines and supported small publishing concerns proved essential to the "snowballing" of Hemingway's reputation.

The Little Magazine: A History and a Bibliography (1947) remains the best general introduction to the role that small magazines played in the early twentieth century, but its tendency to highlight the works of men reflects an approach that many literary histories have used. This tone particularly affects interpretations of the psychological politics behind the creation and promotion of avant garde work. If men have been expected to be bold or experimental, and women have been expected to be emotional or compliant, then post hoc discussions of the bravado that is obvious in much modernist writing will be pitched a certain way. For instance, Hoffman, Allen, and Ulrich choose to characterize Ezra Pound as "truly the 'personality as poet,'" a man whose "critical remarks are characterized by spasmodic penetration, an arbitrary and cocksure forthrightness, and an obstinate refusal to brook what he considered untimely or petty opposition," and who thereby became "one of the most effective sponsors of experimental literature in our century" (21). Their assessment of the *Little Review* notes some of the same energy and individuality but gives these qualities a distinctly different spin; the *Little Review* is characterized as a "personal" magazine that reflected Margaret Anderson's "breathless racing with life" from interest to interest (20): "It was an exciting magazine, quixotic, sometimes immature, but always radiating blue sparks of highly charged feeling. Many were the stars that danced before Margaret Anderson's impulsive vision . . . Inevitably, there was to come

---

[8] This is attested to in the first of Bryher's autobiographical books, *The Heart to Artemis: A Writer's Memoirs* (New York: Harcourt, Brace 1962) 201.
[9] Nicholas Joost, *Ernest Hemingway and the Little Magazines: The Paris Years* (Barre; Barre, 1968) 19–33, 41–42.

a time when she could glimpse no further horizon" (52). The style of Anderson's magazine is equated with her personality and dismissed as a limitation, and Anderson's successes in dealing with "opposition"—most notably in her and Jane Heap's attempts to publish as much of *Ulysses* as they could in the face of legal and economic sanctions—are given little credit even during the more extended discussion of the magazine found in the book. Also, Anderson is often discussed as if she stood alone in her editorship, although readers of the magazine find abundant evidence of Heap's contributions made in her own particular style. In general, the terms applied to Anderson carry heavy connotations of emotionalism, immaturity, and frivolity, which have often been used to dismiss women and their achievements, whereas Pound's strong personality quirks are treated as an important component of the era's powerful experimental urge.

Through such selective discussion of their topics, these and other literary historians often decide, for example, that Pound "took over" or managed literary magazines more ably than the actual editors, and in a broader sense base their discussions on an assumption that only men's literary work merits critical attention. Discussions of women's work are usually predicated upon the work of associated men, or upon the assumption that women's accomplishments occurred in spite of their personalities rather than because of them. Some historians, sharing the viewpoint of many male modernists, see women's literary magazines as "vessels" that carried the "creations" of male writers—an extension of the belief that women's importance rests in "serving men," a figure of speech carrying a negative sexual charge. Such attention skews and reduces the complexity that these historians claim for modernism, even as it marks the prevailing attitudes within which literary women had to work.

Fortunately, some recent scholarship has begun to correct the neglect and misunderstanding that has resulted from a masculine orientation in scholarship and criticism. When scholars decide to evade certain masculinist assumptions by returning to original data, there is much to discover. Women's influence in literary publishing has been persistent even if not immediately apparent. First books by Ernest Hemingway, Marianne Moore, Samuel Beckett, and William Carlos Williams, for instance, appeared as a result of publishing ventures managed or paid for by Bryher, Harriet Shaw Weaver, and Nancy Cunard, while other women, including Caresse Crosby and Maria Jolas, actively arranged for publication of work by Gertrude Stein, James Joyce, and D. H. Lawrence. The extensive influence even of acknowledged little reviews sometimes comes as a surprise. Perhaps the most important example is the English periodical the *New Freewoman*. Under its former identity (the *Freewoman*, started in 1911 by Dora Marsden), the paper had pursued social issues, particularly feminist and suffragist concerns; after an eight-month hiatus resulting from the publisher's bankruptcy and a distributor's boycott, the fortnightly was refunded through the initiative of Harriet Shaw Weaver, who had answered Marsden's call for assistance in the last issue of the *Freewoman* and had become a good friend, interested in supporting Marsden's socialist, feminist, and individualist ideas. In 1913 the periodical's title became the *New Freewoman*, with Rebecca West, who had both contributed to and raised funds for the paper, as assistant editor, and the paper began to print more poetry and fiction. Les Garner notes that West worked tirelessly for the paper and served as a link to the public "Discussion Circles" it had spawned (93). After a few months, she secured the additional services of Ezra Pound as literary editor, although his demanding nature was one reason she decided to resign in October 1913, with the assistant editorship going to Richard Aldington.[10]

But the magazine's most influential era lay ahead, when the *New Freewoman* became the *Egoist* in 1914, with Weaver as editor and Aldington as literary editor, a position that passed to H.D. during 1916 and then to T. S. Eliot in 1917.[11] Gillian Hanscombe and Virginia Smyers note that, under Weaver, "*The Egoist* became clearly a literary periodical" (178); Marsden had effectively withdrawn due to strain and a desire to spend more time with her own writing. The *Egoist* printed the much-discussed "Imagist number" in 1915, as well as many serializations, particularly James Joyce's *Portrait of the Artist as a Young Man* and portions of *Ulysses*. Its literary review provided early critical notice for H.D., Ford Madox Ford, Joyce, Wyndham Lewis, Amy Lowell, Marianne Moore, Pound, Dorothy Richardson, and many other emerging figures. In addition, Weaver developed the Egoist Press in order to publish *Portrait of the Artist* in book form, since no other publisher would do it; some extremely important by-products of the Egoist Press's

---

[10] Hanscombe and Smyers 169–70. See also Jane Lidderdale and Mary Nicholson, *Dear Miss Weaver: Harriet Shaw Weaver, 1876–1961* (New York: Viking, 1970), and Les Garner, *A Brave and Beautiful Spirit: Dora Marsden, 1882–1960* (Aldershot: Avebury/Gower, 1990) 114–16. Marden and West were not particularly happy about the direction Pound seemed to want to take, but both wanted the paper to increase its literary aspects.

[11] Hanscombe and Smyers quote a letter written in 1914 by Aldington to Amy Lowell in which he states, "Hilda is taking over the Egoist. I seem to be a little 'out' with Miss Weaver just now." (176). This piece of evidence suggests that, although Aldington and H.D. worked closely together on a number of literary projects through World War I, H.D. had more influence on the *Egoist* than the "official" date of her literary editorship (1916) would credit. See Cyrena N. Pondrom, ed., "Selected Letters from H.D. to F.S. Flint: A Commentary on the Imagist Period," *Contemporary Literature* 10.4 (1969): 557–86, and my discussion in chapter 4 [*Women Editing Modernism: Little Magazines & Literary History* (Lexington: U of Kentucky P, 1995) – Ed.].

existence included books by Richard Aldington, Jean Cocteau, H.D., T. S. Eliot, Moore, and Pound.[12] Weaver's propitious decision to become editor despite her inexperience not only led to the printing of significant modern writing but also served private purposes: it allowed her to provide a steady outlet for her friend Marsden's philosophical writings, it kept Marsden independent from Pound's antagonism, and it allowed Weaver to expand her skills and knowledge in new directions while still consulting with her friend through frequent correspondence (Garner 133, 135). Marsden and Weaver's cooperation in running the *New Freewoman* and in consulting about the *Egoist* served their ambitions in mutually satisfactory ways.

At almost the same time as the *New Freewoman, Poetry: A Magazine of Verse* appeared in Chicago under the editorship of Harriet Monroe and her first coeditor, Alice Corbin Henderson. *Poetry* presented in its early years an astonishing gallery of new poetry by H.D., T. S. Eliot, Marianne Moore, Ezra Pound, Carl Sandburg, Wallace Stevens, and William Carlos Williams, among others. Although, as Ellen Williams points out, retrospect causes us to expect more from the first issues than they actually contained, the impact of that magazine upon the literary community was immediate (31–33). *Poetry* served as a forum for debate about the Imagists, free verse, international versus national identity in art, and the role of the artist's audience—all issues of considerable importance for the development of modern aesthetic ideas. The early editorial dynamics of *Poetry* included not only Monroe and Ezra Pound, as is usually pointed out, but also Henderson, who assisted Monroe during the first crucial years of the magazine's existence. The relationship between Monroe and Henderson altered and sharpened *Poetry's* editorial policies. Henderson, for example, mediated between Monroe and Pound, discovered and promoted such figures as Sandburg, Edgar Lee Masters, and Sherwood Anderson, and engaged in vigorous defense of vers libre. Henderson and Monroe's interactions, like those of Weaver and Marsden at the *New Freewomen*, demonstrate the kind of cooperative work often found in women's editorial activities, which when viewed in the aggregate suggest that women's community was integral to the development of modern critical sensibility.

In addition to the pioneering work done in *Poetry* and the *Egoist*, numerous other periodicals that were edited, produced, or funded by women provided space and encouragement for new ideas. Among these, two of the most important are the *Little Review*, edited by Margaret Anderson and Jane Heap, and the *Dial*, under Marianne Moore's editorship from 1925 to 1929. The *Little Review*, founded in Chicago in 1914, carried sections of Joyce's *Ulysses* (later published in its entirety by Sylvia Beach in Paris), and pieces by Djunda Barnes, Mary Butts, H.D., Eliot, Moore, Pound, and Richardson; it also served, under Jane Heap's guidance especially in the

---

[12] Lidderdale and Nicholson 459–65.

1920s, to introduce many avant garde visual artists and theorists. The *Dial*, which had already demonstrated a bold modern vision by printing Eliot's "The Waste Land" and work by E. E. Cummings, came under Moore's hand in 1925; she solicited and secured work from such important writers as D. H. Lawrence, Pound, and Gertrude Stein.[13]

Other women such as Ethel Moorhead and Kay Boyle (*This Quarter*), Katherine Mansfield (*Rhythm*, the *Blue Review*, the *Signature*), Florence Gilliam (*Gargoyle*), and Maria Jolas (*transition*) helped to edit and produce small magazines that extended the influence and scope of avant garde art and writing. Women were drawn to work in and support other kinds of publishing as well, most notably through independent publishing concerns founded or operated by Sylvia Beach (Shakespeare and Company), Gertrude Stein (Plain Editions), Nancy Cunard (The Hours Press), Caresse Crosby (Editions Narcisse, At the Sign of the Sundial, and Black Sun Press), and Wyn Henderson (Aquila Press), or through financial "patronage" of fine presses by such women as Barbara Harrison (Harrison Press), Helena Rubinstein (who staked her husband, Edward Titus, for At the Sign of the Black Manikin Press), Harriet Shaw Weaver (The Egoist Press), and Annie Winifred Ellerman—known and Bryher—whose funds helped support a number of avant garde presses in England and Europe . . . Whatever list one might compile of the "masterpieces" of the early twentieth century, it will include a high proportion of pieces for which women provided the forum for first publication, the impetus, the monetary support, or the initial critical reception, which was extremely important because so much experimental writing was going on. The more one looks, the more evidence one finds that, but for women's foresight and resourcefulness, much important modernist literature, art, and criticism might never have been printed.

---

[13] For a discussion of Moore's work for the *Dial*, see chapter 5. I rely heavily on unpublished correspondence in the American literature collections, Beinecke Rare Book and Manuscript Library, Yale University. See also Grace Schulman, *Marianne Moore: The Poetry of Engagement* (Urbana: U of Illinois P, 1986) 9–25, and Taffy Martin, *Marianne Moore: Subversive Modernist* (Austin: U of Texas P, 1986) 48.

JANE HEAP AND HER CIRCLE

by Linda Lappin (2004)

Late one morning in February, 1921, two women followed an Irish police officer through the corridors of the Jefferson Street Police Court of New York City. The men bustling about the offices lifted their heads to observe these two unlikely criminals on their way to be fingerprinted. One was a lady of high fashion, wearing a tailored blue suit and a cloche hat, a string of pearls looped upon her satin blouse, and a pale silk rose pinned to her lapel. She walked with self-confidence and poise, as if striding across a stage to take a last bow. Indeed, she was a gifted pianist accustomed to smiling down upon admiring audiences, but today her face was a mask of disdain: arched eyebrows finely tweezed, nose discreetly powdered, dark red lips. Her right hand was gloved, the left bare. Behind her walked a short squarish woman with close-cropped hair, sporting a man's jacket over a broad black skirt, a black bow tie, and deep scarlet lipstick.

Led to a desk where another policeman awaited, the chic lady in blue balked at the ink into which she was invited to dip her fingers. All morning, on her lawyer's instructions, she had sat docilely through her trial, but now lighting a cigarette in her ungloved hand, she announced that she could not possibly comply unless they assured her no irremediable damage would be done to her person or her manicure. Her requests for fresh towels, scented soap, and a clean nailbrush sent the officers scurrying obediently.

Her companion observed the scene with restrained amusement. Her own hands, calloused and muscular, the nails rimmed with printers' ink and oil paint, were certainly no stranger to stains, and managed carpentry tools or embroidery needles with equal skill. Perhaps she even sympathized with the men flustering about her friend, whose eau-de-cologne added a piquant note in the warm room above the smell of stale tobacco and perspiration.

After depositing their prints, the women were escorted to the exit, wondering all the while where they would find the money to pay the hundred dollar fine they had been charged for distributing pornography through the U.S. mails. At the time, their worldly funds amounted to less than five dollars cash. The man whose charges led to their conviction tipped his hat as they stepped out to the street. John Sumner, head of the New York Society for the Suppression of Vice, had never met such original ladies before. It was a pity they had let themselves become entangled in this dirty business.

These criminals were Margaret Anderson and Jane Heap, the editors of the *Little Review*, and the pornography they had purveyed through the post office consisted of copies of their magazine in which excerpts from James Joyce's *Ulysses* had been printed—the first chapters of Joyce's masterpiece to be published in America. The bone of contention that morning in court had been the Nausicaa chapter, which contains sequences of voyeurism and masturbation. Sumner, speaking on behalf of the good citizens of New York, feared this text might corrupt the minds of young girls and wanted all publication stopped.

Anderson was disappointed they had not ended up in jail, from where she might have circulated some useful propaganda for *Ulysses*, which despite their ardent promotion in America had not yet received critical acclaim. She blamed her own innate refinement for the missed opportunity. During the trial, one of the judges remarked that it was obvious merely by looking at her that she could have no idea what the words she had published actually meant.

This was not the first time Margaret Anderson or Jane Heap had found themselves on the wrong side of the law for their daring publishing ventures or for their association with undesirables such as the anarchist Emma Goldman, another frequent contributor to the *Little Review*. Anderson had once been accused of vagrancy, when, to avoid paying rent, she had camped with a group of friends for several months in tents on private property along Lake Michigan, and even of burglary, in California, when she and Jane broke into an abandoned house that belonged to the local sheriff. It was always Anderson's good looks and charm that got them off the hook.

The *Ulysses* obscenity trial marked a downturn in the history of the *Little Review*, in the public and private lives of its editors, and in the annals of civil liberties and censorship in America. No New York papers came to their defense during the trial, and some donors and subscribers to the *Little Review* withdrew their support of the magazine. Even the *New York Times* admonished them for publishing "lascivious literature." It was not until after the book's publication in Paris that the ban on *Ulysses* was overturned in 1933 by Judge Woolsey in a ruling that was to have far-reaching impact on artistic freedom in the U.S. For Anderson and Heap, the banning of *Ulysses* in 1921 was a serious financial setback and a check on a creative project into which they had poured not only their funds, but their emotional and vital energies for over four years.

Avidly read by a heterogeneous group of subscribers throughout the United States and Europe, the *Little Review* was among the first literary magazines to introduce American readers to feminism, modernist writing, radical politics, avant-garde visual art, and new music theory. Anderson founded the magazine in Chicago in 1913 because, as she claims in her autobiography, *My Thirty Years' War*, there was no good conversation to be had anywhere. A passionate advocate of art for art's sake, Anderson had been introduced to the Chicago publishing world fresh out of college and by the age of twenty-seven had gained the skills and connections to launch her own magazine. Scenting something new in the air after the 1913 Armory Show of post-impressionist painting, she longed to establish herself as an intermediary between the new artists and writers and a new reading public. Her magazine was meant to be a challenge: "making no compromises to the public taste."

When Anderson met Chicago artist Jane Heap, she discovered not only a spellbinding conversationalist, but a promising editor with an acute intellect and pungent humor, if only she could be convinced to put pen to paper. Heap soon joined her as companion, lover, co-editor, and business partner in an adventure that absorbed their personal lives, their creativity, and their finances for fifteen years—the magazine was produced on a shoestring budget and the issues were stacked, wrapped, and labeled for mailing in Jane's bedroom.

In 1917 they moved the magazine to New York because Margaret felt they had exhausted the resources of provincial Chicago. She wanted her magazine to become "an international organ." By this time the *Little Review* had attracted the attention of Ezra Pound, then living in London. In a letter thanking Anderson for a copy of the magazine, Pound criticized the editors for their sloppy proofreading and general bad taste and offered his assistance as foreign editor, dictating the following conditions: "I want an official organ where I and T.S. Eliot can appear once a month (or once an issue) and where James Joyce can appear when he likes and where Wyndham Lewis can appear if he comes back from the war."

Ezra Pound was not the only literary lion who sought to gain editorial control of this seminal review. Poet Amy Lowell had also demanded to be taken on as poetry editor, promising to pay $150 a month for this privilege, but Anderson had refused. Pound's offer, instead, was accepted and in return he obtained financial backing for the magazine from his own benefactor, John Quinn, a New York lawyer. Quinn helped Anderson and Heap through many scrapes with the law, as for example when, in support of anarchist Emma Goldman, they published several editorials against conscription and were investigated by the federal authorities. He later defended them unsuccessfully in the *Ulysses* trial. In addition, Pound put Heap and Anderson into direct contact not only with the expatriate and self-exiled writers from abroad like Eliot and Joyce, but with contemporary French poets like Apollinaire and Cocteau.

Anderson relates that when she scanned the first excerpts of *Ulysses* Pound had sent her, she uttered a cry of delight, for she instantly recognized the most brilliant piece of writing that her magazine would ever publish, which, indeed, it had to publish at all costs. "We'll print this if it's the last thing we do!" she said (as their friend Alan Tanner observed, it very nearly was). Few readers shared their enthusiasm at first while critics ignored or panned Joyce's opus. Still, Anderson and Heap pressed on, despite protests of some subscribers who condemned Joyce's work as "filth" and "slush."

After the trial's conclusion, Margaret Anderson plunged into depression and gradually lost interest in the *Little Review*, seeking consolation in love affairs. Jane Heap, deeply hurt by Margaret's defection, struggled on with the tedious paperwork involved in getting out the magazine. Under her editorship, the *Little Review* gave increasing space to the visual arts. She also opened an art gallery in Manhattan, The Little Review Gallery, where New Yorkers viewed works by Brancusi, Picabia, Kurt Schwitters, Man Ray, and Tristan Tzara. Few historians have noted Heap's continued efforts to introduce America to new artistic trends from Europe, and her importance as transmitter of the avant-garde has largely gone unrecognized. Yet this was only one of her many unacknowledged accomplishments.

In 1924 Heap and Anderson were in the audience at the Neighborhood Playhouse in New York to witness one of the most exotic and esoteric spectacles to reach the United States from Europe: pupils from George I. Gurdjieff's Institute for the Harmonious Development of Man in Fontainebleau gave a mesmerizing performance of Gurdjieff's sacred dances and gymnastics. The announcement published in the local newspapers had promised an evening of "Ritual Dancing, Music, and Supernormal Phenomena," but for Heap and Anderson this event proved to be transforming.

Re-elaborations of postures, dances, and exercises culled from the religious and folk traditions of Central Asia and the Far East, Gurdjieff's sacred dances and movements presented to western viewers stunning feats of coordination and physical awareness. Dancers were accompanied by piano music, performed by Thomas de Hartmann, noted Russian composer, who collaborated with Gurdjieff on the transcription of a corpus of dances, songs, and melodies from Central Asia. It was an exclusive performance, by invitation only, and although no tickets were sold, the house was packed. New York intellectuals and high society crowded the theater, listening to the explanatory lecture given by A. R. Orage, former editor of the influential *New Age*, which had folded just two years earlier when Orage gave up his London life to follow Gurdjieff to France.

Many were drawn to the mysterious Gurdjieff during his American tour when this performance was repeated in other major U.S. theaters. Gurdjieff's appeal cut across class and educational differences, galvanizing rich and poor, artists and businessmen. Leading figures in the publishing and music worlds – including Gorham Munson, Muriel Draper, and Lincoln Kirstein, future director of the New York City Ballet, would soon become pupils. Others were intrigued but wary, like Hart Crane, who described Gurdjieff's costume as similar to "a lion tamer's." Reviewers in newspapers across the nation praised the dancers' "perfect muscular control combined with grace and significance."

Both Heap and Anderson were deeply struck by the ideas expounded by Orage, by the dancers, and by the figure of Gurdjieff who proffered a method of self-development and awareness enhancement, in itself an exciting concept for these two women who dreamed of making life itself an art and had dedicated themselves to the quest for new ideas. Gurdjieff's teaching centered upon the awakening of a higher self lulled to sleep by the mechanical quality of modern life. This project surpassed all Heap and Anderson had known and done before: radical politics, radical life style, and the promotion of the avant-garde. Jane Heap offered her Greenwich Village room as a meeting place where people might gather to discuss Gurdjieff's ideas. Then in the summer of 1924, she sailed for France on the Cunard Line to visit Gurdjieff's institute at the Prieuré in Fontainebleau where she joined Margaret Anderson and Margaret's new partner, the French opera singer Georgette Leblanc.

Over the next decade, both Jane Heap and Margaret Anderson established themselves in Europe, although throughout the twenties Heap traveled back and forth from Paris to New York, putting out the *Little Review* and organizing exhibitions at her Manhattan gallery. In Paris between the world wars they gravitated to the center of several extraordinary communities—the artists' quarter, the expatriate Anglophone community with its writers, intellectuals, and small press publishers, and the legendary literary salons run by the formidable Parisian hostesses: Natalie Barney and Gertrude Stein, among others. But within these communities there lay a more secret and private one: a group of friends—Heap, Anderson, Georgette Leblanc, Kathryn Hulme, Solita Solano and her companion Janet Flanner, the *New Yorker* correspondent—all writers, all lesbians, five of whom were pupils of Gurdjieff and members of a special study group known as the Rope, directed by Jane Heap under Gurdjieff's personal instruction. Flanner, companion to Solano, was the only one to resist Gurdjieff's magnetism and she resented his influence upon the others. Over the years, Flanner grew only slightly more accepting of Solita's connection with Gurdjieff for whom she worked as personal secretary. In Paris in the twenties and thirties, these six women often lived in the same hotel—the Hôtel Saint-Germain des Prés in Rue Bonaparte, and worked closely together, editing each other's manuscripts, furnishing each other with emotional encouragement and financial support. Although in later life they formed new partnerships and were separated by great distances, they remained a tightly knit circle, always ready to rush to each other's aid when needed, even well into old age.

As their private lives moved in new directions and as their involvement in Gurdjieff's school deepened, Anderson and Heap decided to close down the *Little Review* in order to dedicate themselves to their individual projects: Jane Heap would later play an important role in transmitting Gurdjieff's work in England for nearly thirty years while Margaret wrestled to record her experiences of Gurdjieff's philosophy in two books, *The Fiery Fountains* and *The Unknowable Gurdjieff*.

Margaret Anderson has left a detailed account of her personal development in a three-volume autobiography, but Jane Heap has left hardly any record at all: no books, no journals, a scattering of letters, brief essays and editorial comments appearing in the *Little Review*, often signed only with the lowercase initials jh. She strove for a low profile, for near invisibility. Her full name did not appear on the masthead of the *Little Review* until Spring 1925. Heap was an intensely private person, so reticent, Margaret Anderson recounts, that she detested doing the shopping, for she hated having to divulge to the grocer or the butcher what she was planning to cook for dinner.

Nonetheless, Heap's wit and intelligence are legendary. Many of her one-line witticisms and pithy criticisms, later recorded by her pupils as "the aphorisms of Jane Heap," have assumed the status of proverbs. Although her name appears in studies of the *Little Review* and of early radical movements in the U.S., in memoirs dealing with the expatriate community in Paris in the twenties, in encyclopedias of lesbians and their contribution to American culture, and in many memoirs connected to the diffusion of Gurdjieff's ideas in England and America, no biographies of Heap have yet been written. Several feminist scholars have tried and given up the attempt.

One would-be biographer, Susan Noyes Platt, has defined research into Heap's life as "the great dead end," for Heap left few traces. Heap would probably be pleased to know that so far no one has pinned her down to any of her former selves: anarchist, artist, cross-dresser, radical lesbian, modernist editor, champion of civil liberties, gallery owner, charismatic leader of Gurdjieff groups, keeper of a repair shop for antique toys.

Still, a few biographical facts are known: Jane Heap was born in Topeka, Kansas, in 1883, of an English father and a Norwegian mother whose ancestors came from the Arctic Circle—a heritage Heap cherished, for she sometimes boasted that she was not American at all, but Norwegian. These were the days of the horse and buggy, gas-lit parlors, stiff muslin bloomers, and scorching curling irons—a quaint and archaic America she would soon out-strip, and whose values she would come to reject. "Families are only meant to do penance," she grumbled in a letter to her friend Florence Reynolds. What little we know of her early years is to be gleaned from her correspondence with Reynolds, and from brief autobiographical references published in the *Little Review*. Heap's childhood was dominated by an unusual social and architectural environment: the Topeka insane asylum where her father worked, which stood next door to her home. Writing in the *Little Review*, she describes the impact of the asylum on her mental development.

> It was a world outside of the world, where realities had to
> be imagined and where, even through those excursions in
> illusions and hallucinations, there ran a strange loneliness.
> The world can never be so lonely in those places where the
> mind has never come as in a place where the mind has
> gone. There were no books to read in this place except the
> great volumes in the Patients' Library; and I had read them
> all. There was no one to ask about anything. There was
> no way to make a connection with "life." Out there in the
> world they were working and thinking; here we were still.
> Very early I had given up on everyone except the Insane.
> The others knew nothing about anything, or knew only
> uninteresting facts. From the Insane I could get everything.
> They knew everything about nothing, and were my author-
> ity; but beyond that there was a silence. Who had made
> the pictures, the books, and music in the world? And how
> had they made them?

Early exposure to the asylum patients shaped her vision of the adult world and gave her firsthand experience of the strange workings of the psyche. She quickly realized that the boundaries between sane and insane are not always distinctly drawn, a conviction she shared with Gurdjieff. Wandering those desolate corridors, she sensed that a separate reality existed apart from daily life—apart from the sane world of "uninteresting facts." Art in all its forms was the bridge to that transcendent dimension—where one could connect more authentically to life's secret sources. This hunger for authenticity of self is perhaps the touchstone of Jane Heap's existence and she was to seek it in many ways: through art and through the spirit, and also through her private life.

The artist, in Jane's eyes, was a privileged person of superior sensibilities who stood out in the crowd. "Who is there but the artist," she wrote in the *Little Review*, "who is willing to feel in this thing the imminence of something beyond life and personality?" To art, then, she would dedicate her life. She began painting seriously at the age of sixteen. After high school, she enrolled in the Art Institute of Chicago. Graduating in 1905, she then found employment as an arts instructor at the Lewis Institute, while continuing her own arts and crafts studies in night school. At Lewis she formed a strong attachment with a student, Florence Reynolds, daughter of a wealthy businessman. Over the years their youthful passion matured into a deep friendship. Florence gave Jane many forms of emotional, moral, and even economic support throughout her life. In her long letters from New York and from abroad addressed to Florence, first as "Tiny Heart" and then as "Mother," Jane recounted her escapades with Margaret Anderson, her political involvement with Emma Goldman, and the behind-the-scenes story of the *Little Review*, providing titillating gossip about Greenwich Village and the Left Bank, and later graphically depicting the terrors of the London Blitz. These letters, now edited by Holly Baggett and published by New York University Press, are nearly the only personal documentation in print regarding Jane Heap, with the exception of Anderson's autobiography.

The early letters of 1908–9 show Heap's personality in formation. At twenty-five, Jane Heap was dreaming of big things as a Chicago artist, but financial realities brought her back to Kansas to live with her family, who were supportive at first of her "oddness." She could still enjoy family outings: a Ringling show or a visit to the state fair, but tensions pulled beneath. "I cannot be alone in peace for a minute," she protests. "I have not the feeling for my sisters I should have," she confesses to Florence, and adds that she has refused to attend her sister's religious wedding ceremony. Frequently she complains of having her time frittered away by household chores and scorns her sisters for throwing money away on cosmetics. Jealous of her nephew's opportunity to study medicine, she objects that she might have studied art in Paris for a year on the funds set aside for his education.

That her daughter was somehow different from other girls was apparent to Jane's mother, although Jane was shocked by her mother's plans for her future, as she confides to Florence in a letter, "Mother said she never expected me to marry—that when all the kids are gone, she and father would come to live with me, and I could go to school . . ." In young womanhood, Jane's sexual orientation must have been quite clear to her and her circle, other young women who called themselves by men's names and peppered their letters to each other with romantic endearments. Of one (female) friend named "James," she writes, "She said she had been doing some of my stunts—dressing up in men's clothes and making love to girls." To Florence she wrote, "You called our Love—Friendship—it has not got to that has it? Isn't it very like the Love our friends the poets sing about. I think it very strange and different from friendship, or just love with a little letter, don't you?" Later she expressed her perception of "strangeness" to Florence even more explicitly, "Why did I always feel conscious when there were people present—as if it were not fair to you or something to love you publicly or what was it? I think we felt a difference, that others did not suspect." The older she grew, the more she reconciled herself to her "difference," the more her self-presentation moved toward a masculine mode: men's capes, ties, hats, and tailored jackets worn with a skirt or trousers. Ostentation of such a mannish image was an act of courage in those days. Her most conspicuous piece of clothing was a Russian fur hat that dramatically set off the stark geometry of her cheekbones and jaw line. Admirers in Paris praised her face as resembling a young Greek god's: broad forehead, full cheeks and chin, high cheekbones. Margaret thought she resembled Oscar Wilde.

A young woman of powerful feelings and intense moods (she describes herself kissing a photograph of Florence "to destruction"), Jane Heap was a romantic—"I have been playing the moon was you," she tells Florence—and an idealist. "I believe in living a little more than necessary seeing and believing life to be as one wished it to be, creating beauty where it doesn't exist," she claims. At the age of thirty, Jane Heap lacked only one thing: a worthy cause into which her whole being might be channeled.

Jane Heap and Margaret Anderson met in 1916, in the Fine Arts Building in Chicago, where Margaret rented a studio as her office for the *Little Review*. Jane was 33, Margaret 30. At the time of their encounter, Margaret was discussing Eleonora Duse with one of the magazine's potential patrons, a woman aptly nicknamed "Nineteen Millions." Nineteen Millions had just decried D'Annunzio's ill treatment of the great actress, at which Jane, unable to contain herself, let out "a loud and tender laugh" and confessed that Duse had always given her "a large pain." Nineteen Millions stomped out, incensed, but Margaret was entranced by such brave debunking and cultural iconoclasm. Here was a woman ready to speak her mind frankly, toppling the idols of "high culture," infringing the rules of "bon ton,"—another trait Jane would share with George Gurdjieff. To Anderson, Jane Heap was a bracing blast of fresh air, and her conversation was absolutely the most stimulating to be had anywhere.

This perception was not unique to Margaret Anderson. Jane Heap's captivating conversation and charismatic presence were noted by many in America and Europe. One Paris friend commented that Heap radiated a magnetism that was almost palpable to both men and women. Margaret felt that Jane's assistance—her ideas and her talk—would guarantee success to the *Little Review*, but Heap was reluctant. Why try to shape people's opinions about art or any other subject? Why have a magazine at all? she demanded. Margaret responded, "Imagine allowing the intellectuals to stagnate in stupidity when a word or two from her would change their mental life!" Margaret's arguments won her over, or perhaps wore her down, and she agreed to try. Still, Heap did not consider herself a writer. The only way to record her fabulous talk was to dictate it to Margaret, as they could not afford a dictaphone. Jane's irreverent wit added extra bite to the magazine's editorials. Her eye for bold modern type fonts and bright cover designs brought a visual dimension to its innovative message. Soon she was writing her own articles and quickly became the real power—for it was Jane who summed up the magazine's credo: "To express the emotions of life is to live/ To express the life of emotions is to make art." Her critical sense determined the standards by which submissions were judged. Moreover Jane enjoyed the tasks Margaret detested: answering letters from subscribers and would-be collaborators sending in manuscripts, most of which, Margaret claims, were very bad.

Talk was the medium and the substance of Heap and Anderson's relationship. They did nothing but talk says Anderson, for hours, days, years. Their domestic life was sometimes arranged to accommodate this overpowering impulse. In one home, they put their beds in the dining room and dined in pajamas so that after dinner there would be no need to halt the conversation in order to undress. They simply moved from table to bed, and kept talking till dawn, even, says Anderson, while half unconscious. Mainly they discussed art, and "the strange necessity" some human beings feel to create it. At last Margaret had found a sparring partner with whom she "could argue as long as I wanted." For Jane, too, these arguments were a stimulus. She required resistance to make any conversation worthwhile.

Jane saw Margaret as her "comrade" and her "blessed antagonistic complement." To the uninitiated outer world, their contrast in appearances was familiar: the ultra feminine and fashionable Anderson and the austere and trousered Heap. Prior to her relationship with Jane Heap, however, according to the expatriate writer Glenway Wescot, Margaret dressed in a severely tailored masculine manner in her twenties and only later adopted the look of the high society femme fatale immortalized in her portraits by Berenice Abbott and Man Ray. Margaret's alluring makeover was probably not, or at least not only, a response to Jane's male identification in clothes, but a consciously adopted strategy for enhancing her success. One of her main concerns from the very beginning was fundraising for the *Little Review*, and her technique was direct: she marched uninvited into offices of business tycoons, demanding they listen to her plea for patronage. Very often, she walked out again with a generous check in hand. Men found her extraordinarily attractive. Hemingway pursued her futilely in Paris, wrote Jane, like a lovesick rabbit. Women, too, were impressed by Anderson's grooming and style, although for a long period of her life she possessed but one suit and one blouse. For Margaret, economic survival was a question of looking and playing a part. She often criticized Jane's outrageous attire, and would sometimes refuse to be seen in the street with her if she were wearing her wild Russian fur hat.

Teamed up at any social gathering, they were a formidable pair, "much loved" and "much loathed." There was nothing Margaret relished as much as an impassioned argument and she was anxious to display Jane's superior intellectual powers. Eagerly she pounced upon her chosen prey, invented some pretense for dissent, and then in the heat of debate let Jane deliver the final blow to their antagonist. "You are the buzz and I am the sting," Heap once quipped in a brilliant assessment of their mode of social operation. Sometimes Jane was reluctant to ridicule or expose an opponent. Despite her tough exterior, she was sensitive to people's feelings. She liked to argue for fun, and would surprise her interlocutors by taking both sides in order to get an argument churning. Jane viewed strong clashes of opinion as a means of synthesis and union: "We need fights, discussions—hot and impolite, jeering and insulting, to knit the thing together," she wrote in the *Little Review*. Creative conversation required active participation. "Oh come on," she would prod her listeners, "a good answer deserves a good question." Margaret's approach to dialectic was more domineering. She not only wanted to win but to take converts. Anderson was convinced that if she had had more time to talk things over with John Sumner, he would have become a fervent fan of *Ulysses*.

Once Jane had agreed to join Anderson as co-editor, they set out for California on a subscription campaign, although they were desperately short of funds. Prior to departure, they put up posters in the Chicago Fine Arts Building begging for contributions and were richly rewarded with packets of tea and coffee, candy, cakes, gloves, underwear, and other donations to help see them through the journey. In California they rented a ranch house in the Muir Woods where they spent five months talking, riding, and enjoying the mountain air. The afternoons were dedicated to work on the magazine, but the manuscripts they had received were all disappointing. Nothing, they found, was worth printing. When the issue was finally ready to go to press, it contained only a two-page spread of cartoons by Jane illustrating their California adventures and thirteen blank pages, intended as a want ad for literary talent.

Anderson's picaresque account of their California sojourn in *My Thirty Years' War* emphasizes the pecuniary instability that plagued both women for most of their lives. Margaret Anderson had perfected the art of living on practically nothing, and had a knack for asking favors of the right people. She even managed to obtain the free loan of a grand piano for their mountain retreat, but Jane Heap sought solutions to their practical and economic problems in her resourcefulness, manual skills, and creativity. Wherever they set up house, Jane crafted furniture, created exotic environments with cheap materials, and designed and sewed most of their clothing.

While in California, Heap revealed aspects of her character to Anderson: a tendency to brood and pout, morose moods, suicidal thoughts. She craved drama, she relished "scenes," which Anderson abhorred. Shortly after their return to Chicago, Margaret decided to move the magazine to New York, and this proved traumatic for Jane. Train fare was provided by a friend who had just published a piece in *Vanity Fair* and offered them his earnings. Throughout the trip, Jane clutched a sachet, token of her bedroom in Chicago, and kept smelling it for comfort. According to Margaret, she would not look out the taxi window once they were in New York, and when they got to the hotel she threw herself down on her bed and moped for hours while Margaret roamed the streets in search of new miracles to sustain them.

For living space, they found a four-room apartment on West 16th Street, with an undertaker on the first floor and an exterminator in the basement. The editorial office of the *Little Review* was housed nearby in a basement studio in the old Van Buren House at 31 West 14th Street and rented out at twenty-five dollars a month. Once a home had been found, Jane's spirits improved, and they set about redecorating their apartment. Jane's room became a temple of creativity, with walls covered in gold Chinese paper, a dark plum floor, pale cream woodwork, silk cushions in rich colors tossed on a divan suspended from the ceiling by heavy black chains. In this eclectic Wildean environment Jane received authors and artists connected to the *Little Review*.

Cultural life in New York was not all it was cracked up to be. Margaret had expected to be swept away by rhapsodic conversation, but both women discovered that New York's intellectual talk at parties proved to be merely a sterile exchange of information. The only consolation was greater commitment to the magazine, which nearly doubled its number of pages. Margaret tracked down the new contributors, Jane received them in her exotic room with the swinging divan: Hart Crane, Djuna Barnes, William Carlos Williams along with old friends like Sherwood Anderson and Emma Goldman whose work appeared in the review alongside Pound's submissions sent from Europe.

By the time they had established themselves in Greenwich Village in 1917, the honeymoon was over between Anderson and Heap. In her autobiography, Margaret decries Jane's moodiness, while Jane, in her letters to Reynolds, bitterly complains of Margaret's lovers and the "barroom atmosphere of love" she seemed to thrive on. Margaret explained her affairs to Jane as "passing attractions," assuring her anxious companion that she was her one great love, an argument Jane found unconvincing. It was in this period, far from her Kansas home, that Heap began to address Florence as "Mother" and to depend increasingly upon her for moral support. Although Heap may have had a brief affair with Djuna Barnes who wooed her relentlessly in New York, she remained loyal to Margaret Anderson.

Now under the co-direction of Ezra Pound, the *Little Review* grew in scope, authority, and readership. Pound presumptuously dictated the creed of the new masthead: "The Magazine that is read by those Who Write the Others." Despite the magazine's growing reputation as an arbiter of literary taste, its finances were always strained. Although Anderson and Heap engaged the cheapest typographer in New York, Mr. Popovitch on 23rd Street, unpaid bills kept accumulating. Margaret resorted to a strategy of "tears, prayers, hysterics, or rages" to convince the printer to push ahead when advance funds were lacking. Jane's reaction to chaos and stress was quite the opposite. She was seized by "fits of patience" that nettled Anderson. They often spent their Sunday afternoons at the printers', helping read proof, set type, and fold pages for the binders. At home they led a retired life, economizing in every way possible, sewing their own clothes and cutting each other's hair. The only thing they didn't do, Anderson recalls, was make their own shoes.

Such self-sufficiency was vital: a recurring motif in Jane's letters to Florence Reynolds is the constant lack of funds, not to mention the lack of fuel. Jane describes a Spartan Thanksgiving and even bleaker Christmas Eve in 1917: "no money, no presents, no coal, no breakfast, and no tree . . ." The only missive in the mailbox was a catalogue of tombstones and funeral monuments—printed, Heap's keen editor's eye noticed, on exquisite paper. But at the eleventh hour something always saved the day: a letter with cash, a subscription pledge, gifts of food or small luxuries from family or friends, very often from Florence Reynolds, and once again life became the celebration of good things.

The *Ulysses* trial, resulting in heavy economic losses for the *Little Review*, marked the nadir in an ongoing battle with the post office. Joyce was not the only *Little Review* author censored for obscenity. Wyndham Lewis met a similar fate. Whenever a publication was banned after being submitted to the mails, all copies were confiscated and burned. During the serialization of *Ulysses*, of which twenty-three sections, or nearly half the book, appeared over the course of three years, the *Little Review* was banned and burned four times before federal suppression of all further publication. Each episode was traumatic, a "burning at the stake" Anderson claimed, and given the unpaid bills for paper and printing costs, a financial fiasco. Before the trial, Heap published a scathing accusation in the *Little Review*. "The heavy farce and sad futility of trying a creative work in a court of law appalls me." Her prediction that the trial would be a farce proved even more accurate than she first expected: several months later, Jane met one of the judges at a party. Learning she was of Norwegian extraction like himself, he told her that if he had known that fact at the time of the trial, he would have overturned the verdict in their favor. This could hardly have been a consolation, seeing the upheaval the conviction had caused in their lives.

Like so many American artists and intellectuals in the twenties, disillusioned by the puritanical restrictions and cultural aridity of their society, Heap and Anderson turned to Europe in search of fresh intellectual freedom and nourishment. For Anderson, Europe had become the pole of attraction for other reasons. She had fallen in love with opera singer Georgette Leblanc and had decided to follow her to France. Leblanc tried to persuade Margaret to let the magazine die, but Jane would not hear of it, at least not yet. Anderson's name continued to appear on the masthead as editor, but control passed into Jane Heap's hands.

Now that Anderson had stepped aside, Heap also gained greater independence from Pound, who gradually withdrew from his role, but it was Pound who indicated the new direction Heap so eagerly pursued: dadaism. Pound had insisted they respond to the trial by bringing out the most startling European issue possible—and the most startling thing in Europe at that time was the outbreak of Dada. The autumn 1921 issue featured Brancusi, Cocteau, Picabia, and Pound united in a protest against the censorship of *Ulysses*.

Among the Dada artists published in the *Little Review*, Baroness Elsa Von Freytag-Loringhoven—performance/multimedia artist and poet—remains the most controversial, for her status as a serious artist has only recently been recognized. The Baroness, whose prime medium of expression was "corporeal art" and "art-to-wear" costumes, had first wandered into their office in 1917 wearing a tam-o-shanter decorated with long-handled ice cream soda spoons and a necklace of tarnished tea-balls. She soon became one of the most frequent contributors to the *Little Review*. Anderson and Heap's publication of the Baroness' work brought them much criticism from cultural authorities like Harriet Monroe, the editor of *Poetry*, and also from Ezra Pound, but Jane Heap staunchly defended Von Freytag-Loringhoven as the living personification of the dada spirit. By shaving her head and painting her face with postage stamps, the Baroness dared crack the mold of woman's image—which Jane too had broken by cross-dressing—and that Margaret manipulated primarily as a power tool. They could see what the Baroness' critics could not: as a feminist statement, the Baroness' body art was way ahead of her time.

Patronage of authors such as Von Freytag-Loringhoven has often been cited as an indication of Heap and Anderson's dubious tastes and shaky editorial policies when not tempered by Pound's guidance in the later years of the magazine. This view is unfair to both editors' achievements and fails to discern the reasons underlying their enthusiasm for dadaism and, later, for surrealism, which were among the many "great ideas" to which Heap and Anderson were drawn. Dadaism voiced the same spirit of rebellion against bourgeois conformity that had attracted both women to anarchism. Surrealism unlocked the secret contents of the unconscious through which the hidden I revealed itself while questioning our basic assumptions concerning reality. Gurdjieff's cosmology later promised an even greater liberation and revelation of self on a far vaster scale.

Although no longer partners, Heap and Anderson remained united not only by the *Little Review* and their interest in Gurdjieff, but also by a curious family tie: Jane Heap had adopted Anderson's nephews, Tom and Fritz

Peters, after their mother's nervous breakdown, as Margaret had shown no interest in assuming the role of surrogate mother for her sister's children. When Heap traveled to France to study at Gurdjieff's institute in the summer of 1924, the Peters boys were also enrolled as boarders there.

Heap's frequent periods of study at Gurdjieff's Institute in Fontainebleau—with its spiritual discipline, hard work, and illuminating talks with Orage—did not preclude moments of full immersion in Paris. In her letters, she describes the familiar excesses of expatriate life: plentiful cocktails at the Deux Magots, wild dancing in the street till dawn, attending boxing matches with Hemingway, affairs. Heap was also tirelessly at work collecting material for her gallery and for the *Review* and spending hours at the Exposition Internationale des Arts Decoratifs et Industrielles Modernes held in Paris at that time. This proved to be the background research for two exhibitions she would later bring to New York—one on theater and stage design; the other on industrial design and architecture entitled "The Machine Age Exposition" in 1927, where Americans viewed works by Le Corbusier and the Bauhaus for the first time. Her letters also recount evenings with Joyce and Nora, gatherings at Shakespeare and Co., and stimulating visits with Gertrude Stein, who paid homage to Jane Heap in a poem published in the *Little Review*: "Jane was her name and Jane her station and Jane her nation and Jane her situation."

There exists a famous portrait of Jane Heap from this era, at the age of forty-one, taken by Berenice Abbott. Heap wears a tuxedo jacket and a bow tie, hair bobbed savagely short at the back, a thick lock swept across her forehead. Her brooding, deep-set eyes are trained slightly off the camera, the full, unsmiling lips are coated heavily in dark lipstick. She appears remote and forbidding, and thus was she described by the American writer Robert McAlmon, who found her intimidating. Pound was rather more generous, praising her energy and her "ballyhoo." The writer Kathryn Hulme noted another feature—"Warm brown eyes softened the austerity of her masculine countenance."

In 1929, both Jane and Margaret decided it was time to end the *Little Review*. The revolution they once hoped to engender had never got off the ground. The two women no longer shared the same vision of the artist's role. Heap saw the artist more in relation to a collective, or cohesive group, striving for a common aim. Anderson instead tended toward a more personal and inward view, and she began planning her autobiography. Dissatisfied with the state of the arts, they sent out a questionnaire to the writers and artists whose work they had published for over fifteen years. It read:

> What should you most like to do, to know, to be?
> Why wouldn't you change places with any other human
> being?
> What do you look forward to?

What do you fear most for the future?
What has been the happiest moment of your life? The
unhappiest?
(If you care to tell)

Some dismissed the questionnaire haughtily as too naive, or perhaps too nosy. Others, such as Sherwood Anderson, George Antheil, Jean Cocteau, Nancy Cunard, Emma Goldman, Marianne Moore, and Bertrand Russell answered with pondered replies that were published in the final number. Janet Flanner helped edit the farewell issue in their hotel room in Rue Bonaparte, spilling green ink all over the bed. Jane's own contribution read:

> I am bringing the *Little Review* to an end, for my part, because I have found the answers to some of these questions.
>
> The revolution in the arts, begun before the war, heralded a renaissance. The *Little Review* became an organ of this renaissance. No doubt, all so-called thinking people hoped for a new order after the war. This hope was linked with the fallacy that men learn from experience. Facts prove that we learn no more from our experiences than from our dreams.
>
> For years we offered the *Little Review* as a trial track for racers. We hoped to find artists who could run with the great artists of the past or men who could make new records. But you can't get race horses from mules. I do not believe that the conditions of our life can produce men who can give us masterpieces . . .
>
> We have given space in the *Little Review* to 23 new systems of art (all now dead) representing 19 countries. In all of this we have not brought forward anything approaching a masterpiece except the *Ulysses* of Mr. James Joyce . . .
>
> Self-expression is not enough; experiment is not enough; the recording of special moments or cases is not enough. All the arts have broken faith or lost connection with their origin and function . . . The actual situation of art today is not a very important or adult concern (Art is not the highest Aim of man); it is interesting only as a pronounced symptom of an ailing and aimless society.

With this conclusion, Heap had reached a turning point. From now on, she would pursue what she believed was a higher aim, while still paying tribute to Joyce's "near masterpiece" and to the outstanding contribution of the *Little Review* to the culture of her times. "Later magazines," she writes, "had the same intellectual program, but the *Little Review* had the corresponding emotions; and consequently an energy that nothing has been able to turn aside . . . except itself." They had ridden the crest of every new wave—every new artistic movement for over fifteen years. But the waves had all lost momentum and even the society that had allowed such rich aesthetic invention was now crumbling around them. The effects of the stock market crash would soon be felt, first in America and then in Europe, dragging inexorably toward war. The growing crisis in Europe was particularly evident to their friend Janet Flanner, whose "Letter from Paris" in the *New Yorker* furnished an astute analysis of the rise of fascism in Germany, Italy, and Spain, and of its devastating effects on the freedoms and pleasures that had attracted so many Americans to France. While most of their American friends—including Solano and Flanner—would repatriate shortly after Hitler's invasion of Poland in 1939, Heap and Anderson chose to remain in Europe throughout the war, and this decision was to cost them dearly.

Seemingly oblivious to the social deterioration around her, Margaret Anderson had drifted off into a fairy tale with Leblanc. Leblanc's aristocratic relatives had leased the couple a deserted wing in one of the family chateaus, where they lived like lost princesses in the "enchanted gloom," although they often had to do without hot water, electricity, heating, and, as the war approached, even food. Jane remarked to Florence Reynolds that Margaret now dwelled in a strange state of detachment. Margaret paints these years with Leblanc as a slow dream.

Gurdjieff sold the Prieuré in Fontainebleau in 1933, forced by debt to close it down, purchased an apartment in Paris, and entered a new phase of teaching. In 1935, at Gurdjieff's behest, Jane moved to London with her new companion, Elspeth Champcommunal, who had worked in Paris as a designer for British Vogue. Few personal details remain to piece together Jane Heap's life from this point on.

Throughout the thirties, Jane continued corresponding with Anderson and Leblanc, whose "slow dream" terminated abruptly when Georgette discovered a swelling on her arm, signaling a rapidly advancing cancer, just two months prior to the outbreak of the second world war. The ensuing chaos delayed her surgery—and then ended all hope for escape.

Jane, meanwhile, was bearing up under the London bombs, finding refuge at a farm called Gotten Manor. To Florence she describes the Nazi menace as "some horrible, formless, senseless, mass pushing relentlessly against mind and emotion." To the bombing itself she took a stoic attitude, "You can't be afraid. It's either death or not death," she wrote both to Reynolds and to Anderson, while maintaining a sense of humor. "Every day I learn my gas attack lesson, printed in the paper and how to dig a trench in your garden, and then I had to laugh because we have no garden." "There is no where to go if one's time is up, so why worry in the meantime?" she concludes, assuring Reynolds that she has plenty of insulin on hand, should it be needed, and that although the dangers of the bombing were real enough, they were greatly exaggerated by the news reports.

For the first time, her letters bear reference to the diabetes that afflicted her for the rest of her life. Although most of Heap's letters to Reynolds during the war years have been destroyed, from Reynold's answers, which have been preserved, we can patch together a sketchy picture of this dramatic period. Reynolds expresses increasing concern for Anderson and Leblanc, "trapped" in France, and threatened by possible internment in a Nazi camp. A similar fate had befallen two of their friends: the singer Noel Haskins Murphy and fellow Rope member Elizabeth Gordon, who died upon her release.

Anderson's testimony of the last months of Georgette's courageous battle against cancer, recounted in *The Fiery Fountains*, is a lucid if electrifying record of their further withdrawal into a world of their own making. To the very end, they succeeded in making life and even death a work of art: "Our fear of death became quieter. We entered that transition which leads from despair to destiny, which is like the shift that occurs in art—from stylelessness to form."

To read this testimony alongside the correspondence of Jane Heap with Anderson, Leblanc, and Reynolds allows us to glimpse the profound inner transformation that had occurred in this odd triangle—Heap-Anderson-Leblanc—as rivalry and jealousy were replaced by affection and deep respect. To the dying Leblanc, whom she had once detested, Heap writes, "If only we could understand that it is the same Great Self in all of us; that we are only like beads strung on that Great Self—that we have no self of our own until we become one with that self, through work and detachment from our infatuation with the bead that we are now."

Jane Heap spent the last thirty years of her life in service to the Great Self, and to the teaching through which she had encountered its power, conducting Gurdjieff study groups in her house in London, in Hamilton Terrace. Although she had locked the door of her art studio three decades earlier, in London she opened a restoration workshop for antique rocking horses, to give her pupils direct experience of Gurdjieff's method which involved the application of quiet inner attention to crafts and manual tasks. One of her young pupils in the fifties was the theater director Peter Brook, who remembers her thus: "a very unusual person who affirmed nothing other than what she was, which was herself, Jane, all of one piece, living within her own space." The old verve, the expansive mind, the gusto and humor were still there, harnessed into a "a powerful but quiet presence."

One by one the beads of the Great Self slipped from the string that had bound Heap and her circle of intimates. Leblanc died in 1941, Reynolds in 1945, Gurdjieff in 1949, Heap in 1964, Anderson in 1978. Heap, says Brook, had no time for memorials or commemorations. She probably would have frowned upon a biography of her life. Jane Heap strode light years ahead of her contemporaries, given the easy self-confidence with which she lived her life as a lesbian, and the intellectual, artistic, and spiritual adventures in which she fulfilled a destiny as iconoclast and teacher. Many fine writers have attempted to capture the essence of Jane Heap, but Georgette Leblanc, in her imperfect English, sketched this brief portrait, quick and penetrating as a haiku, in one of her last letters to Jane: "You are alone in the strong life—alone in the large mind—alone in the unique and real sky who is on the earth." No one could have described better this woman from the Kansas plains and her search for a great idea.

The author would like to thank Holly Baggett, James Moore, and Peter Brook for their help.

"ALL GOOD DISCOURSE MUST,
LIKE FORWARD MOTION,
KNOW RESISTANCE."
 —James Merrill, *Scripts for the Pageant*

SOME THOUGHTS ON
POETRY

by Ben Leubner (2012)

I.

Poetry is at our mercy. If the most successful of "little" literary magazines were ever in need of humiliation, we would have but to mention the following: T. S. Eliot's "The Love Song of J. Alfred Prufrock" was held in deliberation for over half a year before being published; Wallace Stevens's "Sunday Morning" was mangled and reorganized for its publication (Stevens put up little resistance at the time); Marianne Moore, despite receiving her first American publication there, was apparently so put off by the magazine that she abandoned it for over fifteen years; and William Carlos Williams had to frequently complain to the editor that it was no longer necessary for every line of a poem to start with a capital letter. These, of course, are all early examples and might be attributed to the founding editor, Harriet Monroe, alone (or to her small staff), as opposed to *Poetry* in general. But the errors, oversights, and embarrassments are not editor-specific; they accompany the magazine throughout its history. Take, more recently, the volume *Between the Lines*, the second volume in a history of *Poetry* in letters, compiled and edited by Joseph Parisi and Stephen Young. The volume covers the years 1962–2002, and yet, looking through the index, one notes, amidst the numerous inclusions, the complete absence of, for instance, Frank Bidart's name. Was he simply not submitting?

All of this is as it should be. That is to say, *Poetry*, for its own good, *should* be thus at our mercy, or rather shouldn't forget this host of imperfections which extend back almost a century now, imperfections which constantly resist, or offer material for resistance of, any claim to prestige (and the complacency which may come with it) that the magazine might make for itself, or that others might make for the magazine. It is, in fact, a constant resistance from both within and without the magazine's borders, a resistance that plays the role of gravity to *Poetry's* Pegasus, that has enabled the magazine to become so prestigious in the first place.

James Longenbach begins his 2004 book *The Resistance to Poetry* with the following sentence: "This book is about the ways in which poetry is its own best enemy" (xi). With the help of a capital "P" and some italics, I think we can turn this into a valid assertion concerning Harriet Monroe's magazine of verse: *Poetry* is its own best enemy. What Longenbach's title and opening sentence imply is the fact that the best resistance to poetry comes from poetry itself, both externally, insofar as one poet or poem challenges another, and internally, insofar as poems are composed in "the language of self-questioning—metaphors that turn against themselves, syntax that moves one way because it threatens to move another, voices that speak because they are shattered" (xi). Such resistance doesn't so much inhibit the growth of poetry as provide the grounds for that growth. Similarly, both the external resistance to the small industry of *Poetry* in its early days (offered by, for instance, local Chicago newspapers), as well as the internal resistance that came from the volume's own employees and contributors (most notably in the form of Ezra Pound's hyper-critical letters from abroad, letters which repeatedly accused the magazine for which he was foreign correspondent of publishing trash), fueled even as it constantly threatened the success of *Poetry*, creating a precarious dynamic the maintenance of which was perhaps Harriet Monroe's greatest feat as an editor.

Both the resistance itself and the constant need for it are still there today. When *Poetry* was given over $100 million in 2002 by the philanthropist Ruth Lilly, many people in the literary community openly wondered if such a gift might ruin the magazine. Howard Junker, editor of the journal *ZYZZYVA* in San Francisco, speculated at the time that since *Poetry* was now become a foundation, "sustaining the vision of a venerable little magazine [would] become an afterthought" (*Between the Lines* 383). There may be resentment embedded in these lines, as the editors of *Between the Lines* suspect, but there is also, it seems to me, a legitimate concern. To what extent, that is, is *Poetry*, the "little" magazine, threatened by what T. S. Eliot, as early as 1950, called *Poetry*, "an INSTITUTION" (*Dear Editor* 383)? Ironically, now that *Poetry* is completely financially secure for the first time in its long history of operating, for the most part, on a very tight budget, the need for resistance has perhaps become greater than ever. That is, *Poetry* must resist its own security.

There is little doubt that the magazine will prove capable of this task, its editors and employees having been at it for a good deal of time now, always keeping *Poetry* more or less true to its origins. And yet, as always, there is cause for trepidation. The last two hundred pages or so of *Between the Lines* read more like a history of what is nauseatingly referred to as "po-biz" (the poetry business) than as a history of either poetry or *Poetry*. I found the only sustained redeeming feature of these pages to be the letters exchanged between Donald Hall and Joseph Parisi concerning the sickness and eventual death from leukemia of the former's wife, the poet Jane Kenyon (pages 312–323). Here, at least, was an existential concern, something much more profoundly human than news of financial reports, arts endowments, poetry projects, and the like. One might legitimately argue, of course, that the history of *Poetry* has always been a history of financial crisis and the dilemma of how to enable both poetry and *Poetry* to succeed amidst this crisis (as the letters of *Dear Editor*, the precursor to *Between the Lines*, unquestionably prove), but there is something disturbing, something which indeed threatens to turn the little magazine itself into an afterthought, in the second half of *Between the Lines*. Po-biz seems to be taking over. Still, one cannot argue against the prudence of Ms. Lilly's donation by citing the necessity of poverty in the world of poetry, for it was to counter just such illusions that Harriet Monroe began the magazine in the first place. As John Timberman Newcomb has it, "Monroe's modernist idealism admitted no inherent contradiction between the creation of poetry and the creation of a market for poetry" ("*Poetry's* Opening Door" 18). In other words, financial affluence didn't have to mean artistic destitution; that genius thrived only on poverty was a romantic myth that had effectively barred the poet from earning a living on his art alone. The donation, then, isn't an enemy clothed as a friend, commercial success come to ultimately ruin *Poetry*; to make such a claim invites the fruition of the very thing the claim itself alerts us to, for in shifting the focus of resistance from the concerns of poetry itself to a destitute stereotype, one leaves poetry (and thereby *Poetry*), despite one's potentially good intentions, defenseless.

Nevertheless, *Poetry's* prestige may indeed not be the best thing for contributing poets. Both its excellent reputation and its current affluent state could well prove to be a trap for them. "The literary text," explains George Bornstein, "consists not only of words . . . but also of the semantic features of its material instantiation, [which] include cover design, page layout, [and] spacing" (6). The meaning of a text, that is, or the reputation it will acquire, depends partially (and significantly) on when, where, and how the text is published. Similarly, a poet's own reputation depends not only on the quality of her work but also on where her work is published. Or rather, to put it more accurately, where her work is published determines, in part, the quality of her work. There is, as Newcomb says, an "interdependence of magazine reputation and poetic reputation" (*Others, Poetry* 265). Publishing in a specific journal at a specific time means positioning oneself as a poet, jockeying, however self-consciously, for reputation. "The egotism of poets," Wallace Stevens wrote to Harriet Monroe in 1932, "is disgusting" (*Dear Editor* 301).

And four years later, just after Monroe had passed away in Peru, Stevens reflected, "Her job brought Miss Monroe into contact with the most ferocious egoists. I mean poets in general" (322).

As *the* place to be published, then, for much of the 20th Century, *Poetry* found, and still finds, itself in the position of either shattering those egos via rejection or confirming them via acceptance. In either case, a certain voraciousness is apt to be inculcated in the poet, a hunger for appearance which could perhaps overtake the initial desire to write poems (assuming the presence of such a desire). "I want to prove to myself that I can hit *Poetry*," wrote Philip Booth to Karl Shapiro in 1952, when Shapiro was editor (Oostdijk 354). Booth's ambition to appear in the pages of the magazine, of course, might have spurred him on to write better poetry than he would have otherwise, but one can quite plausibly imagine this scenario working the other way, as well. The solution to this problem, though, clearly doesn't lie in perennially keeping a magazine destitute, both financially and in terms of its reputation. Instead, resistance is called for where it has often, if not always, been present since the inception of the print public sphere: in the poet's own struggle with various forms and modes of publicity. In this matter, one might say, the poet's ego is perhaps his own best enemy.

II.

The imperative for all things *Poetry*, it seems, might be derived from the song of God B in James Merrill's *Scripts for the Pageant*: "HOLD IT BACK AND WE SURVIVE" (78). The history of *Poetry* is a history of resistance in all directions; its early *avant-garde* status was predicated upon its resistance of traditional forms and conceptions of poetry, and its current institutional prestige is steeped in resistance of just that prestige, in, for instance, the editors' ongoing willingness to reply considerately and personally to a significant percentage of the 90,000 unsolicited submissions they receive each year (*Dear Editor* 3), an intimacy not generally associated with institutions. Human culture might have changed significantly in or about December, 1910, but *Poetry* was launched in October, 1912. If one was looking for a specific date to mark the beginning of the modernist era in poetry, this has to be it. One might wish, in the avant-garde spirit of modernism itself, to mark the outbreak of the movement with the launch of a more radical magazine, say *Others*, but then one must remember that *Poetry* itself was hardly less radical at the time of its inception and has only become an institution since.

That one can find the spring of a legitimate poetry renaissance in the founding of a literary magazine raises important questions that, like many of their kind, are fundamentally unanswerable: was the magazine simply fortunate to find itself conceived at precisely the time when Williams, Eliot, Stevens, Moore, and others were cultivating their talents, or did its conception have something vital to do with the formation of those talents? Did the modernists create *Poetry*, or did *Poetry* create the modernists? That there was much in the air and water, so to speak, from the mid-19th century and earlier that led to the formation of both is certain (and illustrated nicely by Robert Scholes and Clifford Wulfman in their 2010 book *Modernism in the Magazines*), but the fact that these questions can nevertheless be asked both ways testifies to the importance of the literary magazine, or little magazine, in general, and to the importance of *Poetry* in particular. One could even go so far as to make the case that the most influential person in the 20th century, in terms of poetry, was Harriet Monroe, whose creation of the magazine and 24-year editorship of it spanned the arc of the modernist era, an arc that generated itself primarily by resisting many of the currents that enabled it, including the currents of received ideas concerning literature in general and poetry in particular.

Richard Aldington said to Monroe ninety years ago, "You have done a great deal in the past years. It would be absurd to expect you to print masterpieces each month and no one but a blind partizan would expect you to cling to one school of poetry; but you can claim, I think, to have published work by very nearly every living poet of talent" (quoted in Williams 245–6). This is both a tremendous compliment and a tremendous back-handed compliment, for implicit in Aldington's appraisal, of course, is an accusation that *Poetry* prints a lot of bad, average, or only merely good poetry, from month to month, decade to decade, and now, editor to editor. But awash on this legion of sentiment, tripe, and mere versification were what have turned out to be many masterpieces. Confirming Aldington's opinion, Joseph Parisi, who edited the magazine from the 1980s into the 21st Century, pointed out, in an effort to disillusion those who might lament the passing of the golden days of *Poetry*, that "a distressing number of dull issues in the twenties and thirties are filled with mediocre and parochial verse" (quoted in Oostdijk 346). One can easily say something similar of the magazine under Parisi's own editorship, with as little disrespect to Parisi as Parisi had for Monroe when he made his comment, which is to say none. Resistance makes the little engine go, and *Poetry* has been adept at overcoming its own shortcomings, oversights, and errors, in addition to its publication of a lot of bad poetry, ever since its debut, largely by recognizing the fact that these things are simply essential to its enterprise.

Billy Collins wrote to Parisi in 1997, "Thanks for taking 'Taking Off Emily Dickinson's Clothes.' I wasn't sure you would go for that one, but I'm really glad you did. How can you not like that title!" (*Between the Lines* 345). But how *can* you like that title, I'm inclined to ask. Apparently, one Caroline Finkelstein did like it, for she wrote to Collins early the next year to tell him she was "looking forward to your 'Taking Off Jorie Graham's Clothes'" (346), a poem which has not yet appeared and I hope never will. Parochial indeed. But these are the poets and poems that serve as poles to keep the magazine's tent standing that one of Marianne Moore's elephants might occasionally wander through it. In *Between the Lines* Parisi writes of his own editorship: "While many decades on we still wanted to keep *Poetry's* door open wide to the latest New Poetry, I felt that we should also return to Monroe's other original aim and pursue audience-building more creatively" (262). One wants to be on the cutting edge, but one also wants, or even needs, from a financial standpoint, at least, to be popular. One of the results of this endeavor on Parisi's part was the Poets in Person audio series, an innovative and successful project that made poetry accessible to "nonspecialist audiences" (296). One of the other results, however, might have been the publication of just such pandering poems as the Collins one mentioned above. In this regard it is important to remember that Monroe's own steadfast insistence on audience-building must have been, at least in part, what led to some of the "dull issues" of the 20s and 30s, but that it is also an important factor in the magazine's astounding longevity and thus not to be lamented outright.

No doubt Pound's extreme audience-be-damned stance played a significant role in the sinking of many little magazines, and it might have sunk *Poetry* too were it not for Monroe. On the other hand, too much audience-building might perhaps result in an even more adverse effect, in a slow degradation of content quality based on too strong of an appeal to a lowest common denominator. A good deal of resistance to reception trends thus seems, even if somewhat paradoxically, quite practical. *Poetry* never could have consisted entirely of the gemmed animals of Marianne Moore, but neither can it be all Mr. Collins and his tricks. That it has been able to walk this tightrope, sometimes nimbly, sometimes clumsily, for over a hundred years is and continues to be its most astounding feat, a feat that consists of even as it generates acts of resistance.

In 1968 one Nan M. Eaton wrote to then-editor Henry Rago: "Dear Sir: I'm a young poet, not an old fogie, and enjoy new and creative writing. However, in thoroughly reading your publication on its arrival today, it's obvious somebody's putting you on. And you as editor are being sucker enough to print it. Probably if I put this letter in lines one inch long you'd print it" (101). There is something both specious and weighty in this letter, leaving alone the writer's assumption that his youth guarantees his taste, for if Eaton were, hypothetically, referring to the October issue of the magazine, he might have had in mind the one inch lines of James Schuyler, in which case he is, in my opinion, merely imperceptive, though if, on the other hand, he were referring to poems that really do utilize one-inch lines as nothing more than a gimmick (plenty of candidates from 1968 alone), his claim could said to be at least partially well-founded, if not well-phrased. Either way, the editor's task upon receiving such missives is to both welcome and resist them, encourage and repulse them, take them into consideration while somehow simultaneously ignoring them. In 1981 a reader by the name of Stephen Sikora wrote to editor John F. Nims: "Rarely do common readers venture out of their own specialization as consumers, and when they do, a few knife thrusts from a skilled professional quickly send us scurrying back to our proper station of voicelessness" (233). It is perhaps unfortunate that there is a great deal of truth in Sikora's claim. I say "perhaps," of course, because those knife thrusts, however rude and arrogant they sometimes can be, are also often precisely what enable the advancement of an art. That is to say, artistic development, while it no doubt does depend to some extent on public support, just as certainly depends on resistance *of* the general public, the world of "common readers" and people who specialize in being consumers. It is a strange symbiotic relationship in which mutual beneficence is achieved in large part by way of mutual antagonism.

Much of what's written in the two preceding paragraphs (and throughout this essay) hinges on that most enigmatic of concepts—taste. What makes the concept so beguiling, of course, is the variety of ways in which it can be employed, from ordinary assertions concerning something being in good or bad taste to metaphysical expositions of what constitutes the faculty of taste. Add to this variety of uses the infinitely complex dynamic of the creation and maintenance of the phenomenon (or phenomena) which "taste," as a category, implies, and aesthetics suddenly seems like a province of chaos theory. One might revise a question asked earlier, then, in this way, fully mindful, here as before, of the fact that in doing so one is drastically oversimplifying the matter: Does *Poetry* reflect good taste or is it the arbiter of what shall and shall not be said to be in good taste? The answer has to be, of course, "Well, both," with little to no quantification forthcoming. *Poetry* no doubt determines to some extent what constitutes good taste in poetry, and it then goes on to reflect that taste in its own pages. This is an ongoing process, from issue to issue, maybe even from one submitted poem to the next. Newcomb writes that Harriet Monroe's primary goal with *Poetry* and her 1917 anthology, *The New Poetry*, was to "form rather than reflect current tastes" ("*Others, Poetry*" 267). While this perhaps remains true even of the magazine today, it seems worth pointing out that the formation of taste can't conceivably happen without its reflection in some fashion, as well. *Poetry's* governing of taste (by which I mean both the formation of new tastes and the reflection of current tastes) via what Bornstein calls "the Politics of the Page" is thus a complicated process, one which is by no means limited simply to the magazine's acceptances and rejections but which includes, also, the various letters of advice and encouragement written by the editors to both aspiring and established poets, as well as the letters written by poets and readers to the editors. The friction generated by these various manifestations of resistance ultimately produces the energy that enables both *Poetry* and poetry to survive.

The painter Fairfield Porter said that it was imperative to see both the figuration in abstraction and the abstraction in figuration. As a primarily figurative painter during the decades dominated by Abstract Expressionism and Pop Art, Porter seems in his claim to be making a plea for a flexibility in understanding which is capable of at least straddling, if not transcending, categories. It seems to me similarly important to see both the acceptance inherent in resistance, and the resistance inherent in acceptance, especially as they pertain to *Poetry*. While we might accuse the magazine of mangling Stevens, being tentative towards Eliot, alienating Moore, and frustrating Williams, it is nevertheless true that *Poetry* did in fact give all of these poets some of their earliest publications. And while Bidart, Graham and Phillips might be mostly missing from the index of *Between the Lines*, they have by no means been missing from the recent pages of *Poetry*, as Bidart's "The Third Hour of the Night" took up an entire, very controversial issue in 2004, while a poem from Graham's latest phase (that of *Sea Change*) was featured nicely in a fold-out in the February 2008 issue (the fold-out being necessary to accommodate Graham's lineation).

Poetry, then, is a bit of a paradox. In the end it seems best to quote Marianne Moore, with the help of a few italics:

Poetry

I, too, dislike it: there are things that are important beyond
    all this fiddle.

> Reading it, however, with a perfect contempt for it,
>   one discovers in

> it after all, a place for the genuine. (266)

WORKS CITED

Bornstein, George. *Material Modernism: The Politics of the Page.* Cambridge University Press, 2001.

Longenbach, James. *The Resistance to Poetry.* The University of Chicago Press, 2004.

Merrill, James. *Scripts for the Pageant.* New York: Atheneum, 1980.

Moore, Marianne. *Complete Poems.* New York: Penguin, 1981.

Newcomb, John Timberman. "*Others, Poetry,* and Wallace Stevens: Little Magazines as Agents of Reputation." *Essays in Literature* 16.2 (Fall 1989): 256–70.

—. "*Poetry*'s Opening Door: Harriet Monroe and American Modernism." American Periodicals 15.1 (2005). 6-22.

Oostdijk, Diederik. "'Someplace Called *Poetry*': Karl Shapiro, *Poetry* Magazine and Post-War American Poetry. *English Studies* 4 (2000). 346–57.

Parisi, Joseph, and Stephen Young, eds. *Dear Editor: A History of Poetry in Letters: The First Fifty Years, 1912–1962.* New York and London: W. W. Norton & Co., 2002.

—. *Between the Lines: A History of Poetry in Letters, Part II: 1962–2002.* Chicago: Ivan R. Dee, 2006.

Williams, Ellen. *Harriet Monroe and the Poetry Renaissance: The First Ten Years of Poetry, 1912–22.* Urbana: University of Illinois Press, 1977.

STORY

by Jay Neugeboren (1983)

In the spring of 1931, Whit Burnett and Martha Foley—American foreign correspondents working for the Consolidated Press in Vienna—mimeographed 167 copies of a magazine they called, simply, *Story*. The previous summer, while Burnett was traveling in the Balkans, a letter for him had come to Vienna from Edward J. O'Brien, asking permission to reprint Burnett's story, "Two Free Men," in *The Best American Short Stories of 1930*.

In her memoir, *The Story of Story Magazine*, Martha Foley tells of that moment, and of her elation:

> "Whit will be so well-known, he will be able to sell every story he writes!" I thought, jubilantly . . . "Now Whit will only have to send his story to an editor . . ." My thoughts raced on. But what editor? Where? Reality intruded like the dash of cold water I needed. Not to *transition*, where "Two Free Men," the story O'Brien would reprint, was published. Gene Jolas had just told us he would take no more stories. Not to Mencken, who had bought two of Whit's stories years ago. He, too, no longer wanted short stories. The other quality magazines in the States now had a puny limit of one or two stories an issue. Goddamn it! Short stories are an important part of literature. Why isn't there one good fiction magazine?
>
> Why, indeed! And then it came to me. Whit and I would start one.

$6.95/$8.95 Canada

STORY

Blechman

Martha Foley and Whit Burnett first conceived of *Story* as a kind of sales catalogue. "We would call it a proof-book," Martha wrote, "because it would be proof of what splendid short stories authors were writing. Once editors and publishers had a chance to see them, they would be delighted to buy them and we could give the authors the money."

Story magazine was first published in Vienna in 1931, but it had its origins six years earlier, in Los Angeles in 1925, when Martha Foley was working as a feature writer for the *Los Angeles Daily News*. Like her managing editor, Douglas Turney, she, too, hoped to succeed as a writer of fiction. Together, during lulls in the city room, they would talk of their hopes, and they would bemoan the dwindling market for short stories. The previous year H. L. Mencken and George Jean Nathan had abandoned *Smart Set*, devoted primarily to fiction, in order to found the *American Mercury*, where they intended to emphasize factual writing and "the sociological essay." Mencken's decision to "depreciate" the short story, in favor of "the sociological article as the important form of literary interpretation of the American mores," was, according to Martha Foley, the major blow to the preeminence of the American short story. "The immediate great success of *The American Mercury*," she wrote,

> made other magazines prefer articles to stories. Quality
> magazines, like *The Atlantic Monthly*, *Harper's*, *Scribner's*,
> *Forum*, and *Century*, which had been printing as many as
> eight short stories in a single issue, began to reduce the
> number sharply. Smaller-circulation literary magazines,
> *The Southern Literary Messenger*, *Southern Review*, and
> *Sewanee Review*, devoted more space to critical than to
> creative writing. Some of the better "slicks," the *Saturday
> Evening Post* and *Collier's*, as well as some of the women's
> magazines, *Pictorial Review*, *Woman's Home Companion*,
> *McCall's*, *Ladies' Home Journal*, continued to print fiction,
> some of it distinguished, but not regularly. "Give me facts!"
> demanded Gradgrind, that "eminently practical man," in
> Dickens's *Hard Times*. "Give us facts!" echoed American
> magazine editors, pleasing the Babbitts and relegating fic-
> tion to the already obscure position of poetry.

Martha Foley tried to get Turney to start a serious fiction magazine with her, but he resisted, and she dropped the idea. When, six years later, Whit Burnett also resisted the idea, Martha became more persistent. She argued with Burnett, she wrote letters to writers and magazines and publishers, she made lists of possible titles (which Burnett disparaged), and she prepared to go ahead with the first issue by herself. Then Whit gave in. "Why," he said one day when they were hanging on to straps in a crowded Viennese street-car, "don't we call it *Story*?"

The first issue of their bimonthly—"*Story*: The only magazine devoted solely to the Short Story"—was published in April 1931; it contained stories by Kay Boyle, Oliver Gossman, Georg Balint, Romer Wilson, Ernst Decsey, and by Whit Burnett and Martha Foley. "The only purpose of *Story*," its first page announced, "is to present, regularly, from one place, a number of Short Stories of exceptional merit. It has no theories, and is part of no movement. It presents short narratives of Significance by no matter whom and coming from no matter where."

Although *Story* magazine continued, in various forms, to be published for the next thirty three years, the time from 1931 to 1941, when Martha Foley coedited it with Whit Burnett, was its great period. Those years were called, by Edward J. O'Brien (founder and editor, for its first twenty-six years, of the Best Short Stories series), "the *Story* decade." For most of those years—in Vienna, on Majorca, and then, from 1933 on, in New York—*Story* was published monthly, ran to more than one hundred pages, and included eight to ten stories per issue. During that decade the magazine also ran other regular features—informal essays ("Notes" and "End Pages" by the editors), best-seller lists, letters (often lengthy story-by-story critiques by readers of previous issues), book review excerpts, and literary essays by writers such as Thomas Mann, George Bernard Shaw, Van Wyck Brooks, and Sherwood Anderson. It also came to print poems, adaptations of plays, photo-essays, film criticism, and—all this without reducing the number of stories—over forty novellas. It ran a readers' literary service, an annual college short story contest, produced a weekly radio program, sponsored a Works Projects Administration story contest (which discovered Richard Wright), and founded and operated The Story Press, a publishing company whose first book was Ignazio Silone's *Bread and Wine*. *Story*'s circulation, in the mid-thirties, was slightly more than twenty thousand.

During these years *Story* discovered and published for the very first time an extraordinary number of American writers, among them Norman Mailer, Erskine Caldwell, William Saroyan, Peter De Vries, J. D. Salinger, John Cheever, Richard Wright, James T. Farrell, Tennessee Williams, Emily Hahn, Frederic Prokosch, Jesse Stuart, Tess Slesinger, James Ramsey Ullman, Dorothy McCleary, Jerome Weidmann, Carson McCullers, Elizabeth Janeway, LudWig Bemelmans, and Nelson Algren. In issue after issue, the editors would point to their discoveries, to the fact that, at *Story*, unknown writers were given the same reading that established writers were given; but they were proud, too, that during these years *Story* also published—for fees of twenty-five dollars—the stories of established authors (who were earning thousands per story from the slicks) and that these authors were usually "represented by stories not identified with the type of work on which [they] have made their reputations" (for example, Faulkner's "Lo!").

During the years from 1931 to 1941, *Story* published, in addition to work by its "discoveries," fiction by William Faulkner, Kay Boyle, William Carlos Williams, Alvah BeSSie, Conrad Aiken, Gertrude Stein, Manuel Komroff, Howard Fast, Katherine Anne Porter, Sherwood Anderson, Meyer Levin, Budd Schulberg, Albert Maltz, Daniel Fuchs, Elliott Arnold, Louis L' Amour, Warren Beck, Wallace Stegner, W. K. Wimsatt, Jr., Irwin Shaw, Aldous Huxley, Dorothy Canfield Fisher, Carleton Coons, Hal Borland, Allan Seager, Zora Neale Hurston, Nancy Wilson Ross, William E. Wilson, Helen Hull, Edita Morris, Mari Sandoz, and hundreds of others whose work was, in varying degrees, already known or beginning to be known. *Story* also published fiction by writers from abroad. It was the first magazine in America to publish the work of Robert Musil, Ignazio Silone, Peter Neagoe, Graham Greene, Malcolm Lowry, V. G. Calderon, H. E. Bates, Alfred H. Mendes, Mikhail Zoshchenko, and Eric Knight. It also published stories (often, for non-English authors, in their first English translations) by Anton Chekhov, Luigi PirandelIo, Ivan Bunin, Stoyan Christowe, Isaac Bein, Abraham Raisin, Flann O'Brien, Sean O'Faolain, Liam O'Flaherty, Morley Callaghan, A. Averchenko, Ralph Bates, A. I. Kuprin, Synnove Larsen Baasch, Romer Wilson, A. E. Coppard, Eric Jens Petersen, Oliver Gossman, and Padraic Fallon.

Many of the magazines that published fiction in the thirties (*Scribner's*, the *American Mercury*, *Collier's*, *Vanity Fair*, the *Hound and the Horn*, and others) have since vanished, and though there are now hundreds of quarterlies (most with very small circulation, and most sponsored by universities) that publish stories of literary excellence, there are, in 1983, less than a handful of magazines—and we can name them: the *Atlantic Monthly*, *Esquire*, *Harper's*, and *The New Yorker*—that both have a wide circulation and regularly publish what has, alas, come, in the literary marketplace, to be called serious fiction. Yet even *Harper's* and *Esquire* have recently published issues containing no fiction. (During the thirties, the *Saturday Evening Post*, then a weekly with a circulation of over two million, was publishing six stories in an issue, and more literary magazines, such as *Harper's*, the *Atlantic*, *The New Yorker*, and *Scribner's*, were often publishing four stories an issue, and sometimes a short novel.)

To list the writers *Story* discovered, then, and to know the history of *Story* in the thirties, is to remind ourselves of how different times were for the short story in America. It was a time when an editor could still hope that a magazine "devoted solely to the short story" could join high culture to a wide audience. (In recent times only magazines of general interest—Norman Podhoretz's *Commentary* or Ted Solotaroff's now-defunct *American Review*—have had such aspirations. And the amount of fiction there—*Commentary* publishes fiction every second or third issue—is exceeded, always, by the amount of nonfiction.) It was a time when, to judge from circulation figures (the *Saturday Evening Post*'s circulation far exceeded that of either *Time*, *Newsweek*, *Life*, or *Look*), readers turned to fiction—and not to the sociological article or the news story—to find out about the life that lay beyond their homes.

It was a time, I would suggest, when serious fiction was still thought of as being a potentially and essentially popular medium—a time when editors such as Martha Foley and Whit Burnett could conceive of themselves as having the mission to bring good fiction to a large audience. And this very sense of mission—the attempt to get the best possible stories to the widest possible audience—accounts to some degree for the great unevenness, the strange mixture of the ordinary and the extraordinary, of highbrow and low-brow fiction that filled *Story*'s pages during these years: daring and original work by writers such as Faulkner, Fuchs, Lowry, Alan Marshall, and Saroyan alongside conventional and predictable stories by writers such as Eric Knight, Mary O'Hara, Louis L'Amour, and Norah Lofts.

Not all the stories, even by the newly discovered writers, were good or innovative or even literary. Many, especially turgid proletarian stories of the Depression, now seem awkward and dated. To read through these stories, and to read through the notes about them and about their authors, is to remind oneself not only of the vagaries of literary styles and taste, but also of the transience of literary reputation. Many authors whose names and works were considered well known (Kressman Taylor, Rachel Crothers, Julia Davis, Eric Knight, Robert Ayre, A. I. Bezzerides) now seem unfamiliar. Writers who, often, *Story* felt were among its great discoveries, writers who went on to have successful careers and to publish several books—Villa Stiles, Constance Bestor, Lewis Carliner, Mary Medearis, I. J. Kapstein—are now, for the most part, quite forgotten.

In Vienna in 1931, Whit Burnett and Martha Foley discovered, everything was expensive, but printing was cheap. What the *American Mercury* paid Martha Foley for a single article—$150—was sufficient to pay for the printing of the next two issues of *Story*, and, to their delight, in hand-set type and on rag paper. Before the second issue went to press, the magazine received crucial encouragement; Edward J. O'Brien wrote again, asking for permission to reprint four stories from *Story*'s very first issue—the most, until then, ever chosen from a single magazine in an entire year.

The number of unsolicited manuscripts multiplied rapidly. The editors received seventy to eighty stories a day and one hundred fifty on Mondays. And they read them all. "We ask *Story* contributors to be patient," they would write in 1934, when they were six thousand manuscripts behind and were receiving one hundred fifty a day and three hundred fifty on Mondays. "Every manuscript is read by the editors themselves. There is no large staff of readers . . . The editors really feel for the authors, and particularly for the newer ones, and *Story* has attempted to avoid any machine-like and stereotyped consideration of what is offered here." (Note, by contrast, a 1978 issue of *Fiction* magazine—which contains work by sixteen authors; is supported by one university and three foundations; has a staff of twenty-two assorted senior, managing, contributing, and associate editors; and which has returned stories it solicited with form rejections.) Martha Foley and Whit Burnett never lost their sense of what it was like to be a hopeful, struggling, and vulnerable writer.

Except to correct misspellings, the editors of *Story* made no changes and asked for no revisions. They accepted or rejected the stories and sent those they liked to the printer. (This, too, helps to account for the unevenness of stories and of prose.) In the summer of 1931, after the first issue of *Story* appeared, Martha Foley and Whit Burnett married. Later that year, shortly before they left Vienna for Majorca, their son David was born. In 1932, when the editors were down to their last fifty dollars, they wrote from Majorca to friends in New York, hoping to find an American publisher who would back their magazine. Manuel Komroff replied that Bennett Cerf and Donald Klopfer of Random House were interested, and that Whit and Martha should come to New York at once. They arrived in America in early 1933, and within days *Story*'s future was decided. It would have its offices at Random House (which was then largely a reprint house and saw *Story* as a good scouting arrangement by which to bring authors to them—they got Saroyan that way). Donald Klopfer would be president, Bennett Cerf, secretary-treasurer, and Harry Scherman (founder and president of the Book-of-the-Month Club), vice-president. Morris Ernst would be the magazine's attorney. Whit and Martha would be the editors, at salaries of thirty-five dollars a week.

The first American issue of *Story* (April 1933) was published on the day before the banks closed. In an announcement to readers ("With this issue *Story* comes to America"), the editors sketched in *Story*'s two-year history—by this time it had published work by Caldwell, Farrell, William Carlos Williams, Musil, William March, Tess Slesinger, among others, and had had dozens of its stories anthologized—and noted that, despite the fact that O'Brien had stated that "*Story* is now the most distinguished short story magazine in the world," at no time "did its circulation ever exceed six hundred copies." The editors, they concluded, "have no wild ambitions for *Story*; they have no illusions that it will suddenly produce a new crop of Conrads or Chekhovs. But they believe deeply that it may easily open the pathway to one or two such, and that it is of infinite importance that a pathway be kept open. Little known as the magazine has been, they have already seen that the stories submitted to them—for honor, apparently, and little more—are more original and in general far superior to the run of those which editors of magazines of large circulation, with fixed notions about their readers, apparently seem to feel they should accept."

Harry Scherman sent out an elaborate test mailing for the magazine to a list of writers, telling them about the magazine and inviting subscriptions. The response was the greatest he ever received. Practically all the authors replied that they would be delighted to subscribe—would *Story* please deduct the price of a subscription from what they were paid for their manuscripts, which they were sending.

Many authors—Algren, Caldwell, Cheever, Tennessee Williams, Cornell Woolrich, Malcolm Lowry—brought their manuscripts to the office by hand. The most heartbreaking, according to Martha Foley, was Lowry, who was then separated from his wife, dismally lonely, and who was having his stories, and a novel, rejected everywhere. "For weeks he visited my office every day," Foley wrote, "sat around for a while, looked at books and magazines I had lying about, and disconsolately departed. Once he disappeared. When he returned he told me he had been placed for observation in Bellevue."

This first two American issues included the first published stories of Nelson Algren, Frederick Scribner, John S. McNamarra, Bernadine Kielty, Linda Henly, Alan Marshall ("Death and Transfiguration," a remarkable story about rural New Hampshire—set in Seabrook—that would elicit as much praise as any story the magazine would ever publish), and the first story published in America by Lowry. They also included stories by Caldwell, Boyle, Komroff, Conrad Aiken ("Impulse"), H. E. Bates, Zora Neale Hurston, Ted Pratt, Faulkner, A. E. Coppard, and Zoshchenko.

By its third American issue (August 1933), *Story* was doing so well that it announced its "expansion from a magazine costing fifty cents an issue and appearing every two months to a magazine which hereafter will cost half that amount and appear every month." ("*Story* was brought to America as an experiment in the presentation of writing which generally was being ignored by the commercial magazines of this country although hailed critically when this same writing appeared in books . . . With this issue's radical change in both price and frequency of appearance, the editors hope to bring *Story* to an even larger reading public.")

For the next issue, Bernadine Kielty, the wife of Harry Scherman, joined the magazine as an associate editor (she would remain for eight years), and George Cronyn, a short story writer and biographer, became business manager. The issue included stories by Marquis W. Childs, A. Averchenko, Alvah Bessie, John Peale Bishop, Whit Burnett, and Gertrude Stein ("A native of Pennsylvania, she prefers Paris, where for many years her salons in the rue de Fleurus have been famous and often deadly").

In this issue Martha and Whit introduced the first of many columns of "Notes"—informal (and often cloyingly cute) remarks about writers and their work, especially about writers whose work was appearing in *Story*. These notes and anecdotes—about the rise of fascism, about the success of *Story*'s authors, and about their personal lives (Kay Boyle and Laurence Vail have "left their Riviera place at *Ville-Franche* and have gone to live in Vienna")—became standard fare for the rest of the decade, and as the magazine succeeded and its enterprises expanded (they announced their first college short story contest in the next issue, and published their first anthology, *A Story Anthology, 1931–33*, at the end of the year), its tone became at the same time, both more intimate and more expansive.

They talked to their readers at length, for example, of their pride in having solicited stories from Ivan Bunin when he was unpublished and forgotten. When he became the first Russian Nobel Prize winner, *Story* had thirteen of his manuscripts, and they finally chose, translated, and published three. They even quoted, at excruciating length, from rejected manuscripts in order to assure readers and writers, as they frequently did, of the earnestness of their own labors.

In the final three issues of 1933, *Story* published work by, among others, Bunin, Faulkner, Fuchs, Isaac Bein, Sherwood Anderson, Eugene Jolas, and, in February 1934, the first published story by a young Armenian writer who would within the next few years become their "star discovery." The writer was William Saroyan, and the story, which had arrived single-spaced on yellow paper (perhaps the most overtly experimental story *Story* would ever publish—their preference was for the realistic and traditional; they never published fiction that, in Flannery O'Connor's words, looked "funny on the page"), was "The Daring Young Man on the Flying Trapeze."

In March 1934, *Story* marked its first anniversary in America with much self-congratulation. "Hardly any" of the seventy-four stories published in the magazine during the preceding year, the editors stated, "would otherwise have seen print . . . had they not been accepted by *Story*." After listing names of new and established writers, they went on to talk about what they saw as a virtual renaissance in the American short story, a renaissance for which they claimed a share of the credit. They wrote of the increasing number of volumes of stories; they wrote of the increased sales of these volumes; they noted that newspapers had begun to print stories; and they were proud that in England two new magazines had appeared, *Lovat Dickson's Magazine* and *New Stories*, both openly modeled on *Story*'s "notable success."

The next few years were *Story*'s most glorious ones. By early 1935 its paid circulation had passed the 21,000 mark; in the same year the *New Republic*'s circulation was 25,000; the *American Mercury*, 31,000; *New Masses*, 32,000; *Scribner's*, 44,000; *Harper's*, 103,000; and *The New Yorker*, 121,000. They had published their second anthology of stories (*Story in America*). They had completed their first college story contest (won by nineteen-year old James Laughlin, later the founder and publisher of New Directions Books); and they had launched the first competition "for the Best Novel written by an Author who has had a story published in the magazine *Story*." The $1,000-prize contest was cosponsored by Doubleday, Doran & Company.

In mid-1935 *Story* moved to new and larger quarters at 432 Fourth Avenue. The general store atmosphere still prevailed ("Our new quarters have a homey air. We are only fourteen floors above Michel's Tavern, at 29th and Fourth. Fourth Avenue is the heart of the America publishing industry. Michel's is the stomach"), but the magazine and the magazine's enterprises continued expanding rapidly. The columns of "End Pages," written, usually, by Whit Burnett, became, in early 1936, a regular and lengthier feature; they ranged over a variety of subjects: Martha's attempts, in Paris, to learn to ride a bike; Whit's meetings with famous writers; anecdotes about David's eighteen imaginary playmates, etc.

In August 1936, with the establishment of The *Story* Service Bureau, the editors, in a wonderfully American blend of idealism, optimism, missionary zeal, and capitalist enterprise, seemed ready to turn the magazine into an industry. The *Story* Service Bureau provided six primary services to *Story* Associates: (1) The *Story* Press-to-Reader Service (for book orders); (2) The *Story* Bureau Information Service (for advice on the selection of book purchases); (3) The *Story* Bureau Study Service (for study groups, classes, and short story clubs); (4) The *Story* Bureau School Service (advice on colleges offering the best courses in modern literature); (5) The *Story* Bureau Reading Service (ten best short stories of the month, etc.); and (6) The *Story* Bureau 'Best-Seller' Service (national best-sellers, most popular books among *Story* readers). "*Story* Associates," the announcement concluded, "will become a powerful factor in assisting people to find the best contemporary literature. *Story* was founded to present good stories. *Story* now takes the next logical step forward in assisting the reading public to find and to buy the best in modern writing."

In October 1936 *Story* announced that Kurt Simon, an exile from Nazism and former publisher of the *Frankfurter-Zeitung*, had become *Story*'s president. The magazine, no longer borrowing office space from Random House, was "on its own independent feet, concentrating solely on its own publishing." In the November issue it inaugurated several new features "with a view to making [*Story*] the most definitive magazine of its kind on the short story and contemporary writing in English."

The new features, which would run regularly until the end of the decade, were (1) essays "on writing and writers . . . from the outstanding short story writers of the world"; (2) regular columns of letters; (3) best-seller lists; (4) "Recommended Reading"; and (5) "Plus & Minus: A monthly survey of the reviews for and against the most significant books of the month." These innovations thrived. During the midthirties *Story* published essays by, among others, Thomas Mann ("Measure and Value"), Sherwood Anderson ("Why Men Write"), George Bernard Shaw ("Fascism"), Van Wyck Brooks, Eugene Jolas, James Laughlin, Dorothy Thompson, and semi-scholarly articles by less familiar names (for example, "Chekhov's Middle Years," by Nina A. Toumanova).

And then in April 1936—their fifth anniversary issue—Whit and Martha announced the establishment of The Story Press, which, "in association with Harper & Brothers, expects to publish in America each year a limited number of books of high distinction." Whit and Martha would edit the books. "Nothing," they said, "will influence the acceptance of a manuscript but its own vitality, freshness, and literary merit." The Press's first book, published a year later, was Ignazio Silone's *Bread and Wine*. Its second book was *Song on Your Bugles* by Eric Knight, a frequent contributor to *Story* (a writer remembered today, if at all, for *Lassie Come Home*, but a writer considered at the time, to judge from the pages of *Story*, to be as distinguished as Silone). Its third book, a collection of four long stories, and the work of a *Story* discovery, was *Uncle Tom's Children* by Richard Wright.

Martha Foley and Whit Burnett seemed, in the midthirties, to be succeeding in their attempt to bring quality fiction to a wide audience. *Story*'s circulation stayed steady at around 21,000; its books sold well (*Bread and Wine* went quickly to more than 100,000 copies); some of *Story*'s discoveries (Saroyan, Caldwell, Farrell) were already reaching large audiences with their books while continuing to publish—for twenty-five dollars a story—in *Story*, and others were finding publishers. Whit and Martha noted in one column that six recent contributors had, largely because of their appearance in *Story*, sold first novels.

At the end of 1936, *Story* also instituted a regular review column, "Firsts," by Horace Gregory, on the "new writers of today and their first books." It emphasized, too, its new commitment to publishing longer stories, for which it used—for the first time in English, according to Martha Foley—the word novella (novelette, she said, sounded too demeaning—like "farmerette" or "flannelette").

The new features continued, for the most part, to appear regularly in the magazine for the rest of the decade, but from 1937 until Martha's leave-taking in 1941, the magazine initiated only a few other innovations, and most of them (photo-essays, play adaptations, and poetry, for example) were quickly discontinued. The magazine's college story contest continued through these years, as did The Story Press. But during these years notice of the *Story* Service Bureau disappeared from the magazine's pages; the magazine returned (without explanation) to bimonthly publication in July 1938; there were—especially in 1938 and 1939—fewer essays by Whit and Martha until, in 1940, there were none at all. And then the magazine's circulation began to decline—to 17,000 in 1938 and 1939, and to 8,000 in 1940 and 1941.

In 1940 the magazine announced what was its only major new addition during these years—"Tonight's Best Story," a radio program broadcast on Tuesday evenings at 9:30 over New York station WHN. Rex Stout appeared in the opening show ("The Night Reveals," by Cornell Woolrich); a few programs later Erskine Caldwell appeared to speak about Richard Wright's "Fire and Cloud." Others whose stories were adapted were Irwin Shaw, Kressman Taylor, Eric Knight, Saroyan, Lord Dunsany, Sean O'Faolain, Sherwood Anderson, and Martha Foley.

Though both the magazine's circulation and its nonfictional departures declined during these years, the dedication to quality fiction by both new and established writers did not. *Story* printed the first published stories of some of its most noteworthy finds: Richard Wright, twenty-one-year-old J. D. Salinger ("He is particularly interested in playwriting"), Mary O'Hara, and Tennessee Williams.

The second issue of 1941—Martha Foley's last year at *Story*—contained the first published stories by two new writers, James Ramsey Ullman ("Still Life") and Hallie Southgate Abbett ("Eighteenth Summer"), one of the runners-up in *Story*'s contest conducted among "budding writers of the Junior League." The latter is worth mentioning, for in 1942 Hallie Abbett would become the second Mrs. Whit Burnett, and she would, from that year on, edit the magazine with her husband. (Her name first appears on the title page, as associate editor, in January 1944.)

The May–June issue of 1941 was the magazine's tenth anniversary issue, and *Story* observed the occasion by reprinting "some of the most significant stories which have appeared in [its] pages since 1931." The editors chose a dozen out of nearly one thousand stories *Story* had published during the previous decade, selecting them, they wrote, "not only for their literary quality but because in addition to being good stories they seem in one way or another, to illuminate the years in which they were published." The stories, they believed, were "almost a literary history of their time."

There remained two more issues of *Story* for which Martha Foley served as editor. The first, in July–August, contained the first story published in America by Flann O'Brien ("Flann O'Brien is a discovery of William Saroyan's, but further than that, at this moment, we know nothing except that he is not William Saroyan"), and the second, and last, in September–October, was "a departure from the magazine's ten-year policy of exclusive devotion to the creative short story." It was an issue dedicated to Sherwood Anderson, "the greatest contemporary short story writer." In addition to selections from Anderson's work, it contained contributions from Steiglitz, Dreiser, Stein, Wolfe, Henry Miller, Saroyan, Kenneth Patchen, Ben Hecht, and others. "In the field of the short story," the editors wrote, "Sherwood Anderson set out on new paths at a time when the American short story seemed doomed to a formula-ridden, conventionalized, mechanized and commercialized concept. When *Winesburg, Ohio* appeared in 1919 it was intensely influential on writers who had either lost heart or had not yet found their way." (How times change! In a recent graduate writing class of mine, not one student had ever read *Winesburg, Ohio*.)

And then, on page 1 of the November–December 1941 issue, appeared the following announcement, signed by Whit Burnett and Kurt Simon:

TO OUR READERS

> With this issue, the name of Martha Foley disappears from the editorial title page of *Story*. Miss Foley is on a leave of absence in order that she may edit the Edward J. O'Brien Memorial Anthology, *The Best Short Stories*.

They wrote of their desire to help continue O'Brien's "great and pioneering tradition" by relinquishing Martha Foley. But the brief twenty-one-line announcement seemed, given all that had passed, strangely impersonal, oddly cold and dry. "After ten years of daily association," it concluded, "it would be impossible in a few brief words here to express our gratitude for and appreciation of Miss Foley's work on *Story*. We greatly regret her loss to the magazine and its readers, but we join with them in wishing her the very best in her new undertaking."

The *Story* decade was over.

In the same issue in which Martha Foley's departure was announced, *Story* printed the winner of its eighth college contest, "Greatest Thing in the World." It was written by an eighteen-year-old Harvard student, Norman K. Mailer. On how he had felt about appearing in *Story*, Mailer later wrote that "probably nothing has happened in the years I've been writing which changed my life as much. The far-away, all-powerful and fabulous world of New York publishing—which, of course, I saw through Thomas Wolfe's eyes—had said 'yes' to me."

Story continued to give such encouragement, intermittently, until 1964 and numbered among its discoveries, after Martha's departure, Truman Capote, John Knowles, and Joseph Heller. Whit Burnett and Hallie Abbett edited it as a bimonthly until the summer of 1948 when it became, briefly, a quarterly. It suspended publication from 1948 until 1951, when it reappeared for a while in book form every six months, still under Whit Burnett and Hallie Abbett's editorship. It ceased publication again through most of the fifties and reappeared in 1960, under the partial sponsorship of the University of Missouri and with a greatly expanded editorial board. "The editors," Burnett wrote, "believe that there is even more demand now for a magazine of distinguished and readable short stories than there was when *Story* first began nearly thirty years ago . . . *Story* enters the sixties confident there are many new writers of power and talent yet to be heard from. And to these as well as to all skilled and meaningful writers of our day, it opens its pages."

The belief and hope—and tone—remained the same, but the times were different. Despite partial sponsorship by the University of Cincinnati, and, for its college contest, by the Reader's Digest Foundation, *Story* suspended publication again—for good—three and a half years (and twelve issues) later, in early 1964.

Story's extraordinary gift for discovery—for publishing those writers and those stories that were being rejected by all other magazines seems to me, from this distance, its most valuable contribution, its most precious gift. It cared about the short story and about the writers of short stories—especially new writers—and it gave hundreds of them what was essential: some confirmation from the world that what they were doing mattered. "Publication of early work is what a writer needs most of all," Erskine Caldwell wrote recently, echoing the sentiments of many of *Story*'s contributors. "By putting me into print when the commercial magazines and book publishers took no notice of what I was trying to do—Whit and Martha gave me the confidence to keep going in my own way, instead of trying to 'write what editors want.'"

Story's openness to new writers and to different kinds of fiction seems, today, especially remarkable. "The editors have refrained from any narrow definition of the short story," it declared in 1935, "from saying, other than by the implication of the published examples, what a short story is or might be. They have no preconceived notions of its limits or its possibilities: they feel it can, perhaps, be better than we know." *Story* was to be, always, "a magazine edited with scant respect for the formulas and taboos created in this century by the magazines of great circulation in their effort to publish a type of fiction that could never offend anyone—much." Thus, in *Story*, one might find a story that could just as easily have appeared in the *Saturday Evening Post*, followed by a story that might have appeared in *transition*.

Story was impressive, too, not only for its openness to new writers and new fiction, but for its success. It published eight to ten stories a month, year after year, for an audience greatly larger than that of any literary quarterly, and it thereby helped give new life to the American short story at a time when the genre seemed in decline. It retained a wonderfully naive optimism and excitement about fiction, and this—combined with the huckstering—enabled it to reach a widely diverse audience with stories of widely divergent quality. It still hoped, as no literary magazine does today, to reach the general public.

Forgotten Pages: Black Literary Magazines in the 1920s

by Abby Ann Arthur Johnson (1974)

I.

Towards the end of his life, Langston Hughes wrote an article about Harlem during the 1920s. In his narration, he paused fondly over memories of Sugar Hill. At 409 Edgecombe, the address of the "tallest apartment house" on the hill, lived Walter and Gladys White, who gave frequent parties for their friends; Aaron and Alta Douglas, who "always had a bottle of ginger ale in the ice box for those who brought along refreshments"; Elmer Anderson Carter, who succeeded Charles S. Johnson to the editorship of *Opportunity*; and actor Ivan Sharpe and his wife Evie. Just below the hill, in the Dunbar Apartments, lived W. E. B. Du Bois as well as E. Simms Campbell, the cartoonist. Nearby was Dan Burley, a black journalist and a boogie-woogie piano player. Hughes recalled the excitement of those days: "Artists and writers were always running into each other on Sugar Hill and talking over their problems and wondering how they could get" fellowships and grants from benevolent organizations. One evening, Hughes and six of his compatriots gathered in the Aaron Douglas apartment and decided to start a literary magazine, "the better to express ourselves freely and independently—without interference from old heads, white or Negro."[14] From that initial discussion at 409 Edgecombe came *Fire* in its one and only issue of November 1926. Two years later, some of the same persons began another literary magazine, this time called *Harlem*.

During the decade, similar conclaves of black artists met throughout

[14] "The Twenties: Harlem and Its Negritude," *African Forum*, I (Spring, 1966), 18–19.

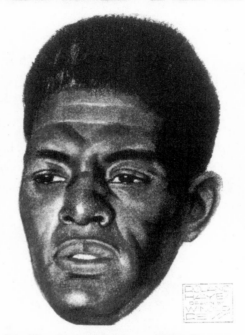

SURVEY GRAPHIC

HARLEM
MECCA
OF THE NEW
NEGRO

MARCH 1925

the United States. These groups, which have received little notice, included Krigwa of New York and other cities, Dixwell of New Haven, the Scribblers of Baltimore, the Saturday Nighters of Washington, D.C., the Writers Guild at Fisk, the Ethiopian Guild of Indianapolis, the Gilpins of Cleveland, the Ethiopian Folk Theater of Chicago, the Book and Bench in Topeka, the Dallas players of Texas, and the Ink Slingers of California. In addition to their other activities, most of these organizations hoped to encourage Negro art through publishing "little magazines." Only a few actually did begin periodicals; among those few were the Boston Quill Club, which produced the *Saturday Evening Quill*, a group in Philadelphia which issued *Black Opals*, and a literary society at Howard University which published the *Stylus*.

Students of the period have not noticed the publications from these smaller groups. Instead, they have concentrated on the NAACP magazine, *Crisis*, founded by Du Bois in 1910; the socialistic *Messenger*, which was started by A. Philip Randolph with Chandler Owen in 1917 and which eventually became a platform for the Brotherhood of Sleeping Car Porters; and the Urban League's journal, *Opportunity*, begun by Charles Johnson in 1923. When discussing Negro literature of the 1920s, scholars usually say little about *Messenger*, seeing the journal primarily as an arm of social action, not of artistic expression. They comment more fully, but still not enough, on *Opportunity* and Johnson's efforts to promote the arts. In Harlem Renaissance, Nathan Huggins noted that *Opportunity* especially "believed its motto—'Not Alms but Opportunity'—to apply to the arts."[15]

Historians pay particular attention to *Crisis* and the role of Du Bois in the Negro Renaissance. Elliot Rudwick stated that "no Negro writer could help but have been stimulated by *The Crisis* editor's lyrical and plaintive pieces." In his journal, Du Bois himself claimed that "practically every Negro author writing today found his first audience through the pages of *The Crisis*." Among his discoveries, Du Bois numbered Jessie Fauset, Langston Hughes and painters Wilbur Scott and Richard Brown. Du Bois did give early publication to many writers. At the same time, though, he maintained ideas which began to separate him from those very writers and from the literary periodicals which would emerge later in the decade. In a controversial statement often cited from *Crisis*, Du Bois disclaimed any notion of art for art's sake:

> [A]ll Art is propaganda and ever must be, despite the wailing of the purists. I stand in utter shamelessness and say that whatever art I have for writing has been used always for propaganda for gaining the right of black folk to love and enjoy. I do not care a damn for any art that is not used for propaganda.

Messenger and *Opportunity* differed in their response to literature and

---

[15] New York: Oxford University Press, 1971, p. 29.

other matters, but all three magazines were significant to the literary Renaissance. As Huggins stated, "each of these magazines saw as part of its role the encouragement of Negroes' work in the arts and the publishing of their achievement for blacks and whites to see."[16]

Few writers have said anything about the literary periodicals of the period—*Stylus*, *Fire*, *Harlem*, *Black Opals* and the *Saturday Evening Quill*. In their studies, scholars customarily indicate no understanding that such journals ever existed. Occasionally, they refer to *Fire*, rarely to *Harlem* and almost never to the other three publications. Huggins, for example, commented briefly on *Fire* and *Harlem*, calling them "short-lived magazines . . . *Harlem*'s attempts at 'little' magazines." He later devoted several lines to *Fire*, quoting material from Langston Hughes's *The Big Sea*. Nowhere did he examine the significance of *Fire* and *Harlem* or mention comparable periodicals in other urban centres.[17] Only Langston Hughes, in his autobiography and his article of 1966, gave significant insight into *Fire*. Hughes did not, though, allude to *Harlem* or the other three literary journals. Despite such responses, these magazines provide particular insights into Negro literature of the 1920s and thus merit attention.[18]

II.

The impetus towards such journals came in the winter of 1915–16 when Professors Alain Locke and Montgomery Gregory organized a literary society on the Howard campus. Called Stylus, the group included students, to be selected from biannual competitions, and several faculty and honorary members. Originally, the organization felt itself in the tradition of the Hartford Wits, an informal club formed chiefly by Yale graduates in the

[16] Leslie A. Lacy, *Cheer the Lonesome Traveler* (New York: Dial Press, 1970), p. 74; W. E. Burghardt Du Bois, "Criteria of Negro Art," 32 (October 1926), 296; Huggins, p. 29.

[17] Huggins, pp. 169, 240–1. John W. Blassingame called the Huggins study "hardly definitive," saying that Harlem Renaissance "ignores the internal dynamics of the black community which fostered and nurtured the movement." Blassingame concluded that there still exists undiscovered "a different kind of renaissance than that which Huggins found." See John W. Blassingame, "The Afro-Americans : Mythology to Reality ," in *The Reinterpretation of American History and Culture*, ed. William H. Cartwright and Richard L. Watson, Jr (Washington, D.C. : National Council for the Social Studies, 1973), p. 69.

[18] With the exception of the last two numbers of *Black Opals*, the Moorland–Spingarn Research Center of Howard University holds copies of the extant issues of these journals. Our thanks go to the Research Center for the use of these increasingly rare copies.

late eighteenth century. Despite initial proclivities, Stylus charted a route far different from that maintained by the Hartford writers. From the beginning, members wanted to encourage artistic expression in the black community, especially among youth. They hoped thereby to stimulate black writing which would be considered on an equal footing with other literatures and which would create respect for the Negro population in the United States. Gregory remembered that the society had "a vision, a vision which embodied in the not too distant future a Negro literature that should secure recognition along with that of other peoples." The *Howard University Record*, in later years, recalled that the efforts of Stylus were not limited to Howard University, but that they extended "to the Negro race and to civilization." Benjamin Brawley noted that the organization "hoped to make a genuine contribution to racial advance." To further their ends, Locke and his associates issued the first purely literary magazine published at any Negro college. Appearing in June 1916, *Stylus* featured student efforts and special contributions by honorary members, such as William Stanley Braithwaite, Benjamin G. Brawley and James Weldon Johnson.[19]

World War I interrupted the work, sending *Stylus* members and supporters to distant parts. Efforts did not resume until peace returned and a handful of old members came back to campus. With that nucleus, Professors Locke and Gregory attracted new student members, including Zora Neale Hurston, and additional honorary members, notably Charles W. Chestnutt, W. E. B. Du Bois, Alice Moore Dunbar and Arthur A. Schomburg. The second number of *Stylus* appeared in May 1921.

In his "Foreword" to that issue, Montgomery Gregory voiced sentiments which would be echoed by "New Negroes" emerging in the latter half of the decade. "It becomes clearer daily," he stated,

> that it must be through the things of the Spirit that we
> shall ultimately restore Ethiopia to her seat of honor
> among the races of the world. The Germans have amply
> demonstrated the futility of force to secure a place in the
> sun. Any individual or people must depend upon the
> universal appeal of art, literature, painting, and music—to
> secure the real respect and recognition of mankind.

Gregory urged his colleagues onward, with promise of better days ahead: "*The Stylus* is on the right track although like all bearers of Truth they are in a minority for a day. Theirs are the future years, rich with the promise of a fulfillment of the visions of those whose love for their race embraces

---

[19] "Foreword: Greeting," *Stylus*, I (May 1921), 6; "The Stylus," *Howard University Record*, 19 (May 1925), 372; "Visions of the Dawn," *Stylus* (June 1934), p. 2. The issues of *Stylus* following May 1921 were assigned neither a volume nor a number.

humanity."[20] *Stylus* reserved further statements for future years. The third number, to be discussed later, did not appear until 1929.

Probably the most outstanding student of the *Stylus* organization, during the early years, was Zora Hurston. In her autobiography, *Dust Traces On A Road*, she traced her literary career from her involvement in the Howard group. She explained how Charles Johnson, who was then planning the first issue of *Opportunity*, read a short story of hers published in *Stylus*, apparently "John Redding Goes To Sea," and asked her to contribute to his magazine. Hurston sent him "Drenched in Light," which he published. Later he published her second story, "Spunk," and counseled her to live in Harlem, the better to find an outlet for her literary talent. Hurston responded enthusiastically: "So, beginning to feel the urge to write, I wanted to be in New York."

After her trip to Harlem and her subsequent involvement in the artistic community there, she began to value Johnson as "the root of the so-called Negro Renaissance": he convinced young writers to come to New York; he encouraged them by accepting their contributions to his journal; he sought out new talent through his *Opportunity* Award dinners. Hurston believed that the much-acclaimed Locke, her former professor, owed Charles Johnson a great debt: Locke's *The New Negro* (1925) was "the same material, for the most part, gathered and published by Dr. Charles Spurgeon Johnson." She concluded that "the so-called Negro Renaissance . . . was his work, and only his hush-mouth nature has caused it to be attributed to many others." In *The Big Sea*, Langston Hughes made similar claims. He stated that Johnson, as editor of *Opportunity*, "did more to encourage and develop Negro writers during the 1920's than anyone else in America. He wrote them sympathetic letters, pointing out the merits of their work. He brought them together to meet and know each other. He made the *Opportunity* contests sources of discovery and help."[21]

Charles Johnson showed much acumen as an editor, particularly when compared with those who founded *Fire* in 1926. In his 1966 article and his autobiography, Hughes detailed the beginning and end of that little magazine. At Aaron Douglas's apartment, Hughes and six others chose a name

---

[20] "'Foreword: Greeting," *Stylus*, 1 (May 1911), 6.

[21] *Dust Traces On A Road* (Philadelphia: Arno Press, 1969), pp. 175–6; *The Big Sea* (New York: Hill and Wang, 1963), p. 218. Shortly before his death, Johnson reflected on the role that he, as editor of *Opportunity*, had played in "providing an outlet for young Negro writers and scholars whose work was not acceptable to other established media because it could not be believed to be of standard quality despite the superior quality of much of it." See Charles S. Johnson, "The Negro Renaissance and Its Significance." in *The New Negro Thirty Years Afterward*, ed. Rayford W. Logan, Eugene C. Holmes and G. Franklin Edwards (Washington, D.C.: Howard University Press, 1955), p. 85.

for their journal, divided up the responsibilities, and made a passing nod in the direction of finances. They selected *Fire* as a title because, in the words of Hughes, they desired to "*épater le bourgeois*, to burn up a lot of the old stereotyped Uncle Tom ideas of the past, and to provide . . . an outlet for publishing not existing in the hospitable but limited pages of *The Crisis* or *Opportunity*." The editorial board included Wallace Thurman, as editor, Aaron Douglas, as artist and designer, John P. Davis, as business manager, artist and writer Bruce Nugent, short story writer Zora Hurston, poet Langston Hughes and poet Gwendolyn Bennett, also affiliated with *Opportunity* and later with *Black Opals*.

The group was certainly talented but surely uninformed in matters of business. They began the journal with very insufficient funds, even for one issue. Each member of the board was to contribute fifty dollars for initial expenses. Because only Wallace Thurman had a steady job, he assumed responsibility for the bills; this was a generous but costly gesture. Hughes wondered how the number ever left the printer's office: "How Thurman was able to persuade the printer to release the entire issue to us on so small an advance payment, I do not know. But he did."

The bills were enormous because the seven chose a needlessly expensive format. Hughes recalled that "only the best cream-white paper would do on which to print our poems and stories. And only a rich crimson jacket on deluxe stock would show off well the Aaron Douglas cover design." As a result, there was money neither for advertising nor distributing the journal. And there was no coherent plan for funding a second issue. On an introductory page of the first number, the editorial board made a limp plea for support:

> Being a non-commercial product interested only in the
> arts, it is necessary that we make some appeal for aid from
> interested friends. For the second issue of *FIRE* we would
> appreciate having fifty people subscribe ten dollars each,
> and fifty more to subscribe five dollars each. We make no
> eloquent or rhetorical plea. *FIRE* speaks for itself.

The editors of those journals which lasted the decade, both black editors and those who were white, such as Harriet Monroe of *Poetry*, knew that a periodical could never sustain itself with such a lacklustre appeal.

After November 1926, *Fire* never reappeared. "When the editorial board of *Fire* met again, we did not plan a new issue," Hughes remembered, "but emptied our pockets to help poor Thurman whose wages were being garnished weekly because he had signed for the printer's bills." Thurman's wages continued to be "garnished" for three or four more years, even after "the bulk of the whole issue" burned to ashes in the basement of the apartment in which it was stored.[22]

---

[22] "The Twenties," pp. 19–20, *The Big Sea*, pp. 235–7; *Fire*, 1 (November 1926).

The end was ironic, particularly because fire had been the unifying metaphor in the periodical. To make the title appear as an alarm, the board placed two exclamation marks after the word—*Fire* ! ! The editor autographed special copies, including the one in the Moorland–Spingarn Research Center of Howard University, with "Flamingly, Wallace Thurman." The "Fore word" reinforced the dominant motif and consequently deserves full quotation:

> FIRE ... flaming, burning, searing, and penetrating far
> beneath the superficial items of the flesh to boil the
> sluggish blood.
>
> FIRE ... a cry of conquest in the night, warning those who
> sleep and revitalizing those who linger in the quiet
> places dozing.
>
> FIRE ... melting steel and iron bars, poking livid tongues
> between stone apertures and burning wooden opposition
> with a cackling chuckle of contempt.
>
> FIRE ... weaving vivid, hot designs upon an ebon bordered
> loom and satisfying pagan thirst for beauty unadorned
> . . . the flesh is sweet and real . . . the soul an inward
> flush of fire . . . Beauty ? . . . flesh on fire-on fire in the
> furnace of life blazing . . .
>
> "Fy-ah,
>
> Fy-ah, Lawd,
>
> Fy-ah gonna burn ma soul!"

The poetry section announced itself with the title from Countee Cullen's poem and appeared as "Flame From The Dark Tower." The issue concluded with "A Department of Comment" by Thurman, called "Fire Burns." In those pages, he cried freedom for black writers, saying "it would seem that any author preparing to write about Negroes in Harlem or anywhere else . . . should take whatever phases of their life that seem the most interesting to him, and develop them as he pleases."

Editor Thurman preferred the less reputable side, as his inclusions in *Fire* indicate. The three short stories featured characters falling far short of standards dear to the bourgeoisie, both black and white. "Cordelia The Crude: A Harlem Sketch," by Wallace Thurman, presented the early career of "a fus' class chippie"; "Wedding Day," by Gwendolyn Bennett, told of the violence and despair in Paul Watson, a black American who emigrated to

Paris because of "his intense hatred of American white folks"; "Sweat," by Zora Hurston, narrated the tragic end of Sykes, a loafer who lost everything, including his life, because of an obsession with fat black women—"Gawd! how Ah hates skinny wimmen!"

The issue also included the first part of a novel by Richard Bruce, called "Smoke, Lilies and Jade." In his narration, Bruce detailed the amours of bisexual black artist Alex, known to his male lover Adrian (alias Beauty) as Duce. One scene, in particular, violated the sensibilities of the middle class on both sides of the colour line: "Alex ran his hand through Beauty's hair . . . Beauty's lips pressed hard against his teeth . . . Alex trembled . . . could feel Beauty's body. . . close against his . . . hot . . . tense . . . white . . . and soft . . . soft . . . soft . . ."[23]

The poetry section began with Cullen's poem. Thurman and the others liked the selection, partly because of its defiant but technically graceful introduction: "We shall not always plant while others reap / The golden increment of bursting fruit . . ." "A Southern Road" immediately followed. Written by Helene Johnson, who later became part of the Boston Quill Club, the poem described the victim of a lynching: "A blue-fruited black gum /. . . Bears a dangling figure,— / Sacrificial dower to the raff, / Swinging alone, / A solemn, tortured shadow in the air."

The section contained "Elevator Boy," a controversial poem by Langston Hughes. The selection bothered many, because the protagonist showed no evidence of the American work ethic: "I been runnin' this / Elevator too long. / Guess I'll quit now." "Flame From The Dark Tower" featured another poet worthy of comment. Lewis Alexander, who was a member of the Washington Saturday Nighters and also of the Quill Club, contributed two poems, one of them about a prostitute ironically called "Little Cinderella," a girl who did not wait for her prince: "Look me over, kid ! / I knows I'm neat,— / Little Cinderella from head to feet. / Drinks all night at Club Alabam,— / What comes next I don't give a damn! . . ."[24]

Reactions to *Fire* were mixed. As Langston Hughes noted, the white press largely ignored the journal, except for *Bookman*, which reviewed the periodical in November 1926. In *The Big Sea*, Hughes called that appraisal "excellent," an adjective he wisely removed from his 1966 discussion of the same material. The *Bookman* review shifted in tone, telling blacks first to lift themselves into the middle class by their own bootstraps and then suggesting that Negro art should be separate and distinct from "American literature." The anonymous writer, who was perhaps editor John Farrar, initially commended *Fire* for appearing "at a time when the Negro shows ominous signs of settling down to become a good American." He continued: "As

[23] *Fire*, pp. i, 15, 48, 6, 25, 41, 38.
[24] "Flame From The Dark Tower," Fire, pp. 16, 17, 20, 23.

the Negro begins more and more to measure up to the white yardstick of achievement, he will gain a merited position in American society . . ." By his conclusion, the reviewer was complimenting *Fire* for encouraging "separate but equal" in the arts: "It is to be hoped that he [the black artist] will find in this new Negro quarterly the thing he needs to keep his artistic individuality"—so much for the white press.[25]

According to Hughes, the black press was more voluble and quite indignant, as the editorial board expected it would be: "As we had hoped—even though it contained no four-letter words as do today's little magazines—the Negro bourgeoisie were shocked by *Fire*." The literary reviewer for the Baltimore *Afro-American* wrote an angry letter to Thurman, saying, "I have just tossed the first issue of *Fire* into the fire." In *The Big Sea*, although not in the 1966 article, Hughes also claimed that "Dr Du Bois in the *Crisis* roasted it," although he provided no supporting quotation. Actually, the reactions in the black community were more complex than Hughes indicated.[26]

In January 1927, the *Crisis* "Looking Glass" commented on *Fire*. Rather than "roast" the journal, the reviewer praised Aaron Douglas's illustrations and the expensive format selected to highlight those contributions. At the end of his note, he even endorsed the publication: "We acknowledge the receipt of the first number of *Fire* 'devoted to Younger Negro Artists.' It is strikingly illustrated by Aaron Douglas and is a beautiful piece of printing . . . We bespeak for it wide support."[27]

Opportunity spoke more enthusiastically about *Fire*. In "The Dark Tower," his monthly column, Countee Cullen endorsed the journal. With the support of Charles Johnson, he called *Fire* "the outstanding birth of the month." He then suggested, tongue-in-cheek, that the number might bother unsophisticated readers: "There seems to have been a wish to shock in this first issue, and, though shock-proof ourselves, we imagine that the wish will be well realized among the readers of *Fire*." He found "ample extenuation" for Bruce's "Smoke, Lilies, and Jade," considered "a reprehensible story" by many, in its technical execution and fine phrasing. He applauded the format, particularly the "startlingly vivid Douglas cover done in red and black," and contributions by Zora Hurston. Cullen thought both Douglas and Hurston "noteworthy for their method of treating racial subjects in a successfully detached manner." He anticipated the next issue: "This sort of success, more than any other, augurs good for the development of Negro artists."[28]

---

[25] "A Challenge To The Negro," *Bookman*, 64 (November 1926), 258–9.

[26] "The Twenties," pp. 19–20; *The Big Sea*, p. 237.

[27] *Crisis*, 33 (January 1927), 158.

[28] *Opportunity*, 5 (January 1927). 25.

III.

The demise of *Fire* educated Hughes in the ways of literary periodicals: "That taught me a lesson about little magazines. But since white folks had them, we Negroes thought we could have one, too. But we didn't have the money." Hughes learned not to involve himself again in such a venture. Thurman responded in a different way—he "laughed a long bitter laugh," as Hughes recalled.[29] But then he quit laughing and began work on another journal. The one and only issue of *Harlem* appeared in November 1928 with Thurman as editor, Richard Bruce as contributing editor, and Aaron Douglas as art editor. The contributors included a panoply of distinguished names: Langston Hughes; Helene Johnson; Alain Locke; Theophilus Lewis, formerly connected with the *Messenger* and a critic of drama; George Schuyler, earlier associated with the *Messenger* and in 1928 the editor of a "new Negro newspaper syndicate"; and Walter White, author and assistant secretary of the NAACP.[30]

Thurman saw *Harlem* as a new type of black literary periodical. In his editorial, he sketched the history of Negro magazines, beginning with "the old propagandist journals," such as *Crisis*, *Opportunity*, and *Messenger*, which had served their day but were "emotionally unprepared to serve a new day and a new generation." All they could offer the aspiring young writer was an occasional page—"But the artist was not satisfied to be squeezed between jeremiads or have his work thrown haphazardly upon a page where there was no effort to make it look beautiful as well as sound beautiful." The only recourse for the black artist, until the latter 1920s, was the white press. Few Negroes, though, would continually buy "white magazines" in order to read an occasional poem or short story by a black author.

In 1926, *Fire* seemed to herald a new day. As Thurman remembered, it "was the pioneer of the movement. It flamed for one issue and caused a sensation the like of which had never been known in Negro journalism before." When it failed, other publications emerged, such as *Black Opals* in Philadelphia, "a more conservative yet extremely worthwhile venture," and the *Saturday Evening Quill* in Boston, which was published by and for members of a literary group. These little magazines had problems, however, as Thurman so well recalled: "The art magazines, unsoundly financed as they were, could not last."

Thurman hoped to solve those problems with *Harlem*, and thus he subtitled the journal, "A Forum of Negro Life." Primarily, he would include short stories and poetry, as he had in *Fire*. He would, though, reach out for a larger audience by featuring essays on current events, as well as more "intimate" essays, and by publishing competent white writers as well as black. The journal "wants merely," he said, "to be a forum in which all people's

---

[29] *The Big Sea*, p. 238.
[30] "Our Contributors," *Harlem*, I (November 1928), 21–2.

opinions may be presented intelligently and from which the Negro can gain some universal idea of what is going on in the world of thought and art." By adopting a conciliatory tone, Thurman hoped to garner support from some of those quarters which had previously rejected him and his efforts. Continuing to use the third person, he explained that "it [*Harlem*] enters the field without any preconceived editorial prejudices, without intolerance, without a reformer's cudgel."[31]

To emphasize his basic approach, he included an essay by the statesman-like Alain Locke. In "Art or Propaganda?" Locke agreed with Thurman that the time for "weeping and moaning" was past. He concluded that "all our purely artistic publications have been sporadic" because they could not consistently meet the requirements of *Crisis*, *Messenger* and *Opportunity*, journals which had been the only recourse to black artists and which were "the avowed organs of social movements and organized social programs." "There is all the greater need then for a sustained vehicle of free and purely artistic expression," said Locke. "If *HARLEM* should happily fill this need, it will perform an honorable and constructive service."

Thurman began his journal with an essay he had solicited from Walter White. At the onset of the article, "For Whom Shall the Negro Vote?" White quoted from Thurman's letter to him, which had asked for a discussion of "'the dilemma of Negro voters today—surveying the attitude of the old guard toward loyalty to the Republican party and the attitude of another group which is openly advocating a bolt from the traditional party of our fathers.'" In his analysis, White adopted a moderate, well-balanced tone, seemingly in keeping with Thurman's approach to his new journal. He acknowledged great inadequacies in Al Smith and Herbert Hoover, candidates for the United States presidency, but he did not call for new political parties. Seeing that black voters held a balance of power in about ten states, he urged Negroes to "trade ballots for justice," to make white candidates listen to the needs of black people.[32]

So far so good. With the first essay, *Harlem* did appear as a journal much different from *Fire*. As the reader proceeded into the journal, however, he encountered short stories and poems similar to those printed in *Fire*. Hughes contributed three poems dealing with drunkenness, boredom and jazz, and a short story called "Luani of the Jungles," which portrayed the fatal attraction between a white European man and a black African woman. The other short stories offered pictures no more appealing to the black bourgeoisie. Roy de Coverly's "Holes" and George W. Little's "Two Dollars" both dealt in prostitution and murder. Only George Schuyler offered a respectable character in "Woof," a story about the courageous and commanding First Sergeant William Glass of Company H, Twenty-Fifth U.S. Infantry.

---

[31] "Editorial," *Harlem*, pp. 21–2.

[32] *Harlem*, pp. 12, 5–7, 45.

Thurman had planned succeeding issues of *Harlem*. With this in mind, he challenged readers to support his effort. In the last page of his editorial he wrote: "It now remains to be seen whether the Negro public is as ready for such a publication as the editors and publishers of *Harlem* believe it to be." He gave further evidence of his plans at the end of the journal, when he listed prominent writers who had been asked to contribute to future issues, such as Heywood Broun, a columnist for the *New York Telegram* and the *Nation*; Clarence Darrow, "noted liberal and attorney"; Eugene Gordon, editor of the *Saturday Evening Quill*; Charles Johnson, former editor of *Opportunity*; Claude McKay, author of *Home to Harlem*; H. L. Mencken, editor of the *American Mercury*, and Frank Alvah Parsons, President of the New York Schools of Fine and Applied Arts.

As a literary editor, Thurman failed once again, and for several reasons. First of all, he had not achieved a journal sufficiently different from *Fire*. Too many readers undoubtedly associated the second periodical with the first. Then, too, the journal materialized just before the financial crash of 1929. In those days, no literary periodicals were finding easy financing and many were quietly slipping out of existence. With the catapulting difficulties of the times, few were in a mood to notice the loss of a once-promising periodical. And so few said anything when they waited in vain for the second number of *Harlem*. Responses in the press were negligible, as were comments afforded later in published reminiscences of the period and in autobiographies. Much research uncovered only sparing references, one of the few stated in the autobiography of George Schuyler, entitled *Black and Conservative*. Schuyler remembered the journal chiefly because it included his story "Woof," which he considered one of his best literary portraits.[33]

The loss of *Harlem* disillusioned Thurman. He never again attempted a literary journal, and he became more and more convinced of the failure of the Negro Renaissance. In *Infants of the Spring* (1932), Thurman compared the black twenties to a scene at a drunken party. Raymond, who represented Thurman, described the situation: "Whites and blacks clung passionately together as if trying to effect a permanent merger. Liquor, jazz music, and close physical contact had achieved what decades of propaganda had advocated with little success." Raymond concluded that "this . . . is the Negro renaissance, and this is about all the whole damn thing is going to amount to." Through his protagonist, Thurman also re-evaluated some of the main figures of the period. He reserved a gentle satire for Alain Locke, who "played mother hen to a brood of chicks, he having appointed himself guardian angel to the current set of younger Negro artists."[34] Parke appeared several times in the novel, always "clucking" after a brood of scattering chicks.

---

[33] New Rochelle: Arlington House, 1966, pp. 169–70.
[34] New York: Macaulay Company, 1932, pp. 186–7, 180.

IV.

While *Fire* and then *Harlem* were making their début, other little magazines surfaced elsewhere on the east coast and also elicited the attention of Alain Locke, among others. In the spring of 1927, *Black Opals* came to the fore under the direction of Arthur Fauset, a teacher in the Philadelphia public schools, and with the support of a group of young, primarily local, Negro writers. Two other issues followed, the Christmas 1927 number under the leadership of guest editor Gwendolyn Bennett and an editorial staff composed of Fauset, Nellie Bright, Allan Freelon and James Young; and the June 1928 number, under the control of the same editorial board, with the exception of Bennett.

The first issue included a statement of purpose: *Black Opals* "is the result of the desire of older New Negroes to encourage younger members of the group who demonstrate talent and ambition." The statement continued, expressing ideas reminiscent of those given earlier in *Stylus*, another magazine directed towards youth: the journal "does not purport to be an aggregation of masters and masterpieces. These expressions, with the exception of contributions by recognized New Negro artists, are the embryonic outpourings of aspiring young Negroes living for the most part in Philadelphia. Their message is one of determination, hope, and we trust, power." The "aspiring young Negroes," who primarily wrote poetry, were students in the Philadelphia public schools and at the Philadelphia Normal Schools, Temple University, and the University of Pennsylvania. With the possible exception of Mae V. Cowdery, then a senior at the Philadelphia High School for Girls, most of these students did not emerge later as established poets. The "older New Negroes" were identified explicitly on the contributors page of the first number: "LEWIS ALEXANDER is a well known New Negro poet..."; "LANGSTON HUGHES is the well known New Negro poet"; "ALAIN LOCKE, author of 'The New Negro,' is the father of the New Negro movement."

From a historical perspective, the most significant material in all three numbers is "Hail Philadelphia," a short essay written by Locke and included in the first issue. The essay deserves examination, partly because it shows Locke as politician, steering cleverly between the old ways and the new, endorsing the new without a flat rejection of the old. To introduce his thesis, Locke criticized the elders of Philadelphia, but with humour:

> Philadelphia is the shrine of the Old Negro. More even
> than in Charleston or New Orleans, Baltimore or Boston,
> what there is of the tradition of breeding and respectability
> in the race lingers in the old Negro families of the city that
> was Tory before it was Quaker. Its faded daguerotypes [sic]
> stare stiffly down at all newcomers, including the New Negro (who we admit, is an upstart)—and ask, "who was your
> grandfather?" and failing a ready answer—"who freed you?"

In his next paragraph, Locke made a gesture towards the "Old Negro" of Philadelphia and elsewhere, saying that "I was taught to sing 'Hail Philadelphia' (to the tune of the Russian anthem), to reverence my elders and fear God in my own village." After a few more conciliatory lines, he turned to the youth, and remained in that direction to the end of his comments. He warned young readers about the past: "I hope Philadelphia youth will realize that the past can enslave more than the oppressor..." To emphasize his message, Locke came towards his conclusion with a metaphor:

> if the birth of the New Negro among us halts in the shell of conservatism, threatens to suffocate in the close air of self complacency and snugness, then the egg shell must be smashed to pieces and the living thing freed. And more of them I hope will be ugly ducklings, children too strange for the bondage of the barnyard provincialism, who shall some day fly in the face of the sun and seek the open seas.

Interestingly, Locke selected the very imagery Thurman would associate with him in *Infants of the Spring*. Quieting his essay, Locke ended with a direct address to young black writers willing to experiment: "Greetings to those of you who are daring new things. I want to sing a 'Hail Philadelphia' that is less a chant for the dead and more a song for the living. For especially for the Negro, I believe in the 'life to come.'"[35]

Locke established a tone for the journal, but he did not control the publication. Arthur Fauset, the moving force behind the journal, was more conservative than Locke, even though he could make a gesture in the philosopher's direction. Fauset was not, to use Locke's image, in a mood to smash the "egg shell... to pieces." Neither was he in a position to do so, publishing mostly the "embryonic outpourings" of interested students. The third and last number of *Black Opals* ends with Fauset's review of *Quicksand*, by Nella Larsen. Fauset began the review with sentiments which could have been endorsed by Locke, and others. He praised Larsen's novel as "a step forward" in Afro American literature: "For the first time, perhaps, a Negro author has succeeded in writing a novel about colored characters in which the propaganda motive is decidedly absent." But then Fauset went on to qualify his allusion to propaganda. In so doing, he stated views which were decidedly conservative when compared to Locke's and Thurman's enunciations in *Harlem*. Fauset claimed that the propaganda novel, like the "pure" literature advanced by many "New Negroes," had its place: "If the 'pure' artist desires to create pure art, then of course let him create pure art; but whoever set up any group of Negroes to demand that all art by Negroes must conform to such a standard?"[36] With such comments, Fauset suggested that *Black Opals*

[35] *Black Opals*, I (Spring 1927), inside back cover, front page, 3.
[36] "Quicksand," *Black Opals*, 1 (June 1928), 19.

was not a radical publication, even though it supported much of the new black literature. Like *Stylus*, it wanted to teach the young, not shock their elders. As Thurman said in *Harlem*, *Black Opals* was "a more conservative" effort than his own, yet "extremely worthwhile."

As "a more conservative" periodical, *Black Opals* never confronted the type of maelstrom engulfing *Fire*. Rather than create controversy, it elicited comments ranging from mild approval to enthusiastic endorsement. In the past, *Opportunity* had encouraged the new magazines more than had the other Negro publications; it proved no exception this time. In a February 1928 column of "Ebony Flute," Gwendolyn Bennett recalled "the rare pleasure" she had in editing the second number of *Black Opals*. More importantly, she noted a proposed visit between the Philadelphia and Boston literary groups, thereby suggesting that the individual societies did not work in isolation from one another: "I understand that the *Black Opals* have been asked to visit the *Quill Club* in Boston in the spring of the year. Such interchange is good." With others, Bennett saw such interchange as a significant event in the evolving Negro Renaissance: "mayhap some year both of these groups with one or two of New York's younger, newer Negroes will get together and go to visit the Ink Slingers in California."

Countee Cullen also found hope in the efforts of these literary societies. In "The Dark Tower," he commended the Philadelphia journal, reserving special praise for poems by Nellie Bright and Mae Cowdery. Like Bennett, he hoped the Negro Renaissance would spread across the land, enveloping urban centres from the east to the west coast. "The *Black Opals* venture is one which," he asserted, "we should like to see sweep the country as the Little Theatre movement has done."[37]

The Boston Quill Club issued the first number of the *Saturday Evening Quill* in the very month when the Philadelphia group brought forth the last number of *Opals*, June 1928. For the next two years, the *Quill* appeared annually, the second number in April 1929 and the third and final number in June 1930. The officers of the Quill Club, and those responsible for the journal, were Eugene Gordon as president, Grace Vera Postles as secretary, and Florence Harmon as treasurer. Gordon, who also served as editor of the *Quill*, was on the editorial staff of the Boston *Post*. Florence Harmon had been a student at the Gordon College of Theology and Missions, in Boston, had contributed a short story to her college year book and had also contributed to the Boston *Post*. The secretary of the Club, Grace Postles, was a graduate of Cheney State Normal School and, when the *Quill* first came out, a student at the Emerson School of Oratory.

Other introductions are in order, since participants in the Quill Club have not occupied many pages in literary histories. Members and frequent contributors to the journal included Waring Cuney, a student of music in Boston who

---

[37] "Ebony Flute," 6 (February 1928), 56; "The Dark Tower," 5 (June 1927), 180.

had been published in the *Black Opals* and had won top prizes in the second *Opportunity* contest for his poem, "No Images"; Alvirah Hazzard, a teacher in the Boston public schools who had contributed several short stories to the Boston *Post*; George Reginald Margetson, a native of St Kitts, British West Indies, who had been published in several anthologies of Negro poetry; Florida Ridley, formerly a teacher in the Boston public schools and an assistant editor of *Womens Era*, who had contributed to *Opportunity* and *Our Boston*; and, among others, Dorothy West, who first published in the Boston *Post* and who won half of *Opportunity*'s second prize in 1926 for her short story, "The Typewriter." In *Infants of the Spring*, Wallace Thurman reserved laurels for only a handful of Renaissance writers; among those few were Dorothy West and Helene Johnson, also a distinguished member of the Quill Club. Through Raymond, Thurman praised the two for their "freshness and naivete which he and his cronies had lost" and for their skill as writers: "surprisingly enough for Negro prodigies, they actually gave promise of possessing literary talent."[38]

With "A Statement to the Reader," printed in the first issue of the *Quill*, Club members expressed their reasons for publishing a journal. As the statement indicated, they did not want to start a revolution; they did not want to make money, never offering the *Quill* for sale until the third issue; neither did they want to exhibit their literary wares before a wide audience. On behalf of his colleagues, Gordon wrote: "They have not published it [the *Quill*] because they think any of it 'wonderful,' or 'remarkable,' or 'extra ordinary,' or 'unusual,' or even 'promising.' They have published it because, being human, they are possessed of the very human traits of vanity and egotism." In other words, they wanted to try their work out, preferably on a close circle of friends. As explained further, they paid for their publication out of their own pockets. Evidently their pockets were more full than those of Thurman and associates, since they could sustain their effort for three years.

Unlike *Opals*, which specialized in verse, the *Quill* printed fiction, drama, poetry, essays and illustrations. Some of the selections had a decidedly conservative message, such as the poem by George Margetson, which lauded Abraham Lincoln as the black saviour—"To every dark-skinned child a hope he gave, / And made four million hearts beat happily."[39] Most of the contributions, though, dealt with themes that had become conventional in Negro literary periodicals of the latter twenties—the problems of unemployment, the resultant tension between husband and wife, particularly when wife alone works, and the temptation to "pass" if one were "high-yaller" or light skinned. The same material had appeared in *Fire* and *Harlem*, but with different treatment. Thurman's writers often employed southern, rural dia-

---

[38] *The Saturday Evening Quill*, I (June 1928), inside back cover; *Infants of the Spring*, p. 231.

[39] *Quill*, 1 (June 1928), front page; "Abraham Lincoln," *Quill*, 1 (June 1928), 34.

lects and included terms like "nigger" and "coon." Eugene Gordon and his colleagues depended on standard educated English, the type of language they used in their everyday professions.

In views aired generally and in the *Quill*, editor Gordon carefully separated himself and his involvements from radical positions in art and politics. Disagreeing with many contemporaries, he refused to see American Negroes as a separate people, as part of an African past rather than an American present and future. He expressed his opinions at length in *The Messenger*, where he said, essentially, that "the blacks of America are beginning to realize that their future lies in America, and not in Africa, or with the dead kings of Egypt; that they are no longer more to Africa, and will never again be more to Africa, than are their white compatriots to Caucasia."[40]

Gordon continued in the same vein in the *Quill*. In his editorial for the first issue, he urged his associates to look to the ground on which they stood, not to hanker after some distant jungle. Basically, he considered the Negro writer to be as American as apple pie:

> The colored artist is trained in the same schools that train
> the white artist, and at the hands of the same instructors.
> He gets the same stereotyped formulas of technique and
> style. He stands to the rendering of the Star Spangled
> Banner, and even, at times, tries to sing it. He salutes the
> flag throughout the farthest reaches of the land; eats baked
> beans and brown bread on Saturday night, in Boston;
> sneers, in New York, at "the provinces"; falls in line to
> shake the President's hand at New Year's, in the District
> of Columbia; laughs at the comic strip; and he worships
> wealth and caste in true American fashion.

Gordon realized that black artists had some rich sources unavailable to whites, but he asserted that Negro writers must use the "same method" and "the same medium" or language available to white authors.[41]

To further his views, Gordon included an essay by William Edward Harrison, Harvard-trained journalist, in the third number of the *Quill*. Like Gordon, Harrison said that American blacks could hardly look for inspiration to Africa, which was surely a "terra incognita" after some three hundred years. Summarizing Gordon's ideas, he claimed that black writers should use materials from their own environment in an effort to reach out to all people, black and white: "This literature must be at once profoundly racial and still universal in its appeal." He then stated opinions which were held by other

---

[40] "Group Tactics And Ideals," *The Messenger*, 8 (December 1926), 361. See Gordon's comments also in "The Contest Winners," *Opportunity*, 5 (July 1927), 204.

[41] "A Word in Closing," *Quill*, 1 (June 1928), 72.

Club members but had not been explicitly asserted in the *Quill*. Looking to the success of the Boston and Philadelphia literary organizations, Harrison asserted that Harlem could no longer be the moving force in the Negro Renaissance. The "Harlem theme" had "grown stale," as had writers like Thurman and George Schuyler:

> Through the efforts of these and their satellites Harlem,
> the Negro quarter of New York, has been relegated to the
> place of a satrapy of Babylon or Sodom; it is the epitome of
> the bizarre and the unregenerate asylum of Vice in capitals,
> if we may trust these literati; k means somehow knowing
> nods and winks, and suggests forbidden *diableries*.[42]

By the turn of the decade, many reviewers agreed that the Harlem theme was indeed "stale." Writers for the New York *Amsterdam News* and the *Commonweal*, among others, called the *Quill* the best of all the Negro little magazines. A reporter for the *Amsterdam News* urged "Harlem writers" to follow the "example" of the Boston group, while the reviewer for *Commonweal* praised the journal for its "admirable absence of jazz and Harlem posturings . . ." W. E. B. Du Bois liked the fresh beginning he saw in the *Quill* and commended the journal in *Crisis*: "Of the booklets issued by young Negro writers in New York, Philadelphia and elsewhere, this collection from Boston is by far the most interesting and the best . . . It is well presented and readable and maintains a high mark of literary excellence." Charles Johnson, in an unsolicited letter, went so far as to call the journal one of the few solid artistic achievements of the decade: "Here we have what seems to me the best evidence of a substantial deposit after the feverish activity of the last few years."[43]

V.

As the Great Depression began, the *Quill* came to an end, as had its predecessors. By 1930, only one Negro literary periodical remained, and that was *Stylus*, which had led the way for the others. During the 1920s, *Stylus* had remained strangely quiescent, presumably in part because Alain Locke and his Howard associates preoccupied themselves with artistic happenings elsewhere, specifically in Harlem, Boston and Philadelphia. After issuing the second number of *Stylus* in 1921, they waited until June 1929 to issue number three. And then, in the middle of the Depression, they reinstituted

---

[42] "The Negro's Literary Tradition," *Quill*, I (June 1930), 6, 8.

[43] "Excerpts from Comments on the First Number of *The Saturday Evening Quill*," 1 (April 1929), inside front cover; "Excerpts from Comments on the Previous Numbers of the *Saturday Evening Quill*," 1 (June 1930), inside front cover; W. E. B. Du Bois, "The Browsing Reader," 35 (September 1928), 301.

the journal on a more regular, annual basis.[44] They were able to continue because of University funding, and also because of the loyal support of such Honorary Members as Lewis Alexander, William Stanley Braithwaite, Charles Chestnutt, Countee Cullen, Langston Hughes, Georgia Douglas Johnson, James Weldon Johnson, Claude McKay, Arthur Schomburg and Jean Toomer.

From his perspective on the Howard campus, Locke studied the 1920s and presented his conclusions in "Beauty and the Provinces," an essay published in the 1929 *Stylus*. He began his remarks with new definitions, calling a capital a centre for creative work and a province a place empty of poets, a place "where living beauty . . . is not." Using these definitions, Locke pointed to New York as the capital of the United States and to Harlem—"the mecca of the New Negro"—as the vitality of that capital. Washington, D.C., on the other hand, was a province, in touch only with the "nation's body." It was not, wrote Locke, "the capital of its mind or soul." The District could have become a true capital only if "Negro Washington" had dropped its "borrowed illusions" and encouraged its wealth of "intellectual and cultural talent." Had this happened, the 1920s could have been known as the Washington Renaissance rather than the Harlem Renaissance. As it was, the District "merely yielded a small exodus of genius that went out of the smug city with passports of persecution and returned with visas of metropolitan acclaim."

Locke blamed "Negro Washington" in general. He never became more specific in his essay, desiring instead to encourage that which merited praise. And thus he turned to "certain exceptions" in Washington, pointing with "collective pride" to the "pioneer work" done by *Stylus*. As Locke remembered, the Howard group was among the first to advocate a Negro literature rooted in racial consciousness, or on "the foundation of folk-roots and the race tradition." Locke also remembered the many groups which had followed in other cities, which he mentioned by name. That very enumeration encouraged him, indicating "what has been accomplished in little more than a decade." The Negro Renaissance was just beginning, he concluded: "The provinces are waking up, and a new cult of beauty stirs throughout the land."[45]

Writing in 1929, Locke could not foretell the shape of the future, even though he knew other Negro literary periodicals had failed and even though he was looking into the face of the Depression. Locke was too close to the times to see them clearly. Those who wrote decades later had a better opportunity to view the 1930s. In his 1966 essay, Langston Hughes commented on the changes wrought by the Depression: "by the time the thirties came,

---

[44] In the years following, *Stylus* appeared in 1934, 1935, 1936, 1937, 1938 and 1941, which marked the twenty-fifth anniversary of the organization and the last number of the journal.

[45] *Stylus* (June 1929), front page, pp. 3–4.

the voltage of the Negro Renaissance of the twenties had nearly run its course." Writers of the new decade would not congregate enthusiastically in the small groups which had sponsored the little black magazines of the preceding years. Rather, they would find sustenance in the Federal Writers Project of the Works Progress Administration. Looking back nostalgically to the 1920s, Hughes called those years "Harlem's Golden Era."[46]

Hughes knew much about the 1920s, but his judgments also need review. Like so many others, he was fascinated by Harlem and thus concentrated on that city in his reminiscences. Such concentration provided valuable insight; at the same time, though, it obscured part of the fuller picture. Harlem did have a "Golden Era," but the Negro Renaissance of the decade was not circumscribed within the boundaries of that urban area. Negro communities from Boston to Los Angeles also had visions of a "New Negro" and a new literature. The record of this broader awakening has been forgotten but it is not lost. The story remains, preserved within the surviving copies of the black literary periodicals of the 1920s.[47]

---

[46] "The Twenties." pp. 11–12.

[47] Abby Johnson wishes to acknowledge the support she has received from the Faculty Research Program at Howard University.

III. AFTER MODERNISM

The landscape of literary magazines changed drastically after the wars. The energy of modernism had largely dissipated, and the burgeoning Cold War brought new uncertainty to the world of art and literary expression, internationally and at home. Many magazines shut down after great success in the early part of the twentieth century—such as *Horizon* in Europe and *Story* at home—and the university was increasingly becoming a stable, fruitful home to existing publications and newly created ones. Television and the movies were increasing in popularity and influence. And, perhaps most importantly, war veterans were returning home, to college, and to the typewriter.

*Sowing
words
for seventy
years*

$15.00 U.S./$15.00 CANADA

ANTIOCH
the # REVIEW

Anniversary Issue

LITTLE MAGAZINE, WHAT NOW?

by Paul Bixler (1948)

I.

Anyone who wants to consider the fate of the little magazine today must give at least preliminary attention to the book on the subject compiled by Frederick J. Hoffman, Charles Allen, and Caroline E Ulrich. This necessity occurs because the little magazine historically has had its sources in many a backwater and obscure literary freshet. The book charts much undiscovered territory and anyone who would set foot in the area now must examine its map although some of the guide marks may prove mistaken. *The Little Magazine* (Princeton University Press, 1946) is an "authority," to be reckoned with even when it is contradictory, confused, or dead wrong.

Hoffman-Allen-Ulrich fix the beginning date of the little magazine movement as 1912. This would take on more significance if the authors had set the fact in its socio-literary context. Although there were a scattering of little magazines before that time, it is true that little-magazine publishing became a phenomenon only after *The Masses* (begun in 1911), *Poetry* (1912), *Blast* (1914), the *Little Review* (1914), *The Midland* (1915), had established a pattern. (It is characteristic of the authors that they chose the year and the appearance of *Poetry* rather than of *The Masses* to fix the movement.) But the years 1910–12 also saw the end of the muckrakers. That the little magazine was preceded by the muckraking journal and by its accompanying literary ferment, Hoffman-Allen-Ulrich seem entirely unaware. From their story one gets an impression of considerable literary excitement, but it appears to be an excitement which arose out of little more than a superior sort of spontaneous combustion.

The book's better part is its bibliography and index, upon which the authors (chiefly Mr. Hoffman and Miss Ulrich) have showed in more than 200 pages a meticulosity and precision well beyond what is normally expected in such matters. The 540 little magazines listed in one bibliographical alphabet and the 96 "fellow travellers of little magazines" listed in another are given life histories (or obituaries) replete with inclusive dates, places of publication, editors, most frequently published authors, and often a thumbnail sketch of policy and contents. The bibliography is obviously not exhaustive yet it has been receptive of anything in English or under American editorship. One of the characteristics of the little magazine in English, too little remarked upon, is its geographical spread. A hundred and thirty-nine of the 540 little magazines and 43 of the 96 "fellow travelers" are listed as published outside the United States. The majority of these foreigners or expatriates appeared in Britain or on the European Continent, but it is interesting, if nothing more, to find three of them published in Mexico, three in Spain, eleven in Australia, three in the USSR (at Moscow). Eric Bentley has shrewdly remarked that the little-magazine movement has not been so much international as homeless. But that truth should not be allowed to obscure the accomplishment of the bibliography, which, after a manner of speaking, documents it.

Not so much can be said of the rest of the volume. In somewhat more space than they have given to the bibliography and the index, the authors have attempted a "history." The plan has been to divide the little magazine into types (about which more later) and to intersperse chapters on each type with chapters of chronology. This turns out to be a kind of glorified expansion of certain items of the bibliography. These pages give evidence, for one thing, of the great inbreeding among many little magazine editors and authors, but that is a fact with which Hoffman-Allen-Ulrich never come to grips; of the social setting within which the little magazine movement took place we get very little. Instead, we are regaled with endless details (interesting enough in their way) of authors, editors, and particular magazines; we are fed gossip and given a grabbag of odds and ends.

In the brief concluding chapter, and even more clearly in the introduction, the authors make a stab at the criticism and the social history presumably necessary to the job they have set themselves. The relationship of the little magazine to the mainstream of literature turns out to be its relationship to commercial publishing. In the literary world, according to the authors, the little magazines are the advance guard breaking the way for the large commercial operators. As they put it:

> The commercial publishers—the large publishing houses and the big "quality" magazines—are the rear guard. In a few instances they are the rear guard because their editors are conservative in taste, slow to recognize good writing; but more frequently the commercial publishers are the rear guard because their editors will accept a writer only after the advance guard has proved that he is, or can be made,

commercially profitable. Whatever the reason for their backwardness, few commercial houses or magazines of the past thirty years can claim the honor of having served the advance guard banner; they have discovered and sponsored only about 20 percent of our post-1912 writers; they have done nothing to initiate the new literary groups. To their credit, it may be said that they have ultimately accepted any author, no matter how experimental, after he has been talked about for a period of years—sometimes a good many years.

Now there is partial truth in this pattern, but nowhere in the book is it examined critically for its social or literary implications. Instead, it is accepted mechanically and "proved" statistically. One would immediately question, as a sample, the idea that the little magazine is a feeder of the big "quality" magazine. For every William Faulkner whose stories have made the *Saturday Evening Post* or the *Atlantic Monthly* there are ten other graduates of the little magazine whose skill in short fiction is small or whose short stories will rarely, if ever, be accepted by the commercial magazines. Book publishers should have their profession correctly represented, too. They do not compete directly with magazine editors—even little-magazine editors. They are looking for books, not short stories or essays, and since the young writer will frequently and sensibly begin with less ambitious efforts, it would be fairly normal for his first work to appear in little magazines rather than between boards.

That 80 percent of our post-1912 writers have been the discoveries of the little magazines is now by way of becoming a literary cliché simply because Hoffman-Allen-Ulrich have asserted it as fact, and because the statement, an easy one to repeat, has been taken up by reviewers. Its documentation is not in the book but in an essay, "The Advance Guard" by Charles Allen in the *Sewanee Review* (summer 1943). Here Allen traced the beginnings of sixty writers "generally accepted as representative of the various literary and philosophical outlooks" whose first work appeared after 1912, and found that 90 percent of them published their early work in little magazines. (He deducted 10 percent "as possible margin of error.") In his selection of writers Allen was partial to poets and he left out of account at least another sixty writers of quite as great importance (such as Bernard DeVoto, F. Scott Fitzgerald, Ring Lardner, John O'Hara, Thomas Wolfe, Dorothy Parker). But it is not so much his figures, faulty enough as they are, that seem strange, but the fact that he used figures in the first place as the basic element in his and his fellow authors' estimate of what the little magazine has been worth.

The little magazine, then, has been historically both more and less than Hoffman-Allen-Ulrich allow. It has a place both in social and literary history which they do not so much deny as neglect. It has been more than "revolt" and experiment, and advance guard. And on the other hand, it was not altogether the great literary hothouse of the '20s and '30s that they make out.

II.

Just what is a little magazine? Allen-Hoffman-Ulrich divide the field into six classes—poetical, regional, leftist, experimental, critical, and eclectic—and all are given chapters in their book. In this pattern they reflect the decision of Allen in his earlier essay, who remarked after setting up his categories: "One can make such divisions provided one does not take them too seriously." (Though most of the rest of the paragraph in the essay was incorporated in the book, this one was dropped.) Elsewhere in their book they say of their categories:

> Each of the six groups of periodicals that we have men-
> tioned contributed valuably to a regenerative literature.
> Perhaps those magazines devoted to the experimental phi-
> losophies and techniques . . . have most clearly performed
> the advance guard function. The regionalists or proletar-
> ians [leftists] might, and sometimes did, attain recogni-
> tion without little magazine help, but the experimentalists
> rarely could rely on such fortune.

In this paragraph the authors offer a strange, hesitant questioning of the structure of their book and of its chief idea as to the nature of the little magazine. I am inclined to agree with the questioning. In spite of all the space devoted to them, the six categories seem to be casual devices not to be taken "too seriously." Three of them—poetical, experimental, and criti-cal—could be better explained simply on form—respectively, on the poem, the short story, and the critical essay. The eclectic type seems to be a kind of cross-section of these three and there are hints that on its upper levels, it shades out of the little-magazine group into what the authors term the fel-low traveler. This leaves the regional and leftist categories, which seem clear enough, but you will note in the above paragraph that it is these two which have not so clearly "performed the advance guard function."

And the performance of this function is, to the authors, of supreme im-portance. It is so important that the word little in front of magazine is not really sound; in fact, "in a sense," the word is "vague and even unfairly derog-atory." The correct term is *avant-garde*. And it is so inclusive that anything outside it falls inevitably into the category of the fellow traveler.

We must, then, have the fellow travelers defined for us. They include undergraduate literary magazines and periodicals devoted to arts other than writing, but the best examples seem to be the quarterly reviews, "not mon-ey-minded," but the "intelligent, dignified, critical representatives of an intelligent, dignified, critical minority... conscious of a serious responsibility which does not often permit them the freedom to experiment or to seek out unknown writers." Except for the *Yale Review* and the *Virginia Quarterly*, whose stability and respectability and advertising are now beyond questioning, the reviews and most of the other fellow travelers could be called little magazines that have made good. Many a little-magazine editor today will be found yearning to join this more or less successful group if only in terms of a relative economic security.

In their "Conclusion" the authors project the pattern of a literary phenomenon of the '20s and '30s into the present and the indefinite future. In their original analysis they inadequately examined the social and cultural background against which the little magazine developed. And at last having saturated themselves in the fascinating lore of personalities and isms and cultural tidbits, they cannot conceive but that the *avant-garde* will go on and on. For the future they briefly examine a number of possibilities, and they wind up:

> Finally, it is possible that the *avant-garde* will become conservative, even reactionary, in its theory and practice. It is not altogether ridiculous to imagine a revolt, sponsored by little magazines, against what are now viewed as revolutionary literary forms and styles. A cry for "Intelligibility!" may arise from the rank and file of unknown writers, who may forthwith establish mimeographed sheets quoting from the poems of John Greenleaf Whittier and other "primary" writers. This, however, is the least likely of all probabilities.

It may be unlikely, but it is not out of character with what the authors have given us on page after page as the core of little-magazine history.

Why, one might ask, does the little magazine have to go on forever being adolescent or, as these authors put it, *avant-garde*? New magazines and young authors will always have fresh enthusiasms. But does all growth take place in a vacuum and has all the experimenting been done in vain? The truth is that there are already, and have been for some time, signs of maturity. Since we are in search of the nature of the little magazine, let's discard such words as *avant-garde* (which has been applied to all and not, as it should be, to some little magazines) and find terms which will apply not only to what the little magazine has been, but what it is today and what it could become. Let me suggest a working description:

Size. It must seem obvious that the little magazine is a small enterprise. Not only is it not brought out with the idea of making a profit, it frequently, even with financial help, is lucky to make ends meet. Its editors often serve without pay, and its contributors, if they do not serve similarly, receive no more than pin money. Its circulation may be a few hundred and it cannot rise to more than a few thousand; many a little magazine has begun with a readership made up of its editors, its contributors, its would-be contributors, and their personal friends. Usually the format is not self-consciously small, but the lack of advertising (such are popular standards) will at least make it seem small.

Stability. Just because a magazine is little it does not follow, as one might suppose, that it must collapse after a couple of issues. One editor of the 1920s put the limit of a little magazine's vitality at two years, but this kind of thing seems an idiosyncrasy of the times, when it was fashionable to let a magazine die and then a few months later to found another with a purpose barely if at all distinguishable from that of the first. The little magazine can live as long as its editors have ideas, good health, and sufficient funds. It usually requires a subsidy. Supplementary funds may be furnished by a university, a book publisher, or a literary-minded fat cat. It has been suggested that the federal government give assistance after the manner of the Federal Theatre Arts Project, but a more logical idea would be for the federal government to allow, or even encourage, authors currently in the money (from Hollywood sales or best-seller successes) to contribute a portion of their heavy income taxes to the support of little magazines or similar literary and artistic ventures. (This at least would furnish a financial connection between the popular and serious literature.) In any case, the little magazine does not serve its purpose by going out of business. And its stability and continuation are probably as much dependent on an annual subsidy as on anything else.

Control. That the little magazine usually needs a subsidy in order to live and grow does not mean that it can safely accept control from anyone but its own editors. Most institutions other than the academic will not assume the role of financial god-father for a magazine without also calling the editorial tune or even attempting to fill the publication with its own publicity. (A notable exception is the Common Council for American Unity which subsidizes *Common Ground*. Allen-Hoffman-Ulrich do not list *Common Ground* even under the fellow travelers, but I should argue that it is a first-rate little magazine.)The university, more sophisticated in intellectual matters, will usually offer a form of editorial freedom, but this, too, may be watered down by academic timidity, lack of conviction, or conventional restraints. Whatever the financial sources, the editors must be strong men, knowing their own minds and their own policy. Two or three editors are better than one, but it does not follow that eight or ten are better than two or three. The little magazine lives or dies in its individual free expression, and for this result the editors must be both free and responsible.

Content. The little magazine cannot be a professional journal nor the organ of a professional society, but this does not mean that it cannot have standards of intellectual and artistic judgment. There has been a conventional decree that the little magazine must serve the cause of revolt. That decree comes down from the time when freedom was conceived principally as an opportunity for "blowing the lid off." So far as content is concerned, the little magazine is a small enterprise because its material is minor or unpopular or of limited appeal. Its fiction, through strangeness in form or subject, may be somewhat difficult to read. Its ideas may be socially (read "conventionally") difficult of acceptance or they may be hard to understand; they do not have to be half-baked nor must they be confined to the literary. If this definition does not seem to apply fully to the little magazine of the '20s and '30s, particularly in the area of ideas, please remember that I am speaking also of what the little magazine may become. I shall follow this up further on.

III.

Let's look at the content of the recent little magazine. Of the total enervating mass of periodical journalism, the little magazine, though it reaches a relatively tiny audience, is no insignificant part. No one can pretend to complete knowledge of all of it unless he gives attention to little else. But a fair sampling should afford sufficient clues.

The pattern of little-magazine fiction is difficult to establish. It may be said for one thing that its form is no straitjacket; gone are any strictures about the well-made story, the O. Henry or any other ending, and even the necessity of rebellion, revolution, or experiment. At first glance, also, the subject matter may seem to show as much variety as the form. Twelve of the thirty short stories selected by Martha Foley for *The Best American Short Stories*, 1946, and ten of the thirty which she chose for 1947 were taken from little magazines. They share with the stories from the quality commercial group (*Harper's, Atlantic Monthly, New Yorker, Harper's Bazaar*) and from a scattering of the slicks (*Good Housekeeping, McCall's*) an emphasis on the theme of children (usually in relation to parents or teachers), on the individual's isolation from society, and a certain nostalgia for times past. But these little-magazines elections differ from their fellows chiefly in two respects. They exhibit a greater awareness of social problems; eight of them, as against two from other magazines, include race relations as a major or minor theme or as part of the psychological atmosphere. And their characters and fictional situations are frequently unlovely and unpleasant. This latter characteristic would not be accounted bad if it did not sometimes seem to be cherished for its own sake—as though the authors were employing their writing as a defense against the outside world or even as a weapon whereby they could vicariously attack the unhappiness of their own childhood. I do not want to exaggerate this tendency; it is by no means generally true. But at its worst, in such a story as "The Cocoon" by John B. L. Goodwin, a horror tale without any philosophical, moral, or social significance whatever

VQR

THE VIRGINIA QUARTERLY REVIEW
A NATIONAL JOURNAL OF LITERATURE AND DISCUSSION
AT THE
UNIVERSITY OF VIRGINIA
SPRING 2008

IN THIS ISSUE

Bill Sizemore on
PAT ROBERTSON

Lawrence Weschler on
ROBERT IRWIN

Geoffrey Hayes on
RORY HAYES

Chris Ware's
JORDAN W. LINT

SPRING FICTION
SUPERHERO STORIES

and with a lonely frightened child as the chief character, publication would hardly seem justified.

In Miss Foley's collections, the fictional products of the little magazine have the special advantage of being placed side by side with some of those in the commercial journals. But they cannot be other than highly selective and they are chosen by one person with special ends in view. A better perspective is possible if one examines the more inclusive work of particular magazines as made accessible in *Accent Anthology* (Harcourt, Brace, 1946) and *The Partisan Reader* (Dial Press, 1946).

Accent, begun in 1940, is one of the best of the academic little magazines. Its campus background (it is published at the University of Illinois) has not noticeably affected its freshness or given it literary inhibitions. Forty percent of the bulk of six years' publication have been squeezed between boards. The fiction section indicates that the editors are hospitable to work of a considerable variety. It includes stories of social problems, of poetic mood, of experiment in form. There are psychological studies and fragmentary snapshots of Life. There is some tendency towards the foreign or unfamiliar setting, towards the nostalgic or quaint. The best story of the group is Walter Van Tilberg Clark's "The Indian Well," a perceptive, brilliantly told narrative of an old prospector in the desert country. It might have appeared in a quality magazine or with a few minor changes (today possibly with none at all) in the *Saturday Evening Post*.

Partisan Review, of "bohemian" or extra-academic extraction, might be called the bellwether of all little magazines. (It has just become a monthly and may in the future pass into the quality group.) Its history covers a period of more than ten years, but the bulk of selections in the *Reader* parallel the years of *Accent*. Its fiction shows many of the same characteristics—flashes of insight, frequent attenuation and intellectualization, some interest in form and experiment. But something else has been added or imposed. These stories are more of a piece. They show a definite philosophy and a consistent outlook on life. Their authors have business with middle-class mores, and they are aware of a *Partisan* thesis, that the intellectual is alienated.

The outstanding story, Mary McCarthy's "The Man in the Brooks Brothers Shirt," which concerns an affair between a woman intellectual and an American businessman, is a modern masterpiece. It has both conflict and substance, elements so frequently missing from little magazine fiction that their absence might almost be assumed to be a hallmark. Yet it could have appeared nowhere but in a little magazine, and most particularly in *Partisan*.

From this and other evidence, one cannot say that little-magazine fiction is all it might be. Yet it stands up well with other fiction. If honest short story writers find it difficult in a confused world to organize their material into meaningful patterns, so do modern novelists. Too seldom are either able to develop major relationships or major situations. Too often they seem to stand on the rim of the real world grappling with aberrations and abnormalities, with wild dim shapes of a scarcely-ever land. One may hesitate to attempt a diagnosis of this weakness. But I would hazard a guess that at least part of the difficulty comes from a lack of the wisdom necessary to understand or handle such ideas—a lack for which the American "pragmatic" tradition bears some responsibility.

At this point it is worth taking note of what has happened to book publishing. Traditionally, the creative writer has very often depended upon the book publisher for assistance in his early development. His publisher (whenever he has shown promise as a novelist) has assisted him both with money and advice, given him an advance at the psychological moment, and held his hand or carried him psychologically past the first novels which do not make their keep. This relationship is now being interfered with by excessive publishing costs. Where the publisher could once count on breaking even on a novel with a sale of 2,500–5,000 copies, he cannot do so now short of 6,000–10,000 copies. And that is only one of a number of forces turning the publisher's attention away from the development of new writers and from the best publishing practices. The result is to throw greater responsibility for literature upon the little magazine—a responsibility which it was never designed to bear except in part.

The little magazine does a good job of publishing fiction. What is to its particular credit, there was never a time when the serious short story writer had a better chance to be published regardless of his manner or inclination. (Miss Foley records that 1946 saw a new record set in the number of published short stories and that 1947 broke that record both in the number of stories and of new authors writing them. Although she is not explicit about it her conclusion would seem to apply more to little magazines—or at least no less—than to others.) This does not mean that the author of fiction is properly paid for his effort, or that he can make even a partial living out of writing for the little magazine. But the little magazine cannot be expected to pay properly. It is doing its primary job when it publishes, and when one takes account of the growing quality market (which includes *Tomorrow*, *Commentary*, *Harper's Bazaar*, *Mademoiselle*, and others as well as *Harper's*, the *Atlantic Monthly*, and the *New Yorker*) it appears to be publishing its full share.

IV.

One cannot say so much for its nonfiction. Nearly all the articles appearing in nearly all little magazines are concerned with literary criticism. By and large such criticism has become very cozy and intimate, a pursuing of the tortured word until it yells for mercy and a squeezing out of meaning until it is too thin and isolated to be understood short of an occupational lifetime. One gets an uneasy feeling that some of these little-magazine critics like a particular poem for the very difficulty it presents to the layman. In our broken world such a solitary or isolated pursuit of technical literary efficiency has come to resemble more and more a special kind of division of labor. In its exercise it seems like the pleasure of the armchair detective in solving a crime or, on a somewhat lower level, of the Monday-morning quarterback who replays Saturday's game. So much of the criticism is technical that when it does, on occasion, rise to philosophy, it turns out to be a technician talking philosophy—than which nothing could be more misrepresentative.

Literary criticism monopolizes the nonfiction pages of the little magazine—and too much of it is confined to the type described above. But the little magazine is a large mansion and it could accommodate even an atomized literary criticism if occasionally it housed something else. Almost alone among its fellows, *Partisan Review* has made some pretense to breadth. It began in 1936 out of a political interest—and it has been unsteadily losing that interest ever since. It has published the brilliant philosophic group of essays, "The Failure of Nerve," and after the war the political series on "The Future of Socialism," but more and more the battle for any other than literary values has become a losing one. Perhaps the final blow came in 1943 when Dwight Macdonald left the magazine to start his own journal, *Politics*—which itself, after a brilliant interlude, seems to have entered a period of innocuous desuetude.

Partisan has constantly plugged the line that the intellectual is alienated. But one wonders how the intellectual can gain morale when he turns out to be, nine times out of ten, a writer or an artist? Where are the lawyers, the doctors, the scientists, the engineers, the technicians—yes, even the philosophers? The intellectual, it seems, is not even a whole intellectual but a literary one—which is something pretty special.

Partisan has served the cause of general ideas better than any other little magazine. The overwhelming majority have served it not at all. Last year there was published a new anthology, *American Thought 1947*. Its aim was to publish "a small encyclopedia of the annual crop of thinking in America," to "display the major 'trends' of ideas." Its point of view was serious; the slick commercial magazines were barred from consideration and journalism was included only to the extent that articles were to be understood by the intelligent reader, "yet not outraging the sensibilities of the expert" in the particular area treated. One might have thought that such an opportunity would have provided a field day for the little magazine, but not so. Out of thirty-eight selections only thirteen came from that quarter, and of these, eight were from journals unrecorded in *The Little Magazine*. Four selections (the limit set by the editors for selections from any one) came from the *American Scholar*, three from the *Antioch Review*, one from *Science and Society*. It may be argued from my own criterion that the last is not a little magazine but I should include it in spite of its academic dullness.

There are other projects, either in progress or contemplated, that use this big collection of littles for their home base. It needs not much imagination to perceive in this wealth of material the seeds for articles, bibliographies, doctoral dissertations, and books. Students in Cultural History have shown as much interest—from ideological, historical, sociological, and psychological viewpoints—as have students in Contemporary Literature; and a young lady in Art History has begun a systematic examination of *The Masses* for the political cartoon work (particularly Art Young's) that magazine featured. An up-to-date revision of the basic work in the field, Hoffman, Allen and Ulrich's *The Little Magazine: A History and a Bibliography* (Princeton, 1946–1947) might advantageously be based on this assemblage of original sources, and I have had consultations with a doctoral candidate about his plans for writing an interpretative history of a single significant journal, such as *The Southern Review*, to investigate its role and influence over the years, its political and artistic change of character, and the causes and consequences of those changes. And, following the anthologistic trend of our time, the idea of culling the best from the great little mags of the past and present, and presenting it in book form, is certainly tempting, though not altogether new.

The ordering of current little magazines presents problems that are apt to baffle the staff of Serials Acquisitions Departments. The streamlined business methods to which they are accustomed fail to work in the domain of unbusinesslike and usually impecunious individualists. Ordering through agents is practically out of the question; subscriptions need to be placed directly with the one-man (as a rule) trinity of publisher-editor-distributor—a trinity that is likely to go "on the road" without further notice, or change its editorial address at the spur of the moment from Brooklyn to San Francisco. Most of those editors have very decided ideas about the poetry of William Carlos Williams and Wallace Stevens but are extremely hazy on the merits and purposes of invoices in triplicate. Nor are they unduly bothered by the implications of terms like "quarterly": unexpected hitches and delays are always expected in this un-business, and a double issue is an accepted way of skipping an issue and yet giving the subscribers their money's worth, causing never a murmur of discontent among them but many a groan out of a university library's serials checker. In the cases of the more affluent littles that are distributed by DeBoer's "Selected Outlets," the situation is somewhat less irregular.

Acquiring back issues to fill existing gaps is a perennial task that can be met through purchases from private collectors and the few dealers mostly on the East and West coasts, who specialize in little magazines and avant-garde literature in general; or through exchanges with libraries and individuals; and sometimes through gifts and public auctions. Vigilance and the spreading of the word about one's interests and lacks can yield happily surprising results. (One of the Sukov collection's needs, for instance, is a run of *The*

Double Dealer, an important journal published from 1921 to 1926 in New Orleans.) "Desiderata lists" are periodically sent to likely sources, and as a last resort one can reproduce missing issues by "Xeroxing" or other photocopying methods, if one can locate the original issues and get the consent of the owner. A bibliography giving the holdings of six participating libraries is the *Union List of Little Magazines*, published by the Midwest Inter-Library Center in Chicago in 1956—a useful tool for locating copies. And the excellent annotated bibliography in the back of the Hoffman-Allen-Ulrich work is of inestimable value in checking on the completeness of one's holdings and in establishing *desiderata* files ...

ANIMA RISING: LITTLE MAGAZINES IN THE SIXTIES

by Len Fulton (1971)

The little magazines and small presses of the decade enormously affected and, in turn were affected by, all the major social issues of the time: peace and war, race, education, censorship, explosion of underground papers; and later in the decade: ecology, Indian rights, Women's and Gay Liberation and so forth. An even slightly informative discussion of the entire spectrum of forces running into the small print media would take much more (hopefully recycled) paper than I have here been issued. But, so confined, it is my belief that the general frontal pressure of small presses in the sixties was created by the emerging action ethic of youth, which evolved quickly into a do-it yourself praxis and a search for generational identity. Then, there were three more particular influences which I'll take up at length, one technological and economic (offset printing), one aesthetic (concrete poetry), and one spiritual (mimeography). True to the thirst for wholeness and relatedness that pervaded the decade, these influences remain inseparable except under the most academic analysis, rolling together in an incessantly overlapping and altering pattern. And other influences are as well strung into the current: freedom of language and the belief that it belongs to the person using it; the proliferation of *book* publishing; poetry pamphleteering by the small periodicals to a point of blurring the distinction between book and magazine (*The Outsider* is called a "book periodical," for example), and the eventual interchangeability of the terms "little magazine" and "small press," just one manifestation of the liquidizing (not liquidating) of traditional boundaries between genres and media, and a redefinition in *process* rather than structure; an alienation from the austere and isolated scholarship of the university—for any austere and isolated scholarship—or any austere and isolated *anything*—

The Black Mountain Review

Charles Olson
        Against Wisdom As Such

    Robert Hellman
            The Quay

René Laubiès
        Eight Reproductions

Spring 1954
75 cents

and an increasing suspicion of university or institutional sponsorship or of those publications so sponsored; the falling into general disrepute of the old "school" phenomenon which made the critic's life so easy and smart; the appearance of definite if some times evanescent regional influences; the indurate poetry of Charles Bukowski; the organization of the small presses in 1968 into the Committee of Small Magazine Editors and Publishers (COS-MEP). The decade with which I am really concerned here now is not in fact a ten year period at all, but more like four or five years, starting in 1963 and 1964 with the sudden inception of so many important small presses, and coinciding incidentally with the inception of the first underground newspapers. Nevertheless, some of the immediate forerunners of the small presses of this time in the United States were Tuli Kupferberg's *Birth* (started in 1957 and carried well into the decade as Birth Press); Ed Sanders' *Fuck You/A Magazine of the Arts*; Robert Bly's *The Fifties* (started in 1958, changed to *The Sixties* and now *The Seventies*); LeRoi Jones' *Yugen* (1958 1962); and John Bryan's *Renaissance* (1961).

Although the form of printing known as "planographic" (flat surface) can be traced back to Germany in 1796, it was not until photoengraving methods were developed in letterpress printing that the offset process became a reality. In 1904 a lithographer in New Jersey named Ira W. Rubel came upon the modern offset process through an error of his press feeder. He discovered that to run the image from its original cylinder onto a rubber blanket and thence to the paper greatly increased clarity of the printing. The process was used and developed up into the fifties but, because of expensive investments in letterpress machinery, the big newspapers and periodicals did not convert to offset. There were no offset presses on the magnitude of the giant, web-fed letterpress machines, and no type setting or accessory equipment equal to the Linotype machine, the Ludlow typecaster, and so on. As far as I know the first offset daily newspaper in the U.S. was the *Middletown* (N. Y.) Daily Record (1956), which had to have its press custom built. There followed, apparently, the production of larger offset equipment which had the effect of throwing the smaller, used machinery onto the market. As advances were made quickly in the technology of first-line items, these used presses became more plentiful, cheaper, and better. They began to land in garages, cellars and front parlors.

The conversion from letterpress to offset printing in the sixties by the small presses is statistical fact. The proliferation of these presses early in the decade is the basic technical stimulus to the entire small and underground press movement. In 1960 some 78 per cent of little magazines were letter press-printed, 17 percent were offset; by 1969 only 31 percent were letter press, 54 percent were offset.

This process was made-to-order for the fluid, "do-it-yourself-*now*" current that began to engulf the sixties. It took no accessory equipment on the order of that required in letterpress, and the advent of direct platemaking and direct masters simplified things still more. Little space was required for storage and operation, and many smaller models could be moved by one man quickly and entirely. Most of all, however, for the little magazines justified typesetting could be done for a nickel a line—or for just about nothing by the editor on his own typewriter. And if a given contributor's work went beyond the usual "straight matter" (prose or poetry) toward visual art, this could be re produced faithfully at little or no extra cost, and with little or no condescension to the intervening printing technology. This last of course is critical, for finally the experimenter and his editor (often one and the same) were wholly *free* in point of technological fact. Freedom in that decade, as we know, was a thirst touched off by something far deeper and more universal than the coming of the print medium into proletarian hands (and things were happening in light and sound, too). Freedom was the mid century *Zeitgeist*, with its taproot in the early-century failures of industrialization, the sundry dehumanization that started with the First Great War and reached its most imposing moments over Hiroshima and Nagasaki. As always that *Zeitgeist* expressed itself most exquisitely in the arts, and especially those arts with little "to lose" from the truth—the avant garde, the experimental, the underground—the arts to which commercial viability was not a founding consideration. In the print media nothing stood readier as a vehicle than the little magazine.

The spiritual essence of the poetry that came to be known as "concrete" lay in the evolution of perception and theory in this century from static towards dynamic modes. The development of quantum physics, of behavioral and Gestalt psychologies early in the century are evidences of this in the sciences and humanities, whose premises are infinitely simpler than those of art. In the literate arts early moves toward Dadaism, surrealism and later antirealism were in this direction, as were surrealism and abstract expressionism in painting, and "atonality" and Serialism in music. Expanded communications, increased mobility, and simply population growth itself contributed to a general sense of fluidity that blossomed after mid-century, which led inevitably to the notion that there was no one way to do any thing, only many ways with varying probabilities of betterness. This relativeness led to exploration of intermediary areas ("energies" would be a term more in keeping with the spirit) and a seeming irreverence for old and static categories and terms. Much here is a tremendous if technologized *re-turn* toward what the styles of "primitive" man must have been. This thought is important, at least, in considering concrete poetry as it developed into the sixties in Europe as a virtual renaissance.

It began in the late forties and early fifties with the "ideograms" of Brazilian Decio Pignatari and Diter Rot of Iceland; and with the "constellations" of the Swiss Eugen Gomringer, whom the American Emmett Williams refers to in the foreword to his massive *An Anthology of Concrete Poetry* (Something Else Press, 1967) as "the acknowledged father" of it all. Gomringer and Pignatari met in 1955, and out of this meeting came plans for an anthology titled *Konkrete Poesie*, which was unfortunately not published. During the fifties similar and often independent work was being done by Haroldo de Campos of Brazil, Kitasono Katue of Japan, Ian Hamilton Finlay, a Scot, and Pierre Gamier of France. Essentially though, the early efforts in concrete poetry began on either of two continents, Europe or South America, and their convergence provided the nucleus for an international poetry Gomringer called "supranational." The ideogram was based on a visual syntax and an analogical method of composition rather than, as in traditional poetry, a grammatical syntax and a logical or discursive composition. The semantic elements in an ideogram cannot be separated from the visual elements. This latter is also a basic force in the Gomringer constellations. For Gomringer the poem was a functional object held in dynamic balance "as if it were drawing stars together to form a cluster." It would seem that the dynamic quality of the poem for Gomringer was slightly more critical than the visual presentation of an idea (as in the ideogram). The convergence then produced a poetry universally called "concrete," a term that only in the last year or two seems to have come to be less than descriptive of the work being done. Concrete is "a poetry far beyond paraphrase," says Emmett Williams, "a poetry that often asks to be completed or activated by the reader, a poetry of direct presentation—the *word, not words, words, words* or expressionistic squiggles—using . . . semantic, visual and phonetic elements of language as raw materials."

A number of small magazines published this work in the fifties. These included *Vou* (Tokyo), *Noigandres* (Edicoes Invencao, Sao Paulo), *Ideogramme* (Switzerland), *Bok* (Reykavik), and *Bord-dikter* (Stockholm). This last published work by Oyvind Fahlstrom as early as 1952; and *Vou* was founded in 1935 as a Japanese avant-garde magazine. *Noigandres* was produced in the fifties by a group of Brazilian poets of whom Haroldo de Campos was one of the most brilliant, emergent international figures.

In the sixties the concepts and arguments of the concrete poetry of Gomringer and Pignatari provided a departure point for a new revolution. Whereas these early concretists were interested in crossing the traditional boundaries between the literary and visual arts—itself a revolutionary proposition—those of the sixties moved out almost recklessly (and certainly courageously) in such flamboyant directions that virtually all art forms were affected. It came to Great Britain, to Canada and to the United States, though its main vanguard, at least as concerned its original inclinations, remained in continental Europe and South America. The experiments in "word plastics" of J. F. Bory, editor with Julien Blaine of *Approches*, and with J. Gerz of *Agentzia* (both Paris) and Ugo Carrega, editor of *Tool* (Milan) are outstanding. Bory uses word conglomerates and expanding, exploding characters to communicate feelings such as fear and ideas such as time. His work covers an enormous range, from such photographic experiments as *"erotographie"* (*Approches* 2), to the handprinted per mutational Chinese script of *Beche* (Approches, 1966), and *Whispering* (*Approches*, 1966) in which the voice volume implied for the words (in English) is rendered by light-to-lighter shades of yellow, with a typical expanding-contracting arrangement. The magazine carries work by Use and Pierre Gamier, editors of *Les Lettres* (Paris), whose concern is with spatialism and a supranational poetry (see "Pour Une Poesie Supranationale"), and includes an essay or spatialism, plus spatialist work by the Garniers, "Poemes mechaniques architectures" (in *Approches* 1), some plastic poems by Kitasono Katue of Japan, excellent collages by Claude Pelieu of the U.S., and much else.

Ugo Carrega of *Tool* (Milan) is another brilliant artist in "the world of verbal-phonetic signs (of the words apart from their meaning or sound) and the world of graphic signs (their physical appearance, the 'matter' of the word on the page)." Carrega's work often takes on organic, map-like qualities (as in *non principio e fine* or the card set *mikrokosmos*) but can also be expansive and flamboyant like Bory's (as in *idea rotore* and *segno vita*). In *Tool*, a large and beautiful folio, Carrega has used work by Julien Blaine, Herman Damen, Luigi Ferro and many others.

Other directions on the continent have been sought by Martino Oberto, editor of *Ana Eccetera* (Genoa), who connects graphics, words and their analogical equivalents, and seeks "the operational awareness of the specific exercise of linguistic terms, integrative levels for a type of language programmed to philosophical abstractism." Daniela Palazzoli and Gianni-Emilio Simonetti, editors of *Da-a/u dela* (Milan), verge toward musical experiments such as Sylvano Bussotti's "The Rara Requiem" which, in all its complexity, fits on a 4½" X 10½" card; Carl Weissner, editor of *Klactoveedsedsteen* (Heidelberg), has published tape recorder mutations by William Burroughs, Claude Pelieu and himself, and is interested in cut-up art, tape experiments, "word/sound bruitage."

In Great Britain one of the most important forces in this movement has been Ian Hamilton Finlay, a typographer and sometime toy maker, publisher of Wild Hawthorne Press and a concrete magazine called *Poor. Old. Tired. Horse.* He has worked in environmental poetry, sculpture poetry, glass poetry (his "wave/rock" as photographed by Patrick Eagar is well known) and a series of standing poems. He has divided his work into "fauve" and "suprematist" poems, apparently to distinguish between those which make reference to events outside themselves, and those which are unified semantic and graphic forms. He has also published kinetic poems and a series of kinetic booklet poems. His 1960 book, *Glasgow Beasts, An A Burd Haw, An Inseks, An, Aw, A Push*, caused an uproar among literary Scots.

Elsewhere in Great Britain, Cavan McCarthy devoted his mimeo mag, *Tlaloc*, to visual-concrete poems, and to communication between, and information about, concretists throughout the world; John Furnival and Dom Sylvester Houedard of *Openings* published poster poems, graphic scores, cards and folders of concrete poetry; John J. Sharkey who, with his wife Sonia edited *Loc* and *Lisn*, published "post-concrete" poetry—semiotics (code poetry introduced by Decio Pignatari and Luiz Angelo Pinto in 1964), computer poetry, nonverbal poetry, spatial poetry. The poster and cartoon poetry of Christopher Logue has been outstanding.

South America has, of course, continued to be a place of great experiment and invention in concrete poetry throughout the sixties, as can be seen by the constant references in the preceding text. The founding of the Noigandres Group (1952) and the "pilot plan for concrete poetry" (1958) together with the work of such internationally brilliant poets as Haroldo de Campos, Augusto de Campos, and Decio Pignatari provided Brazil with as rich a heritage in the genre as any nation in the world. It was largely through proselytization by these Brazilians that concrete poetry came to the attention of such artists as Ian Hamilton Finlay of Scotland, Kitasono Katue of Japan and Dom Sylvester Houedard of England; and it was these same Brazilians who suggested the term "concrete" to Eugen Gomringer in Switzerland in 1954, launching the international poetry. What is now a tradition continues, centered largely in Sao Paulo, Brazilia University, and Rio de Janeiro. The Argentine magazine *Diagonal Cero* (Buenos Aires), edited by Edgardo Antonio Vigo, has been highly influential in the South American and international concrete movement throughout the entire decade. The work of Vigo himself in stylish geometrical and punch poetry has pressed ever outward against any limits the genre possesses. *Diagonal Cero* is associated with Guillermo Deisler of Chile and Miguel Angel Fernandez of Paraguay.

The Canadian movement in concrete poetry has rested largely in the hands of a multimedia Toronto group centered at Ganglia Press (*Gronk, Synapsis*) and Coach House Press. Work by bp Nichol, David Aylward, David Harris (also recently bylined "David uu"), Rah Smith, Bill Bissett, and Jon Riddell has appeared. A good example of this work is bp Nichol's *Journeying and the Returns* (1967), a package containing a book, a record and assorted small pamphlets called "skoobs" by England's Cavan McCarthy, which is "books" spelled backward. The Toronto group has been interested in "concrete sound kinetic and related borderblur poetry," and has been allied both spiritually and materially with the Cleveland mimeo work of the late d. a. Levy, and that of D. r. Wagner's *Runcible Spoon* (now in Sacramento, California).

In fact, any discussion of the concrete poetry movement in the United States beyond the extraordinary work of New York–based editors such as Emmett Williams and Dick Higgins of Something Else Press, or Jerome

Dada-like, always saying it the way it comes down to him, incessantly fascinated with the very act of making the poem and often cataloging the environment in his last several lines. He published stories as early as 1944; his first poem was printed in 1956 in *Quixote* (Cornwall on-Hudson); by 1959 his poetry began to appear widely in little magazines such as *Epos* (Crescent City, Florida), *Coffin* (Eureka, California), and *Wanderlust* (Metairie, Louisiana). His first collection of poetry, highly surrealistic, was *Flower, Fist and Bestial Wail* (Eureka: Hearse Press) in 1961. He was named "Outsider of the Year" by Jon and Gypsy Lou Webb's *Outsider* (New Orleans) in 1962. His first important collection was published by the Webbs in 1963 (*It Catches My Heart in Its Hands*). His stock rose considerably in 1964 and 1965 when the mimeo publishers, then just starting up, seized upon Bukowski and structured a poetry and a dialogue around him. Chief among these was Douglas Blazek of *Olé* but it also eventually included Steve Richmond of *Earth* (Santa Monica), d. a. Levy of Cleveland, and Charles Potts of *Litmus* (Seattle-Berkeley) among others. The two important collections *about* Bukowski and his work are Hugh Fox's *Bukowski* (Abyss Publications, 1969) and Blazek's *A Bukowski Sampler* (Quixote, 1969).

Neither unrelated to Bukowski nor the meat poets nor mimeography nor anything else in small press publishing was that thing known as free press and speech. Though the breakthroughs made by, for example, the "beats" in the fifties are to be remembered and cited, the sixties saw its share of busts, starting perhaps with the prosecution in Marin County, California, of Henry Miller's *Tropic of Cancer* and running on through Lenore Kandel's *Love Book* in San Francisco toward the latter part of the decade. These cases had the benefit of huge publicity at least. Yet throughout the decade the small poets and publishers and booksellers were busted at a rate far greater, and with far more painful results, than their larger brethren: d. a. Levy, John Sinclair, Steve Richmond, James Lowell, John Kois, Robert Head, rjs, Dave Cunliffe, Malay Roy Choudhury—the list goes on round the world and back into the heart and soul of Western reason and constitutional guarantees. At this present moment Allen Ginsberg is collecting such documented evidence for *P.E.N.*

A number of black presses sprang up by mid-decade (there are now dozens): Dudley Randall's Broadside Press (Detroit), which has published several dozen very fine one sheet poems and some full-length books (*Black Pride* by Don L. Lee; *For Malcolm: Poems on the Life and Death of Malcolm X*, edited by Randall and Margaret Burroughs); *Soulbook* (Berkeley), one of the earliest magazines (1964), "dedicated to all our black ancestors who have made it possible for us to exist and work for a LOVE SUPREME of BLACK PEOPLE"; *Journal of Black Poetry* (San Francisco), edited by Joe Goncalves; and *Black Dialogue* (San Francisco), edited by Arthur Sheridan, Edward Spriggs and Abdul Karim. Because of the political and social imperatives of the black movement in this country, it must be said that the underground newspapers have served as a more immediately effective medium. Black poets and writers have insisted on coming to the small magazines more as poets and writers than as blacks. Andrew Curry (*Dust*), Al Young (*Love*), and Ed Bullins (an editor of the now defunct *Ante*) are cases in point.

As part of the attack on tradition and taxonomy, many small magazines coveted nonspecialization as a policy; among them foremost was Harry Smith's *The Smith* (N.Y.C.), "the most general magazine," now occupied in the promulgation of Smith's "Anti-Civilization League"; Curt Johnson's *December* (Western Springs, Illinois); Morris Edelson's *Quixote* (Madison); Margaret Randall's *El Corno Emplumado* (Mexico City), a magazine of great range, quality, and influence; Marvin Malone's *Wormwood Review* (Storrs, Connecticut); and *Dust* (El Cerrito, California) which I myself founded with others of widely disparate (too widely, it turned out) interests in 1964. The "imagism" of the fifties was carried into the sixties by Robert Bly's *Sixties* (Madison, Minnesota) and George Hitchcock's *Kayak* (San Francisco), among others. A poetry written after the spirit of the American Indian appeared on the West Coast about 1966, exemplary of which are "Shaman Songs" by Gene Fowler and Norman Moser, published in Moser's *Illuminations* and in *Dust*.

Though in the times few magazines could maintain any genuine regional flavor for long, some did at least in part covet a geography or what might be called a "geo-sociology." These would include such magazines as *Foxfire* (Rabun Gap, Georgia), edited by G. Eliot Wigginton; *South and West* (Fort Smith, Arkansas), edited by Sue Abbott Boyd; John Sinclair's *Artists Workshop Press* (Detroit); d. a. Levy's *Marrahwannah Quarterly* (Cleveland); John Simon's *Aldebaran Review* (Berkeley); and R. R. Cuscaden's *Midwest* (Geneva, Illinois). Also, as mentioned previously, the northwestern mimeo publishing of Ben Hiatt's *Grande Ronde Review*, Mel Buffington's *Blitz*, and Carlos Reye's *Prensa de Lagar* exuded a regional quality.

Shortly after mid-decade, government money began to appear for the small magazines from both the National Endowment on the Arts and the Coordinating Council of Literary Magazines, a New York-based nonprofit association; and George Plimpton and Peter Ardery brought out their first *American Literary Anthology* in 1966, designed to print the best work each year from the small magazines. As might be expected, of course, the small and truly independent magazines were the last to benefit from these programs, and a number of things have conspired to make even dimmer the hope of future beneficence. Largest is the insistence on Congressional and other administrative meddling ("auditing") in the programs and, as per Representative Scherle's remarks cited earlier here, a gross intolerance for letting art go its way. This has led to the virtual shut-off of funds in the Plimpton project and to a Washington-based audit of the Coordinating Council. There is also in the National Endowment itself a new leadership, oriented more toward community programs, and away from support of individual artists or independent (let alone clandestine) efforts. Finally there is, in the face of any and all institutional interference, beneficent or otherwise, the irascibility and impatience of the small pressman himself, who cherishes his freedom more than his very life. Those well meaning administrators caught between these impulses and a government which cherishes the opposite have a thankless, bitter, and probably failing task. And then the small presses organized themselves in 1968 at Berkeley into the Committee of Small Magazine Editors and Publishers (COSMEP), a difficult undertaking given the above-mentioned editorial attitudes. Yet COSMEP has somehow stayed glued together despite periodic financial emergencies, has in three years held three annual conferences (Berkeley, 1968; Ann Arbor, 1969; Buffalo, 1970), and has published a *Catalogue of Small Press Publications* in 1969 (free to libraries) and a *Bookstore Survey* (1969) for members. It also issues a periodical newsletter (five dollars per year to nonmembers).

This getting together, however tenuous at present, has been one marker at least that the sixties are gone and that a new era is upon us. I believe that government support in the future will run from spotty to nil, and actually be less and less significant to the small presses. *At the same time* I look for continued consolidation along economic lines as editors rework and harden the increasing power of their numbers. I suppose this process is bound to affect them editorially, though if they stand clear of institutional sanction, these effects are not likely to be serious. What *is* likely, however, is that small pressmen will find themselves with growing power as a pressure group, and what lies beyond *that* is anybody's guess. Certainly individual presses and editors will be less and less at the mercy of commercial printers, the post office, cheating bookstores, and county prosecutors. In addition to COSMEP's 250-member publishers there is the Underground Press Syndicate of newspapers which, with its associate, Canadian, and European presses, has nearly two hundred members; the Association of Little Presses in the United Kingdom has about sixty members; the COPLAI group in Argentina (Confederacion de Publicaciones Literarias Independentes) has an unknown number; additionally, there are many more "specialized" magazines and presses dealing with the interests of blacks, Indians, women, Mexican Americans, and gays, and with issues of ecology, educational reconstitution, GJ. antiwar movements (seventy-five of these last in the United States alone).

Put it all together by, say, 1975, and you will indeed have a new age.

DAILYW🌐RLDBEAN

SPEC I A L!

FRISCO, 22-574 — SECONDS AFTER YOU KNOW WHEN THIS AFTERNOON EVEN YOUNG AN ALLEGED EXPERT MEMBER OF A SIXTIES ERA MOD SQUAD GOT A SLUGSTRAIGHT OFF INTO THE CLEAR BLUE SKY A-

PAGE AS THE BACK OF A DOLLAR FOOD COUPON WITH THE SECOND EPISODE WITH . . . YOUTH HAS REMINDED OUR FRIENDS ACROSS THE BORDERLESS THAT A HANDFUL OF BO-OZE GOLF SEEKERS DO NOT NECESSARILY AN ACCESSION HAVE

Sara Moore

BOYE KNOB HILL AND EL PRESIDENTE SWALLOWED HIS BUBBLE GUM FOR THE LAST TIME IN THE REPUB-LIC OF CALIFORNIA. HE WAS CARRIED TO AF I IM-MEDIATELY, HIS FACE AS

not xochimoco, ma ihica nichuana tehuatla xochit 🌸 yehene ye iman poyocur ma ihtoc timalnih-tihuara 🌸 nenohpal aychene ve atem zan tlachu cuetotla moyahua 🌸 moazquetlal moxxo yehuatl nepapan xuchitl 🌸 zan comoni huehuetl mava cehuatlo 🌸 in queztzalpovconati a l xcuilihue noyal, necnemict 🌸 in xochitl a va nzetzelihuipanetel nicaiva, nenonaliuram 🌸 zan noyoline entlapani oa noyoline tel ahxa-moyahni in co ixtla 🌸 cuicail ye comovi anthea ya in queninan iuan 🌸 ac in moval ihte noyol-lno yolcan nocoui in terecutin in 🌸 zin ye ic nicloca in queu-montan 🌸 zao nicayahtea noxo-chitevo nocuicatoca 🌸 nictlah-tehuaz in queunanian 🌸 xochi-nenehiahtiaz noyollae yehuan te-pilhuan in terecutin in. 🌸

THE LETTERPRESS IN THE MIMEO REVOLUTION

by Kyle Schlesinger (2007)

Typography is the visible language of modern American poetry—the horizon where the literary and visual arts meet, and I feel that too little has been written on the role of the literary fine press as a genre distinct from artists' books, the genteel tradition of private press publishing, and the mimeo revolution. Loss Glazier, among others, has argued that the mimeo revolution of the sixties was not limited to magazines that actually used Edison's machine. For aspiring poets, activists and publishers, the allure of the mimeograph was its approachability, immediacy, affordability, and no-frills DIY aesthetic.

Given that the parallel proliferation of digital type and electronic publishing have perpetuated one another since the end of WWII when the letterpress became commercially obsolete, a grassroots renaissance in fine printing began in America during the nineteen-forties that rivaled the works of the European Dadaist, Cubists, and Futurists of the early twentieth century. The countercultural politics of print in postwar America follow in the historical trajectory of the revolutionary potential that has stimulated cultural, religious, political, and aesthetic transgressions since Martin Luther.

Like many young poets, my mentor Robert Creeley began corresponding with his significant peers and elders by inviting them to contribute work to a magazine. His first experience as a printer came rather unexpectedly: "I had tried to start a magazine with the help of a college friend, Jacob Leed. He was living in Lititz, Pennsylvania, and had an old George Washington handpress. It was on that that we proposed to print the magazine. Then, at an unhappily critical moment, he broke his arm, I came running from New Hampshire—but after a full day's labor we found we had set only two pages, each with a single poem. So that was that." The magazine never materialized, and he eventually gave Cid Corman the work he had collected, including poems by Denise Levertov, Paul Blackburn, Charles Olson, and his own poem, "Hart Crane" for the first issue of *Origin*. Their dispute over the printing of the first issue serves as a particularly insightful rift because it sets the stage for the charged debates between the things we have come to associate with letterpress (quality, prestige, sensuality, beauty, authority, tactility, etc.; as represented by Creeley) and the renegade DIY aesthetic of an emerging mid-century counterculture that Corman endorsed.

Letterforms are nothing if not controversial. In the early fifties, when letterpress printing was not entirely obsolete but certainly on the decline, Corman felt that it was pretentious, and opted for a combination of varitype and photo offset printing, much to Creeley's dismay. Although Corman felt that the first issue was "no marvel of printing," its reception was more than favorable: Vincent Ferrini, whom Cid had gone to join in Gloucester to celebrate the occasion, was thrilled. Olson, whose contributions claimed the bulk of the issue, was ecstatic. To read the magazine had given him the fullest satisfaction he'd ever had from print. However, the most exuberant praise, first by telegram of 20 April, then by letter, came from the poet who had but a single poem in the issue. It was a very fine job, Creeley admitted, clean, wonderfully flexible, and altogether without pretension.

Today I'm going to talk a bit about the "letterpress in the mimeo revolution," highlighting the books and periodicals of a few magpie poets who, dissatisfied with the mainstream academic and new critical culture, decided to take the face of contemporary writing into their own hands by teaching themselves how to print and set type in order to publish the writing they wanted to read.

According to Len Fulton's *International Directory of Little Magazines & Small Presses* the number of poetry magazines soared from 250 in 1965 to 700 in 1966. Coincident with this swell, the phrase "hypertext" was coined, Vietnam became the first televised war, Xerox introduced the first Telecopier fax machine, and Kodak introduced Super 8 film for home movies. Not only did these developments change the way people saw themselves and the world around them, but they gave them more control over the ways in which they chose to order and introduce an ever-escalating quantity of information—particularly visual. By the time President Nixon resigned from the White House, there were 2,000 magazines in circulation, Steve Jobs had sold his Volkswagen microbus to raise funds to build the first Apple computer, and Edison's patent on the Electric Pen turned one hundred years old.

War isn't everything, but it changes everything: how we write, what we read, how we think we feel about what we see or "know." In America, the war industry has done more to advance, and define the role of media and technology than any other force of the twentieth century. As co-curators Steve Clay and Rodney Phillips demonstrated in their relentless scavenger hunt for mimeo magazines featured in their Secret Location on the Lower East Side exhibition, there is more to be learned about the history of letters at large through the study of the minor events in publishing than subscribing to the ideology of the great books club. History is not only written by the victors, but for the victors, and distributed in the medium and language of their design. Studies of popular media such as handbills, posters, and magazines offer an account of the past that interrogates the barbarity of power struggles, transcends the boundaries of the working class and the social elite, and mends the violent ruptures of official histories. As the narrator of French filmmaker Chris Marker's *Sans Soleil* reminds us, "history throws its empty bottles out of the window."

The Untide Press was conceived in the midst of a broken world. William Everson was stationed in a conscientious objectors' camp in Oregon when he published his own poetry in an unofficial mimeographed newsletter entitled *The Untide*—launched in 1943 with the assistance of other like-minded artists, activists and writers including Adrian Wilson, who went on to become a successful printer and writer working with independent theatres in the Bay Area, and the actor, poet, and playwright Kermit Sheets. In a time of political unrest, Everson and company produced *The Untide* as a response to the camp's official newsletter, *The Tide*. Its purpose was decisive and tersely stated in the first issue, "This is the time of destruction, against which we offer the creative act." *The Untide* is a threshold between art and activism, poetry and politics, pre- and postwar life, books and periodicals, and the technologies of the mimeograph and the letterpress. Everson and company ran the mimeograph machine to produce his own *X War Elegies* and other small volumes before realizing their collective abilities in the production of Kenneth Patchen's *An Astonished Eye Looks Out Of the Air* in 1945 as the war was ending. In a letter to his wife Joyce dated 13 September 1944, Wilson expressed his reservations about Patchen's poems, which was the last, and most sophisticated book The Untide Press produced in Waldport.

> The Patchen poems—thirty-four of them that will take at
> least fifty pages—arrived. To me and Bill they were a great
> disappointment and Bill wanted to send them back even
> if Patchen did have a fit, but the rest of the Press wants
> to publish, perhaps for the name . . . Of the movements
> of the Allies I am unaware. It's insane; the arts, the forest,
> and the ocean here are a direct antithesis . . .

At mid-century, burgeoning dialogues between artists and writers took a postmodern twist, and journals played a key role in creating a sense of community among American poets living outside of metropolitan literary hubs. The magazines of the mimeo revolution had a disposable allure; they were easy to produce, inexpensive to purchase, fun to give away, and could literally materialize overnight. The mimeo was the perfect medium to efficiently advance experimental writing and art into public domain. Mimeograph magazines are characterized by their standard dimensions, side-stapled spines, non-archival paper, hazy typewriter fonts, and lingering inky odor. Editors frequently published visual art, promoted collaborations between artists and writers, and solicited artists such as George Schneeman and Joe Brainard for images to spice up the covers of their journals. For example, early issues of the Irving Rosenthal's Chicago-based Beat mimeo *Big Table* featured the art of former Black Mountaineers Aaron Siskind and Franz Kline, as well as the polemic anti-war artist Leon Golub on its covers.

As editor of *The Black Mountain Review*, Creeley published poets and artists—some of whom were in direct affiliation with the experimental college in rural North Carolina, others not. Following Pound's suggestion, Creeley thought of the *Review*, ". . . as a center around which, 'not a box within which / any item . . .'" could appear. Akin to Pound's dictum, "verse should consist of a constant and a variant," the *Black Mountain Review* had a group of regular contributors, while Creeley made a point of introducing new writings from emerging and marginal authors to insure a balance between the familiar and the unknown. The first issue appeared in 1954, and Jonathan Williams sold copies on the road with his Jargon Society books, while Paul Blackburn took responsibility for distribution in New York City. Reproductions of images by visual artists Philip Guston, Harry Callahan, Jess Collins, Franz Kline and Aaron Siskind were featured in a specific signature, accompanied by a brief introduction from the editor, whose friendships and collaborations with these artists and many others sustained three generations. It was modest, handsome, and affordably printed letterpress by Mosen Alcover, the jobbing firm in Palma de Mallorca who also produced the books he published as the editor of his own Divers Press. The College closed in the spring of 1956, and Williams became the publisher of the final issue. Allen Ginsberg (whose poem "America" appeared here for the first time) became the contributing editor, and published "Book III" from "William Lee's" (Burroughs') *Naked Lunch*. Creeley moved from the rural South to the arid Southwest, and his proximity to the West Coast poets, combined with Ginsberg's editorial sensibility, is reflected in the selection of writers whose works appeared in the seventh issue: Jack Kerouac, Gary Snyder, Phillip Whalen, Edward Dorn and Michael McClure.

One of the most radical small press operations to emerge from California was the brainchild of Wallace Berman, the visionary artist behind nine issues of *Semina* (1955–64). Berman acted as a regular contributor, founding editor, printer, designer, and distributor. Berman's admirable autonomy may be at least partially attributed to his desire to keep a low profile, to avoid entanglements with authorities on the grounds of censorship. Following his first exhibition at the Ferus Gallery in Los Angeles in 1957, he was arrested, tried and found guilty of exhibiting "lewd and lascivious pornographic art" by the same judge who had convicted Henry Miller on similar grounds. In December 1957, Berman explained the journal's circumstance on a small card pasted to the back of the second issue:

> During the second month of a scheduled exhibit of my paintings and sculpture, members of the vice squad entered the Ferus art gallery & confiscated a copy of 'Semina no. 1' which was used as an important part of a work entitled 'Temple'. Brought before the righteous judge Kenneth Holiday, who, taking the allegorical drawing in question out of context, declared me guilty of displaying lewd matter. I will continue to print Semina from locations other than this city of degenerate angels.

According to the colophon glued to the rear, inside cover, this issue was stapled and "handset with miscellaneous available type and papers." The poems are printed on a variety of paper swatches in numerous inks and founts, creating a sensual collage of colors and textures that reflects the discrepant content. Its hand-wrought character is accentuated by the astonishing amount of time it must have taken Berman to tip all of the poems into the otherwise blank, craft brown pamphlet.

Semina 3 was devoted to Michael McClure's "Peyote Poem," the first issue devoted entirely to the work of a single author, giving it the feel of a chapbook. The poem is printed letterpress on a single sheet of white paper, folded into fourths and glued into a brown folder made of construction paper. The title is printed in black ink on a card bearing the image of two peyote buttons. In future issues of the journal, Berman constructed folders, or portfolios with envelopes inserted (not unlike those that secured the check-out cards that used to appear in library books) to hold a hodgepodge of loose poems and pictures together. *Semina* had a decidedly non-commercial element; it contained no advertising and copies were not available in any bookstore. It was distributed through the mail, and in a sense, Berman's mailing list circumscribed the scope of the magazine's underground audience. Editions were small, ranging from two to three hundred, and much of the printing was performed on his own wonky letterpress in Los Angeles, San Francisco, and a handful of places he inhabited briefly in between. Very few copies of this obscure publication remain—a friend in Rochester tells me that Berman gave him a suitcase of *Semina* to take to Woodstock where he distributed them to hippies "tripping" in the mud. More were lost in a landslide that destroyed Berman's home in 1964, about twelve years before his sudden death in an automobile accident on his fiftieth birthday in Topanga Canyon. Robert Duncan recollects:

> *Semina* was a cult magazine. It meant to reveal the possibility of the emergence of a new way of feeling. Cult means

the cultivation of something . . . Wallace Berman gathered writers and artists he knew that gave him a sense of his own personal identity, and taking hold of the personal beginnings of his art.

Bean News was a tabloid-sized newspaper edited by Ed Dorn in collaboration with Holbrook Teter and Michael Myers of the Zephyrus Image Press in San Francisco. To the outsider, *Bean News* is a dense and cryptic compilation of, ". . . letters, articles, poems, puns and rebuses." In addition to the newspaper, that included a lightweight overseas version printed on Bible tissue paper, the dynamic duo behind the Zephyrus Image Press also produced press passes, letterhead, business cards and other miscellaneous ephemera to make the paper seem as true to its mythology as possible. Copies are extremely rare, both in special collections libraries and among rare book dealers. Few would know anything about it if not for a bibliography by Alastair Johnston, who writes:

> To my mind, the paper is so full of in-jokes and self-indulgence that it doesn't hold up. The form is amazing, but the content is rather opaque. When I expressed this to Raworth, he replied: 'One of the things that made that period work for me, and probably the reason *Bean News* doesn't wear well (and after all, these things were meant to be ephemeral) for you now, was that total feeling of open mind (with Ed, Holbrook and Michael) . . . there needed to be not even the minutest break between thought and language . . . and even beyond language; gesture . . . a finger movement would communicate. It certainly moves things along.'

Now that I teach typography at the university I feel that I must reconcile my incongruous affinity for mimeo culture. I spend my days scolding students and preaching the golden rules of legibility while secretly waiting to go home to read my decaying, illegible, "dirty magazines." Why should I condemn aspiring graphic designers for making the same mistakes I not only condone, but celebrate in mimeo magazines?

Making clear distinctions between: art and craft; craft and design; and design and art has never been easy, and the standardization of the personal computer in the home and office over the last two decades has made these distinctions even more complex—but why define? Look up 'DIY' in Wikipedia, and you will find the following warning at the head of the page: "This article or section does not adequately cite its references or sources." Sites like this are forums for direct democratic meaning-making free from the scrutiny of the 'experts' responsible for manufacturing 'authoritative' sources. *The Oxford English Dictionary* defines DIY as: "The action or practice of doing work of any kind by oneself, esp. one's own household repairs and maintenance." Simple enough, but not entirely satisfying. This speaks to the postwar era when people canned their own food, fixed their own engines, and darned their socks. These skills and values are, as they say, a thing of the past.

Before Stewart Brand became the Stewart Brand, the young countercultural figure rented a state-of-the-art IBM typewriter to create issue number one of *The Whole Earth Catalog* in 1968. It was subtitled: Access to Tools. The *Catalog* was designed to enable independent thinkers and backto-the-landers to lessen their dependence on conventional modes of passive consumption. For better or worse, the personal computer and Internet have given almost everyone the opportunity to perform the tasks of a publisher with (and more often without) the professional credentials that would have been necessary for publishers of the first half of the twentieth-century.

In closing, I would like to return to Glazier's claim that the literary fine press has more in common with the mimeo revolution than the private press tradition if only to get at the state of DIY publishing today. Due in no small part to desktop publishing software, the transformation from consumer literacy to producer literacy has become irrevocably blurred. The word 'design' once implied that a product was ultra-hip: designer jeans, designer teapots, and even designer drugs were all the rage. In Yuppie-times, The Sharper Image was where it was at—but although 'design' still summons notions of slick sports cars, sleek interior decorating, and seductive websites, the mimeo revolution was not about shopping, decorating or perpetuating the myth that our world has been designed by professionals endowed with specialized tools, skills, and knowledge. DIY is about making decisions and asking questions about who we are, what we do, and how we live, because writing, like printing, is both a thing and an activity.

In Exile and Against Criticism: *The Paris Review* and the Branding of Contemporary Literature

by Travis Kurowski (2012)

In the late nineteenth and early twentieth centuries, American literary magazines were more commonly referred to as "little magazines." George Plimpton, editor of *The Paris Review*, famously loathed the phrase. "I wish I could get you to say 'literary' magazines rather than 'little,'" Plimpton jokingly chided an interviewer in the late 1970s. "'[L]ittle' referring to a magazine," he continued, "would . . . refer to its physical dimensions—which suggests that a 'little magazine' editor is responsible for those fat little numbers, that you ripple fast with your thumb, and you can see Carl Hubbell throwing a screwball . . . or, in sleazier neighborhoods, Popeye doing something to Olive." As Plimpton was well aware, the phrase "little magazine" was in reference to *The Paris Review*'s—and all literary magazines'—small circulation numbers, and not its physical dimensions or respectability. Small circulation numbers for literary magazines have always been common. Mid-nineteenth century American literary magazine ancestor, *The Dial*—edited by Margaret Fuller and Ralph Waldo Emerson and arguably the most influential literary magazine in American history—never had more than 300 subscribers.

Literary magazine publishing by definition ventures on the margins of popular literary production and the publications are often referred to as a home for the avant garde; George Hitchock, editor of *Kayak*, famously described them as "the furnace where literature is being forged." According to Princeton University Press's landmark and often-cited 1947 literary magazine history, *The Little Magazine: a History and Bibliography*, these magazines "have lived a kind of private life of their own on the margins of culture." Not that the marginalization of literary magazines is anything which needs to be argued—on the contrary, their relative marginalization might be the only trait that all literary magazines share. Allen and company went on to define the little magazine as, "a magazine designed to print artistic work which for reasons of commercial expediency is not acceptable to the money-minded periodicals or presses." This is a common definition for literary magazines, as the modern literary magazine was born during the crush of magazine advertising (and with it a drop of magazine prices and an increase in circulations) in the late nineteenth and early twentieth century; literary magazines were a reaction to this drastic change. So *The Paris Review*, which wanted to be both a large circulation magazine and was willing to market itself in order to do this, was a quite different twist on the medium to date.

1. Defining the Brand and a Brief History of the Medium

The American literary magazine *The Paris Review* (1953–present) was something of an anomaly in its early years—even in the world of literary magazines, where there generally exists greater diversity among magazine editors and layout formats than similarity. What was notably unique for *The Paris Review,* and what propelled the magazine into unprecedented literary magazine success and influence during the second half of the twentieth century, had much to do with an initial implementation of three then-unique editorial choices for literary magazines of the time, this combination resulting in what became essentially *The Paris Review* brand. These three traits have since been emulated by a great number of literary magazines (from independents like *McSweeney's* to university sponsored magazines like *The Missouri Review*) due to their success for *The Paris Review* under the editorial guidance of the ever-energetic Plimpton, an eager and effective promoter of his magazine. *The Paris Review*'s insertion of these traits and certain branding techniques within the literary magazine structure brought the niche market of literary magazine publication into the consumer twentieth century.

Many would assign and have assigned the twentieth century success of *The Paris Review* almost wholly to Plimpton, as for fifty years he was a constant voice and editorial overseer for the magazine, while at the same time never taking a salary for his position as editor, and his editor calling card doubling as a subscription card for the magazine, one which he left "on bus seats and slip[ped] . . . into the occasional pocket," telling the pocket's owner, "No harm done. No harm filling one out." He was a constant and dedicated proselytizer of the literary. It is also well known that, due to Plimpton's (and many other *Review* founding editors') prep-school upbringing and connections within the literary, economic, and political world, he was able to introduce the magazine to, and solicit money from, many people who would be initially unavailable to those not born into such an upper-class society. For example, Plimpton's father was a United Nations diplomat and both Adlai Stevenson and Robert Kennedy were close friends. Nonetheless, giving entire responsibility of the magazine's success to Plimpton would be shortsighted. The majority of literary magazine ventures have been initiated and run by people from the middle and lower classes. But it is also true that other people from high society have begun and edited literary magazines (such as Scofield Thayer on *The Dial* and Francis Ford Coppola with his *Zoetrope: All-Story*), and none have yet gained the influence or longevity of *The Paris Review*. It was through a combination of *both* the magazine's editorial choices and Plimpton's own vigor and connectedness that kept the magazine solvent and influential in literary circles. Without specific and effective editorial choices, Plimpton might easily have been a mouthpiece for yet another type-heavy critical review, which still saturated the literary magazine market in the early 1950s.

The three important choices *The Paris Review* editors instigated for the magazine were the following (listed in no particular order, as all three were accepted and initiated by the magazine's staff right from the start). First: established in 1953 in Paris, *The Paris Review* saw itself and promoted itself as an expatriate literary magazine, even though most of its issues were sold in the United States and nearly all its editorial staff were U. S. citizens, thus giving the magazine the gilding of literary Paris and the foreign (as well as giving the magazine the freedom to experiment with its concept away from the prying eyes of their audience); Second: unlike the majority of literary magazines then and now, Plimpton and the rest of *The Paris Review* staff (aided by a small army of eager interns) were more than willing to actively and openly market their magazine—a commercial literary endeavor Malcolm Cowley favorably termed in his introduction to *Writers at Work: The Paris Review Interviews* as, "Enterprise in the service of art." Finally: the editors made an early decision to keep the magazine politically ambivalent and free of any literary preconceptions about what type of writing needed to be published; along these lines, their first and only manifesto announced that they had no manifesto, so they would be allowed instead to focus on creating the artistry of the magazine through the publishing of creative work and design. These three choices might be summed up as: the cosmopolitan choice, the commercial choice, and the procreative choice.

Early managing editor for the magazine, John Train, summarized this last, procreative choice quite succinctly, noting that early *Paris Review* editors were "convinced that theories, both literary and political are the enemies of art." All in all, the focus of *The Paris Review* was on a holistic idea of a magazine-as-art, while what at the time mainly produced were literary magazines whose focus was on criticism, such as *The Partisan Review* and

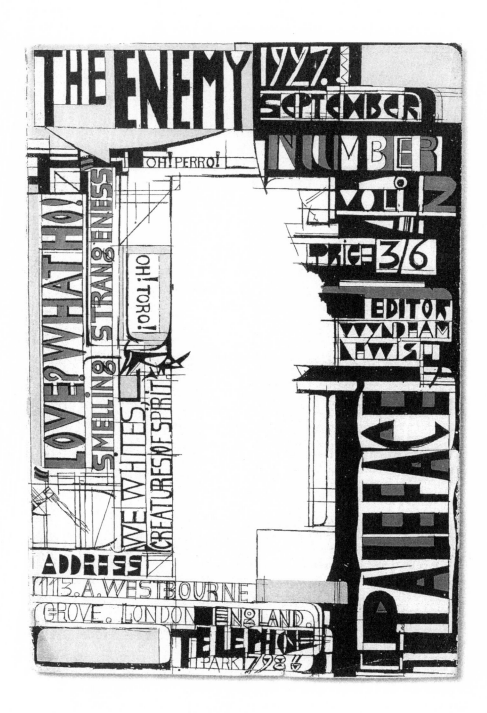

The Kenyon Review. It was an "Age of Criticism," as described by Randall Jarrell in an essay published the same year *The Paris Review* published its first issue. Along these lines, Malcolm Cowley described the literary magazines of the 1950s as "mature, solid, academic." It would be a decade in which *The Paris Review* and the later Beat periodicals emulating it (such as *Evergreen Review*) were to be a breath of fresh air.

Now certainly none of these editorial choices were by themselves unique. Literary magazines have before *The Paris Review* been concerned with the magazine as object and its public appearance. Other magazine editors in the past—such as those I've mentioned and others: *Blast, The Little Review,* and *The Enemy*—have employed creative uses of typography and design to create a more artistically produced periodical. And magazines such as *The Masses* and *Direction* have used idiosyncratic or eye-catching images to draw attention to their publication. As well, magazines such as (again) *The Little Review* (in Paris) and *Story* (in Vienna) have either begun or emigrated overseas, yet kept their main audience in the United States (most of these moves have been for the lower production costs overseas—another connection between the literary magazine and the modern brand). Many individual magazines before *The Paris Review* exhibited at least one of the three above editorial choices, but none assumed all three.

The success and ingenuity of these three key editorial decisions put together (each of which I will devote a section to later) work to show how Plimpton, novelist William Styron, and the other initial *Paris Review* editors seemed to understand better than these other magazines seemed to about the medium they were working with—the literary magazine—and, then, how to best manipulate that medium. They understood that the medium of the literary magazine was not just a pamphlet of literature, as it had been most often treated by literary magazines from *The Dial* and the *The Egoist* in the late nineteenth and early twentieth centuries, to *The Partisan Review* and *Kenyon Review* in the mid twentieth century, the writing of which was to be digested and enjoyed, while the vehicle of the magazine was to simply serve as a surface for the writing, and so treated as largely irrelevant. (This wasn't the case for such short-lived modernist magazines as Wyndham Lewis's *Blast,* but such ventures were always short lived and might be better referred to as works of art first and literary magazines second.)

What *The Paris Review* editors understood of the literary magazine venture was that *it functioned best as an enterprise rather than as a chapbook*; it needed to be widely and not centrally focused. (Plimpton often boasted that *The Paris Review* had the second longest masthead in magazines, just behind *Rolling Stone.*) For *The Paris Review* the entire literary magazine venture was important: distribution, marketing, printing, and so forth. Anything that *The Paris Review* brand touched—from the Revel parties, to the magazine covers, to the prints the magazine sold in order to raise money, to its famous World Fair booth, to the anthologies it began to print, to the literature it published in the magazine itself—was part of the brand and mattered equally.

This above is the limitation of my focus here: to explicate the effectiveness of *The Paris Review* in understanding and manipulating the medium of the literary magazine. This essay is only a brief pass over the history of *The Paris Review*, which is inarguably an important and much underexplored area in the history of American and world literatures.

The Paris Review's focus from early on was on getting the magazine—and therefore the literary art—into readers' hands. The marketing and the art *The Paris Review* invested themselves in were not antagonistic (as with most other literary magazines at the time), but co-creative elements. Styron says that they strived for an "attractive balance" of the elements (14). In a 1999 interview with the Canadian literary magazine *Pagitica*, Plimpton describes how he saw *The Paris Review* as something larger and different than other literary magazines:

> I was studying at Cambridge and I wanted to possibly teach or get involved in television, which at that time was just beginning. And then I was called by my old friend Peter Matthiessen and I think that from the very beginning, we had ideas on how we could make the magazine sell. We put a fancy cover on it, comparatively. Most of the journals at the time had what was inside the magazine, on the cover–period. They were like law-school journals. But we had an art editor, William Pene Dubois, which was quite rare for literary publications. And criticism. We took that out of the magazine. When it really got going, we thought about getting it distributed. We had people on the street with it; we put posters up everywhere.

Plimpton goes on in the interview to explain the Revels, parties the magazine threw to promote interest in the publication, and other things the *Review* editors did to attract attentions. As Plimpton asserts, the editors concluded early on that, if a literary magazine was going to effectively publish and disseminate works of literature, it needed to be seen as something larger than simply a sounding-board for political or theoretical views, or as an inert publishing venue, both of which the literary magazine medium had been previously used for and viewed as by editors from *The Dial* to *The Masses* to *The Partisan Review*, not to mention the plethora of university-based literary magazines that often relegate design and promotion to an afterthought. *The Paris Review* editors knew that they needed to be something essentially, and not just marginally, different from those other magazines, and seemed to come to the conclusion that the magazine itself had to be seen as the source of interest and attention itself, and not simply expecting the good writing within it to garner sufficient attention. The editors saw that, in order for any readers in America or abroad to notice it during a time both color television and the hydrogen bomb came to fruition, when advertising had begun its stranglehold on culture, they had to work hard to develop interest and trust in the magazine through the magazine's content, image, and overall concept.

The medium *was* the message, as media theorist Marshall McLuhan was to say eleven years later in *Understanding Media: the Extensions of Man*. Though this is not a new concept for publishers, it was one greatly shunned (and much still shunned) by the majority of literary magazine editors in the past. For the majority of literary magazine editors, the content *itself* was supposed to be significant enough. And for the early *Paris Review*, the content of the magazine was still primary, but to get that content into the minds and hands of readers they had to do various things to make the magazine a marketable venue for new and experimental works of art—to "make the magazine sell," as Plimpton put it, and, in doing so, make new and experimental literature a part of the culture.

What I am talking about basically is branding and how it worked for *The Paris Review*. A brand, as described by Naomi Klein in her study of the United States advertising industry, *No Logo*, is the ephemeral concept of an enterprise as opposed to the products it produces. The products *can* be labeled or associated with the brand, but then so can anything: an event, a statement, a person, etc. This is the power of branding; a person can represent a car, a rock concert can represent a computer, a book can represent a vodka. Though as far as I know this has not yet been expressed in writing about the magazine (other than in Cowley's above-mentioned phrase, perhaps), what *The Paris Review* editors were realizing in 1953 was that *the literary magazine is a brand*. In a sense they were retooling the medium, which had been in existence, and remained largely the same, since its formal beginnings in the early nineteenth century. As Naomi Klein so persuasively and simply explains in *No Logo*, thoughts about branding turned in the 1940s "away from individual products and their attributes....since corporations may manufacture products, but what consumers buy are brands." Plimpton and the rest seemed aware of this, for what *The Paris Review* sold wasn't just pieces of writing, but the concept of literature.

I will now describe the three editorial decisions in detail that formed the background of the first fifty years of *The Paris Review*'s editorial policy, the creation an artistically designed and marketed literary periodical.

2. MAKING AN AMERICAN LITERARY MAGAZINE IN PARIS

The Paris Review was created by United States' citizens who had recently moved to Paris: Peter Matthiessen, Harold "Doc" Humes, William Styron,

Hemingway, Faulkner, Gass, Dickey, Rebecca West, PR History
25th Anniversary Double Issue

The Paris Review

79　　　　　　　　　$10.00 £4.50 55F

George Plimpton, John Train, Donald Hall, Thomas H. Guinzburg, and William Pène du Bois. First discussion of *The Paris Reveiw* began when, in 1952, Humes approached Matthiessen and asked if he wanted to work as fiction editor for Humes's magazine, the Paris *News-Post*, but the two quickly agreed that the stories they had received for the *News-Post* were too good for the publication and decided to begin a magazine of their own specializing in creative work. Matthiessen had no experience in publishing at this time, but was just recently out of Yale and at work on his first novel, *Race Rock*. Plimpton and Guinzburg were recruited, and, along with Styron, all five of them sat and discussed—over two bottles of Plimpton's absinthe—the direction and name of the magazine in Matthiessen's apartment, described by Styron as,

> on a Utrillo-like back street in Montparnasse; spacious, airy, its one big room filled with light, the Matthiessen pad...became the hangout for many of the mob of Americans who had hurried to Paris to partake of its perennial delights, to drink in the pleasures of a city beginning to surge with energy after the miseries of the recent war. "U. S. Go Home" was painted by the Communists on every wall—it was probably the most ignored injunction in recent history.

The name for the magazine was debated, and rumor has it that, since Plimpton came up with the name *The Paris Review*, he was named as the magazine editor.

There has long been a certain romantic aura of the literary associated with Paris, and it certainly behooved *The Paris Review*'s early reputation as *the* magazine of literature to have the name of the city in its title and to be located there. In his book, *News of Paris*, Ronald Weber describes the writer-mystique surrounding the city after the Second World War: "For...literary dreams, Paris was an obvious destination. It was the literary capital of the world—where James Joyce was and where *Ulysses* was published, in time where Hemingway, Scott Fitzgerald, Ezra Pound, John Dos Passos, and other literary luminaries had been....Paris was where the twentieth century was." *The Paris Review*'s early self-exile in such a city helped them hone the image they were constructing for their magazine, at least until finally returning to New York and their United States home for good in 1974. For the first twenty years, the city of Paris did much of the branding work for them: it brought with it connections to Joyce, Hemingway, Montparnasse, the famous artist cafes located there (La Dôme, La Rotonde, La Closerie de Lilas) and the mystery of the expatriate writer. As Weber claimed, Paris was the literary center of the world, and some of that history was bound to brush off on the boys at *The Paris Review*.

Besides the literary aura of Paris, there were likely many other attractions for the young editors beginning a new literary magazine. Historically, being an American expatriate literary magazine during the early years of the cold war helped them keep out of politics, and so keep their brand clean and completely literary. (It has only much more recently been tainted slightly with connections to the CIA through Peter Matthiessen.)

The tradition of an expatriate American literary magazine goes at least as far back as Margaret Anderson's *The Little Review* (1914–1929), which moved to Paris in 1922, and also included other less well-known magazines, like *transition* and *Merlin. The Paris Review*, by name and location, was also associated with this group of magazines, who were, incidentally, the first American literary magazines to publish some of the works of Joyce and Beckett, possibly two of the largest non-American literary icons in America of the century. Craig Monk wrote a study of *Merlin* and *transition*, in which he explains something of the attraction of literary magazines to exile in the French capital:

> A resurgence in English-language journals provided a valuable outlet for the young writers of a new generation plying their trade in post-war Paris. While these expatriates were drawn to France by example, they also wished to slip from under the shadow of those artists whom Gertrude Stein most famously described as the "lost generation." The modern little magazine, characteristically defiant, provided an excellent vehicle for the work of Americans.

But the Parisian affair could only last so long for the reputable American literary magazine. In the late sixties and early seventies the French economy and currency began to improve, and *The Paris Review* took a year off, packed its bags, and headed home. In the introduction to their first issue of the magazine from their new New York office in 1974, Plimpton wrote about his version of *The Paris Review*'s reasons for publishing from overseas and why they had, after twenty years, picked up editorial anchor and headed home:

> A firm policy of *The Paris Review* has been to stick to the tradition of the expatriate paper...to stay abroad the better to find and publish material largely out of the mainstream of literature, to offer works which in the phrase sanctified by *The Little Review*, the distinguished expatriate magazine of the '30's, "makes no compromise with public taste." But this attribute, while absolutely appropriate, no longer seems a matter of geographical location. The ease of travel and communication has lessened the need for a magazine serving a "colony" of writers living abroad, and indeed such a colony, while in evidence in the 1950's when *The Paris Review* begun, no longer survives to such a degree.

But, of course, the name was to still remain *The Paris Review*, a name often commented on since 1974 as being strange, as the magazine is no longer created in Paris and has never published reviews. And yet, neither the name or the location of *The Paris Review* had ever really summed up who they were or what they were doing—Americans publishing creative work from a host of international writers and artists—but it summed up how they wanted to be perceived: cosmopolitan editors in France, working in that esteemed tradition of writers and editors in Paris who came before them.

3. The Literary Magazine as Enterprise

Malcolm Cowley was not only a critic and novelist of the modern artistic era, but also a pronounced critic and scholar of literary magazines. His 1954 book, *The Literary Situation*, roundly criticizes the state of literary magazines in the middle of the century. In his introduction to *The Paris Review*'s first anthology of interviews (soon to become a very popular anthology series), Cowley famously expressed what he saw as the difference between *The Paris Review* and all the literary magazines before them, both in Paris and at home:

> *The Paris Review* took a different direction from that of
> other magazines....Like them it wanted to present mate-
> rial that was new, uncommercial, "making no compromise
> with public taste,"...but unlike the others it was willing
> to use commercial devices in getting the material printed
> and talked about. "Enterprise in the service of art" might
> have been its motto. The editors compiled a list, running to
> thousands of names, of Americans living in Paris and sent
> volunteer salesmen to ring their doorbells. Posters were
> printed by hundreds and flying squadrons of three went
> out by night to paste them in likely and unlikely places
> all over the city. In June 1957 the frayed remnants of one
> poster were still legible on the ceiling of the lavatory in the
> Café du Dôme.

Cowley goes on to explain that *The Paris Review* interviews—arguably the single thing that the magazine remains most well-known for—were created "as another device . . . for building circulation. The magazine needed famous names on the cover, but couldn't afford to pay for the contributions of famous authors. 'So let's talk to them,' somebody ventured." Novelist E. M. Forster, their first interview subject, gave much more thought and depth to the interview than was initially planned by the editors, and therefore, in Cowley's opinion, gave a new direction for the endeavor, "furnish[ing] the best of patterns for the series that followed."

2 **2003**
$7.00
$8.50 Canada

A TRIBUTE TO
WILLIAM PHILLIPS

Partisan Review

In this same vein, Plimpton has said that, "In fact, one of the reasons I think we chose the name *The Paris Review* was because we thought maybe we'd be mistaken for the *The Partisan Review* and people would subscribe." Though this remark was maybe made in jest, alongside Cowley's explanation of "enterprise in the service of art" it begins to explain Plimpton's early understanding of the importance of branding and promotion. As Cowley expresses, this knowledge was vastly different than that expressed by other literary magazines.

Since its inception, *The Paris Review* has used commercial tactics to promote their magazine, while many editors still today "proudly refuse to adjust to one well demonstrated marketing fact—that literature alone is not appealing to broad audiences." *The Paris Review* editors, on the other hand, have continually taken measures to widen their audience and promote literature through non-literary means. Some examples of this are *The Paris Review* booth in the 1964–65 New York World's Fair, the soliciting of magazine covers and prints to be sold from the most popular painters and graphic artists of the time (such as de Kooning and Lichtenstein), and the famous Revel parties the magazine would throw, whose guest lists included up-and-coming writers along with the nation's most famous artists, intellectuals, and politicians.

Of course, there is and was a very specific reason for editors to distrust the sort of self-promotion and image consciousness *The Paris Review* experimented with. As I mentioned earlier, in the beginning of the twentieth century magazines were the main purveyor of advertising, and the modern American critical and artistic literary magazine began as a reaction against such heavy commercialism as demonstrated in larger circulation magazines such as *McClure's* and *Ladies Home Journal*, which, because they sold so many ads, were able to drastically lower their cover prices and subscription rates below cost. As literary magazine editors did not participate in the new magazine ad economy, their cover prices and subscription rates were much higher in comparison. Ezra Pound pointed this out in his often-cited 1930 "Small Magazines" essay from the *English Journal*: "In the new system the contents were selected rigorously on the basis of how much expensive advertising they would carry." Content under the control of finance, a relationship thought highly antagonistic to the literary arts.

But it wasn't advertising the *The Paris Review* pursued—it was the brand, which became the abstract foundation of the economy of the 20th century. And today a great number of literary magazines have begun to follow *The Paris Review*'s lead, launching side projects to increase interest in the magazine, such as the creation of book imprints. And nearly every literary magazine today throws parties, offers up swag at literary conferences, or sells print T-shirts or some other wearable logo. Honestly, it would seem strange for a literary magazine today not to be an enterpriser in the service of literary art.

4. Creativity and Politics: Editing the Silent Generation

"Art for art's sake" is an aesthetic dating back to the mid-nineteenth century, and this aesthetic generally sums up what *The Paris Review* wanted the public to understand as their artistic mission. In his preface to their first issue (neatly described as a "Letter to the Editor," and so seemingly not the manifesto it clearly is) that became the mission statement for the magazine, William Styron expresses the apolitical and atheoretical stance that the editors wanted for the magazine:

> I think that if we have no axes to grind, no drums to beat,
> it's because it seems to us...that the axes have all been
> ground, the drumheads burst with beating. This attitude
> does not necessarily make us...the Silent Generation (the
> fact of THE PARIS REVIEW belies that), or the Scared
> Generation, either, content to lie around....It's not so much
> a matter of protest now, but of waiting; perhaps, if we have
> to be categorized at all, we might be called the Waiting
> Generation–people who feel and write and observe, and
> wait and wait and wait. And go on writing. I think THE
> PARIS REVIEW should welcome these people into its
> pages–the good writers and good poets, the non-drum-
> beaters and no-axe-grinders. So long as they're good.

Styron's preface was composed by him and edited by Plimpton, but was certainly influenced by all of the editors' long, absinthe-infused discussions about the magazine in Matthiessen's apartment, and so it can be relatively assumed that this preface represents all of the editors' opinions, not just Styron's. Moreover, it was often cited by Plimpton to describe the magazine's editorial mission, and is today prominently displayed on the magazine's website.

What is most interesting about the preface, and the editorial stance it describes, is that it is clearly a political and theoretical position, though it tries to rhetorically disguise itself otherwise. It needs to be examined in its historical context.

Styron's preface flat out rejects pieces that are political—that have an axe to grind, in Styron's terms. No matter if these pieces are good, they are *de facto* not allowable on *The Paris Review* page. "We have critics, not creators," Styron says in condemnation of what he saw as 1950s publishing trends, at the same time asserting that *Paris Review* is a reaction to the era's "age of criticism." What is contradictory here is that Styron—and with him, *The Paris Review* editors—are actually in this *taking a very political and theoretical stance*, no matter Styron's attempts to write his way away of it. In other words, *The Paris Review* is a part of the age of criticism that it denies. Their political stance is one of non-involvement, which is a highly charged political stance in the 1950s, a time when artists like Arthur Miller, Elia Kazan, and countless others, were to be soon brought before committees on conspiracy charges. In this beginning of the Cold War (the hydrogen bomb was invented as *Paris Review* editors were laying out their first issue), as political prosecution intensified in the United States, *being apolitical was political for an American artist*. And certainly declaring that art wasn't political and that there were no drums to beat was about as political as one could get. As Albert Camus famously noted, if you're not on the side of the victims, you're on the side of the executioners.

But—and here is my point—if you are publishing works of art and want to sell issues to a broad audience (which has always been, remember, abnormal for literary magazines), an apolitical stance would be the best stance to take, or at least the best stance to promote.

5. THE FUTURE LITERATURE

On November 10, 2007, the American journalist and novelist Norman Mailer died. The next day, *The Paris Review* put up a message regarding his passing up on their website, along with a link to the texts of two extensive interviews the magazine did with Mailer (1964, 2007) and a piece Mailer published in the magazine in 1961 (an interview with himself). Earlier in 2007, *Paris Review* had honored Mailer with their Hadada Award for "his lifelong commitment to the arts," and he was a special guest for that year's spring Revel. When Grace Paley died just months earlier, the magazine did a similar thing, highlighting writings Paley published in the magazine and her *Paris Review* interview. The same when Kurt Vonnegut died a few months before: pieces published, interviews done. Even the idiosyncratic Hunter S. Thompson was noted and hyperlinked.

What is simply astounding about *The Paris Review* is not that it publishes good writing—that work successfully accomplished by most literary magazines—but that it has managed to do so with such a consistent and unparalleled track record. Looking back over the past six decades of its publishing record, literary history and *The Paris Review* history so overlap that it is hard to distinguish whether *The Paris Review* created the contemporary literary canon or, due to historical conditions, what has become the canon became connected to *The Paris Review* brand. It is the chicken and the egg dilemma, a rhizomatic mass of causes and effects perhaps forever intermingled, overlapping, and indistinguishable from each other.

What is clear is *The Paris Review*'s constant efforts of promotion and its influence on the literary magazine industry. From early on, *The Paris Review* editors wanted the publication to be more than just words and images on a printed page, but rather to integrate everything available to them in regards to magazine publication, literature, art, and enterprise into something much larger than a single magazine: an idea. Now this is the norm. In a 2000 *Print* magazine article on the current emphasis of graphic design in literary magazines, the author Tom Vanderbilt concludes with the assertion that, "Branding is everything these days."

*The expectation of failure is connected with
the very name of a Magazine.*
—Noah Webster

THE EXPECTATION OF FAILURE: AN EXCERPT FROM *ARTISTS' MAGAZINES*

by Gwen Allen (2011)

In 1788 the American publisher and dictionary writer Noah Webster, founder of several short-lived periodicals, lamented the precarious enterprise of publishing a magazine.[1] The average lifespan of a magazine in the United States between 1741 and 1850 was only eighteen months, and it was not until well into the nineteenth century that the advertising industry made magazine publishing a reliably profitable business.[2] Yet the ephemerality that defined the magazine at the dawn of its invention has remained fundamental to the social possibilities inherent in this particular form of printed matter. To publish a magazine is to enter into a heightened relationship with the present moment. Unlike books, which are intended to last for future generations, magazines are decidedly impermanent. Their transience is embodied by their unprecious formats, flimsy covers, and inexpensive paper stock, and it is suggested by their seriality, which presumes that each issue will soon be rendered obsolete by the next.

During the 1960s and 1970s magazines became an important new site of artistic practice, functioning as an alternative exhibition space for the dematerialized practices of conceptual art. Abandoning canvases, pedestals, and all they stood for in the established institutions of modernism, this art sought out lightweight and everyday media, and relied heavily on texts, photographs, and other kinds of documents. Conceptual art depended upon the magazine as a new site of display, which allowed it to be experienced by a broader public than the handful of people actually present to witness a temporary object, idea, or act—or in the case of earth art, ambitious enough to make the trek to the remote locations where this work tended to reside. As the art historian David Rosand observed of the pivotal new role of the art

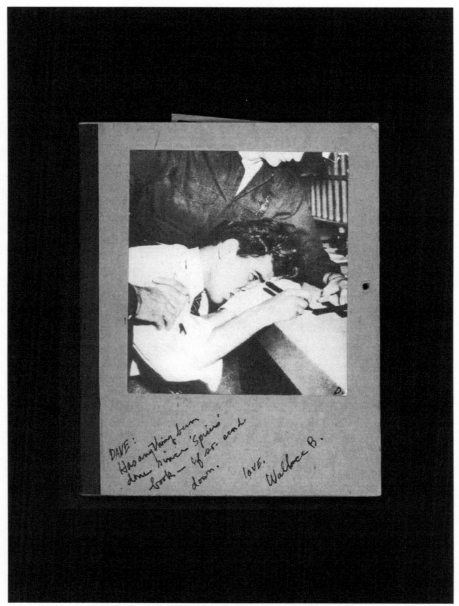

Semina 8, inscribed to Dave Haselwood of the Auerhahn Press.

magazine during this period, "you read it. But you read it because it told you what was going on partly because so much of what was going on was *not* to be seen in the galleries."[3]

While artists used the magazine to document their work, they also began to explore it as a medium in its own right, creating works expressly for the mass-produced page. These original artists' contributions (sometimes called artists' projects, artists' pages, or magazine art)[4] investigated the distinct materiality of the magazine as well as its unique properties as a form of communication. The everyday, throwaway form of the magazine mirrored art's heightened sense of its own contingency in the 1960s and 1970s: its insistence on the actual time and place in which was it encountered. Inexpensive and accessible, the magazine was an ideal expressive vehicle for art that was more concerned with concept, process, and performance than with final marketable form. Indeed, the ephemerality of the magazine was central to its radical possibilities as an alternative form of distribution that might replace the privileged space of the museum with a more direct and democratic experience. As Joseph Kosuth described his *Second Investigation* (1968), which took the form of advertisements in various newspapers and magazines, "people can wrap dishes in my work."[5]

Artists' magazines functioned as important alternatives to the mainstream art press and commercial gallery system during the postwar period. These publications, scores of which began—and more often than not ended—were driven not by profit motives but by an earnest and impassioned belief in the magazine's capacity to radicalize the reception of art. As Benjamin Buchloh recalled of *Interfunktionen* (a magazine that he took over in 1974 and edited for just two issues before a controversial work within the magazine's pages led to its financial undoing): "I think you have to be very young and very naive and very lunatic to do a magazine in the first place."[6] If this observation captures something of the utopian hopes artists and critics pinned to the magazine during this time, it also suggests how these aspirations paradoxically acknowledged—and even in some sense depended upon—the very fleeting and precarious nature of the magazine itself.

Like the relationships and communities they embody, artists' magazines are volatile and mutable. They seek out the leading and precarious edges; they live at the margins rather than in the stable and established center. They thrive on change and impermanence, favor process over product, and risk being thrown away. They court failure. Yet, such failure should be understood not as an indication of defeat, but as an expression of the vanguard nature of these publications and their refusal of commercial interests. Moving beyond the literal failure of magazines, this quality took on metaphorical and ideological significance as a rejection of standard measures of art world success, and as a different way of imagining art's power and potential.

DESIGNED FOR REPRODUCIBILITY

Walter Benjamin was among the first to observe that when art is reproduced and distributed through the mass media, it becomes a qualitatively different form of communication, one with profound aesthetic and political repercussions. In his 1936 essay "The Work of Art in the Age of Mechanical Reproduction," he argued that when a work of art is mechanically duplicated, it loses its aura, or its unique existence in time and space. However, at the same time, he insisted, it gains a new—and highly ambivalent—political function, one that is predicated upon its greatly expanded public. Speaking of the new technical capabilities of photography and film, Benjamin declared that "the work of art reproduced is now becoming the work of art designed for reproducibility"[7]—a phrase that presciently describes many of the artistic practices that are discussed in this book. Benjamin's understanding of the social possibilities of art and media was rooted in his nuanced attention to the material conditions of production and distribution, and the way these structure the social relationships between the author or artist and the audience—ideas he also discussed in "The Author as Producer" (1934). (In fact, Benjamin even planned, along with Bertolt Brecht, to publish a magazine, *Krise und Kritik* [Crisis and criticism], that would have allowed him to explore these ideas not only in theory but in practice—a project that unfortunately never materialized.)[8]

Benjamin's observations shed light on the important role of magazines in the history of art—a role that has arguably been as vital as that of the works of art themselves. One of the first artists' periodicals was the *Propyläen* (1798–1800), founded by Johann Wolfgang von Goethe and Johann Heinrich Meyer. As Goethe explained, its title referred to "the step, the door, the entrance, the antechamber, the space between the inner and the outer, the sacred and the profane, this is the place we choose as the meeting-ground for exchanges with our friends"—a description that indicates the magazine's important role as both a portal and gathering place for people and ideas.[9] *The Germ*, another important early artists' magazine, which was started in England by the Pre-Raphaelites and published for a mere four issues in 1850, likewise suggests the formative role of magazines: it was here that artistic ideas were not only recorded and exchanged, but germinated; here that avant-garde movements originated and gained momentum. With the development of new printing technologies, the twentieth century saw a flourishing of periodicals for which artists served as publishers, editors, writers, typographers, and designers. Some of the most important of these included prewar avant-garde magazines such as *Lacerba* (1913–1915), *Blast* (1914–1915), *291* (1915–1916), *Cabaret Voltaire* (1916), *The Blind Man* (1917), *Dada* (1917–1921), *De Stijl* (1917–1932), *L'Esprit Nouveau* (1920–1925), *Zenit* (1921–1926), *Mécano* (1922–1923), *Merz* (1923–1932), *Lef* (1923–1925), *La Révolution Surréaliste* (1924–1929), *Tank* (1925), *Novyi Lef* (1927–1929),

Internationale Revue i10 (1927–1929), *Minotaure* (1933–1939), *View* (1940–1947), and *VVV* (1942–1944), as well as the postwar abstract expressionist periodicals, including *Iconograph* (1946), *The Tiger's Eye* (1947–1949), *Possibilities* (1947–1948), *Instead* (1948), and *It Is* (1960–1965).[10] Important avant-garde artists' magazines, such as the Japanese periodical *Gutai* (1955–1965) and the Argentine magazine *Boa* (1958–1960), were also being published outside of Europe and the United States during these years.

Even as these publications implicitly questioned the division between fine art and design, insisting upon the magazine as an important site of artistic production, they remained, for the most part, a means to an end—vehicles for defining artistic agendas and circulating ideas, rather than works of art in themselves. Clive Phillpot stressed this difference in a 1980 article, noting of these earlier periodicals that artists "simply used their skills to produce magazines, however handsome or unconventional they might be. Unlike artists in the '60s they were not consciously using the production of a magazine to question the nature of artworks, nor were they making art specifically for dissemination through a mass-communication medium."[11] By contrast, he argued, artists' magazines in the 1960s manifested "a wholly different attitude of artists towards the magazine and towards the nature of what constituted art."[12]

Indeed, while the magazines featured in this book are in many ways heir to these earlier artists' periodicals, they also signal something different, demonstrating an unprecedented experimentation with the formal and conceptual possibilities of the magazine, and a new kind of self-reflexivity about its status as a medium. This novel understanding of the artists' magazine can be traced back to several periodicals from the late 1950s and early 1960s, including *Spirale*, *ZERO*, *Gorgona*, *Revue nul=0*, *Revue Integration*, *Diagonal Cero*, *KWY*, *Revue Ou*, *material*, *dé-coll/age*, *V TRE*, and *Fluxus*, as well as Wallace Berman's *Semina*. These publications, many of which had exceedingly small print runs of just a few hundred copies per issue, exemplify a radical new kind of experimentation with the formal and conceptual possibilities of the magazine, as artists utilized unbound, die-cut, and embossed pages, glued objects onto pages, tore them, and even burned them. Bernard Aubertin, for example, glued three matches to a page of *Revue Integration* and lit them, leaving three scorched marks on the page. Such investigations of the materiality and temporality of the printed page (which very much overlapped with the practices of concrete poetry) coincided with new understandings of artistic medium itself in the postwar period. As the meaning of art was increasingly seen to reside in a performative, temporal, and conceptual experience rather than a strictly formal, visual one, artists found new ways to express these experiences in the magazine, breaking away from the traditional limits of the static, two-dimensional page.

In the late 1960s and 1970s, artists approached the magazine with the same inventiveness with which they embraced other media in the "expanded field." They experimented with format, design, and typography, reveled in the materiality of language and print, emphasized the tactility and interactivity of the magazine, and foregrounded the acts of reading and turning the page. Robert Smithson, for example, understood the magazine as a quasi-sculptural medium, likening its dense layers of texts and images to geological strata; Sol LeWitt invited viewers to draw on the page; Vito Acconci conceived of the magazine as a performative realm within which language was an event as much as an object; Dan Graham explored what he called "the physicality of print" as well as its social and economic conditions.[13] Other artists explored unbound, multimedia formats that challenged the very definition of the magazine itself. Whereas Benjamin argued that reproduction ruins the aura of the original work of art, replacing its unique existence in time and space with a mediated experience that at once diminishes its authenticity and renews its significance and potential in the present, these experiments open onto a new set of possibilities. In some cases, artists imbued the reproduced page with a new kind of auratic presence; in others, they destabilized the hierarchy between original and reproduction altogether.

For these artists, as for Benjamin, the social and political implications of art's reproducibility were paramount: their understanding of the magazine as a new kind of artistic medium was accompanied by a profound recognition of its possibilities as a distribution form that might circumvent the expertise of the critic and the exclusivity of the gallery space, and thus radically transform the reception of art. Yet the possibilities of the media for artists during this time were also vastly different from those that Benjamin identified—not only because of their remove from the political conditions of Europe in the 1930s that gave his writing its particular urgency, but also because of important changes in media culture itself. The reproduction of art was no longer the relatively new and uncharted phenomenon it had been in Benjamin's time, and artists' understanding of the magazine in the 1960s and 1970s was modulated by an entirely different set of historical circumstances. The reproduction of art had become ubiquitous within an advanced spectacular media culture in which not only works of art but social relationships more generally were increasingly mediated—a situation about which Guy Debord famously observed, "Everything that was directly lived has moved away into a representation."[14] At the same time, advances in printing technology made processes such as offset, mimeo, and Xerox inexpensive and widely available to nonspecialized producers, leading to a burgeoning alternative and underground press.

Artists' investigations of the magazine took place within this context, internalizing the new possibilities of mass communication technology, whether utopian or dystopian. The very notion of the work of art and of artistic medium and how they might express meaning to an audience were understood differently against and within this new media culture. Magazines were certainly not the sole site for such investigations—similar and overlapping concerns attended artists' explorations of film, video, and television, as well as cybernetics and systems theory (not to mention more traditional mediums such as painting and sculpture) during this time. However, the magazine played an especially pervasive and pivotal role in the dramatic transformations in artistic production, reception, and distribution in an age of information. Conceptual art's use of the magazine as a medium and distribution form engendered a critique of art's audiences and institutions. By approaching this art through the lens of the magazine's distinct material conditions and social relationships, we can more fully grasp the successes as well as failures of these practices, while complicating the way in which these very terms are mobilized to assess art's significance and value.

ENDNOTES

1 Noah Webster, "Acknowledgements," *The American Magazine*, February 1788, 130; quoted in Frank Luther Mott, *A History of American Magazines, 1741–1850* (New York: D. Appleton and Company, 1930), 13.

2 Mott, *A History of American Magazines, 1741–1850,* 21

3 David Rosand, interview by Amy Newman, in Amy Newman, *Challenging Art: Artforum 1962–1974* (New York: SoHo Press, 2000), 140

4 Clive Phillpot coined the term "magazine art," defining it as "art conceived specifically for a magazine context, and therefore, art which is realized only when the magazine itself has been composed and printed." Clive Phillpot, "Art Magazines and Magazine Art," *Artforum*, February 1980, 52. Also see Anne Rorimer, "Siting the Page: Exhibiting Works in Publications—Some Examples of Conceptual Art in the USA," in Michael Newman and Jon Bird, eds., *Rewriting Conceptual Art* (London: Reaktion Books, 1999), 11–26; and May Castleberry, "The Magazine Rack," *Afterimage*, March 1988, 11–13.

5 Joseph Kosuth, interview with Patsy Norvell, April 10, 1969, quoted in Alexander Alberro, *Conceptual Art and the Politics of Publicity* (Cambridge: MIT Press, 2003), 49.

6 Benjamin Buchloh, interview with the author, May 29, 2008.

7 Walter Benjamin, "The Work of Art in the Age of Mechanical Reproduction," in *Illuminations*, ed. Hannah Arendt (New York: Schocken Books, 1986), 234.

8 See Peter Uwe Hohendahl, *The Institution of Criticism* (Ithaca: Cornell University Press, 1982), 25.

9 Johann Wolfgang Goethe, "Introduction to the *Propyläen*" in Charles Harrison, Paul J. Wood, and Jason Gaiger, eds., *Art in Theory 1648–1815: An Anthology of Changing Ideas* (Oxford: Blackwell Publishers Inc., 2000), 1044.

10 For a survey of avant-garde periodicals, see Steven Heller, *Merz to Emigre and Beyond: Avant-Garde Magazine Design of the Twentieth Century* (London: Phaidon Press, 2003). For an excellent history of abstract expressionist periodicals, see Ann Eden Gibson, *Issues in Abstract Expressionism: The Artist-Run Periodicals* (Ann Arbor, Mich.: UMI Research Press, 1989). Also see Pamela Franks, *The Tiger's Eye: The Art of a Magazine* (New Haven: Yale University Art Museum, 2002).

[11] Phillpot, "Art Magazines and Magazine Art," 52.

[12] Ibid.

[13] In a set of unpublished notes, Robert Smithson wrote, "The Magazine as a quasi-Object: If we consider a magazine in terms of space and form, we discover rectangular sheets composed of strata." Robert Smithson, Notebook 3 [Microfilm reel 3], Robert Smithson and Nancy Holt papers, 1905–1987, Archives of American Art, Smithsonian Institution; Sol LeWitt, "Page Drawings," *Avalanche* no. 4 (Spring 1972): 18–19; see chapter 2 for a discussion of Acconci's performative understanding of the printed page; Dan Graham, interview by Mike Metz, *Bomb*, Winter 1994, 24.

[14] Guy Debord, *The Society of the Spectacle* (Detroit: Black & Red, 1977), n.p. This shift, located around 1968 in various accounts, designates the change from an industrial capitalist society to what has variously been called a postindustrial, post-Fordist, postmodern, spectacular, or information society. All of these terms point to how communication has superseded the factory not only or even primarily as a site of production, but more significantly as a model for productive processes of all kinds. See Daniel Bell, *The Coming of Post-Industrial Society: A Venture in Social Forecasting* (New York: Basic Books, 1976); Manuel Castells, *The Rise of Network Society*, vol. 1 (Oxford: Blackwell Publishers, 1996); Fredric Jameson, *Postmodernism, or, The Logic of Late Capitalism* (Durham: Duke University Press, 1991); and Michael Hardt and Antonio Negri, *Empire* (Cambridge: Harvard University Press, 2000).

As an unreconstructed anarchist, I still must consider the solution of this issue [proprietary control of the media by the tribe of intermediary bureaucrats] easy, easy in theory, easy in practice; if we do not apply it, it is for moral reasons, sluggishness, timidity, getting involved in what is not one's business, etc. The way to get rid of dummy intermediaries is by direct action. —Paul Goodman, "The Chance for Popular Culture" (1949)

WHY ASSEMBLING

by Richard Kostelanetz (1973)

Assembling grew out of an oppressive crisis in avant-garde literary communication; for while experiments in writing seemed both possible and necessary, genuinely innovative manuscripts found increasing resistance from both book and periodical publishers. *Assembling* was established in 1970 by Henry James Korn and myself, two young writers who had known each other since childhood. Five years older than Korn, I was already a full-time freelance, hyperactive mostly as an essayist and anthologist. I discovered that, in contrast to my expository prose, my visual poetry and comparably eccentric fiction encountered considerably more difficulty in getting published. Even the best of these pieces seemed to take at least two years to get into any sort of public print (at which point, curiously, a few would be anthologized with remarkable speed); and I had good reason to suspect that, as often as not, the periodical editors accepting them were implicitly honoring, or flattering, my critical-anthological activities. The problem was scarcely personal, however, because other work in such veins, including much that I critically regarded as excellent, was similarly blocked. Korn, on the other hand, had produced some remarkably witty and inventive fictions, only one of which had ever been publicly published; and his work as a museum administrator made him aware of grave problems in cultural communication. I suppose that my own anthological experience also gave me a compiler's passion for making available a goodly amount of avant-garde literary material that might otherwise be lost.

It also became clear, at the onset of U.S. publishing's most severe recent depression, that commercial houses were less and less inclined to take risks with any kind of counter-conventional work and/or unestablished authors.

Among the principal reasons are not only editorial ignorance and opacity but a gross rise in the costs of book production and the increasing profit-hunger of even the more "enlightened" publishing firms. The best seller has become their all-engrossing ideal, while interest in commercially more modest work, such as anything avant-garde or unknown, had declined dangerously. Only one one-man collection of visual poetry, for instance, has ever been commercially published in the United States, even though "concrete" is reportedly "faddish"; and since that single book, N. H. Pritchard's *The Matrix* (1970), was neither reviewed nor touted, it seemed unlikely that any others would ever appear—another example of how the rule of precedent in literary commerce produces de facto censorship. Established literary periodicals, on the other hand, were dying or retrenching, while few of the new ones were open to experimental work. For several reasons, therefore, the future of avant-garde writing seemed increasingly doubtful.

In the preface to our initial issue, I noted:

> As young writers of stylistically "different" poetry and prose, we faced not only the inevitable objections to our youth, but also the equally inevitable resistances to our wayward literary purposes. And so we wanted an institution that would publish alternative work by imaginative artists who genuinely believed in what they did. Since rejections often came with the excuse, particularly from those editors pretending to sympathy, that "our printer can't handle this," it seemed best to overcome this obstacle by direct action—by becoming one's own publisher, which is more practicable in this era of photographic reproduction processes; for the oldest truth is that, when other demands are more pressing, the writer must do more than just write.

Somewhat influenced by a beautiful German book called *Omnibus* (1969), we hit upon what we think is the most appropriate structure for a cooperative self-publishing channel. In brief, *Assembling* invites writers and artists whom we know to be doing unusual work, which we broadly characterize as "otherwise unpublishable," to contribute a thousand copies of up to four 8.5-by 11-inch pages of whatever they want to include. Since each contributor is responsible for arranging, by whatever means and funds available, for the production of his own work, he becomes his own sub-self-publisher, so to speak. There is no doubt that writers should usually be paid for what they do; but just as serious poets often give much of their work away gratis, so there are times when every artist feels it worth a few dollars and/or a little effort to put into public print a work that he likes but could not otherwise place. (Indeed, self-publication at such modest cost could stand as an ultimate test of creative seriousness—not just in Russia but in the United States too.) In practice, self-printing turns out to be less forbidding than it initially seems, for not only do academics have access to photocopy machines (and did one writer call upon a family printing business), but recently developed offset and Itek processes can commercially reproduce one side into a thousand sheets for less than ten dollars and both sides for less than fifteen. We advised our invited collaborators to put their names on their work, as we ran no table of contents, and to center their contributions toward the right, leaving at least an inch on the left-hand margin, because *Assembling* promised to collate the contents alphabetically and then return three bound books to each contributor. The remaining copies would ideally be sold through bookstores and the mails, hopefully defraying the costs of binding, mailing, etc.

Since all copyrights, which are the literary form of "property," were returned to the contributors, *Assembling* could make no money from subsequent reprints; and once the thousand copies were gone, it would be impossible to "reprint" the entire issue.

Since both Korn and I were inclined to transcend the boundaries of writing, we opened the book to artists of all sorts. Our form letter invited "poetry, fiction, graphic art, designs, architectural proposals, or any other ideas adaptable to print." As we were also trying to abolish the restricting prerogatives of editorial authority, we agreed to accept everything contributed by those invited. (Our invitation mentioned our "reserving the right to exclude a contribution for reasons unforeseen or in case of libel." I was thinking of egregious slander when I wrote that, but it remains an option we have never considered exercising.) We abrogated editorial authority not because we were lazy but because we wanted a structural contrast to the "restrictive, self-serving nature of traditional editorial processes." Since we are collators rather than true publishers, we customarily refuse requests to handle the printing, for necessity demands that counter-conventional writers learn some essential points about reproduction, such as discovering the method(s) most conducive to their particular work. As a result, each entry ideally represents the best that each contributor can do untouched (or unretouched) by grubby editorial hands. As "compilers" rather than true publishers, we also avoided the editorial pains (or pleasures) of rejecting anything, along with the anxiety of needing to fulfill a predetermined concept; and given the elasticity of our production methods, we never faced the predicament of accepting more material than could be "accommodated by our precious space."

The only editorial control left to us was the invitation itself, so that just as unfamiliar would-be collaborators were asked to contribute examples of their work (before receiving an invitation), so a few contributors to one *Assembling* were not invited to the next. The almost paradoxical reason was not that we thought their work "no good," whatever that might be, or that we wanted to impose a particular style or taste, but that we were obliged, in principle, to keep the medium committed to alternate, otherwise unpublishable imaginative work—a domain that was, to be sure, elastically defined. (None of these unreinvited people ever asked to contribute again, perhaps because of awe or disgust with the rest of the book; and none, to my knowledge, have founded their own collaborative periodicals.) "Don't hesitate to send material that has made the editorial rounds," our initial invitation said, "but remember that there's a difference between manuscripts that are just too freaky to get published elsewhere and those that are simply not one's own best work." It continued: "The long-range goal of *Assembling* is opening the editorial/industrial complex to alternatives and possibilities. The short-range goal is providing the means for unpublished and unpublishable work to see print light, partly to see what kindred spirits and spooks are doing." We also promised to type and print, at house expense, biographical notes, in part to introduce the contributors to each other.

Large cartons poured into our homes and post-office box during the summer, as our one hundred fifty invitations produced forty responses. Late in August, two months after our announced deadline, Korn and I rented a small panel truck and lugged a half ton of paper to a commercial collator (whose services cost us three hundred dollars). The bound books came back a few weeks later, and contributors' copies were immediately put into the mail. (The post office remains an innocent collaborator in the development of experimental writing, for it is largely by posted print that most of its creators know each other's work.) We sent possible reviewers a query, since available copies were so few; and though we honored all requests received, only four reviews appeared, three of them positive—in a Belgian new-poetry journal, a New York undergraduate newspaper, and a Detroit rock magazine. (The single negative notice rather dumbly criticized the absence of editorial authority!)

Our copyright line read: "(c) 1970 for automatic assignment with the printing of this notice to the individual contributors." However, we subsequently discovered that this was invalid. Since copyrights must be connected to a particular name, it should have said: "(c) 1970 by Assembling Press. All rights reassigned to their respective authors upon request." We also made the mistake of incorporating (which cost us another hundred), in part to protect against personal liabilities; but we later discovered that this precaution was unnecessary, as long as we published an editorial disclaimer (for "the views expressed herein") on the title page. Indeed, since we eschewed editorial authority, responsibility for all material definitely belonged to the individual sub-publishers. We disincorporated simply by letting Gnilbmessa, Inc., which is assembling spelled backwards, die of bankruptcy. We also opened a checking account, which was both needlessly expensive and, in practice, rarely used.

The results of such self-publishing license not only confirmed our initial polemical point—both *Assembling* itself and most of its contents were unlike anything seen before—but the book also showed the possibilities and productivity available to society if artists were granted absolute creative freedom. Some pieces were poetry or fiction, while others were visual graphics or words mixed with pictures. Some contributors resorted to commercial reproductive processes (of varying quality), while a few used handpresses. Scott Hyde contributed an especially elegant multicolored photograph. Ed Ruscha's contribution must have been individually hand-stained, as the shape of each brown blot was different. The well-known rock critic Richard Meltzer sent us, as he explained, "a thousand pages of all different shit (including the only copy of the only novel I ever wrote) so each one-page thing is gonna be a whole different show-stopper." Some contributors exploited such anti-editorial opportunity to surpass their earlier work, such as the novelist Nancy Weber, whose handwritten story, "Dear Mother and Dad," was subsequently anthologized. Others, like the poet David Ignatow, introduced work (an excerpt from his journals) that would later appear in a book. The stipulated page size became an inadvertent constraint, as one writer offered a thousand artistically doctored baseball cards, "each with a literary move." We were embarrassed to tell him that the available collating machines could not handle such work.

What was most impressive about *Assembling* was the sheer variety of counter-conventional alternatives, as individual contributions could be roughly characterized as visual poetry, verbal poetry, abstract photography, playlets, minimal poetry, verbal collage, stream-of-consciousness narrative, representational graphics, picture-accompanied words, scenarios for happenings, sculptural documentation, personal journal, esthetic manifesto, etc.; for the hundred flowers blooming here were really different. A few pieces could best be termed "other"; and the only signature on one poem, its face suspiciously turned backwards, read "Richard M. Nixon." The overall constraint of alphabetical order generated some peculiar juxtapositions that, in turn, made the whole book resemble a loony montage. It struck me afterwards that very few contributors portrayed sexual experience, partly because the liberties that artists now want to take and that are blocked by established channels, deal not with content but concept and form.

The contributions were uneven, to be sure, in both artistry and technology (printing quality), but such discrepancies epitomize *Assembling's* characteristic style and integrity, as well as perhaps its charm. "If you don't turn on to something," one contributor noted, "all you have to do is turn the page." Such blatant chaos marked *Assembling* as a counter-book or anti-book (though not a "non-book") which nonetheless gains its cohering definition (which is approximately repeatable) from its unprecedented diversity. In my admittedly biased opinion, more than half of the material has been uncommonly interesting, while a few contributions are awesomely extraordinary. It is more important to judge that very few pieces, if any, would have otherwise gotten beyond private musing into public print. (Korn and I also awarded, in total secrecy, a booby prize to "that contribution most likely to have appeared elsewhere" and thus needing *Assembling* least—a rather fine story by a sometime contributor to the slicks.) Collaborators in the first *Assembling* included such eminences as the painters Edward Ruscha and Arakawa; the poets Robert Lax, Keith and Rosmarie Waldrop, Vito Acconci, and Bernadette Mayer; the playwright Lee Baxandall; the novelists Marvin Cohen, George Chambers, Arno Karlen, and Raymond Federman; the composer Arthur Layzer; the polyartists Liam O'Gallagher, Dan Graham, and Alan Sondheim; along with a few artist-writers making their initial public appearances.

Most of the contributors were pleased, not only with the collaborative concept but with individual works, so that we decided to do the book again in 1971. *Second Assembling*, as we called it, materialized out of nothing in response, like its predecessor, to a summer's correspondence. Many of the same artists and writers joined us a second time—Elizabeth Ginsberg, Tom Ahern, Gay Beste, Jan Herman, Rosalie Frank, and Roni Hoffman; but more than half of the fifty-two contributors were new, including such eminences as the film-maker Stan VanDer Beek (who neglected, however, to send enough copies); the poets Robin Magowan, C. P. Graham, Tom Ockerse, and Ruth Krauss; the fictionists Russell Edson and M. D. Elevitch; and the polyartists Ken Friedman and Bern Porter. Michael Metz, a process-documenting artist who contributed to the first book, took charge of production for the second, not only designing a stunning cover (which, this time, wrapped around the spine), but also joining Korn and me as a "co-compiler." And its preface became yet more assertive, if not strident, in part because the closure crisis had become more severe, but also because I had spent most of the previous year drafting *The End of Intelligent Writing* (1973). In the second preface, I said:

> Anyone who gets [experimental] writing frequently into print is bombarded with requests for advice: Where can one publish? Who? Why not?

> And while one could give specific suggestions before [in the sixties], now the answer is invariably "nowhere," accompanied by a brief and inevitably bitter analysis of the current predicament . . . The terrible point is not that "one can't get published," but that nobody is publishing anymore. The fresh fruits we bear are turning into sour grapes, while the only money falling from those trees of dollar bills is counterfeit and/or confederate; and terror of a kind rules the roost. As writers largely lead isolated lives and have excessively sensitive egos, they tend to take rejections

as strictly personal; but when nearly everything in certain veins is kept unpublished, the problems are not individual but collective—and, thus, amenable to political, or more specifically literary-political, solutions. Since it would be naïve to solicit help from elsewhere, the initiative in introducing any New Art to the reading public must first of all come from the artists themselves. Our guiding rule in an acclimating task comparable to that confronting Ezra Pound and his allies sixty years ago must be this: WHAT-EVER NEEDS TO BE DONE, WE, AS WRITERS, SHALL PROBABLY HAVE TO DO OURSELVES.

After years of courting established publishers on behalf of experimental writing—not only my own but that by others—I am reluctantly coming to the conclusion that more than half of the consequential literature produced in this country today remains unpublished. The more closely one examines the situation, the clearer it becomes that only temporary idiosyncrasy or lapse can explain the commercial release of such genuinely innovative works as Pritchard's *The Matrix* and *Eecchhooeess* (1971) , Richard Horn's *Encyclopedia* (1969), Madeline Gins's *Word Rain* (1969), Kenneth Gangemi's *Olt* (1969), Raymond Feder-man's *Double or Nothing* (1971), G. S. Gravenson's *The Sweetmeat Saga* (1971). Indicatively, most of these conse-quential novels came from smaller commercial publishers. But it is a more telling fact that some of the past decade's most important American avant-garde texts were self-published: Edward Ruscha's widely admired picture books (especially *Thirty-Four Parking Lots* [1967]), Dick Higgins' *Jefferson's Birthday/Postface* (1964) and *Foew&ombwhnw* (1969), Russell Edson's *The Brain Kitchen* (1965), John Giorno's *Raspberry* (1967), Charles Henri Ford's *Spare Parts* (1968), Dan Graham's *End Moments* (1969), Wally Depew's *Once* (1971), Vito Acconci's *Book Four* (1968), among others.

"Ahead of us, especially if the censorship presently implicit in the edi-torial/industrial complex becomes complete," my second preface concludes, "is a writing situation comparable to that current in Soviet Russia, where nearly everything consequential is Samizdat, which means 'self-published,' and circulated from hand to hand. The practice of experimental writing in America is thus coming to resemble private research, like that in science, where new discoveries are first announced on stapled photocopies mailed to one's professional friends rather than trying to generate a demand for his product." We did a *Third Assembling* in 1972 with over ninety contributors, most of whom, once again, had not contributed before; and we expect to do a fourth in 1973.

Assembling has set an initial stone in the implicit edifice of International Cooperative Self-Publishing—a growing, unorganized, artistic movement that includes Dana Atchley's comparably pioneering *Space Atlas* (1970, 1971), which was done with the help of art students at the University of Victoria, British Columbia; Ely Raman's *8 x 10 Art Portfolio*, which began in lower Manhattan in 1971; and Jerry Bowles' *Art Work, No Commercial Value* (Grossman, 1972). Notwithstanding similar concepts in editorial production, these media differ in several crucial respects. Atchley collates his hundred-plus contributions into two hundred fifty loose-leaf clipbooks and sends two apiece back to the contributors, thus having nothing left to sell; and he has recently taken to traveling the country, collecting spare work in one place (usually academic) and then, like Johnny Appleseed, distributing it gratis elsewhere. This extraordinary service implicitly extends his earlier aim of open-ended, unfettered artist-to-artist communication with a different kind of inseminating activity.

Raman's periodical, which appears sporadically, asks for only two hundred copies of one's text, returning two cardboard folders apiece to the thirty-or-so contributors and then selling off the rest to subscribers, who are asked to pay what they can. Bowles' one-shot resembles Raman's and Atchley's in favoring graphics over literary (or post-literary) work, and its large loose-leaf binding was issued, to much publicity and after a gallery-sponsored collating party, by a commercial publisher that, even though it minimally reimbursed its paper-producing contributors, expected to make a profit. Thus, *Assembling* has three clear distinctions: its literary emphasis (in response to an initially literary predicament); its ideological underpinnings (elaborated in the prefaces—a feature indicatively lacking in the others); and its stapled binding, which we feel creates the sense of a fortuitous community united in process, though disparate in style.

What is most important about all these media, in spite of difference, is their common anti-authoritarian structure—quite literally, a participatory democracy that successfully redistributes both initiative and responsibility. In addition to epitomizing the humanist theme of ultimate self-determination, this collaborative concept represents, in my opinion, an important development in literary communication, precisely because it transcends "dummy intermediaries," and it has a further advantage of easy imitation. (Its commercialization also signals a certain, perhaps dubious success that probably explains why Bowles' enterprise rejected a duly submitted contribution, albeit an outrageous one, that went instead into *Third Assembling*.) In the mail recently came *Clone*, which is comparably produced by students at the Rhode Island School of Design, and another pile of unbound pages from British art students, along with independent invitations to send self-published packets to Holland, Germany, and Italy.

Unless the crisis in literary communications is radically solved, it seems likely that self-publishing, both individually and collaboratively, will continue to be necessary and respectable, and xerography paper may at times become more honorific than letterpress printing. Especially since the means of production have become more accessible, the pressing problem now, for all alternative publishing, is how to distribute the results beyond one's immediate acquaintances (or mailing list). The best solution is so obvious it remains visionary: a national network of art-conscious wholesalers and retailers capable of handling small, probably slow-moving quantities. At last count, the enterprise has cost us several hundred dollars that we can theoretically recoup.

We were pleased to discover that *Assembling* has been read, not only by fellow contributors (who comprise a most ideal audience) but by its purchasers; and even those who browse in literary bookstores. The last tell me that they were intrigued by a subtitle that reads, "A Collection of Otherwise Unpublishable Creative Work" and they quickly discovered that the book's contents are, at minimum, clearly unlike anything they had read/seen before. There are good reasons to believe, as I wrote elsewhere, "that the magazine's distinctiveness caused it to be enthusiastically possessed, if not securely lodged within the imaginative memories of many readers; for as the anthropologist Edmund Carpenter observed, 'It is one of the curiosities of a new medium, a new format, that at the moment it first appears, it's never valued; but it is believed.'" Most important, in our judgment, is *Assembling's* realization, simply by existing, of our initial threefold commitment to individual opportunity, unhindered communication, and creative adventurousness, for both the contents and its structure finally reflect values intended by, and hopefully intrinsic to, the process. Behind such a cordial gathering of genuine idiosyncrasy is a freedom and anarchy I personally find exemplary. "Assembled we stand," runs our reiterated motto, "disassembled we fall," and for the *Third Assembling* I added: "POWER TO THE PEOPLE WHO DO THE WORK."

An *Assembling* Bibliography

Assembling (1970), 162 pp., the opening salvo, including Ed Ruscha's "Chocolate" stain

Second Assembling (1971), 180 pp., (with a Stan VanDerBeek fold up only available in a few copies)

Third Assembling (1972), 280 pp.

Fourth Assembling (1973), 274 pp.

Fifth Assembling (1974), 284 pp.

Sixth Assembling (1975), 288 pp.

Seventh Assembling (1977), 396 pp.

Eighth Assembling, A–J, (1978)

Eighth Assembling, K–Z, (1978), to serve an increased number of contributors, the Eighth number appeared as two volumes, alphabetically divided, the first becoming mysteriously scarcer than the other

A Critical (Ninth) Assembling (1979), an assembling printed (instead of compiled) of camera-ready critical commentary on experimental literature around the world

Tenth Assembling (1980), produced with the St. Paul visual poet Scott Helmes

Eleventh Assembling: Pilot Proposals (1981), "If you could apply for a grant of $500,000, what precisely would you propose to do?"

Twelfth Assembling (1982)

Thirteenth Assembling: 2 (1983), 14" wide in an horizontal format, velobound

Assembling Assembling (1978), a retrospective produced on the occasion of our retrospective exhibition, 96 pp.

Complete Assembling (1970–82), approx. 3,000 pages, collecting the first thirteen volumes

On the Conjunction of Editing and Composition

by Peter Gizzi (2000)

I remember the first time I saw the reissue of Wyndham Lewis's "Review of the Great English Vortex," *BLAST*. I was twenty-one, walking home, sweaty, exhausted, and alive with the noise of the city after a Pere Ubu concert at Irving Plaza. In the window of St. Mark's Bookshop I saw a fluorescent pink volume with the word BLAST in gigantic bold sans serif type printed diagonally across the cover. The Sex Pistols had nothing on this. I had moved to New York in part to check out the punk/new music scene of the late seventies, early eighties and to go to NYU. Before college I had worked in a factory winding resin tubes and in a residential treatment center caring for emotionally disturbed adolescents. When I did overnights I would stay up late reading *The Cantos*, the then-new *Collected* Oppen and Zukofsky's *A*, as well as H.D., Stevens, Williams, and almost anything published by Burning Deck. I was becoming disgruntled with the vicissitudes of rock & roll. So when I saw the *BLAST* in shocking pink and read the manifestos, I was home in that synthesis—Punk and Poetry had merged and I knew at once I wanted to edit my own journal. It was in the foreword to that volume that I first came upon the writing and the expansive editorial imagination of Bradford Morrow, and I've always wanted to thank him for his role in that magical evening. In fact, it would be hard to imagine the past twenty years without his unstinting work on behalf of so many writers, known and unknown.

Novels and essays aside, Morrow is a practitioner of the art of conjunction. He has edited and introduced a number of important projects through the years: *A Bibliography of the Writings of Wyndham Lewis*, *A Bibliography of the Black Sparrow Press*, reissue of *BLAST*, various editions of the poems,

translations, and essays of Kenneth Rexroth, the fiction of Coleman Dowell, *The New Gothic* (with fellow novelist Patrick McGrath), and most prominently *Conjunctions*, a magazine with enough literary ammo to stage its own revolution. *Conjunctions* is not "little" in any sense—its issues are often 400+ pages, it's distributed widely, and its editorial focus is international—but it has maintained the intensity, intimacy, and cohesion of the classic "little magazines" of Pound's time. The more I've seen of Mr. Morrow's labors in the years following my initial discovery of his work, the less isolated my experience of reading has become, and the more I've come to find a conjunction, as it is defined in my Webster's, as an act of conjoining or state of being conjoined, bound together, belonging to, made up of, or effected by combined elements or persons: a union, association, combination.

In the introduction to *Conjunctions: 1* (a double issue celebrating James Laughlin and New Directions), Morrow gives us a template for reading not only his own project but the process of editing itself as a form of cultural affiliation and recombination. His initial dedication to Laughlin's legacy signals the scope, range, and ambition he has sustained for his thirty-three volume, ten-thousand-page, eight-hundred-author work-in-progress, or "living notebook" as he calls it. Describing the effect of his discovery of New Directions books when he was in college, Morrow recalls the transformative effect of reading Pound's "Canto 4." The choice is not arbitrary, as Morrow himself has added to the scholarship of this poem in an issue of *Paideuma*, and the poem itself is emblematic of his process. In "Canto 4" Pound traces his own trajectory—on a walking tour of Provence—but more significantly he gathers an international assemblage of figures whose stories overlap, intersect, and "rhyme," to create a lasting, inclusive aesthetics that arises out of his wide reading—a performative bibliography.

Editing, like writing, is fundamentally about composing a world. The writers one reads inhabit one's life, haunt one's imagination, daily walks, conversations with friends, dreams. They give one coverage in the world, a sense of place, a shared tradition. In editing, one argues for that constituency. Emily Dickinson wrote "The Soul selects her own Society." In editing, one selects the culture one wants to endure. Or as Pound wrote: "What thou lov'st well is thy true heritage."

Editing is a gift, and Morrow has the ability to work a feeling for how various disparate pieces might fit together, a way of creating a city of peers or a mix of sensibilities that can become mutually generative, catalytic. What makes a work is something both lasting and ephemeral—something that reflects and shapes the period, but that goes beyond the concerns of the period. It is built architecturally, of substantial and fragile design. One has to maintain the delicate play between aesthetic consistency and openness. It is interesting to look at Pound's advice to the young Robert Creeley, as it begins by discussing the way verse operates and how one composes a maga-

CONJUNCTIONS:52

Betwixt the Between

Impossible Realism

zine in very much the same way; that is, journals work like poems. Creeley recounts: "He proposed that verse consisted of a constant and a variant, and then told me to think from that to the context of a magazine. He suggested I get at least four others, on whom I could depend unequivocally for material, and to make their work the mainstay of the magazine's form. But then, he said, let the rest of it, roughly half, be as various and hogwild as possible." In his making of *Conjunctions*, Morrow has published a core group of established writers from John Hawkes, Robert Coover, William H. Gass, Paul West, Walter Abish, Gilbert Sorrentino, Lydia Davis, and Guy Davenport to John Ashbery, Robert Creeley, Barbara Guest, Nathaniel Tarn, Susan Howe, David Rattray, Robert Kelly, Ann Lauterbach, Mei-mei Berssenbrugge, along with twenty years of emerging writers like Ben Marcus, William T. Vollmann, Diane Williams, Can Xue, Mary Caponegro, Robert Antoni, Martine Bellen, Forrest Gander, Peter Cole, Elaine Equi, Mark McMorris, Cole Swensen, Myung Mi Kim, Thalia Field, and me, among others. And, like Laughlin (and Pound), he's consistently maintained a focus on world literatures.

Editing is a creative act, a form of composition that demands an attention to subtle aspects of both the world and the text—the production, the arrangement, the formal or thematic connections between the work of various writers, as well as the leading between lines, the depth of margins, the length of submissions, the viability of various typefaces—concerns which are so minute and so important that they take on the weight and intensity of any made thing. Maybe this is why so many great editors are also great writers. Think of Pound's indefatigable editorial input to various journals, Marianne Moore at the *Dial*, T. S. Eliot at Faber & Faber, Ford Madox Ford's the *English Review*, Apollinaire's *Les Soiree de Paris*, Creeley's the *Black Mountain Review*, Ashbery's *Art and Literature*, Lyn Hejinian's *Tuumba*, Nathaniel Mackey's *Hambone*, to name just a few. Within this rich tradition editors build on each other's work while adding their own innovations. One might argue that *Conjunctions* arises partly in response to Laughlin's *New Directions in Prose and Poetry* annual which built directly on Eugene Jolas's *transition*: all dedicated to "the revolution of the word."

We could call editing a labor of love, but it's more than that. It's labor intensive, and there are always more strings attached than can be imagined. It can be bone bruising, putting you on the line with friends, writers you admire, other editors. Good issues piss people off as much as they attract people—especially when the focus is on just good writing rather than on stylistic politics—and *Conjunctions* boasts some of the most exceptional writing from a myriad of traditions. It's a bit like juggling imaginary worlds. The more successful the journal, the harder it gets; editors get much more work than they can ever accommodate from issue to issue, and the process of selection and arrangement gets increasingly difficult. To edit is to serve

MR21

MISSISSIPPI REVIEW 7/3 $2.50

two muses. As writers we can be blind to what's immediately before us, but years later when the noise of our own egos subsides, we're able to read things within a larger context. Editing requires one to read in this way, to step outside one's own noise and tune into the finer frequencies in front of one.

Even though *Conjunctions* has grown in size from issue to issue, Morrow maintains the same meticulous attention to detail throughout. Since issue 14, *The New Gothic*, he has found a remarkably useful way of preserving the intimacy of a small journal by giving each issue a thematic focus. He also expands his own editorial range by collaborating with co-editors. In a wonderful essay on the history of the little magazine, Cyril Connolly writes that "little magazines are of two kinds, dynamic and eclectic. Some flourish on what they put in, others by whom they keep out. Dynamic magazines have a shorter life and it is round them that glamour and nostalgia crystallize. Eclectic magazines are also of their time but they cannot ignore the past nor resist good writing from opposing camps." To his credit, Morrow seems to have achieved the impossible: balancing the scope of the eclectic with the energy of the dynamic. Some of my favorite issues have been *The Music Issue* (#16); *Fables, Yarns, Fairy Tales* (#18); *Unfinished Business* (#20), which published generous selections of novels in progress; *New World Writing* (#23); *Sticks and Stones* (#26); *The Archipelago* (#27), featuring new Caribbean writing; *Tributes* (#29), writers on their favorite writers; and *Radical Shadows* (#31), previously untranslated and unpublished works by nineteenth- and twentieth-century masters.

In *Critical Mass* (#24), published in silently provocative tandem with his novel *Trinity Fields* on the fiftieth anniversary of the atomic bomb, Morrow writes that the issue "is abundant with work prompted by the spiritual as much as the bellicose" and that, "above all, the title suggests that here is a mass of material we consider to be of critical value." This work is real and is successful first because the editor means it to be real. Having begun this tribute with World War I's *BLAST* and writing this while the "Allied Forces" continue their bombing campaign in Kosovo and Belgrade is again on fire, I return to Pound's edict about verse being composed of a constant and a variant, and I can't help but think that war is the constant and we are the variant, that the survival of culture is a function of how we read and what we compose, that these are the real issues. Real issues.

The Web Is a Gun: An E-mail Exchange with Frederick Barthelme

by Ralph Lombreglia (1997)

To: Ralph Lombreglia
From: Frederick Barthelme
Subject: Literary Publishing on the Web

Ralph Lombreglia: Could you say how you view the Web and its literary prospects?

Frederick Barthelme: There seem to be two basic views of the Web among literary folk. The first and most common is that the Web is a wasteland, another television, a form of advertising—all utterly unsuitable for literary activity. Among these folk there is a curious parallel between response to the Web and response to alternative literatures. Those who are terrorized by any change in the habits, practices, and product of writers, any change that might tend to disenfranchise them, are also, and perhaps not surprisingly, terrorized by the rise of the Web as a publishing forum. The second common view is the giddy "it's all experimental" approach that proclaims that anything on the Web is a fabulous extension of literary activity as we have known it and will clearly destroy all not up-to-date literary activity in about twenty minutes.

Both these views are, even in their most sophisticated disguises, silly.

My sense is that the Web is a gun. It's all potential, what we do with it; it's a device, a system, a "site" in the linguistic sense, a prospect. How we use it over the next decade or two will define it. At the moment it's politically and socially semi-neutral, uninflected, a tool for, in our case, the distribution of literary information. Years ago Charles Newman wrote a series of acute essays for *TriQuarterly* in which he discussed at length the power and potential of literary distribution systems. I know he didn't have the Web in mind, and who knows what he thinks about the Web, but the Web certainly qualifies as a stunning development in distribution systems.

RL: Why did you decide to put your literary journal [*Mississippi Review*] on the Web? What do you hope to see happen?

FB: The simplest answer is that the Web was there. I've been working on computers since the very late seventies. They've always intrigued me. When the Internet got out of the geeks-only stage in late 1993 and the Web emerged, I got involved. My main interest in it was as an extraordinary new delivery system that put stories and poems right into readers' homes and offices.

I've edited a literary magazine for twenty years, partly because I did my time among the unpublished and thought-to-be-unpublishable, and partly for the joy of finding a wonderful story or poem or essay that I know will not be allowed to show its face in *The New Yorker* or *The Atlantic Monthly*. It's a not undesirable duty. When the Web came along, this duty compelled me to move the magazine online.

Certain things became clear at once. It's a great deal easier to publish online than on paper. This may not be true if you're a publishing Goliath, but for mom-and-pop lit mags it is absolutely true. Because it's easier, you can do more of it—we print the paper magazine twice a year, and even that is hard with no staff, no money, no time. By contrast, the Web magazine is a monthly, it's relatively easy to produce (everything is digital, first to last, so there's no typesetting, no scanning, no paste up), and the production costs next to nothing.

Sure, we've dispensed with niceties such as paying contributors, but literary magazines don't pay enough to count anyway, and, in some sense, the fundamental idea of art is that art should be free. The artist makes a gift for the world. It's a book, a story, a painting, a piece of music. With the Web we've got a delivery system with such a radically reduced overhead that carrying out the idealized notion of giving the art away becomes practical.

RL: Are you doing (or planning to do) anything on the Web that you can't do on paper?

FB: Yes. We're getting a literary journal out once a month. We're reaching a much larger audience than the paper magazine does. As far as the writing goes there's not much difference—we find curious fictions and poems, curious written artifacts, and we provide a public venue.

There are a hundred obvious things about the presentation that are different. The most interesting of these may be that Web publishing allows, even encourages, the kind of tinkering that paper publication prohibits. Often I add a story mid-month, or redesign the site, or add graphics, or change the way I'm treating type. The Web allows much more hands-on activity than paper printing. This has the potential for making the Web a more pliable and responsive medium than print. I'm also adding a few typical Web bells and whistles. Sound is something I'm very interested in. I hope to deliver new music of some kind on the *MR* site. It's no good simply to pipe in some Muzak, or some comfortable jazz, so I'll use Koan to produce the music to start with, then try to get involved with people who are making interesting hearable things. The prospects for doing similar things with visual material are slimmer at the moment, but I expect that to change.

RL: Has your journal's Web site changed anything about the way you design or produce the paper publication? If not, can you foresee changes down the road?

FB: It hasn't had much impact on the paper magazine. It has changed the way we look at the magazine, and I suppose it must be admitted that for me the Web version is now the real *Mississippi Review*. The paper version is vestigial. I should add that this isn't a widely shared view—there's still a premium among writers in appearing in a paper publication over a Web publication. But I expect this to pass also.

RL: Web publishing isn't free, and nobody seems to be paying to read what's published online. Do you see a workable financial model besides killing the paper magazines to feed the Web sites?

FB: The only reason Web publishing isn't free is that some larger sites are paying editors. For those of us who work in small-scale publishing, the Web is free, or close enough. I don't have to do a Web magazine, and the university I work for isn't paying me more because I'm doing it (and wouldn't pay me less if I stopped tomorrow). If I were operating outside the university, publishing a Web magazine might cost me $20 a month, unlike paper publishing where paper and printing and distribution would make doing a magazine impossible.

Slick magazines will no doubt build big editorial staffs, paying many people for doing little work, and this will necessitate that the Web be profitable. What many of us are hoping is that this sort of publishing will just die, leaving the Web to the rest of us. That said, I know well enough that this sort of publishing won't die, that money will be made, and made in abundance, and made in the literary business, on the Web. What I don't know yet is whether this will destroy the Web by reducing it to another mechanism of cultural control of the many by the few, though this is what I fear. See next question.

RL: How do you see the long-term impact of the Web on the literary life of the country?

FB: This is tricky. The answer depends more or less on whether the Web is essentially taken over by large publishing and media corporations. If it is not, then the Web will be the most powerful agent of change since the printing press, and the changes that it will bring about are not readily foreseeable. On the other hand, if the Web is gobbled up by the standard purveyors of culture (magazines, newspapers, television, and so on), then it will become another means of control, like television, and the long-term impact will be to enhance the dominion over the culture by its established "owners."

RL: Do you see your journal ever sponsoring or publishing "multimedia literature" that cannot be experienced without a computer, or a collaborative ongoing literature created by many writers in some networked "groupware" situation? Or some other experiments impossible in a paper-based magazine? Or would you rather keep doing more or less what you've always done on paper? And why?

FB: This is a dicey area for me, since I started off as a visual artist, and came into literary work through the then multimedia door (here I'm referring to the sixties, Fluxus, happenings, indeterminacy, books with graphics, photos, objects, peculiar texts, odd ways of meaning, and so on). Thus many things now presented as hypertext do not interest me. It's a grave indictment of experimental literature, and in particular hypertext, that the best work on offer so far pales by comparison to the elegant work of Alain Robbe-Grillet (and a dozen others) who took uncertainty as a central system of construction and as a central thematic interest some thirty years ago and made successful literary art. We can't simply rehash all these old ideas and present them as the fabulous new art of hypertext.

I've seen a few things worthy of attention. In particular the work of Christy Sheffield Sanford seems to be an authentic step. There's also a site at http://www.jodi.org/index.html that confuses the boundaries of literary action on the Web in an interesting way. I'm sure there are others working at the edges and genuinely changing the definition of literary art, but I wouldn't expect there are many such artists. So far, the tendency has been old messages in new bottles.

IV. PRESENT & FUTURE

Literary magazines today seem to be both everywhere and invisible, depending on your perspective. Ever easier access to new publishing technologies—from Xerox machines to Wordpress.org—alongside the proliferation of creative writing programs in higher education have made creating a literary magazine ubiquitous, sometimes for reasons other than idealistic early modernist notions of the avant garde. At the same time, the entertainment industries of movies, video games, television, and music capture an increasing amount of the public's attention to the detriment of reading—where, nonetheless, a handful of immense media corporations dominate the publishing landscape. Most recently, the apparently instant connection of the Internet to nearly every aspect of our lived experience is increasingly changing how, and how much, we read, with new reading devices being introduced into the market at a rapid clip. So where does this leave the literary magazine, the independent, the university supported, the corporate imprint? And—maybe most interesting to readers, writers, and publishers today—just what do all of these new developments mean for the literary magazine of the future?

NINTH
LETTER

[VOL 5] ISSUE 1   SPRING + SUMMER 2008 $14.95

ninthletter.com

UNIVERSITY OF ILLINOIS AT URBANA-CHAMPAIGN

81

0 74470 05097 1

The Changing Shape of Literary Magazines; or "What the hell Is this thing?"

by Jodee Stanley (2008)

I imagine that everyone reading this who's familiar with *Ninth Letter* and our distinctive format expects me to write something along the lines of "literary publishing needs to be more experimental! more design-heavy! just heavier in general—we need more magazines you can hardly lift!" And it's true, *Ninth Letter* is a journal that stands out, literally, on the shelf: oversized, full of color, elaborately designed, packed with inserts, foldout posters, and other gadgets. Some readers adore this; others very vocally do not. The response we most often get from people seeing *Ninth Letter* for the first time is, "This is a literary magazine?" The answer is yes, if by "literary magazine" you mean a publication which primarily exists to publish poetry and prose of extraordinary quality. But it's true, we do things a little differently from everyone else. Our mission, in addition to providing a forum for great writing, is to find ways to utilize graphic design so that it illuminates and enhances the literary experience. When our experiments are successful (more often than not, I hope), *Ninth Letter* becomes a new kind of reading experience. We have been credited with, or accused of, attempting to "redefine" what a literary journal is—maybe we've even made that claim ourselves somewhere along the way. But I don't think "redefine" accurately describes *Ninth Letter*'s goal. What we really want to do is experiment with what a literary magazine can be. In this new millennium of crossed genres and blurred boundaries in art and media, ever-evolving technology can provide endless opportunities for creative work. Design and writing seem a natural partnership, both in print and online. At least, that's how we see it.

Looking at the bigger picture, and our place in it, I think what keeps literary publishing vital and relevant are editors with visions. Plural. We need new magazines that explore new territory, of any kind—*One Story*, for example, which broke new ground on the far end of the spectrum from where *Ninth Letter* sits, but which is one of the most exciting journals happening right now. Or *Hobart*, which takes a more traditional approach in print and also utilizes the Web to publish great flash fiction. Or the gorgeous new little letterpressed poetry journal *Tuesday; An Art Project*. Or *Zoetrope* and *McSweeney's*, our predecessors in experimenting with graphic design. Beyond the most basic definition of "literary magazine" as a forum for literary writing, the concept of how this forum is created, shaped, and distributed will always be broadening and changing, as long as there's a desire for the stories and the poems.

I don't believe there needs to be a manufactured push toward innovation, though. Literary publishing has always adapted naturally, over the decades, to embrace or at least acknowledge cultural change. Movements and trends will always make their way into literature because that is one of the purposes of writing—to reflect our world, to challenge our perceptions and help us make sense of what's happening around us. Likewise, the venues for new writing themselves will flex and bend, evolving along with the content they provide, in whatever way suits them best.

Experimental publishers, online journals, podcasts, publications produced on DVD, all of these make literary publishing a curious and more exciting place, but there's no danger that they'll completely replace traditional publishing formats, nor could they. In a healthy literary environment, the old guard and the new guard in all its myriad forms will co-exist peacefully, encouraging our readers to explore, learn, and take enjoyment from as wide a variety of media as possible. As always, I think, the most important thing for literary editors, both experienced and new, to do is to find a way to express their passions, whether it be in traditional forms and formats, experiments with design and content, new technologies, or something entirely different.

The Future Is a Magazine: A Roundtable on the Contemporary Literary Magazine

With Jill Allyn Rosser (for *New Ohio Review*), Speer Morgan (for *The Missouri Review*), Marco Roth (for *n+1*), Raymond Hammond (for *New York Quarterly*), Adrian Todd Zuniga (for *Opium Magazine*), Eli Horowitz (for *McSweeney's*), and Aaron Burch (for *Hobart*); moderated by Gary Percesepe and Travis Kurowski for *Mississippi Review* (2008)

Mississippi Review: Literary mags are small magazines that publish less well-known writers and serve as stepping stones for writers who eventually go on to become highly regarded, a kind of "Triple A" farm system where younger writers publish their work and learn from that process. Is this any different now than at any time in the past?

Jill Allyn Rosser: I think, with the advent of the creative writing boom, it's even more important than it had been before. It's crucial for me to find someone I am interested in reading that's a fresh voice—that's why I cruise the magazines. I don't go to the big publishing houses to find what my students will respond to and what I, personally, might learn from and be excited by.

Speer Morgan: I think that literary magazines have been important throughout the twentieth and the beginning of the new century. They've been important since the teens, really, when *Poetry* magazine kept poetry alive. You know, the newspapers were publishing poetry but it was all pretty bad poetry. [Laughter] There's a long history of literary magazines that are discoverers of

HOBART
another literary journal

issue <u>no.</u> six

summer '06 / ten dollars

new talent and of them taking material that just wasn't readily available in the commercial crest. Even during the strength of the magazine—which in America was between the 1880s and the 1950s—there was still need for it.

Marco Roth: I think the question is: How far do we want to go back historically? What kind of literary magazines are we looking at? Because I came up with a list of the magazines that includes us when we were starting *n+1* and they were all movement magazines. That minor league baseball analogy is so tempting and also so horrifying [laughter] because you want to be the major leagues. There were these magazines, particularly in the early part of the twentieth century—*Blast*, *Poesia*, futurist magazines, *The Fugitive* in the south, the *Agrarian* and of course parts of the *View* and T. S. Eliot's *Criterion*—which were also, of course, critical magazines since they published literature and criticism together. Also, *Tel Quel* in France in the 60s, which published a lot of new writing. And then it seemed like every naturalist movement in the early part of the twentieth century had a literary magazine or several. There was a whole rise of national literature in Ireland and Scotland. If you wanted to be a nation, you had to have a literature, but then you had to have literary magazines that would publish the emerging literature of that nation. And then you can go back even to *Lockwood* magazine in England that published George Eliot. And these are also critical magazines, a lot of them. I think what's changed in the literary magazine is the narrowing of it since Clifford Joe called it the "great writing boom." And I don't know when we want to start dating that.

Rosser: Yeah. [Laughs]

Roth: Now there is this sense that these small magazines were just an artifact of modernism, and that we moved beyond literary modernism because we've moved beyond ideology, and so what's left is a kind of cultivation of new talent, but talent for what sake? What are the major leagues that literary magazines are serving? Is it publishing, which has become risk adverse? Who is willing to take risks? At this point it is the small magazines who have to take the risks. So, in some ways, it's more like a talent scout. But I think that histories go around. We could live in an age in which a movement magazine is still possible that published literature along with political essays and non-fiction criticism—and that's what we were really trying to do, to kind of break down the necessary "willed minor-ness" that literary magazines have put themselves into.

Morgan: Here's the thing about movement magazines. The advantage is that some of them can be very historically important, like *The Fugitive*, which was one of the ones you mentioned. And several of the ones you mentioned, they're historically important, and they are remembered as markers and be-ginners and significant in the history of literature. The problem with move-ment magazines is that they tend to have short life spans, and that's not necessarily a terrible thing, but it is a fact.

Rosser: When we look back to the earliest stage of the literary magazine, that was a time—well into the 1920s even—when people were gathering in hot beds of creative activity. There was Paris and Hemingway and Stein. I don't think that really happens anymore—the salon—and the magazine has become a replacement for that. Now that we have such a vast network of writers, they can't gather in one city. They do tend to gravitate towards, say, Boston and New York, and, I suppose, L. A. You need to have these maga-zines because we're all so spread out, and I don't think that has changed at all. To go back to the original question, I think the need is stronger, if anything.

Raymond Hammond: Since the phenomenon of the creative writing pro-gram has blossomed since the sixties, I think that one of the functions of the little magazine has become to be a stalwart against homogenization of the work. We are the magazines that take the risks and put different voices out there as opposed to the larger presses that tend to be more homogenous.

Morgan: I fully agree with that. We've published so many people over the years for the first time. Maybe the simplest way to put it is that we are the ones who actually read the manuscript. The presses love us because we do their work for them. [Laughter] And it's a massive amount of work, when you think that we [*The Missouri Review*] receive fifteen thousand manuscripts a year, and literary presses, even the big presses, just simply can't afford to read that many manuscripts. So you hear all of these terror stories of them—the young editors, assistant editors—just throwing stuff down the stairway and making big jokes of actually reading any of the stuff.

Roth: This raises the question whether small magazines should unionize, given that we provide an outsourcing function for major publishers. This has allowed publishers to cut back, let go of a lot of their editors. They can always rely on the little magazines to make the calls for them. Maybe there should be a union movement among literary magazines in the beginning of the twenty-first century.

MR: Lit mags have tiny circulation, perhaps even smaller readership. Is there anything wrong with that if the magazines still serve the purpose of a practice field for younger writers?

Hammond: I work the night shift at the Statue of Liberty as a federal law enforcement officer and that's how I make my money. I don't make it here, and that's true of many people in lit mags. Some people do, which is fine, and, hopefully, one day I will. There are many people where I work who ask for the magazine who wouldn't normally be reading poetry magazines. One magazine might see ten people as it gets passed around. Readership always tends to be higher than circulation and I definitely don't see anything wrong with that. I actually see it as being necessary for what we're doing.

Morgan: I agree. We've paid attention to circulation over the years and the truth of the matter is that every issue of our magazine goes out to what used to be considered a reasonable quality publication number. Certainly thirty years ago, the number six thousand was considered a reasonable number for a literary book. It's not now because of the economics for publishing, but if you consider the fact that there's also the internet and library subscription services, every issue of the magazine including the website gets seen by several thousand. So it's not as if we're hidden in the shadows. In fact, the Internet has made us quite available. We have five hundred readers a day on the Internet site and they have been going up steadily.

MR: Online literary magazines get much more attention from prospective readers than print magazines. A print magazine might have a press run of five thousand copies per issue, whereas the online site of the same magazine might get 125,000 visits quarterly. These figures aren't perfectly comparable, but they're in the ballpark. Yet most writers say that they'd rather publish in print journals. What are your thoughts on this?

Adrian Todd Zuniga: This is one of the great ironies of literary publishing. But I think the real factor is that there's endless space on the web and ultimately anybody can get published. Somebody I know might start a little magazine that has fifteen people reading it, but someone might submit to that and get accepted. I think that what it really comes down to is that there's limited space in the print world and so that's value—and I think that editors of publishing houses say, "Well, you're in a print magazine. That's better."

Hammond: I think that as the internet evolves and things become more permanent—with the generation coming up who are more accustomed to reading online—I think we'll see a shift in that. Maybe that prestige element will change. Maybe it won't. One of the things we [literary magazines] do is—we do preserve. We take a snapshot of this historical time period for future generations to take a look at. Storage, archiving, providing access for reading by future generations, having all of our issues available to them in the future, is important.

THANKFUL · EMBOLDENED

M^cSWEENEY'S

FULL TO BURSTING! FULL TO BURSTING! FULL! BLOOD OF US ALL!

& — HOT-BLOODED — PERPETUAL — &

THE PRESUMPTION OF GOOD WILL

LIFE-SAVING

IRRATIONAL (OR MORE LIKELY, IRREDUCIBLY) RATIONAL)

A momentary respite.

NO. **9** PROMPTLY

NO. 9 WITH GUSTO

DOUG DORST
Greed. Lust. The burden of being endlessly wrong.

JEFF GREENWALD
Conflict without reason or result. This is the problem.

A. M. HOMES
A new creation myth. A flight into a lesser life.

Gabe HUDSON
Corrective! | The greatest of battles. | Bring it back!

Denis JOHNSON
Depravity. | The curves of a true enemy. | For whom?

Roy KESEY
The possibilities of possession, of ruin. | Balance!

K. KVASHAY-BOYLE
Flailing. | Winching. | The responsibility of accusation.

NATHANIEL MINTON
Being lost. | Being buried. | Lumping. | Heat. | Topography.

ELLEN MOORE
Listening to music with headphones next to the person you love.

VAL VINOKUROV
Russians barking. | Russians flailing. | Russians marching.

W.T. VOLLMANN
Catacombs. | Corpses. | Of course there are jokes.

TRUST
THIS GODDAMN LAND

TAKE: *your aggression.* QUESTION: *your aggression.* REMOVE IT: *from the company of others.* WALK WITH IT: *to a faraway place.* ALONE? *Yes, alone.* LEAVE IT: *under a great wide sky, exposed, apart.* DO NOT: *bury it.* DO NOT: *live with it.* NEVER: *in your home.* NOT: *in your life.* IT IS: *viral.* IT GROWS: *like a shadow.* WE MUST: *carry it away.*

HOLD
THEM CLOSE

KNOW THEM. KNOW THEM. THEY CAN TALK! THEY CAN TALK! CARRY IT. CARRY THEM. KEEP IT SWEET. DO NO HARM. HARM IS HARM IS HARM. *And yet:* YOUR HARM IS OUR HARM.

CANNOT. WILL NOT. CANNOT. WILL NOT. CANNOT. WILL NOT. CANNOT. WILL NOT. CANNOT. WILL NOT. CANNOT LIVE THAT WAY AGAIN.

REMEMBERING! WRAP YOUR TINY AND ATROPHYING RARMS! WEAK & RUBBERY BUT YOURS. REMEMBERING! YOU MUST— REMEMBERING! MORE FOR YOUR SAKE THAN THEIRS.

Breathe. *Breathe.* *Breathe.*

EFFLORESCENCE

BLOOMING OR RASH? · THE HIGHEST POINT · OR SOMETHING · THAT ITCHES? · HE IS GONE

Our motto this time: "WE GIVE YOU SWEATY HUGS."

Do you sense it?

GEGENSCHEIN

NO MORE

Alternate motto: "WE ARE OUT LOOKING."

$15.00 U.S. $22 CANADA

ISBN 0-9719047-5-8

9 780971 904750   90000

LATE SUMMER EARLY FALL **2002** WE WILL DO FOUR THIS YEAR

FRIDTJOF

Rosser: My students still want print mags. Online publication is great, and, sure, *Poetry Daily* or *Slate* get way more hits than any of us can hope to have. On the other hand, they're hits. I don't mean to denigrate that idea. It's just that when I read online, and I do quite a bit now, it always feels to me like provisional reading. Later, I'll get to the real immediate intimate experience with text. Maybe it's my generation. But I see young people walking around with books, holding them like friends. When I was recently in Paris, they had a vending machine with books in it and I was so moved and gratified by that—because you think of vending machines as providing staples, like food or Snickers bars, or Pepsi and condoms. Immediate, the stores are closed, got-to-have-it stuff. And there were these books. They were novellas mostly, like Kafka's *The Metamorphosis* and Dostoevsky's *Notes from the Underground*, and children's books, poetry books. I was so excited. I kept walking by. It's still needed, the physical object, and I think it lasts longer than any archive. Well, we don't know yet, but the online archiving systems could all go kablooey one day, whereas the book is there as long as the library doesn't burn down. [Laughter] I believe online submissions are becoming more important, but I think that the print journal still has a very strong place in 2008 and probably into, oh, 2040. [Laughs]

Roth: I want to agree with Jill because I think there is something to the book itself. As a writer, I know I would rather be in print than online, although I've written for online publications. There is still a kind of aura and, if anything, the aura is growing because of the advent of the new technology. We're in a kind of moment of nostalgia for the book and we're starting to think more about what it is that books do that computers can't. When you have a book, there's a great feeling of orderly progression from beginning to end, or there's a feeling of actual acts of transgression if you skip around. And there's a smell to the pages, there's a feel. You can read in all kinds of strange positions, physically, that you can't read in when in front of a computer. [Laughter] There is this movement towards planned obsolescence in America of everything that's of value—except nobody wants to make cars obsolete yet, which would be the one thing that would probably save us. So, I hesitate when people want to rush literary magazines towards technological oblivion. And books. As long as they can be made available and as long as we still have public libraries, the question of access is really an economic question. It's not going to be solved by giving everybody a computer.

Morgan: I fully agree with what you just said about the cooperation of the two forms. I don't really think they vie with each other. I think they help each other, and we've philosophically believed that since we put up our first website. Before the web existed we had a site in the mid eighties. It was on a pay net and *The Missouri Review* has always believed that one promotes the other. The more action that we have on the internet site, the more magazines we sell. The downside of all of it is that it's labor. I mean, it's a vast amount of labor [laughter] to keep a website going, and for many of us that is an issue. It's an issue for all of us. And so we pay again, we pay with labor, just as we do in reading manuscripts.

Eli Horowitz: We try and think about the capabilities and the possibilities for each of the forms. We're not deciding whether or not to put our journal online. We do totally separate things or somewhat separate things that hopefully support each other. When we're making a book and when we're making a print journal, we're making a thing, and so we tend to try and make the thingiest thing possible. [Laughter] The website lends itself much more to shorter pieces and later pieces and so forth, but also presents all these possibilities. You get the instant feedback. You get a community with your readers. It's not a matter of just shifting from one to the other—and so one's inherently the future and one's inherently the past, or one's inherently pure and one's inherently dirty—they just present possibilities.

Zuniga: I think what's interesting is the prestige of having a print magazine to go along with the website. Literary websites are great, but from a viewer's perspective once you have print you've gone to that next level. *Opium* started online. We are four years online and we've been in print and online for three years after that. The print magazine has definitely legitimized the online experience for our readers. And the website without a doubt promotes the magazine. It gives us a lot more freedom to promote in different ways, but at the same time we're publishing content we're proud of. I'm curious just why we do the print magazine. Because what we're hearing here is we get 125,000 visits? If you've established a brand, then why are we doing the print magazine?

MR: Frederick Barthelme brought *Mississippi Review* online in early 1995. He didn't use the website as a teaser for the print magazine. He feels strongly that's been the right idea and he's never thought of the online and print magazines as different kinds of things, rather just magazines in different packages.

Aaron Burch: I think *Mississippi Review* is an excellent example of something that has a print version and is online and they have the same kind of feel. They complement each other, but without having just the same material, or just teasers or excerpts. They're two mediums that are better suited for different things.

Rosser: I think that the online advantages have not been exploited in the way that they should be. The performative aspects of some kinds of writing could be viewed. You could have the author actually reading. You can watch the author perform it. You can hear it. That's the sort of thing that I think the online publication should push for more of. They can complement each other and they don't have to compete exactly.

Hammond: I agree. I would hate to see *The New York Quarterly* go completely online because of economics or for any other reason. I hope that won't happen in my lifetime. I think we as editors are seeing things that haven't been seen since the advent of the printing press. I mean, this is really a revolution in thinking and medium that is completely new to everyone, and it's our responsibility to navigate into this new territory as best as we can.

MR: Is everyone an artist and everyone an editor? Has the internet democratized writing and publishing to the point where we're seeing a decline in quality, or is this a canard?

Morgan: There has always been bad writing. [Laughter] Since the beginning of the press, the first things that sold were descriptions of executions or semi-poetic descriptions of executions. In the history of printing, 99.9% of the stuff that's printed is junk and so it's really a waste of time to talk about the possible negative effect of online. The excellent stuff and literary stuff has always been a tiny percentage.

MR: So maybe we're just putting bad writing in more hands.
[Laughter]

Roth: I think always, no matter the age, the great stuff just finds its own perseverance and shakes itself out.

Zuniga: We publish daily on the web. Sometimes we go to three days a week because we just don't feel like the content's good enough. When we're publishing five days a week—and I know *McSweeney's* does this—I don't feel like every day we're publishing the next greatest thing that's ever going to be published. Where in the print magazine I do feel like we're much more careful and specific about what we publish—which I think is sort of fascinating for a couple of reasons, but I'm not sure what they are. [Laughter] We [also] have comments, so giving the audience a chance to voice their like or dislike of it. I think that's the community building aspect of it.

Roth: That's interesting. Whether the audience decides what is good writing or bad writing, that's of course the American idealization of literature. This is a problem with literature and democracy that's playing out on the web, which is who gets to decide what is good literature. Previously, it was a

The Missouri Review

The Coming of the
Little Magazine in America

bunch of intellectuals or people based in New York. Certainly what the web has done is opened up this sphere of judgment and, to some extent, fractured the authority of critics. I don't think there should be artificial restrictions of class or where you went to college that allows you to comment on what good writing is, but to use the fact that you didn't go to a particular college, that you're not from one of the central regions, as an excuse to promote yourself—which is what happens a lot of the time—that's just reversing the process. So then you have a kind of, "I'm a better writer because I'm not from one of the traditional leagues." There are things that we would all agree on that constitute good writing. What's missing often from critical conversation on the web is what that is. And when you ask people to prove it, they can't quite prove what they think is good writing or why their writing should be published on the web and why they're a neglected genius. The editorial function is still very important. Yes, now anybody can become a writer, but you're not a writer by virtue of simply being a citizen of America in the Internet age. And that's a distinction that probably needs to be enforced, unfortunately.

MR: Enforced how?

Roth: People need to be called out. [Laughs]

MR: Just told they're bad?

Roth: Yeah. [Laughs]

Hammond: I still think that things will just tend to shake themselves out. As things start to naturally settle, the crap will float to the surface and float away. [Laughter]

MR: What an image.

Hammond: Yeah. I think in a sense that is "calling it out." Those things will just kind of naturally die by their own accord and then the things that are worthwhile will survive.

Horowitz: I think it's a mistake to think of the Internet as some sort of monolithic something that we can even discuss as a single entity. It's the rise in people writing dumb things, the rise in people saying dumb things. I say plenty, and, you know, any website just is some kind of weird space between those two forms. I think it can be dangerous to give it too much authority or too much of a capital letter status. It's really just a thousand points of stupid lights [laughter] and, you know, some of us are stupider than others.

Morgan: You can consider the small magazine as the leader in the area of Internet use because the presses don't use it nearly as well as many of us do. In that sense, we're ahead of commercial publishing. Commercial publishing uses their websites strictly for PR, strictly for advertising. We use it for content.

MR: We have a long interview with Bob Fogarty, editor of the *Antioch Review*, in this issue [*Mississippi Review* 36.3]. He's very clear that he did not want ever to take the *Antioch Review* online. So, there is another perspective on this question.

Burch: I would agree with Raymond that I feel it kind of shakes itself out. The cream rises. And I think one of the interesting things with online is—this is starting to change—but it's still so new that I think some of people's hesitation with it is that shakedown hasn't happened a lot in places yet, and so it's hard to know where the quality is. I think it's easier to judge that sometimes with these print magazines that have been around so much longer. Maybe some of it has already shaken down. There are established reputations there.

Roth: I'd like to believe that what Raymond and Aaron are saying is going to happen, but I don't. The world of publishing is not a natural world and it's not [adherent to] the mechanism of Darwinian natural selection. That's not how canons got won in literature, either. Shakespeare did not rise to the top because he was the best. You had a period in English literature where people were like: Are Beaumont and Fletcher better than Shakespeare? And that might be the period we're in. But what pushes a certain kind of literature forward—that we then look back on and recognize, that all kinds of people can then find value in—is a strong critical voice and a sense of judgment and I think that's what still needs to happen. The Internet has created this kind of Petri dish feeling. You do get exposed to much more bad writing. It's one thing to be sitting in a bar next to people having a dumb conversation that's in one ear and out the other. But, then, when it's on your computer, and the computer is a writing machine and then it's also a listening machine, then—who put this stuff on my computer? You still have this sense that what's in print is somehow being given a value just by being in print. And we still make these analogies between what's on our screen and what's in print, so it feels like there is a lot more bad writing out there.

MR: What do literary magazines want and why do they want it? What are the impediments you face in getting what you want?

Zuniga: What we want is to continue to exist. I think in the literary journal world, longevity really is the prize. I've been published in a couple of magazines that now don't exist—so what does that mean to my story? Does that mean I need to take them out of my bio? I think it means so much to writers to be in a magazine that, first of all, they're excited to be in and, secondly, that is going to be around so they can feel proud of that—not when they get published, but three years down the road when they meet somebody else that has been published in that magazine. And the impediments? I publish a magazine and I pay for it. I try to do my own things and live my own life and travel and do things like that. So the impediment for me is money, and I think everybody probably has that impediment.

Rosser: I think what all of the literary magazines want is to discover the great new voice, and how you get the great new voice to send his or her work to you. If writers know you have a smallish circulation or you're new, they're not probably going to send you their most exciting work. How do you get them to send the stuff that's going to make you really sit back and gasp? That's what we all want. How do you get the person to send their best stuff to you and not the famous magazine, say *Poetry* magazine, or *The New Yorker*, for example. How do we get that stuff? The impediments are manifold and the funding is a big problem. Promotional budgets are small. The list is endless. But I think that's what we all want; we want it to be the venue where poet X, the great poet X of the future, first found a place for that voice, and nurture it and bring it forward and promote it.

Morgan: I think that the way you do it is by continuing to exist and continuing to discover new writers, and by gaining a name that people recognize. Over the years we've published quite a few firsts of later well-known writers. William Gay and Joanna Scott. We actually published one of Naguib Mahfouz's first stories published in the United States, and of course he won the Nobel Prize. You just do it by working hard, by reading everything you get, and by gaining a reputation.

Hammond: When I first read this question, the first thing that leaped to mind for me was a broader audience, and that's not necessarily from the standpoint of selling more magazines. It's from a standpoint of wanting a society where people read and understand poetry on a greater level than what we have and the small market share that we're all trying to reach. I think it would improve society as a whole, just a poetic sensibility for people. The great impediment to that is—I would love it if the majority of our readers also read the *New York Post* as opposed to *The New York Times*. I mean that would be a great accomplishment to me. But it's not going to happen, and the greatest impediment to that that I've seen is the public education system. Everybody thinks that poetry is just something that is like a cryptic quote in the Sunday paper and it's to be figured out and they can't figure it out, so,

Opium
MAGAZINE

7

$10.00US $12.00CAN

07>

0 74470 22269 9

therefore, they don't read it. Like I said before, I go to work and one of the boat captains who hasn't read poetry since he was in middle school asks for the magazine because he enjoys it. He told me, "I thought this stuff was supposed to be figured out." And I explained to him, no, you just read it and get out of it what you get out of it. And he did.

MR: Is anyone here unhappy with what literary magazines currently are and do?

All: Yes. [Laughter]

Zuniga: At *Opium*, we really try to create a community and to do things that are exciting. Feeding into the last question, I think that one of the impediments of what's happening with literary magazines is that people are busy. There's the Internet. There are video games. There's television. There's so much entertainment. I really feel we're living in this weird space and time where we've become an entertainment culture. You can get a job making movies and then people watch those movies—it's a cyclical thing, where entertainment is the focus of our society. The one thing that makes me unhappy about literary magazines is that I don't know that they're really trying to find an audience, to really be unique, and to live in a world where things are so brand-oriented and people are so busy. In the modern era I think we really have to sort of compete with [these] other things, and I think literary magazines tend towards just hanging low. I think that's a very high risk position. I still love what's happening in literary magazines, but I also grew up on them, so I'm curious what's going to happen. I want them to change and evolve, and I'm not certain that they are evolving.

Hammond: I agree wholeheartedly. We're undergoing a branding discussion right now at the magazine trying to do just that, to think about the future, and it goes back to what I was saying about trying to broaden that readership to people who wouldn't normally read literary magazines.

Rosser: I think one of the things that I don't like about the current literary magazine climate—and I don't know how long it's exactly been going on—but it's a response to the glut of books that are being published, poetry books and fiction books and nonfiction. The omnibus review has become so pervasive and I think it is often a degradation of the review form. I miss the in-depth review, and I think that editors are less willing to publish an in-depth review of, say, five or seven or ten pages on a single author's single book because they think: Is anybody that important anymore? People want to hear, what's new? It's that MTV feeling of so much stimulation that we've got to cover everything, and I wish that that would reverse itself a little bit.

Roth: I want to follow up on what Jill was saying by asking if literary magazines should think about publishing more reviews. I think the answer to the problem of too many books is for literary magazines to de-specialize, and to publish more in the way of non-fiction and personal essays, and also political essays and journalism, because there's a dearth of real in-depth investigative reportage out there. And the newspapers have all cut back, especially on foreign correspondence, so there's the question of seizing the opening. I would love it if somebody published more long reviews. And, there has been, of course, a firewall between literary magazines and critical magazines because of the sense that you may be insulting somebody's friends if you review them negatively.

Rosser: Right.

Roth: Everybody now wants to have a book review and start a book review. Maybe, since literary magazines are already in place, especially in universities, there can be kind of more of a conversation between creative writing departments and English departments. You can get people who read contemporary literature who don't actually want to write [it] and that would be very interesting as an experiment in reviewing. So, these are things I would like to see, too.

MR: How much does good design matter?

Horowitz: Matter for what? How much does it matter to get someone to pick it up? I think it matters a lot. None of us are actually designers, but I think you want to create a context that honors the work. That's not necessarily about making a whole issue out of ice or anything like that, but it is about, if the story mentions, you know, a monkey in it, don't just put a big picture of a monkey that obscures half of the words of the story. [Laughter] So, I think it matters on some level, but I think the most important things about it can be navigated by anybody as long as you just give it a little time and care and give it what the story deserves.

Zuniga: I think we're competing with things and I think good design really does matter. You go to a magazine rack that has lots of literary magazines and it's a little overwhelming, so which one do you pick up? I think the one with [the] bright, pretty cover might be the one you go to. There's the one that just has a great cover so you pick that up and then you flip through it and it has good design and that's exciting for people. I just think we have to do something to the work to say: This is worth reading. Look at the care we put into designing this. This is fun. This is something that you want to look at, you want to read the words in this. I think *McSweeney's* is a great example of that. They're beautiful and I think so many people, with every issue of *McSweeney's*, they're excited because they're going to get something fresh and new, and I think that informs what's inside to them. I think a lot of times it's just about getting people to pick it up and if they pick it up, then they start reading something. And that's what we're hoping for, and hopefully what they read, they like, and they buy the magazine or they read through the story.

Burch: Whether it's completely valid or not, there's definitely a correlation in people's minds—I know there is in mine—if somebody's taking care in design, then they're going to be taking care in the stories that they're choosing and editing. And some of that crosses back over to the plethora of online journals, too, and how easy it's become to put up a website. Anybody can do it. But if it looks like you just threw it up and didn't take a lot of care, then I'm going to assume that the stories were chosen with the same amount or lack of care, and I'm going to move on to something that looks better. I might not even read it before determining that this story wasn't worth my time if it looks sort of invalid.

MR: How do environmental concerns factor into your work as a lit mag editor?

Rosser: I'm obsessed—as I think we all are—with global warming and the problems of proliferation of print pages. Losing trees. I certainly want to move into online submissions and get that moving, and I think that is the future, probably, for most magazines, and this is something we can do even though we still want our print, we still want the physical object. This is something I'm committed to moving into.

Roth: We publish a lot on global warming—not as much as we would like, and we obviously want more essays on the subject. But I worry that we're entering into this kind of culture—you know, Dick Cheney says environmentalism is a problem of personal virtue. Where this question is going to be solved is at the political level, and a literary magazine is not going to produce as much pollution as a bunch of automobiles or crop dusting over grape fields or the amount of cows producing methane. [Laughter] That's where the problem is. The problem is not us. Certainly one can do what one can to reduce the amount of paper. I tend not to print things out, but often I also find that even when we get submissions online, if it's something that I'm seriously considering, I have to print it out. There are many things to feel guilty for in life [laughter], but really this is a political issue that needs to be resolved at the political level, and if literary magazines also become more political and more engaged and call readers' attention to the need for a comprehensive environment policy, that would be the best thing that could happen, because we do deal with a mountain of ideas.

Zuniga: In the next two days, hold your breath, we're [*Opium*] launching our "Go Green But Save Me First" issue. I wanted to make fun of the green movement because I don't think anybody's making fun of it "properly." But what was fun about doing this issue was—at the same time while we're poking fun at it—we wanted to show that we were serious about it and we did all this research on how to create a more green issue, not to ship our issues via flight, you know, make sure they're ground shipped. I'm glad this question came up and I'm talking to you guys about this, because now I see the value in publishing a piece on this, to show the different tactics to make your magazine more environment-friendly. We did all this research trying to figure out how we can do it right. You know, not just recycle paper, but having it shipped from a place closer to us. I think it's important, but important like it's important for us to recycle on an individual level. We each have to do what we can and hopefully the world doesn't fall apart before, you know, you meet your 100th anniversary.

MR: *The Paris Review*'s 50th anniversary issue posed the question: What has been the darkest moment in your magazine's history? How would each of you respond to this question today?

Rosser: Aren't they all going to be money answers?

Hammond: I think the darkest time for us is when our founder [William Packard] passed away. And we've been recovering from that ever since and trying to do a lot of the behind-the-scenes work to get that recovery accomplished. Of course, part of that is money [laughter], but that's not the only part of it.

Zuniga: Something happened recently with money. It was about two-and-half years in, when we were still just a website. I was exhausted. I had spent so much time doing this, and the value of it didn't seem to pay off at that moment. I had a drink with a friend who is up for a Pushcart Prize for a story in *Opium* now, which is exciting. So, I was sitting at the bar and I was just like, I can't do this anymore. I'm worn out. I'm going to shut it down. And he said: No, you have to. People read it. You have to continue it. And I listened to him. And then, when we both walked out of the bar, I was like, okay, I'm going to continue it. And when he walked out of the bar, he never had to do anything else. [Laughter]

Rosser: The darkest moment in our three-issue history. [Laughter] We really just didn't know if we were going to be able to scrape up the funds to continue to publish it. It's very simple. No more to say about that.

Horowitz: It's boring—that's just it. It's money, money, money, run out of money. Or, you know, like twice a week, just getting grouchy. [Laughter] There's nothing worthy of a movie or anything like that.

Zuniga: What about when you guys had the whole meltdown around the distributor?

Horowitz: Yeah, well, that was money. When our distributor went out of business and owed us a lot of money and so we didn't have it. That wasn't so dark, it was just, "We need money, what can we do about it?" It all worked out. We were really fortunate, certainly, but it didn't feel dark. It just felt like a problem, you know. It just felt like a challenge.

Roth: We also had money problems. We had $3,000 stolen from our fund-raiser, a couple of years ago. But that was almost so absurd that, you know. Fortunately, we've only been publishing for three years, six issues, and we haven't had anything catastrophic. We haven't had to grovel on our knees. Although we are planning in our next issue "corrections and things we regret." We had a caption that put Pyongyang in South Korea. [Laughter] A small caption error with potentially disastrous global consequences. So I think there are darker moments ahead, unfortunately.

MR: What is needed to maintain a literary magazine in today's environment?

All: Money, readers.

Rosser: Way beyond money, it's dedication, passion, energy, volunteers. I don't know how many magazines can pay everyone who is working for them. I think that's a rare magazine, if it even exists, and I'm constantly having to hand people large piles of manuscripts with a big smile and think: Can you fit this in? There's not enough remuneration. But if people are passionate enough about what they're doing and love the stuff, it can get done and you can find people to do it. And that's it. It's all about dedication and believing in what you're doing: providing a venue for lesser-known writers. For example, there are many writers who do not publish everything [that] they publish in literary journals [also] in their collections, in their books. This [a literary magazine] is the only record we're going to have of those works that, for whatever reason, fell to the wayside. As we know, writers are not always the best judges of their own work. We have a lot of work by Philip Larkin, for example, that he put in journals but he did not deem worthy of his books, and I might have differed with him on that. I think that we do provide a valuable service to the literary community of present and future for archiving this sort of thing. Looking at early versions of stories and poems that appeared in a magazine but that were later revised—I think that's an education in itself.

Zuniga: I somehow have to figure out how to make at least one in four persons that submit also subscribe, because I think the ratio is like 1 in 400,000. [Laughter] If we could figure out how to make any of these people actually recognize that we're doing this for free. I'm not going to bang that drum because—who cares. But if any of these people thought, "I'm going to send in my story," and then it gets rejected or accepted—mostly it gets rejected—I don't think they're like, "You know what, I should be supporting this magazine. I shouldn't be just sending my stories in." That doesn't happen. I just think there's like disconnect more and more nowadays where you download stuff for free off the Internet all the time. Not me, of course, everybody else but me. [Laughter] And an audience. You have to have an audience. You have to have passionate people doing the main thing. You have to have people willing to do a lot of work for what seems like little, but I think the payoff is pretty significant in the long run.

Hammond: I completely agree with Jill. I think passion is the key because money will follow that, somehow, someway. I would love to have one in four of the submitters be subscribers [laughter], but I also realize that's not exactly practical with the number of magazines and the number of submissions that these people are going for. So I don't know. I don't know if there's an easy answer to that one.

Zuniga: You just have to do things to build an audience. I think that we're all trying to have web presences or we try to throw parties or whatever, just to sort of build an audience that's excited about the product or excited about the magazine. (Product is sort of a weird thing to call it.) I think the key is creating community around the magazine and trying to get people that are readers and writers and fans of the magazine and editors—everybody together in a room. I think that feels really good. It feels really good to me to have that opportunity. Like I said earlier, we're competing with all these different media. Maintaining is largely about making enough noise to let people know you're out there so they can discover the magazine.

Roth: Following up with Jill, I want to thank publicly all of our interns who do an enormous amount of work for us and for free and they've been great. We cannot have made it without them. And, the last question—I feel like it is: "From Triple A to Field of Dreams." [Laughter] There are two versions of that. One is that if you build it they will come. And the other that artists are supposed to create the taste by which they are justified, which was quoted from a great poet. I think to do that is the only task of a literary magazine. I think eternal life is a strange desire for anything, and maybe certain magazines do have a limited life span. To go back to the issue of movement magazines, if you can fulfill an important function for ten years and launch a certain number of writers and change the tone or dynamic of the cultural conversation, you've succeeded. And everything after that is great but not necessary. To think we survive may not be the only goal of a literary magazine.

Zuniga: I like what you just said. That's true too.

Rosser: Yeah.

MR: How might literary magazines be different in the future?

Zuniga: I don't know if this will happen, but I think some of the things that Marco has been talking about would be a nice thing in terms of a greater mix of contents and a greater sense of necessariness and vitality and reporting, and really the full range of things as opposed to being too content to just fill one box or one genre or one traditional model. I don't know if there's any reason to think that will happen, but it would be nice.

Rosser: *The Virginia Quarterly Review* and *The Paris Review* seemed to have changed radically in a direction: more widespread concerns, not just literary community. I think that's a good sign. We do need more of that. However, the literary magazine, I hope, stays what it is. There are plenty of magazines that will cover these other issues, and if we cover them, they're going to be done in a literary manner, whatever that means. [Laughter] In a way in which the language itself is more exciting and electrifying perhaps than the content, or matches the content in terms of its appeal and aesthetic appeal and so forth. I would like to see more broad-mindedness in terms of what kinds of essays we're going to publish, and trying to—when we think of *Newsweek* and *Time* and the slicks—trying to provide a little more of world news in our literary magazine. I don't know if that's really possible without the quality taking a strange dive towards reportage of a different kind than what we want. I'm being very inarticulate here but I see a literary magazine opening itself up to more territory.

Zuniga: I just think the real push is going to be in the web, intelligently. I think the future of literary magazines is to have podcasts of authors reading their work or video of authors reading their work or video or audio of authors interviewing one another—just really expanding what is already being done that's great, but just doing it in a new way. Specifically with the interview aspect: you have the magazine, you read the stories and you go to the website, you download the podcast and you listen to the podcast, and then go to the end of that podcast where it's an interview, then maybe it says: Read this story. It sort of cycles. I think *Boundoff* and *Dublit* are two things that are doing some really exceptional stuff—not just presenting, but really doing it in an interesting way, especially *Dublit*. It's just magnificent. It looks magnificent. You just want to poke around and listen to things just because it looks so good. Personally, what I'd like to see is more literary parties with great-looking people. [Laughter]

Roth: Amen. When Todd was speaking, I had a vision. There are about four possible utopias, but one of them is a return to oral culture, which is what the web seems to be turning into. And then, when we say, more interviews, more visual . . . you know, authors aren't supposed to look great. I would rather have a stand-in read for me if it was going to be on video. I'm trying to come up with my actor alter ego who will volunteer. [Laughter] But this could happen, in the sense of if we abandon the silent reading or personal reading completely and go for a kind of community oral poetry or oral epic experience. There may be some literary magazines that make that their mission in the future. And then the other version would be, of course—as Jill was saying, I think—an expansion of literary journalism that, you know, journalism could do a bit more of the literary. And by literary, I mean, I would say a focus on language, and of course subjectivity, inner experience, the inherents of modernism and literary modernism and also the 19th century novel. We could get this kind of movement in which professional boundaries are being crossed more liberally and the borders are opening up in literature that were previously closed— by, in fact, the avant-garde movement that would say: We're going to go for concrete language poetry. So you would have a magazine that would publish nothing but concrete language poetry. Or only what's called "experimental fiction." And now the techniques have kind of been made available to everybody, so that chapter in the history of literary magazine publishing, the avant garde magazine, may be closed or closing, and what will come in its place is a more open mixture of genres, and it will be up to the magazine to pick among them or to ask which ones work. It will be the laboratory in which a lot of mixed genres start to appear, and that would be very interesting.

Rosser: The literary insularity that I was trying to refer to earlier—I don't think it's a bad thing. In fact, I think we need to think more about art than we already do, because the whole point of the literary magazine as I see it is that you want the more obscure, bold, risk-taking work to get seen, and the literary magazine is the one venue where it's not about: Can I sell this? Even we have to worry about, you know: Will people read this? Will they subscribe? Art is not going to evolve if we continue to just see the stuff that's in the more accepted, the more prominent literary magazines and glossy slicks. It's going to stagnate and die if we don't have this constant infusion of the new, the new vision. So we're so essential that I hesitate to say, "Well, we should branch out and become more journalistic," but I want also the magazine to feel relevant to anybody at a newsstand. This is not just about the small, exclusive literary world, a little club, but we also are thinking about the things that everyone should be thinking about. I would like to see a little more of that. I think that's possible in the future. And anybody here who has an online magazine that's different in content from the print, I would love to hear what those differences are other than brevity, if there are any other concerns, because we don't have that at *New Ohio Review*. We just have feed-highlighted features of the actual print magazine. I guess that's another question I'm throwing into the hopper.

Burch: The biggest separation is in brevity. *Hobart* started strictly online and then went to print, and for a while I was doing both, primarily myself. Then at some point I handed off the website to other editors. So there's definitely an entirely different editorial selection, but I think overall we're looking for similar stuff with the difference being in brevity. The most exciting thing that I've done personally, that I've gotten most excited about and that I want to do in the future (I have only done it for one issue thus far because of its time constraint)—but for one issue we did an entire corresponding online issue. It was a little gimmicky. It was kind of like a DVD bonus materials issue and so there were a couple of the people reading their stories, the podcast type thing that we've been talking about. I know a couple of writers sort of rewrote scenes from a different character's perspective or completely rewrote an ending. A couple of people actually had a photo essay that they put together to correspond with the story that we couldn't print in the issue, so we put that online. It was a bunch of additional materials that sort of fed into the same idea as the print, and so, hopefully, if they were looking at that online, they would be curious about the additional stories in print and vice versa, so there was kind of a back-and-forth dialogue between the two there.

Zuniga: I'm going to just declare that actually is the future, because that's awesome and I think that gives people what they want. They want to have interactivity. If they buy a magazine, they're going to be online later, so I think just going to a different destination, having a new experience with something, especially when you think of stories in magazines as these unchanging things. I mean that's incredible. I love that, Aaron.

Hammond: I agree wholeheartedly. I think that the dialogue, the possibility of the dialogic, is really going to expand the future for everything.

Zuniga: We've got an Opium Studio thing that's going to be an art focus thing, and that's going to be storytelling through art, basically, cartoons and things like that. And then we're planning on watching Opium Live soon after we get the studio done, and that's sort of a YouTube. I think what's interesting about that is that YouTube is just a mess. I never want to look at anything 'cause I never know what it is. There's no editorializing. That's something we're trying to do. Who knows how it's going to work, but we'll see how that goes. I think that's an attempt at the future on our part—but then again, money . . .

Hammond: At *The New York Quarterly* we've started a site that's interactive for our poets. It's basically an online index to the magazine, but when you pull up the poet's name, they can go in and build an entire profile and, you know, sell all their books through different venues, all sorts of different things, as well as interact with the magazine, do their galleys; they can submit online, all sorts of things. So that's one thing we've done, but we need to do more for the reader end of things in the future.

Some Comments on the 2008 *Mississippi Review* Roundtable on the Literary Magazine

by Herbert Leibowitz (2008)

As one of the oldest editorial kids on the block, let me offer some comments from the perspective of longevity. First, the question of money. *Parnassus*, which recently published its 30th Anniversary issue, was going to shut down because it lacked the funds to continue. When Willard Spiegelman, the editor of *The Southwest Review*, heard the news, he decided to publish a eulogy for the magazine before it was lowered into the grave—in *The Wall Street Journal*, of all places. As a result of his eloquence, a benevolent stranger stepped forward and gave us enough money to publish two more issues. Unless one has private wealth or receives an unimaginable legacy from a Ruth Lilly, as *Poetry* did, we all have to struggle to scrounge up the money to pay the printer, the landlord, the post office, the contributors, and ourselves. But money has, ultimately, little to do with literary quality. *Parnassus* can't begin to match the fees of *The New Yorker*, but some distinguished writers have written regularly for us because they've admired our stringency, stylishness, and eclecticism.

All editors like to think that had Walt Whitman sent "Song of Myself" to them, they would have immediately recognized its wild originality and clamored to publish the poem. We all wish to be the impresarios, talent scouts, clairvoyants, and angel Gabriel who bring the glad tidings to readers that a remarkable experimental novelist or lyrical poet is appearing in our pages. But the truth is, as many of the editors point out, such work is the exception: in our 1976 Bicentennial issue, we had the good fortune to publish Adrienne Rich's essay "Vesuvius at Home," which radically altered the way we viewed Emily Dickinson's poetry. There were other excellent essays in that issue, along with perfectly competent ones. That was a winning percentage. But sometimes the harvest is sparse. We are all familiar with the toxic poems and middling stories that fill our aptly named slush pile. We wade through them in search of a pearl or a diamond in the rough. There's nothing new under the sun about that. *Poetry*, our longest running poetry magazine, published landmark modernist poems by T. S. Eliot, Ezra Pound, Wallace Stevens, William Carlos Williams, and the Objectivists, but Harriet Monroe also chose reams of dull regional verse we no longer remember. Pound had to coax and strong-arm her into printing "Prufrock" and an exasperated Hart Crane had to explain "At Melville's Tomb" before she reluctantly agreed to publish it. Elizabeth Hardwick, a writer of fierce intelligence, once wisely admonished me to avoid the word "risky," because it is so subjective and imprecise—and self-congratulatory. What is caviar for one editor is trash fish for another. Small presses do sometimes put on stage voices of startling freshness and the trade houses sometimes do feature voices that have grown frayed and wobbly. I'm wary, though, of assigning all virtue to the small presses; their taste is not infallible, they can be rather clannish, enthroning one kind of poem. Perhaps the most brilliant book of poems of 2007, Cathy Park Hong's *Dance Dance Revolution*, was brought out by W. W. Norton.

Who gets to decide what's good literature? Certainly not a cadre of New York intellectuals, San Francisco "Language" poets, academic pontiffs, or the *vox populi* of poetry slams. Deciding what standards are applicable is a thorny issue for American democracy, with its long anti-intellectual tradition and its paranoid suspicion of elitism. Susan Jacoby has tried to rescue the word from its latest narrow definition "snobbism" and to remind us that The Founding Fathers were all elitists, well read in the classics and philosophy and adept in political disputation. In a culture's nonstop conversation and debate as to whether this novel or book of poems deserves praise or brickbats, all opinions are not created equal. An editor must judge the intellectual force or laziness of an argument, the accuracy or sloppiness of a critic's language: the insularity and factionalism in American poetry often leads to absurd *ex cathedra* pronouncements that poet A is a dreary formalist and poet B is the Second Coming of Yeats or Emily Dickinson. That is mere brand labeling, low-level polemics.

Space is a luxury most literary magazines do not have. But for a review magazine like *Parnassus*, I have long held that an author writing a retrospective of Zbigniew Herbert's or Kenneth Rexroth's *Collected Poems*, tracing the history of the ballad or the epigram, reinterpreting Surrealism or lovingly elaborating the glories of Classical Arab poetry needs ample room to make his or her case and to cast an enchanting spell. The Internet, of course, is the realm of vast cyberspace and black holes. My crystal ball is in the pawn shop, so I won't resort to prophecy, but this much I'll venture. Like all new technologies, it can be a medium for innovation or mindless grading, like most of the reviews on Amazon.com. In the blogosphere, I have read postings at stimulating sites and at boring ones. But the standards so far seem to me extremely loose and commonplace, too often a sort of infomercial or special pleading for one idea. I miss the pleasures of style and the provocations of making the reader set aside his prejudices and habits.

Nobody has mentioned the marvelous intangible of editing a literary magazine: foremost, the forging of friendships, first through an exchange of letters, then at a coffee shop or wine bar table talking about a Bosnian poet and baseball, the Bayeux tapestry, and a recipe for melon soup: one imagines he's sitting in The Mermaid Tavern with Keats, Hazlitt, Leigh Hunt, and Benjamin Haydon. Equal to that pleasure are the informal colloquies with the young poets who've come to intern at *Parnassus*, where we talk shop, assess reputations (irreverently), swap jokes, puns, clerihews, listen to a Schubert song. Such, such are the joys.

William Carlos Williams often said that he would have failed as a poet without the help of the little magazines. He founded *Contact* with Robert McAlmon, served as Consulting Editor to *Others*, submitted poems to the rigorous editorial eye of Marianne Moore, even invested some of his hard-earned cash in journals with tiny circulations whose life span was that of a mayfly. *Kora in Hell*, his Dadaist experiment, ran in *The Little Review* along with Joyce's *Ulysses*. I don't think literary magazines will disappear unless culture itself is obliterated. So, editors, sharpen those red pencils and make sure the delete button is working on your computers.

Too Many of Us, Too Much Noise

by Roxane Gay (2011)

It is very easy to start a literary magazine in this day and age. You don't need money. You don't need experience. All you need is Internet access and a few people who are willing to let you publish their work. A great many things have been democratized by the Internet and few more than publishing. But democracy is not always sustainable and this too has been proven by an explosion of literary magazines of varying degrees of quality, few of which are able to actually function as profitable endeavors.

There are few clever options for funding a magazine editors haven't tried—publishing big name writers, holding subscription drives, giveaways, and on and on. Editors sometimes come up with something really innovative but then that innovation wears off and it's back to the drawing board. Even most university-supported magazines are struggling. At *PANK*, our funding varies each year and it was never that much to begin with. We're lucky in that we do pretty well with sales, especially at conferences, but also via our website.

My co-editor and I also regularly ask ourselves, "How are we going to survive as a print magazine?" We have no earthly idea but I must also tell you I've started emotionally preparing for some day having to say, "We are not going to survive as a print magazine." Sales are good but are they enough? Not likely. We've branched into electronic offerings but is that enough? Not even close. We have some advertising but 80 percent of it is ad exchanges. We are distributed by two different distributors and have yet, in three years of distribution, to see one single penny. We're essentially giving the product away. It's maddening. With every issue, we have to compromise or consider compromises—should we stop publishing a two-color interior (yes); should we use a lesser paper (not yet); should we print fewer pieces in each issue (yes); should we change the size to a more traditional size (not yet). I won't even get into the nightmare of shipping costs but a nightmare it is—envelopes, postage, international rates, damaged issues, people who don't update their addresses, and on and on and on. It's all about money and there's never enough no matter what we do and it's mostly okay because we love what we do enough to do what needs to be done to keep it out there in the world.

I love the print magazine, the heft of it, the shape of the content we put in each issue, seeing the issue on my bookshelf and knowing that this artifact exists, that it cannot be deleted or unpublished. This is not nostalgia. I love the Internet and embrace electronic books but I also love opening a box of new issues and inhaling the smell of ink. I love taking the magazine to a coffee shop and reading through it even though I am already familiar with the work and I especially love attending conferences and fairs where I can talk to people about the magazine and put it in their hands and let them browse and ask questions. When something catches their eye, I love being able to talk to a new reader about why I fell in love with that piece. I often wish there was a way to do what I do at AWP, for example, online—a way to sell the magazine in a personal, passionate way. Something about a blog post or blurb on the digital screen is simply not the same because there's too much digital noise. There are too many editors writing about how awesome the work in each issue is and they mean it, they believe what they're saying, but so does everyone else in the virtual room saying those same things about their magazines.

If you ever get a chance to see Chris Newgent sell books at the Vouched Books table, you should. He started this small book concern where he has a table of books he's willing to vouch for. We've talked about it here [htmlgiant.com] before, but you have to see him in action at a reading or other event to really get how awesome the idea is in practice. People hover around the table and listen to him talk about the selections he has with him that day and more importantly, people actually buy the books. He's not getting rich off this but he is able to move books in a way that is personal and connected. He has a manageable inventory so you're not overwhelmed by 10,000 choices. You have twenty or so books to consider and someone who can tell you what you should know about each of those books so you are better informed to make a buying decision. It is concierge book selling at its finest. It's the kind of service you can get at an independent bookstore, only his enterprise is mobile. There is a lot to be said for curation, for saying, I'm not going to sell everything, I'm going to sell what I love most.

I went to the Borders store in the weeks before it closed down in a town about fifty miles from where I live, the closest thing to civilization in these parts. The liquidation had started and the store was a sad, sad place. I kind of wanted to step in front of a bus after a few minutes in the store. The stench of failure was everywhere. The coffee shop was already closed, empty chairs turned over on empty tables, most of the signage taken down. The bathrooms were permanently out of order and blocked by a large bookcase and an angry sign. The employees were in IDGAF mode and who can blame them? The ceiling was dripping with placards advertising shallow discounts on merchandise. Even with the discounts, Amazon was cheaper for many of the books I looked at. I checked on my phone. The store was a real mess, books everywhere, out of order, and more than books, there was a bunch of crap. That's the only word for it—toys and games and movies and bullshit you don't need to find in a bookstore. People milled about the store like buzzards feasting on carrion and hey, I was there too, looking for bargains. I almost bought a copy of Emily Griffin's *Something Borrowed* but the sticker price was $14.99 and the discount was 10%, and I was interested in paying like $2.99 for the book because the movie was terrible. As I looked around the store, even in its diminished capacity, I thought, "This is too much." How could anyone possibly know what to read in that store swollen with books, too many of them mediocre? How could any reading experience be meaningful amidst so many choices?

This is a question we face when we buy books online too but online you can read about a book on a blog, or in *Bookslut* or in a *Fancy Newspaper Review of Books*, for however long those last, and then you can consult Google and find a writer's website and see what other people are saying and you can have something to go on before you buy that book.

When it comes to literary magazines, you can visit that magazine's website and maybe they have a blog and maybe they take the time to update that blog with some regularity. Maybe they're on Facebook and Twitter and now, Google Plus, and maybe they update those because to get anywhere, you have to be everywhere online. You can also consult Google and see what people are saying about a magazine, if people are saying anything about a magazine, though let's be real, most of the time, it's just the writers published in that magazine. You can consult Duotrope and learn some statistical information. In a few cases, you can go to an actual bookstore and browse that magazine but there's a lot to keep track of. There are so many damn magazines. I subscribe to too many. I subscribe to more magazines than I can possibly read. The only ones I read with regularity these days are *American Short Fiction* and *The Paris Review* and with everything else, I read single issues and do the best I can but I can't keep up because there are also online magazines, you see, and let us not forget, there are books, which I also enjoy. We are inundated by content because we are inundated by content creators, all clamoring to put themselves in front of an audience who will see them hear them feel them touch them. I don't think there's anything necessarily wrong with all this but it's something that has to be acknowledged.

I read something about a writer who staged a fake kidnapping or something like that to get the attention of an agent so he might sell his book. That depressed me too, the idea that he didn't believe in the strength of his writing, he believed in the strength of his psychotic ploy. He believed that in order to stand out, he had to do something absurd. Is this what we have come to? I've said it before and I still believe it to be true—cream rises to the top. If the writing is there, what you want for your writing will come, maybe not in the timeframe you want or in the package you originally envisioned, but it will come. Perhaps I tell myself this because like most writers, I'm putting in the work and I'm waiting and I am hoping something comes of it. When I read about writers staging fake kidnappings, though, I wonder. I wonder what the next crazy writer is going to do to satisfy that need to have your work read.

I've often seen the argument that if literary magazines were selling what people wanted, they'd be able to financially sustain themselves, placing the blame on content or aesthetic. Sometimes that might be the case but I don't believe it often is. I also don't believe that writers not supporting the magazines is the problem. That's a tired argument. Writers support magazines just fine.

Are literary magazines selling something people (beyond writers) don't want? I don't know. I guess, based on how dismal the financial outlook is for nearly every literary magazine in the country, the answer is yes. What do we do about that? How do we get readers who are not writers? I personally have no problem with writers as the primary audience for a magazine because so many people want to be writers. Saying writers are the only audience for literary magazines is like saying people who like to swim and go to the beach are the only market for bathing suits.

Sometimes, I think there are too many magazines just like I felt, that night in Borders, that there were too many damn books in the store. Everyone wants to be a writer, but increasingly, everyone wants to be an editor, too. Everyone thinks that they have some special vision only they can usher into the world. Almost daily, I get an e-mail from an editor saying, "Hey, I'm starting a new magazine." You look at Duotrope and know the one thing we have in surfeit is magazines. Not all of them are great but my goodness, if you want to be published, start working your way through the list. It's going to happen. As an editor, I get it, the desire to start a magazine. Editing is awesome, and being able to discover work and shape issues the way you want is fun and interesting. I've learned so much as an editor and hope I have the privilege of doing it for a long time to come.

And yet, I also think, another new magazine? Another RandomAss-Magazine.blogspot.com run by an editor who doesn't care enough to even spend $10 on a domain name and maybe a little more on a Wordpress installation? Another magazine where the editors don't know how they're going to fund each print issue? Another magazine where the editors don't bother to even copyedit the content let alone show a little editorial direction by actually working with writers? Are these magazines, multiplying exponentially, really going to offer something we've never seen before? Is becoming an editor really that important?

One of the primary challenges with getting people to buy magazines is that there are too many. It's not that magazines aren't doing great work or that editors aren't marketing their product well or that they haven't found the right price point or whatever magical solution we're all desperately searching for. People want to read the exciting work in Magazines A, B, C, D, E, F, and G through Z but it's not financially feasible to subscribe to all those magazines and there's so much noise that it's hard to find a way of saying that Magazine P is worth buying over Magazine V. The audience is there for magazines, but too much product is available. Look at the annual book fair at the annual Associated Writing Programs conference. The book fair is insanity. It's a thrilling insanity, but there are more magazines there than you could possibly read in a lifetime and at each table two or three people stand there and tell you, "We love great writing," and each of those people is telling you the God's honest truth. Most of them are committed to leaving the literary world better than they found it but none of us want to admit that we're running out of oxygen in the room. The good news, I think, is that we (writers, readers, editors) love this literature thing so much, we'll endure the tightening in our chests as long as we can.

Cate Marvin Discusses the VIDA Count: An Interview

by Marcelle Heath (2011)

In February 2011, VIDA, an organization for women writers, released what has been called the VIDA Count, a totaling of male vs. female writer bylines for 14 of the top 2010 literary-type magazines. The numbers found the—perhaps expected—much greater representation of male writers in these publications. VIDA has also "counted" female writers in other publishing venues, and has done more counts since 2010: www.vidaweb.org

Marcelle Heath: VIDA's 2010 Count has caused quite a stir in the literary community, generating debate about VIDA's findings on the number of women contributors and reviews by women authors at the top magazines in the country. Many writers and editors were shocked by the glaring gender disparity in publishing. Others, like myself, were (unfortunately) validated by the pie charts: they represented both our personal experiences and deepest fears about institutionalized and pervasive sexism. While many expressed support and offered new ways to include more women, there were some who criticized and dismissed VIDA's methodology.

What was your initial reaction when you saw the data? Were you surprised by how it's been received by both the editors at the magazines in The Count and the public at large?

Cate Marvin: A SHORT ANSWER:

I was both surprised and not at all surprised by the numbers. I think I may have hoped to be surprised. That I hoped the numbers would not turn out as they did. Even though I fully suspected they would.

We at VIDA were gratified by the attention the "2010 Count" received, and especially pleased to find that so many editors were willing to re-assess their own "numbers"—because a great many venues have taken it upon themselves to conduct their own counts.

THE LONGER ANSWER:

I didn't have what one could call an "initial reaction" to the numbers because the process of acquiring the data was so lengthy and time-consuming.

The idea for VIDA's "2010 Count" was conceived almost immediately once the organization was formed, back in August of 2009, at which point I was in conversation with several female writers; it soon became apparent that the practice of "counting" was nearly uniform among us. I was then directed to Juliana Spahr and Stephanie Young's essay "Numbers," which looks at gender disparity in the representation of women in anthologies of avant garde poetry. (This is a terrific essay, by the way, one that I urge anyone interested in "counting" to make a point of reading.)

We at VIDA were still in the process of figuring out how to launch "The Count" when *Publisher's Weekly* "Best Books of 2009" list came out. This required an immediate response on our behalf and provided the impetus for our first press release regarding the omission of women authors from prominent "best of" lists and awards. However, we'd always planned to address a number of different venues in our "Count." VIDA's "2010 Count" is only one of several we have underway.

We're presently in the thick of counting The Best American Series, for example, the numbers for which we'll be posting on the VIDA site mid-April.

The "2010 Count," in particular, was dreadfully ambitious from the beginning. We pulled together a list of prominent literary venues and review venues; I then made it a personal project to acquire the table of contents for these publications. One assumes it'd be easy enough to access much of this information online; however, the content of a lot of magazine websites tends to be difficult to dissect due to the merged display of print content and online content. Some magazines require a subscription for accessing online content. And while one may also acquire access to media content via databases such as JSTOR and Lexus-Nexus, it's nearly impossible to turn up a decipherable table of contents pages. For these aforementioned reasons, I ultimately resorted to photocopying print versions of numerous TOCs at my local library.

Throughout July and August of 2010, I spent much of my free time counting. I had opted to not put my then 18-month-old daughter in daycare in order to save money. So, during the days I cared for her, I all too often lugged said daughter along with me to the library. During the evenings, while she slept, I counted.

Thus, by the time VIDA's "2010 Count" appeared, in early February of 2011, I'd already spent a lot of time with the numbers. And it's a very troubling affair. Like you, many of my suspicions were confirmed. But I was also pretty surprised at just how consistent the findings were. I honestly didn't think *The New Yorker* would count the way it did: the evening I counted the *NYer* (I think I finally went to bed at 4 a.m.), I remember feeling distinctly demoralized. I'll admit: I'd entertained hopes of publishing a poem within its esteemed pages someday. Yet, after counting, this aspiration seemed ridiculous. I felt like a bit of a fool for having believed it possible. So, in answer to your initial question, seeing the numbers depressed the hell out of me.

In fact, I often (jokingly) say that VIDA will end up giving me cancer, as my smoking habit escalated with all of the counting I was doing during last summer, so often late into the night, by which I really mean into the early morning.

And it was a bitch to track down all of the magazines. My local library simply wasn't cutting it. So I finally relented and put my daughter into daycare, headed up to Columbia University's library, where I was able to find much of what I needed. That's one heavenly library. Later, I'd have the wisdom to hit the New York Public Library. They have everything. It was fascinating to see the history of certain venues, such as the Best American Short Stories, which was launched as a "yearbook" in 1915. Looking at the authors who were published in the volumes from the inception of the series really struck home the fact that it's a career-making publication.

As I moved on to counting other venues, I began to feel the shadow of cynicism cross over me. I began to develop the suspicion that I was the butt of a huge joke. I'd be in the city, riding on the subway, or sitting in a restaurant, and notice women of all types and ages reading *The New Yorker*, *Harper's*, *The New York Review of Books*; photos of male authors seemed to peer out at me from the pages, gloating. I wanted to ask these female readers if they were, in fact, enjoying what they were reading, ask if they noticed that nearly every article they perused was written by a man, that nearly every review addressed a book by a male author. And, if they did realize this, how did they feel about it?

September rolled around and I was back to teaching. I began to procrastinate when it came to counting. Frankly, the project had become distasteful. I had piles of TOCs scattered all over my house, stacked in my closet, piling up in my office at school. It was too much! I began to despair as to whether the project would ever be completed.

I then wisely enlisted the help of several women from VIDA. We divvyed up the TOCs and began counting in earnest. We were very careful: at least two or three individuals counted each venue, then cross checked their results with one another.

Some have derided the VIDA Count as "unscientific." It's true that we just presented the numbers. But we made every effort to ensure the numbers were accurate. The night before we launched, I stayed up till dawn on the phone with a close friend (and VIDA intern) who has bookkeeping expertise. She re-tabulated all of our data to ensure its accuracy.

By the time we completed VIDA's 2010 Count, I no longer took offense at the numbers. I know this may sound strange, but I actually found the whole affair funny—no, hysterical. What were these editors thinking? Or, perhaps they were not thinking. About their readership. I came to the conclusion that the female readership is largely ignored, which is also funny, given that we make up such a large percentage of their readers (and, as such, we are the primary consumers of their product). If these editors were financially savvy, wouldn't they include more female contributors? Wouldn't they review more books by women?

I began to wonder why I ever considered myself an appropriate reader for these magazines in the first place. It suddenly seemed so clear that their content was never intended for me. But this also struck me as absurd, given the fact I'm an English professor and writer; wouldn't I be among their targeted readership?

The fact is, I often felt bored when reading these publications. (And I felt guilty for being bored!) Now I know why (whereas before, I felt I ought to be interested). I don't subscribe to any of these magazines. Anymore.

Just as the 2010 Count was making its debut in February of 2011, several persons from the press contacted me. Before founding VIDA, I'd had very little contact with the media. One individual congratulated me on a "great story." As a writer, this struck me as odd, because as far as "stories" are concerned, the VIDA Count required absolutely no imagination.

Heath: There are many vital conversations taking place regarding The Count, including the perception that women's writing is less than: less interesting, less intellectual, less serious, less relevant, etc., etc. In addition, many people have essentialist notions of identity in relation to women professionalizing themselves as writers: i.e., we don't send out stuff because we're insecure, we're not as aggressive as our male counterparts, etc., etc. What surprises me is how little attention is given to the fact that we live in a society that devalues women in all aspects of our lives, that these "essential" ideas about women and men are rooted in the fiction we continue to create—in language, in politics, in literature, and that these myths perpetuate inequality.

What do you make of the disconnect between perception and reality in terms of how women are perceived as writers and the fictional narratives both women and men create to perpetuate these myths?

Marvin: This is a question I'd like to pose to anyone who believes that literature plays a significant role in our culture. It is, in fact, the question that we at VIDA hoped the Count would prompt. But, here, you are asking me to speak to how I understand it. And, to be honest, I don't. I don't understand how people aren't generally taken aback by evidence that is presented daily in media that women are tremendously undervalued, and often dismissed. This is, of course, the root of the problem.

And isn't it awfully funny that we're having this conversation in 2011? But it's not funny, at all. It's pretty scary, especially if you're a woman. Even if you're a woman who's never intended to write and doesn't much care for reading.

I personally think that women, as an entity, are quite adaptable, and that we've managed to accommodate the falsehood of "equality," and much of this has to do with being "polite." We are quite literally trained by society to understand ourselves as less significant than men—and even when we know that we are capable of greatness, we have also learned our place—and we know we will be criticized for being too outspoken or ambitious. From my experience with those who work on VIDA, women enjoy productive discussions, and would prefer to leave the arena when things get unnecessarily combative or ugly. I think it's time we express our experiences and perceptions candidly, that we raise our objections when we feel them rise within ourselves. Too many women feel uncomfortable expressing themselves. I think the root of this lies in that we fear we'll be disliked, or that we'll be shunned. I think we should model the behaviors we wish to see enacted by others. I hope we can more firmly and cogently express our viewpoints, without apology, and that we will work to support one another. We really need to support one another. We need to learn as much as we can about one another's work, about the different genres we're working within, because we all share the same obstacles. And I don't think men are outside this conversation. A great many male editors and writers are themselves deeply interested in bringing women's voices to the forefront. I think the sooner the conversation becomes "about" gender, and less "between" genders, we'll recognize that we're all interested (one hopes) in a shared goal: parity.

Heath: What are VIDA's expectations and goals for The Count? What are your goals for the organization as a whole?

Marvin: We at VIDA want to create a conversation. Many conversations. We wish, quite simply, to create a forum in which people who are concerned about gender disparity in literature can speak to one another. As such, we are about to launch a "forum" on our website in which members may carry on such conversations.

We're also about to launch a blog, which we're calling, after the Sexton poem, "Her Kind." We plan to invite two writers at a time to conduct an extended exchange of ideas in response to specific questions provided by our blog editors, Rose Ben-Oni and Arisa White, who will serve as curators of these conversations.

We've also spoken a lot about establishing fellowships for female writers who are interested in engaging in critical discourse. We'd very much like to provide a substantial stipend, in addition to offering a retreat for such writers at which they would be mentored by writers with experience in this field. We want to help women writers become major players in the field of criticism, reviews, op-ed pieces, etc. It's become obvious that we need more women presenting their critical prose to the literary world at large.

Finally, one of our ultimate goals is to host a national conference that focuses solely on women's writing and its cultural reception, and we intend to include the genres of fiction, creative nonfiction, poetry, as well as playwriting and children's literature. We'd like for this conference to be less commercial than, say, AWP or MLA. By which I mean, we hope to offer a flat rate for all participants (rather than providing institutional memberships, which ultimately favor academics). It would be great if we could provide housing at a low cost; this might be made possible were we to conduct our conference at a university campus. Most obviously, we would want to provide daycare. We wish to host a more intimate conference, one that isn't so much focused on networking, as it is on building community.

Heath: I am often challenged to confront and question my own privilege in my work as well as erroneous ideas about women in general. Often, I fail. What informs your work as a poet and professor? How do you articulate your identity, and what vision(s) do you have for your writing?

Marvin: I prefer that my poems don't answer to identity; rather, I desire that they create their own identities. The most seductive and wondrously empowering aspect of writing is that one can own the page. I personally work with the assumption that I'm not required to be faithful to the actual. And, for me, that's what's writing's about. Escaping the body. Becoming autonomous through being anonymous, and thereby finding a space within which the mind and heart may engage the page.

When writing, I don't think about numbers.

COUNTING BODIES: NOTES FOR FURTHER CONSIDERATION

by Marcelle Heath (2012)

When newly appointed Yahoo CEO Marissa Mayer says that she is not a feminist, she is telling us why VIDA's work is critical for feminism. Historically, the privileges conferred for writers whose work appears and is reviewed by editors in *NYRB*, *Harper's*, *New Yorker*, *Atlantic*, etc. have been readings, grants, fellowships, awards, and employment. Historically, works that appear in and are reviewed by these publications have been edited, curated, anthologized, canonized, taught, sanctioned, appropriated, rewarded, criticized, censored, commended, and so forth. The canon and the publishing paradigm that supports it is, of course, expanding into new modes of critical inquiry and engagement with technological changes. Is there a connection between the resistance to digital publishing and the proliferation and inclusion of women writers within online platforms?

Since the publication of my interview with Cate Marvin, VIDA has published two more counts, the 2011 Count and Best American Count, both with largely dismal numbers. Many editors have taken up VIDA's call. *Granta* issue 115, "The F Word," included well-known luminaries alongside talented newcomers, and I appreciated its attempt to contextualize feminist projects across the globe, but felt it was lacking in scope and vision. Iman Quershi rightly notes in her review of "The F Word" that "More often than not, writers dredge up the same old arguments, air grievances in the same old ways and portray women in the same stereotypical manner which pop culture does ad nauseam." *PANK*'s Queer Issues have been more successful in presenting new and exciting work. In September of 2012, *Brevity* will be publishing *Ceiling or Sky: Female Nonfictions After the VIDA Count*. Roxane Gay's 2012 essay "We Are Many, We Are Everywhere" in *The Rum-*

pus brought a breath of fresh air when she provided a comprehensive list of writers of color to make the point about the ways in which people see, quite literally, what they want to see. The popular site We Who Are About To Die recently began their Ladies Represent column.

Some editors have looked to more problematic assumptions about women writers, such as the reason behind the existing gender disparity. *Tin House*'s Rob Spillman echoed a tired and facile argument when he noted that women are less aggressive than men when it comes to marketing and responding to solicitations. There were darker and more hilarious responses to VIDA in online comments and on websites and blogs, everything from calling out VIDA for using red to depict male writers to denigrating women authors as male-hating chick lit opportunists to declarations of inaccuracy and fraud with VIDA's methodologies. One of the most revealing answers to the issue of sexism in publishing came when I asked Jarrett Haley of *BULL: Fiction for Men* about Laura Miller's article in *Salon* on the exclusion of women in *Publishers Weekly*'s 10 Best List of 2009. Haley said, "As to whether women get their due share of critical recognition and prestige, well, I just don't have a dog in that fight." Actually, we all have a dog in the fight. Every reader who cares about literature and the multitude of ways it is and is not disseminated and consumed has a dog in this fight. The bodies are lined up, waiting to be counted.

"If ever there appears on this earth such a thing as an editorial art, it will be when commercial timidity is removed from the inner office and a spirit of free and genuine sport is enshrined there," wrote *Max Eastman in his 1916 book,* Journalism Versus Art.

THE NEW GRAPHIC LITERARY JOURNAL: AN INTERVIEW WITH STEVEN HELLER

by David Barringer (2006)

The new graphic literary journal is a transitional species in the evolution of a book to a magazine. The traditional lit journal aspires to the artistic permanence of a book while the new graphic lit journal willingly risks the disposability of a magazine by cavorting with contemporary graphic design. Lit journals define themselves by an emphasis on the short story, essay, and poem. By engaging contemporary visual culture, they have a new dimension in which to strive for Eastman's "editorial art."

The risk is the same one identified by Eastman ninety years ago: "the aim of a money-making magazine is to give neither intense pleasures nor intense displeasures to a few, but to please everybody a little all the time." The traditional lit journal occupies a small niche of the magazine market, greatly pleasing a very few. The new lit journal aims to enlarge its audience and, through the use of contemporary graphic design, please a whole lot more.

David Barringer: With your knowledge of design (especially given your book *Merz to Emigre and Beyond: Avant-Garde Magazine Design of the Twentieth Century*), what do you think makes for successful "editorial art" in the realm of the little magazine? Are you on the same page with Eastman, or is he outdated?

Steven Heller: Max Eastman was a smart editor. Interestingly, when he edited *The Masses,* the "editorial art" was decided upon by the contributors: George Bellows, John Sloane (the art editor), Art Young, Boardman Robinson, among them. According to histories of *The Masses,* these contributors

EMIGRE

é·mi·gré (em'ə grā)

The Magazine That Ignores Boundaries

Keeping
Myths Alive
Issue
....
Featuring
....
Henk R. Elenga
....
John Fante
....
Escape Mechanism
....
Motown over
Moscow
....
Pull-Out Poster
....
Magritte's Hat
....
The Cremation of
Sam McGee
....
George Sand

4

Price $5.-

presented their work to people assembled in the editorial offices in Greenwich Village on a specific night. The approval or disapproval came more from these huddled masses than the editors. That for me would be a nightmare. I'm all for art for the people, but having the lumpen determine what is good art is dangerous, if not foolhardy. I think Eastman finally took more control later on, but this kind of democracy can be injurious to any art. Granted the art of *The Masses* was meant to be polemical, but individual expression can be extremely polemical, too, without neophytes offering their uneducated opinions. I think successful "editorial art"—which includes typography, illustration, ornamentation, and other visual matter—is best when the artist has free reign to create. An art director or art editor can push, pull, and otherwise make better (if necessary), but the initial impetus must come from the artist or designer, who, after all, is the expert. An editor (indeed many editors) may feel they know about art, but rarely are they truly fluent enough to make a mediocre piece good, and often make good work mediocre.

Barringer: How did, say, one or two great little mags of the past express this "editorial art"?

Heller: There are so many little magazines, and each has or had unique ways of creating content. I am reminded of the anti-fascist magazine *Direction*, published in the late '30s and early '40s. Paul Rand did many but not all of its covers, and had the freedom to do what he wanted. He was paid a small sum in return (and given some original art by Le Corbusier as payment, too); he dictated what the look and feel of the covers would be. Inside, the magazine layout was rather simple and pedestrian, but the covers set the memorable tone. Similarly, in the '60s a French magazine called *Opus* allowed a single artist, Roman Czechlovitz (wrong spelling), to design almost each cover. His work was bold and smart—sometimes conceptual, other times not. But his continued contribution insured their identity, and also gave the artist a chance to grow. There are many magazines past and present that allow individuals to carry the graphic weight. I think this is very beneficial. But there are other little magazines, like *The Ganzfeld*, for example, that are rooted in visual content, and employ many different artists, cartoonists, and designers. Since the magazine is a visual entity, the variety is expected, even if the various expressions are surprising.

Barringer: What can today's lit journals, who are embracing graphic design, learn from these great little mags of the past?

Heller: Trust! Trust the designer or artist to do good work for the benefit of the journal. Dave Eggers accomplishes this with *McSweeney's*. Moreover, even though his journal is word-driven, his design and choice of artists are

key to the success of his identity and content. He makes the selections—he is the final arbiter—but it starts with a basic, fundamental, and overriding trust in those who make the visual decisions.

Barringer: Lit journals are periodicals that look like books, some of which are now trying to look more like conventional magazines. The forms can be at odds because, as you say, the magazine is primarily a visual entity while the lit journal is word-driven. One compromise might be to focus on typography. What little mags in the past have successfully embraced typography as a means to enhance the graphic while still emphasizing text?

Heller: Going back in history, typography was always important. It just wasn't flashy or illustrative the way magazine typography is today. *The Little Review* back in the '30s was typographically sophisticated—some issues were even risqué in a Dada or Constructivist sense. The original *Playboy* of the '20s was likewise ambitious. And as I've noted, *McSweeney's* is very much about its typographical scheme, as is its sister publication, *The Believer*. Take a magazine like *The New Criterion*: it is typographically bland but nonetheless pristine. It obviously chose not to be overt, but uses a limited palette of elegant faces. Some editors understand type; others do not. Some little magazines can afford a typographic stylist; others cannot. It's a crap shoot.

Barringer: Many of the aesthetically strong avant-garde magazines in your book *Merz to Emigre* are politically motivated or they are propounding a new literary or artistic movement. This critical attitude seems to galvanize a visual identity which in part consists of a struggle to achieve a new relationship between word and image. Is there something about strong emotion (outrage, anger, resentment) that fuels good magazine design?

Heller: Not at all. But first can you define what good magazine design is? The Dada journals were not good—in the conventional sense—design, but they served their purposes: to shock (at first) and to convey material in an irreverent manner. Design can be used for ideological reasons which may, in turn, define a periodical's stance. But I've seen many politically radical magazines in which the design stinks. That said, in retrospect, a periodical like, say, the Black Panther Party newspaper or *The East Village Other* are badly designed or non-designed, but now have a patina of history, which makes the design less onerous and more understandable.

Barringer: Wyndham Lewis's *The Enemy* No. 2 (1927) could serve as an inspiration for the lit journals of today: personal, idiosyncratic, and more like a book than a periodical. What were the graphic contributions of the Futurist/Vorticist periodicals, like Lewis's, to the development of the little magazine?

Heller: Those were the days when little magazines and journals were the first lines of "offense" in the war against complacency. So they had a huge impact on each other. Like the internet, many of these magazines were the connective tissue of a movement, given out at exhibitions and passed from one art group to the other. I doubt they had a big influence on major mainstream magazines, although some of the visual conceits rubbed off. The French *VU*, for instance, was heavily photomontaged, just like the Communist party's *USSR in Construction* or *AIZ*, the German communist paper.

Barringer: For the editors of traditional lit journals, looking down on graphic art is often still part of what it means to be literary. In the *2006 Artist's & Graphic Designer's Market* book, for example, one journal sniffs that they use art, not graphic art, and only for their covers. This view stems from an ignorance about the history of graphic art and its relationship to the little magazine. I'm fascinated, for example, by the relevant examples of *Minotaur* (1930s), *View* (1940s) and *VVV* (1940s). What was so unique about how these magazines managed to pack up art, culture and literature in their designs?

Heller: Have you heard the term "The Whole Work of Art"? I can't remember it in German, something like *Gestemswerk*. There were few distinctions between art forms because that was the nature of these art movements. The Futurists saw advertising as a mass-appeal medium and sought to engage in it as they engaged in painting. Of course, fashion, architecture, packaging, etc. were also part of this equation. The magazines of which you speak were born out of this sensibility. They did, however, reject mass-market magazine conceits and traditions, but replaced them with their own versions of "applied art." They also wanted to make statements that could be best presented in multiple mediums. Graphics were poetic, words were conveyed through graphics. It was also cheaper to produce these magazines back in the late '30s and early '40s. By the '50s and '60s, costs mounted for halftones and color separations.

Barringer: When lit journals go graphic, some seem driven not by an obsession to create "editorial art" but by a desire to increase their audience. So they look to popular magazines for reference. Using more graphics is the very strategy for becoming more like popular magazines. What are the dangers here?

Heller: The danger of emulating the mainstream is always the slavish perpetuation of cliché. That said, little magazines like *Poetry* (with its long tradition) or *Story* use or used great illustrators who also work for mass-market mags. *Poetry* uses a lot of the excellent conceptual illustrators—like Henrik

Drescher—and *Story* (while it was still publishing) had each cover done by R. O. Blechman. I don't think they were copying the mainstream as much as using great talent that can be found more readily in media than those starving painters who hang in garrets.

Barringer: *Tin House*, for example, uses a recognizable magazine format both in their covers and their layouts. *Zoetrope-All Story* invites guest designers to give each issue a visual look, but, as I understand it, they can't touch the text. Even *Ninth Letter*, a remarkably ambitious periodical produced by students and faculty at the University of Illinois, uses graphics mainly as background framing for untouched columns of text. The graphics are uniformly pleasing, pretty, and safe. What strategies can get a little magazine out of these design *cul de sacs* (assuming it wants to turn itself around)? Or do commercial aspirations doom a little magazine to the aesthetics of emulation?

Heller: Good art directors and designers can make a big difference (of course, that's a self-serving answer). One of my favorite little magazines today is *Esopus* (I even contributed to it, and may be on the advisory panel). It is edited and designed by Tod Lippy, a former editor of *Print* magazine and *Scenario*, and former publisher of another little magazine. He was never trained as a designer, but he's one of the most creative art directors I know. The magazine is a cinematic experience because he was also a filmmaker in a past life. I also love *Zembla*, which regrettably has stopped publishing. But it was brilliantly designed by Vince Frost, a remarkable designer. It was actually a joy to behold and read.

Barringer: Eastman thought a freedom from commercial timidity could unleash a sporting spirit, and you've said the work is best when a creator has "free reign." So here are these transitional lit journals with a perfect opportunity to be sporting, to be polemic, to serve as the vehicles for strong critical creativity. Without pressure to maintain high circulations, without the need to compete with the slick glossy magazines, and with funds for a year or two of a little magazine, how can an obsessive creator make the most of this opportunity?

Heller: Avoid being rigid. Too often rules are established at the outset and they're the wrong rules. I don't believe in anarchy, but I do support license at least until a personality is well established. Brodovitch's motto was "Astonish Me!" The design for his magazine *PORTFOLIO*, which lasted only three issues, was truly astonishing. It was risky, because the editor/publisher took no advertising, and the money dried up. BUT for the moments it existed, the creative sky was not even the limit.

There is a compelling value to staying in print...producing and circulating...[books and journals]
that maintain a monitory presence and therefore a psychic weight. A gravitas, in the subculture of
serious readers.
                                                                    —*Laurence Goldstein*

PRAIRIE SCHOONER'S TRADITIONS OF TRANSPORT: LITERARY PUBLISHING IN THE ACADEMY

by Hilda Raz (2003)

I'd like to talk about the venerable literary quarterly *Prairie Schooner*'s history as a scholarly work-in-progress, then turn to some questions about the place of belletristic (or creative) writing in the academy, the role of journals in the mission of university presses, their value to academic departments, and our increasing interest in creative writing in a time of shrinking student enrollments. I'll cite some statistics, make some conjectures, and close with my favourite joke. Today I speak as a professor, a past member of the board of the Associated Writing Programs and a past president, a past member of the executive committee of the College of Arts and Sciences at the University of Nebraska, a writer, and the Glenna Luschei endowed editor of *Prairie Schooner.*

Nothing much was said to me about *Prairie Schooner*'s long history when I took over as the fifth editor. We were too busy to look back. I assembled staff, read manuscripts, called and attended meetings, read proof, wrote letters, and enjoyed most of academic life. The best part of each day was the mail. One day I opened a letter that began,

> What might interest you is the fact that I was one of the founding fathers of your fine magazine. I worked my way through university as a reporter on the local paper and was a friend of Lowry Wimberly's [a professor of English]. He was not a dour man, but that is how he looked. One day in 1926, as I was crossing campus, he called out, 'Don't you think we ought to have a literary magazine?' I said, 'Of course. Good idea.' And Lowry said, 'Good. I'll put you on the committee.' Which he did. I can't remember that

Prairie Schooner

Summer 2004 $9.00

we ever did meet, but I suppose we did. I think there were
five of us. Ed Morrow [Edward R. Murrow, the reporter]
was probably another.

The letter was signed 'Edward Stanley,' and the enclosed photo showed a white-haired man sitting by a swimming pool. Stanley's letter was a surprise. No one, to my knowledge, had heard his name. But when we looked, our files showed that the early committee of *Prairie Schooner* included the famous Loren Eiseley, as well as Weldon Kees and another less familiar name, a student named Volta Torry, who became editor of *Popular Science* magazine. The files also showed that Don Weldon, a friend of Torry's, who wrote for *Prairie Schooner* in the early days as Weldon D. Melick, later wrote 'Personality Pieces' for *Popular Science*, interviews with famous people—Jack Benny and George Burns, for example—that apparently made him famous. He went to Hollywood straight from university and became the youngest contract writer there, with fifty movie credits and a charter membership in the Writers' Guild of America.

Long before anyone here present was born, the editorial staff of *Prairie Schooner*, a magazine begun in 1926 with the support of the land-grant University of Nebraska, was filled with young people who would become successful writers. Another was Jim Thompson. His twenty-nine novels have had a revival, and three of them—*The Grifters*, *The Kill-Off*, and *The Getaway*—were made into movies; it was Thompson who wrote the screenplay for Stanley Kubrick's powerful anti-war film *Paths of Glory*. In 1993, when Robert Polito called the office, we recovered another piece of our history. (Polito's biography of Thompson, *Savage Art*, won the 1995 National Book Critics Circle Award.) From 1929 to 1931 Jim Thompson was a member of the committee, one of 'Wimberly's Boys,' as the group of talented kids he identified and encouraged came to be called. Another was pioneering folklorist Ben Botkin, later at Harvard and the Library of Congress. And Edward Stanley, the writer of the letter that started this inquiry, whose nickname was 'Tuck,' after his favourite stage role, became division editor of the AP and AP Wirephoto. For eighteen years he was head of NBC's Division of Public Affairs and Education, where he started the first television series for college credit, *Continental Classroom*, and then *Meet the Press*. Three thousand other programs were his initiatives, and he published two novels, published in Harriet Monroe's magazine *Poetry*, and interviewed Robert Frost and Carl Sandburg on TV, as well as William Butler Yeats, his favourite, whom he remembered as 'young and vigorous and, in fact . . . on the edge of his second blooming.' Tuck Stanley himself had a second blooming, but that's another story. He died on May 17, 1989, but not before we'd become good friends through the mail. We have his letters and photos in our files. His son endowed our annual Stanley Prize shortly after Tuck's death.

The dour Professor Lowry Wimberly—our third editor, Bernice Siote, who'd been his student, told me he suggested 'The Decay of the World' for her thesis, but she declined—apparently had the gift of inspiration. The complete list of his committee is too long to give here, but it includes Robert Lasch, later a Rhodes Scholar, who worked on the *Omaha World Herald*, then the *Chicago Sun*, and was for many years editor of the *St. Louis Post Dispatch*; and Mari Sandoz, another one of his 'boys.' Sandoz's short story 'The Vine,' written when she was an undergraduate and published under her given name, Marie Macumber, was the first story in volume one, number one, of *Prairie Schooner*. Not long after, we were publishing the first stories of Eudora Welty.

If local professor Lowry Wimberly was in fact our first editor, Karl Shapiro, the Pulitzer Prize-winning poet, was our second, from 1956 to 1963. Sandoz, by then a famous writer living in New York, took quite an interest in the search. Although some contemporary accounts say that she brought Shapiro to *Prairie Schooner*, in fact she was as surprised as anyone else by this Maryland-and-Virginia-raised Jew in Nebraska. He stayed until a censorship dispute provoked his resignation, at which time his poetry editor, Professor Bernice Siote, a poet and scholar whose book on John Keats won the 1958 *Explicator* Award, became editor. Siote brought a new staff member to *Prairie Schooner*: her friend and partner, editor-in-chief of the University of Nebraska Press, Virginia Faulkner, who had been the ghost writer of at least one best seller—the famous madam Polly Adler's memoir, *A House Is Not Home*. She'd been a writer for *Duffy's Tavern*, too, the popular radio show of the forties, and had come home to Nebraska to avoid the distractions of city life.

Professor and scholar Hugh Luke was named editor in 1980. His very first essay to be submitted for publication was published in *PMLA*. In 1987 I became the second woman editor and the fifth editor of *Prairie Schooner*, one of the oldest literary quarterlies in continuous publication in America.

When Michael Cornett, president of the Council of Editors of Learned Journals, asked me to speak today, I wanted to suggest that a literary journal is like a coffee house. Writers and scholars use the space to converse and—in the double sense of the word—to collaborate, sometimes with enemies. We editors are proprietors of such a space. I wanted to use this trope because my family owns a coffee house near the university where many academic writers work. Also, because my father was a pioneer in the transportation industry, a truck driver, I wanted to invoke poet and scholar Alicia Ostriker's observation that in Athens, trucks display on their sides the word *metaphoros*, Greek for 'truck,' a metaphor in this case, a rhetorical vehicle to carry meaning from one place to another with dispatch and wit. I wanted to conflate these tropes to extend and also distort the meaning of *Prairie Schooner*'s name. It might then invoke the spirit of the frontier, the desire to push ahead into *terra incognita*—which, at MLA in San Diego in December, might be said to be scholarly enterprise in the guise of belletristic writing.

I am aware, as you are, that rage over such an endeavour led to Matthew Arnold's famous epithet, 'An unlearned, belletristic trifler.' Certainly for many years scholars in the academy had dismissed living writers and their more personal concerns to valorize their own professional obsessions. This line between poet and analyst was described by Anne Sexton, in a slightly different context, when she wrote in 1960, 'My business is words. Your business is watching my words.' Now we note a difference. Literary journals are gaining the attention of scholars, both as repositories for the writing of their subjects and also as publishing opportunities. The line between scholar and writer has grown thin. Scholars are writing fiction and poetry; writers of distinction are critics and scholars. For example, in 1962 we published a very young fiction writer and poet. Decades later, at the *Prairie Schooner* Seventy-Fifth Anniversary Conference and Celebration, a panel of scholars discussed these texts as the author stood in the back of the room, informally supplying information previously unavailable. That night, just a few days after 9/11—we didn't think anyone would fly, much less attend this special occasion—nearly one thousand people filled a hall to hear Joyce Carol Oates read from her work.

Successful scholars often write so well that literary journals are eager to publish their essays and reviews. In our forthcoming spring 2004 issue, we feature a piece about the Federal Writer's Project that uses the work of Rudolph Umland, an early staffer of *Prairie Schooner*, as a lens for viewing the national enterprise. We have a forthcoming essay called 'Jane Heap and Her Circle' [Page 77] on expatriate publishing in the 1920s. We've published important and highly articulate essays on Willa Cather by Judith Fryer, Susan J. Rosowski, and others, as well as work by Cather herself; on Steven Crane by major Crane scholars, as well as a holograph page of a Crane poem discovered in the 1980s; on James Fenimore Cooper; on Margaret Drabble; on and by Weldon Kees (two articles by poet Howard Nemerov); and a special issue on Loren Eiseley with essays by him and about his work. And these are only a few examples.

Prairie Schooner has published the documents scholars need in order to preserve them and bring them to scholarly attention. Professor Siote inaugurated a series of issues containing source material and criticism of American writers, among them Malcolm Lowry, a writer who lives on in many guises, not least in an online periodical called *zEtna—Magazine under the Volcano*. Its name is an anagram based on the name of the city where the magazine is published (Zenta, Serbia-Montenegro) and its subtitle refers to Lowry's novel: this "non-profit and independent portal, or magazine, [is] in other words a 'digital volcano'." *Prairie Schooner*'s Malcolm Lowry issue sold for years as a photocopied packet that cost more to produce than we charged. We couldn't afford to reprint the issue.

Siote also published "a Latin-American sampling with one of the few reports ever to come out of Paraguay, [and] two 'Letters from Selma' in which a businessman and a nun reported their visit South." We published the PEN keynote speech given by Maxine Kumin when she and Carolyn Kizer resigned as chancellors of the Academy of American Poets in protest of the lack of diversity in the leadership (Lucille Clifton was chosen as her replacement). In fact, for many years, literary journals have published a rich mix of creative and scholarly work. As our thirst for the personal grows keen, increasing numbers of scholars construct and claim identities through which to speak, much as writers of fiction do. The rhetoric of the scholarly essay has changed. Literary journals provide larger audiences than scholarly journals can—and new audiences, too. In the new issue of *Profession* 2003, published by MLA, Natalie Zeman Davis, Henry Charles Lea Professor of History Emeritus at Princeton, says, 'a . . . personal history, but one, I think, characteristic of the experience of other social historians of my generation or younger who began to relate to literature in a new way.' In 2001, Lindsay Waters, executive editor for the humanities at Harvard University Press, wrote in the *Chronicle of Higher Education*,

> Our publications need to be more like those of Swift
> and Voltaire—proper humanistic emanations that offer
> persuasive accounts of the world . . . rather than empty
> exercises of scientific competence designed to please two
> men in New Haven and no one else in this world . . .Think
> of the people whose best work appeared in [belletristic]
> essay form: Barbara Johnson, Nina Baym, W.K. Wimsau,
> Cleanth Brooks, T.S. Eliot ...

Publishing these kinds of essays is part of the literary journal's mission. Waters was arguing for revised standards of promotion and tenure in the academy, standards that, in fact, already have changed.

Creative writers in the academy are bound by the same standards for promotion and tenure as our scholarly colleagues. Our publications are reviewed with the same diligence as those of scholars. We study our own and others' writing with the same tools and intellectual rigour as our colleagues study the texts of Eudora Welty, Willa Cather, Cyrus Colter, Tony Cade, Tennessee Williams, and others published in the pages of literary journals that are the gold standard for creative work refereed by editorial staff and boards. (And here it's interesting to note that the endowed Franklin chair in literature once held by esteemed critic Hugh Kenner at the University of Georgia is held now by writer Judith Ortiz Cofer, whose work has earned for *Prairie Schooner* more permission fees than any other in our huge archive.)

If the academy now offers writers as well as scholars a professional home, editors have the same shelter: the very act of making a journal has come to be considered an act of scholarship. In my four years on the university's Advisory Committee, I saw journal editing, which had long been considered 'service to the profession,' revised as 'scholarship/creative activity,' a change editors wouldn't have thought possible ten years ago. Journals like *Prairie Schooner* make contemporary literature the site of their editors' scholarship; when we publish individual pieces of good writing, we identify and describe trends—certainly in the marketplace, but also in the preoccupations of our individual writers, the changing nature of our societies, their intersections and divergence. Special issues may signal the results of our inquiry. Literary journals have been invited into the academy, where we have always been, and now we have been given a seat by the fire.

But long before the Council of Editors of Learned Journals recognized the place of literary journals in the academy with the initiation of its new award for journals that 'especially feature belletristic writing,' *Prairie Schooner* and other literary journals chose to pay dues and nominate issues for prizes awarded by the Council of Literary Magazines and Presses (CLMP). Why? Because we participate in scholarly conversation and we support our organizations. One also might ask why a literary quarterly editor and a poet has been asked to speak to the editors of scholarly journals at the annual meeting of MLA. Perhaps because creative writing has grown exponentially in the academy: from twenty-one graduate programs in 1975 to 141 MFA and PhD programs in 2002, figures reported by the Associated Writing Programs (AWP). Consider the headline in a recent *Chronicle*: "English departments add programs as more students push to write fiction and poetry." According to this report,

> more than 50 colleges have added creative writing to their list of offerings for undergraduates, bringing the total to well over 300 at both public and private institutions. These are not elective courses, but full-blown programs . . . that allow students to earn a BA with a major or minor in creative writing.

Oberlin College notes that they have "three times more applications for positions in our courses than we have available spaces."

To serve student interest, academic programs hire successful writers and give them tenure. Four years ago, Dr Jonis Agee, author of three *New York Times* Notable Books, joined our University of Nebraska faculty, which includes seven creative writers. We have a new summer Writer's Conference that invites, for example, Pulitzer Prize-winning author Robert Owen Butler, the Francis Eppes Professor holding the Michael Shaara Chair in Creative Writing at Florida State University, as well as Rita May Brown, who has never joined the academy, to teach with poets Mark Doty of the University of Houston and Carl Phillips of Washington University, along with agents and commercial publishers. MacArthur Fellow Eleanor Wilner, often a visiting writer in academia, has joined us during the year to teach our graduate students. We have a lively reading series.

In the United States, forty-one PhD programs in creative writing grant degrees; the University of Nebraska's is one. Our students are part of a traditional graduate program that includes the study of medieval as well as postcolonial literatures, composition, and feminist theory and modern and postmodern literatures. Our writers work in a tradition of scholarly endeavour and values. We are well-educated in the most traditional senses. Some of us were trained as and by literary critics; the return to text-centered reading is comfortable for us even as we expand our digital sites. Of course, as writers join scholars in the academy, journals publishing their work provide one of the means of assessing value and assigning rewards—tenure and promotion.

To serve the growing numbers of writers in the academy, the Associated Writing Programs was started in 1967 by fifteen writers representing thirteen creative writing programs. Now AWP serves 330 college and university creative writing programs and 22,000 individual writers, teachers, and students—even as the total number of undergraduate English majors has declined (by as much as 23 per cent since 1970, according to the latest available statistics).

Long ago, when I first arrived at *Prairie Schooner* and worried about the long-term value of our efforts, Bernice Siote said that ninety-nine per cent of the work we publish will not survive the issue—but it's the 1 percent that makes us indispensable to the enterprise. We editors are in a good position to identify both the ninety-nine per cent that may signal cultural change and the one per cent to change the canon, which has become increasingly various and unbound.

Of what other use is a literary magazine to a university and its press? We serve by publishing new literature; we provide a measure of excellence for academic advancement; and we train future editors for the field. Our staff has included Kevin Prufer of *Pleiades*; Ted Genoways of *Virginia Quarterly Review*; Ladette Randolph, senior executive editor at the University of Nebraska Press, whose American Lives Series has twice won Discovery Awards; Suzanne Poirier at *Literature and Medicine*; Kathleene West, poetry editor of *Puerto del Sol*; April Ossmann, director of Alice James Press; and others—including W.G. Hegier, who as a graduate student was book review editor of *Prairie Schooner*. Regier, also a writer and critic, was director of the University of Nebraska Press and then Johns Hopkins University Press. Now, as director of the University of Illinois Press, he writes as follows in response to my question about how journals serve university presses:

> Journals were the foundation for Johns Hopkins University
> Press, the oldest continuously operating university press
> in the United States, and have been a reason that major

presses are major presses. The University of California Press, the University of Chicago Press, the MIT Press, not to mention Oxford and Cambridge, receive much of their vitality—editorial and fiscal—through their journals. Presses that have built up their journals programs in recent years, including Duke, Illinois, Indiana, Nebraska, and Texas, did so in the faith that journals are where new ideas are tested, new talents emerge, and new fields stake out their territory.

Paul Royster, director of University of Nebraska Press, comments,

> For the presses, [journals] serve as a farm system or proving ground for the development of book ideas, and they help a press to establish its identity as a publisher of note in specific fields. In some cases, journals programs grow to a size that adds considerable revenue and/or intellectual clout. In our case, the journals we publish dovetail usefully with our book and monograph publishing programs in creative writing and nonfiction.

And Ladette Randolph, once managing editor of *Prairie Schooner*, observes,

> By their nature, journals are in a unique position to publish more writers faster. As such, book editors use journals as a means for discovery, both for including new writers/ scholars and for keeping current with new trends. Recognizing new talent and cultivating early relationships with the writers we find in journals allows book editors to play a more active role in developing articles into manuscripts or finding worthy finished manuscripts in advance of the curve.

And what use is the literary journal to an academic department? Linda Pratt, former president of the American Association of University Professors (1992–1994) and in 2002 president of the Association of Departments of English, is chair of English at the University of Nebraska–Lincoln. Pratt says the following about the importance of a literary journal to a university department:

> Two reasons stand out in my mind when thinking about the importance a literary journal can have to the department which sponsors it. First, a literary journal brings national visibility to a department. Everybody who reads that journal or submits material to it will know where the journal is located. The better the journal, the better the

national profile, which is one reason to invest in the quality
of your journal. Every career in a department is enhanced
by the department's national reputation, so an investment
in a journal is really an investment on behalf of all the
members of the faculty. Second, a literary journal is an
instrument of disciplinary communication. Through it, the
department will have a deeper and more current sense of
the literary world at any given historical moment. Writers
communicate to their audiences through publication in the
journal, and the department that is publishing the journal
is in communication with all the active writers. Access
to the discourse of the writing world opens through the
work of the journal and its staff, and this becomes part of a
cross-fertilization process between the creative writers and
the members of the discipline of English whose interest is
the study of literature.

No surprise, then, to learn that some literary journals are expanding, as
is *Prairie Schooner*. With the support of the university, we've started a Prize
Book Series in poetry and another in short fiction, with an award of $3,000
to each winner and a standard contract for publication and distribution by
the University of Nebraska Press. And the best for last: you may know the
philanthropy of poet and writer Glenna Luschei, editor of Solo Magazine
and Solo Press, who served *Prairie Schooner* as an editorial assistant for Karl
Shapiro. She has endowed the magazine, and its editors, in perpetuity. We
look forward to the changes made possible by Dr Luschei's gift and cherish
her example as an editor, publisher, and writer.

The best reason we find ourselves at MLA is this: our readers and writers
are your colleagues, but they are also your audience, members of promotion
and tenure committees, lawyers, acrobats, taxpayers, and potential donors.
Often literary magazines are used in classrooms as textbooks. The traditional barrier between student and text, critical commentary and belletristic
essay, is fluid and changing. The work itself is evidence of this change in
and outside the classroom, evidence of the dissolving distinction between
scholarship and belletristic writing and their makers—scholars and writers,
practitioners and teachers.

I'll close with a riff on my favourite joke: A scholar dies and goes to
heaven. St Peter meets him at the gate. "You've been so productive and helpful to the profession," he says, "we've decided to give you a choice between
heaven and hell." "Oh," says the scholar, "how do I choose?" "Try both," says
St Peter. He snaps his fingers and they descend. When the scholar opens
his eyes he sees bank upon bank of scholars chained to their desks being
whipped by devils. "Not my idea of an afterlife," says the scholar. "Okay, says
St Peter, and he snaps his fingers and they ascend. When the scholar opens

his eyes, he sees bank upon bank of scholars chained to computer desks being whipped by angels. "Oh," cries the scholar, "what's the difference?" "Hmmmm," says St Peter—"Here, you get published."

CAVE WALL

Number 8

Serial Killers: Toward a Future of the Literary Magazine in America

by Ian Morris (2010)

It is never good when the man from administration has a letter addressed to you on the desk before him. In such instances the letter isn't handed to you but is instead pushed in your direction by the tip of a manicured finger. So was it that Susan Firestone Hahn and I had our editorial positions terminated at *TriQuarterly* magazine, a concern we had sustained for, in my case, twelve and, in Susan's case, thirty years, and were told that the name *TriQuarterly* would continue to exist atop the masthead of an online, open access journal to be operated by students and faculty of Northwestern University's School of Continuing Studies. And so was it that the miasma of global human activity in an age of chaotic technological innovation and change was rippled by yet another barely perceptible disruption of its ether.

Experiencing sensations similar to those I felt when my wife and I were once mugged at gunpoint, I went home that evening and posted, on the *litmagslji listserv* (a forum of editors moderated by the Council of Literary Magazines and Presses), an email I titled, melodramatically, and, upon reflection, I believe aptly, "The Death of an Institution." In the time it took for my Webmail page to auto-check for new messages, my inbox was filled with replies echoing my original header, *Re: [litmagslji] The Death of an Institution* and containing expressions of condolence, anger, support, and above all questions about the university's press release, which referred to *TriQuarterly* in the context of "scholarly" publishing for reasons known only to its authors and to Susan and myself not at all. Over the next few days the discussion on the listserv shifted from *TriQuarterly* specifically to the broader issues raised by this action, regarding new technologies, the intrinsic value of a literary magazine, and the benefits and perils of university support.

TriQuarterly

NUMBER SEVENTEEN · WINTER 1970 · $1.95

for
Vladimir
Nabokov
on his seventieth
birthday

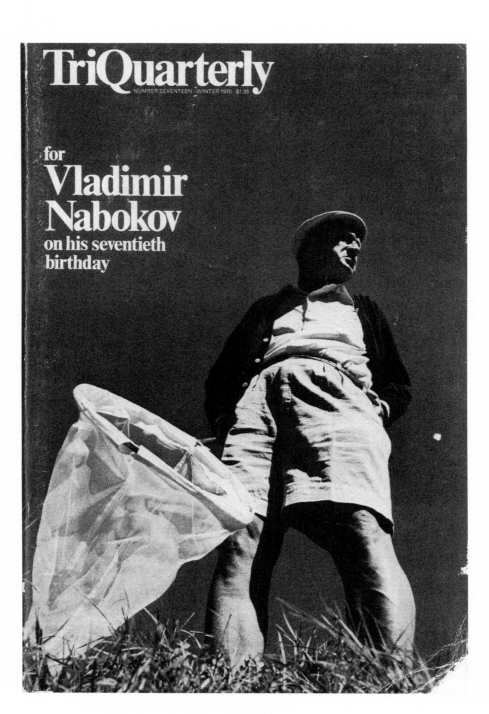

Prior to getting chucked out of my job on the premise that the future of the literary magazine lay online, I didn't have a rooting interest in any one vision of the future of literature delivery systems over another. I prefer reading books to reading on the computer, but that is a personal preference, probably linked in some way to a high school memory of dashing down a city block to catch a bus with a paperback copy of *Flappers and Philosophers* in the back pocket of my Levi's. Maybe it's just that, as one editor of an online journal conceded at last year's conference of the Associated Writing Programs, "The book is market tested." Or, more to the point, someone long ago perfected a book that doesn't run on batteries.

At the same time, while my imagination has never been drawn to new digital technologies, I am no Luddite. We have at *TriQuarterly* a dwindling core of older, well-known authors who submit typewritten manuscripts and communicate only by phone or United States mail; however, we as editors do not have the luxury to resist progress, even if we were inclined to. More and more journals are adopting automated submission systems and perhaps more are scrapping traditional mass-mailed subscription renewals in favor of email-based subscription renewal systems. And, most significantly, there does not exist an established literary journal that does not have a fully functioning website that provides guidelines for submissions, an automated method for subscribing, and some sample of content (in many cases, some of that content appears only online).

In other words, anyone in need of a model for what the future of literary magazine publishing might look like may be surprised to learn that we are already living in it. If I were to found a new literary magazine tomorrow (a dicey proposition these days, no doubt) I'd urge the board to call it *A Respected, Widely Read Print Magazine That Pays Its Authors to Publish Them.* The enchanted readers of its first issue would open the cover to find this subtitle on the title page: *That Also Has a Website That Posts Content (Some of It Exclusive) and Has a Lively Blog on Which an Insightful and Engaging Editor Frequently Posts.* This model, or something similar, has been adopted by many of the most respected journals, including venerable publications such as the *Kenyon Review* and *Agni*, upstarts like *Tin House* and *A Public Space*, and, perhaps most successfully, at the *Virginia Quarterly Review.* It was such a model that we were pressing to expand upon at *TriQuarterly.* The appeal of this approach was driven home to me in reverse you might say through recent conversations with editors of online journals, all of whom seemed to be pushing a publication that might be generically called *An Online Journal That Hopes One Day to Publish an Annual Print Anthology of the Year's Best Work.*

In his cheeky introduction to the first issue of *TriQuarterly*, in the fall of 1964, our founding editor Charles Newman wrote, "It may be that in the expanding university, we are witnessing an affluent democracy's oblique answer to the patronage system of the old world—though we could not afford to call it that yet." Certainly from the time one Cro-Magnon demonstrated an aptitude for manipulating pigments beyond that of his clan, and he was excused to some degree from the exigencies of hunting and gathering in order to record the results of those activities upon the cave wall, many, if not most, artists have relied on some sort of institutional support. Those of us who make our livings in institutionally funded arts are all keenly aware of the debt we owe to those institutions. (Indeed, should we forget, there is always someone in the provost's office eager to remind us.) However, little— and I fear increasingly less—credit is given to what the institutions receive in return. What is interesting in the case of *TriQuarterly* is that the administration has not withdrawn, but rather shifted, its patronage not even to a different art form, but to a different portal (to use the word of the day), and indeed one that, for the foreseeable future, will be entirely dependent upon the university for its support.

It may be that the print/online model is just bridge technology between the book and some as of yet unknown medium, in the same way that hybrid cars will be made obsolete by cars propelled by a reliable, affordable power source that has yet to be perfected. But I suspect that the future, when it does arrive, will look unstartlingly familiar, more *Flintstones* than *Jetsons*, in that we are more likely to be bickering with our can openers than owning robot maids. Ultimately, the little magazine continues to outlive its obituary not because of the medium or the editor, but because of the most confounding mechanism in any model of literary production: the writer, its perpetual engine of invention.

THE LITERARY ECONOMY IS PATHETIC: A VIEW FROM SOCIALIST EUROPE

by Megan M. Garr (2012)

Behind the lines of a literary journal are a lot of things, but one of those things is money. Whether you run a letterpress printed wonder or a blog-based journal, whether you print 1,000 copies or offer PDFs, money—or better said, value—underlies every single pixel, every drop of ink, every bind, every envelope. Is your journal run on volunteers' time? Value. One-man show and credit card debt? Value. University funded? Value. Community funded? Value. Kickstarter? Value. Did you just print fifteen poems and seven stories that were given to you for free by writers? Value.

For the last few years, the small press and literary journal world has been slowly waking to the reality that the literary economy is basically pathetic. Journals cost money—but on the whole they do not bring in money. Instead they rely on university support, grants, philanthropy, or the determination and credit cards of their founders. They also, in turn, rely on the donations of writers: millions of poems and stories gifted for the love of the page. On one side of the equation, there are gifts of love and dedication; on the other side, there are printing bills, postal fees, and the barter of values.

A "young Fugitive" writer in nineties Nashville, I came to know the literary journal as an unadorned paper-and-glue booklet beyond the days of its once-glory, backed by local colleges and universities, publishing writers from the area, and run by men. Though not explicitly, I was taught that the literary journal was a means to an end, a stepping stone into whatever

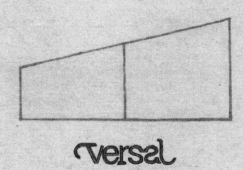

versal

8

currency a writer could garner through "real books," a credit thus, nothing more, removed from any economic mercantile, where supply and demand were simply a trade between editor and contributor and perhaps a few interested others.

Probably because *Versal* began in tiny Amsterdam, hoisted by a skeleton crew of expatriated writers amidst an unresponsive Dutch literary scene, its story had to have different plotlines. When I moved to town in 2001, the literary scene ignored the seemingly few and far between non-Dutch writers here. I started *Versal* as a way to find them, to create enough gravity to pull a new, international literary scene together. So it followed, in my mind, that the journal had to be aesthetically beautiful, something with an inherent and manifest value beyond a publishing credit, beyond a means to an end. The journal for Amsterdam *was* the end.

As *Versal* began to form, other new plotlines showed themselves. *Versal* did not fit into grant applications on either side of the Atlantic; it was neither "located" in America nor was it in the Dutch language. We had to find another way to make money, so we began putting on events and workshops to fund the journal. Submissions also quickly became a site of innovation. The common submission SASE was useless; US stamps, of course, don't work in a Dutch mailbox, and the international reply coupon seemed to confound 80 percent of submitters, as well as Dutch postal workers. Before long, we were 100 percent email submissions, and within a few years had rigged up a PHP-based project management system online to track those submissions—well before online submission managers became so common. These types of early challenges kept us on our toes, and probably for that reason kept our eyes focused on *Versal* as more than just paper and glue with writing in it. *Versal* was our veritable flagship.

What follows is the story of steps *Versal* took in 2011–2012 in our pursuit to survive amidst changing economic circumstances. The text has been adapted and expanded from posts I wrote on our blog over the course of the developments, which led us not only towards a more straightforward and inherent funding model than we had before, but also towards a model where funds flowed to contributors. In other words, towards an actual literary economy.

THE GRATIS JOURNAL

In the summer of 2011, just after *Versal* 9 hit the shelves, I realized that out of all the *Versal*s that had left our stock, only about 30 percent were actually sold. The remaining 70 percent were simply given away: to contributors, as review copies, to various definitions of editorial contacts—70 percent of 750 for promotional purposes to sell the other 30 percent.

Many editors believe deeply in the purity of this inventory spread. The work we collect must be in the world, in whatever way possible. Rogue copies on coffee counters. Slipped between politico gibberish at the chain book-store. Swaps with other editors as a virtual handshake. Donated *en masse* to fairs to raise money for other literary organizations. Sales, I have been implicitly and explicitly taught and told, run contrary to the literary modus operandi. We are made to write, to edit, to appreciate. We are not made to sell.

This attitude is fine, of course, if money is coming from somewhere—namely, from a university or grant system, or from the pockets or credit cards of the editors. But in the last ten years, at least, there has been a growing middle, journals which can rely neither on philanthropy nor on celebrated debt. These journals, *Versal* among them, are looking to the crowd, and from the crowd trying to secure funding to operate. We are leveraging the trade of the journal between hands, one currency for another, in (gasp!) a market-place.

For the first ten years of *Versal*'s existence, we relied on our local com-munity for funding. We put on a hero's share of workshops and events at ri-diculously low costs to participants. Even the teachers donated most of their earnings back to the journal, and of course all of the administration and or-ganization were handled by volunteers. This "circular funding", as I called it, worked fine for a while (especially when we were all younger; I started *Versal* when I was twenty-two). But a lot changed in those ten years. Because of the airline crisis, and because the Dutch privatized its postal service, and be-cause that postal service changed owners at least five times, by 2008 the cost to ship one *Versal* to the USA was almost two times the cost of the journal itself. The financial meltdown hit paper prices, so printing costs soared. The crisis also slowed the flow of expats into Amsterdam, which leveled out our already small community, and reduced the local audience, which attended our events and bought the journal.

Midway through 2010 we looked at our cost base and made some chang-es, switching to a courier service for bulk shipping to reduce postal costs. But the major problem we faced was not directly financial, it was personal. Our team was tired. We were running around Amsterdam trying to put on enough events to fund the journal, and we were losing steam. One exciting outcome of our now more stable local community was that the community had come together more, and as a result more events and workshops were being organized. But from a purely "market" standpoint, that meant our own events and workshops faced competition. We found ourselves in an odd position, forced to compete within our local literary economy or change our activities altogether. We had backed ourselves into a corner. It was time for a change.

This brings us to the summer of 2011. I managed to get a team of upper-level strategy consultants from a major global firm to talk to me, pro bono, about *Versal*'s survival. After my first meeting with them, with a list of ideas and a better understanding of the math behind the line breaks, I realized how much in the marketplace we actually are, how desperately we have been ignoring that fact, and how my utopian literary mindset was just crashing against some fairly basic economic realities. Were we going to change the fact of money? No. Were we going to move to a desert island? No. Did we want to continue the journal? Of course.

Then we had to join, maybe even help build, the small press literary economy.

JOINING THE LITERARY ECONOMY

One of the best Dutch words is *relativeren*. It is a verb that means "to put things into perspective." Our brainstorm with the consultants did just that. The consultants gawked at the clichés we take for granted: that writers are poor, that people submit to journals they've never read, that bookstores buy the journal at a 40% discount, that bookstores don't even buy it, but take it on consignment. In their eyes, the literary world, and *Versal*, were hightailing it from anything money related, on every front. And as the conversation deepened, I realized we were not actually running away—we were running in circles.

Some of what came out of the brainstorm we already knew; much of it surprised us by virtue of its simplicity. This list is by no means comprehensive, but it summarizes the major points that arose from our work with the consultants, and can serve as a starting point for new and established journals looking to build or rebuild towards a more sustainable and self-reliant future.

1. Bring your retail price in line with your journal's added value, or at least make sure there's a profit margin between your retail price and your cost price. If you survey literary journals in your region or around the USA, you'll also gain a sense of the average price—you'll want to stay within this range. When I benchmarked a sampling of American literary journals in the summer of 2011, the average was $11.40.

2. Increase economies of scale. If a company increases the number of units produced, then the cost per unit decreases, as fixed costs (i.e. production costs) become shared over a larger number of units. In journal terms, if you print 2,000 copies instead of 500, the cost per copy (i.e. cost price) goes down. The catch? You need some serious distribution muscle. Since *Versal* is currently run out of my apartment, we're not in the position to pursue this just yet.

3. POD or online publishing can be considered in some cases, but not in *Versal*'s, for reasons that would be obvious to anyone who has touched a copy. But every literary journal has its own "added value," its own unique selling point (i.e. its own *raison d'être*), and for some, switching to cheaper publishing methods could be a boost rather than a step back.

4. Adjust wholesale pricing. The consultants were appalled that most bookstores only take literary journals on consignment, and were additionally floored by the standard 60/40 split. They encouraged us to renegotiate all of our contracts with bookstores, an action I would very much like to take—if I thought it had any way of going anywhere. Changing our own practices is one thing; changing industry practices like the consignment tradition and the heavy price tag just seem out of our current galaxy of influence. Larger journals or consortiums of journals could, however, begin such a lobby.

5. Expand your sales and reach into the broader community. Target art communities, local CSAs, theatergoers, small artesian retail shops; take the audience out of the box. In the last few years, for example, our editorial reach into the arts community has expanded considerably. Translating that into copy sales is a no-brainer next step. Many literary journals out there have similar potential, especially if locally active.

6. Professionalize. With the consultants' help we could give form to a *Versal* that is run not like a non-profit, but like an enterprise. Here's the point where most of us will run for the hills. But I can see some advantages: a bank start-up loan or investors, for example, might allow us to rent office space, get a few editors on a payroll, and help us inch towards economies of scale. One potential path to professionalization would be members of the editorial team becoming shareholders—essentially buying *Versal* and realizing later financial return from the investment. This model is especially interesting for new journals, which can start on a blank page: each editor joins with an investment of funds, and once the journal reaches profitability the editors see returns.

7. Leverage your "contact moments" and engage your personal and literary networks. "Contact moments" is marketing-speak for the times when a literary journal comes into contact with a person. Each of these moments is a sales opportunity. For example, you can leverage the online submission process by offering ways to buy an issue within the steps of that process. All journals should have a database that keeps track of the people it has come into contact with: buyers, subscribers, and contributors, of course, but also submitters, other editors, and people met at conferences and events. All of these folks could mean later sales if you handle it right (and I'm not talking about spam). Making sure they remain connected in some way, through newsletters or social media, means you can contact them when a new issue comes out. Your contacts also have valuable information about how you're conducting your journal and succeeding in your goals; well-constructed surveys and social media engagements can build valuable feedback loops.

8. Charge for submissions. Born and raised in the Netherlands, the socialist, morally bereft and pothead Dutch consultants recommended we charge for submissions. Of course they had no idea that this was and still is a major taboo in the literary community. But the idea was one of the first to arise. Their thinking? The fee would "channel" writers' participation in the literary economics that we all face, whether we like it or not. If the journal can offer writers added value for considering their work—in the case of *Versal*, for example, a high percentage of personalized feedback, where 100 percent of submissions are read by fully-fledged editors rather than interns—then the flow of funds is not manipulative, but conscientious of the values being offered on both sides of the editorial table. If a literary journal can additionally offer transparency about its finances, then submission fees are a viable option, especially in conjunction with contributor payment.

9. Build or engage literary journal consortiums to accomplish certain goals, such as lobbying distributors and bookstores for fairer contracts, placing journals on academic reading lists, ensuring representation at important fairs and conferences, and discussing and disseminating

industry best practices. CLMP does a great job in this regard, but many of the smaller, non-university affiliated literary journals are often still left out, simply as a result of available resources on both ends. Better leveraging the potential of such groups for a wider range of journals will make important strides in improving the literary economy on a larger scale.

10. Stop giving things away for free. Many of us grew up as writers believing our world was a utopic free for all. As much as we love our work, we should question the trope that glorifies our poverty and tolerates this economy of constant donation. I say this to writers who are not paid for their poems and to editors who make beautiful journals by squeezing hours between "real" jobs and family. Here at *Versal,* we used to give copies away for free to just about anyone. But your journal is not your business card. It's the thing you and many, many writers have made together. If you need a business card (which you don't anymore), just make one.

11. Harness your added value and build your business model around that core. Whatever makes your journal unique and wonderful is the center of gravity from which you move. Every decision you make—how you operate your journal, your editorial process, how you engage with potential contributors, how you build your website, the copy on your site, the look and feel of your tables at confer-ences—comes down to whatever is at your core. Stay in line with that. Stay with that. And stay with that finan-cially, too. The less you deviate from your core, your *raison d'être,* the more likely you are to survive in the long term, no matter the external circumstances that may, and will, arise.

In the months that followed our discussions with the consultants, we initiated a range of changes at both operational and philosophical levels. If community and aesthetics are central to the *Versal* ethos, our "business mod-el" needed to continue to reflect that ethos, even if the model itself had to change. So rather than relying on events and workshops for funding—and the goodwill and time of our editorial team to put them on—we looked to the journal itself, where our energies and hearts really lay. We carefully adjusted our shipping methods and charges. We reprogrammed our submis-sion manager to accept multiple types of payments during the submission process, which gave us the ability to charge a small submission fee as well as offer writers the chance to preorder an issue. We also worked out a way to pay contributors; though an initially small amount, our longtime, personal commitment to our contributors (our community) needed to translate into funds as well. And, importantly, we engaged publically in the debates swarming the literary internet at the time and contacted organizations such as CLMP to open up new dialogues. In short, we made sure the flows of money were originating from the journal's core, and that those funds were similarly directed outward. In a microcosm, we created a literary economy.

GOING DUTCH

But.

The literary economy is saturated with presses and journals, and it is fair to assume the consumers in this economy are consuming what they reasonably can. Revenues are spread so thin that, in general, few presses and journals seem able to start or even survive without external cash injections from grants, Kickstarter, or credit cards. These are not sustainable circumstances.

By no means do I think that solutions like the submission fee are the silver bullet to turn our literary economy around. Such initiatives do, however, put literary journals on more sustainable footing, and have the ability to bring the literary economy as a whole to a new level, where new solutions and new models can take shape. If we all agree we're committed to seeing writing in the world, then does it not follow that we all join in the economics to make that happen? And thus change our minds a bit on what that looks like? The world has changed drastically since I was taught to detest submission fees and vanity presses. Can we not change as well?

Inhoudelijk, as the Dutch would say, means the value of the journal is maintained by the value of the journal, means its funding is inherent to its operation, and means it can move forward on two feet of its own making.

A little bit socialist. A little bit bootstrap. If I've learned anything from living around the Dutch, it's that both are possible. Simultaneously.

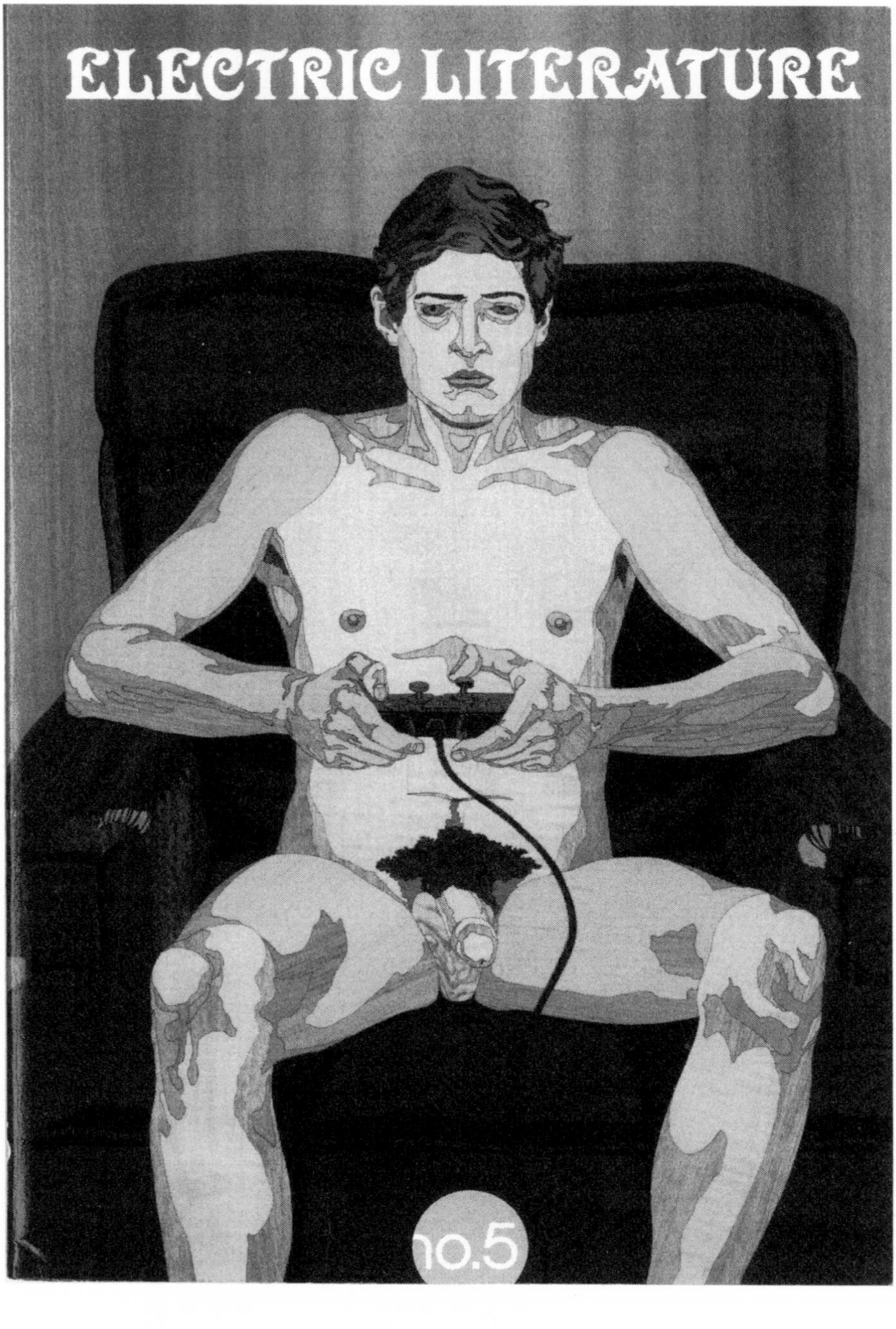
ELECTRIC LITERATURE
no.5

Recommended Reading

by Benjamin Samuel (2012)

Humans are, by nature, storytellers. In any medium, from cave paintings to Twitter fiction, we're compelled to share our experiences and insights of the world. No surprise then that fiction has been encoded to HTML since the dawn of the Internet. So why did Electric Literature, an innovator in publishing, start *Recommended Reading*, a free online magazine? How is *Recommended Reading* keeping us on the cutting edge of publishing?

Cutting Through the Noise

Imagine the sound of cyberspace, with every bit, every site, every tweet, all of it emitting its own audible frequency. Think about how loud it would be, all that data rushing around transmitting the latest *buzz*. It would all coalesce into static, crescendo into white noise.

There's so much content and information in competition, it's become indistinguishable—trying to find what you're looking for is like trying to hear one piccolo player amid the world's largest symphony. But the truth is, if you can filter out the noise—the disruptive tumult of LOLcats, the same *New Yorker* articles that are already cluttering your coffee table, the photos of your friend's fancy cocktail, and the seething vitriol of anonymous commenting—the Internet does indeed harbor good content, even good fiction.

Despite the general frenzy, there is content that is more patient, more thoughtful. Content that doesn't threaten to disappear or surrender to Brownian Motion. The difficulty, however, is finding it.

The Fight for Attention

As I write this, the Internet is raging with the news (or, for those who'd already suspected as much, "the confirmation") that Amazon reviews are not just fallible, but corruptible. David Streitfeld broke the story in the *New York Times*, revealing that a company called GettingGoodReviews.com had commodified the rating system. Self-published authors both small and large (including John Locke, the first writer in Amazon's 1 million-eBook sale club) were buying five-star reviews by the bushel, buying their way into literary fame and fortune.

The rationale: in order to get noticed, a writer needs momentum, at the very least a surfeit of positive reviews. "No matter [how] great your book is, it is fighting against a tidal wave of cheap eBooks on Amazon," wrote Andrew Shaffer at the *Huffington Post*. If you can just break out, get ahead of the pack, you'll find an audience who will carry you into the bestseller list, and there you'll stay.

The scandal is being compared to sports doping, and, although it doesn't account for the fact that the challenge of writing is actually *writing*, it's an apt comparison. If everyone is gaming the system, is it really cheating? Not to mention, how can anyone compete with this level of competition?

According to Bowker, in the last five years, the number of self-published titles has increased 600 percent, with 300,000 titles published last year alone. Writing a book is still a challenge, and writing a *good* book is still a tremendous accomplishment, but publishing is easier than ever before. "It used to take the same time to produce a book that it does to produce a baby," wrote Streitfeld. "Now it takes about as long as boiling an egg." Finding an audience, however, takes time (or, in some cases, money).

Writers in the digital arena aren't just fighting with each other; the battleground hosts all sorts of threats: streaming media, social circles, irrepressible memes, and myriad other non-literary forms of entertainment. But the fact that literature is in competition, that it's even on the Coliseum grounds, is encouraging news for the future of publishing.

It's clear now that the Kindle wasn't the doomsday device publishers prophesied it to be. In fact, it's enriched the landscape in many ways. But there is a new threat to the publishing ecosystem: overpopulation. Just as writers struggle to get noticed, literary magazines and small publishers must emerge from obscurity, must find an audience, and ensure that their voice is distinct and loud enough to be carried above the ruckus.

That's where Electric Literature's new publication, *Recommended Reading*, steps in.

V. WRITERS ON LIT MAGS

Without writers, there would be no literature. The pyramid of editor/writer/reader has made up the economy microcosm of the literary magazine since its origins, with the writer sitting in the imaginative center of the literary arts, generating the content driving editors to produce and readers to consume. What then does the contemporary writer think about the literary magazine today?

unmuzzled OX

HANNAH GREEN ON JOHN WESLEY. RAY JOHNSON.
POETRY BY KOCH, ATWOOD, GIORNO, MALANGA
DI PRIMA, BOWERING, BUKOWSKI, SIMIC, HOROVITZ.

$1.00

Publishing What We Are Trying to Write

by Aaron Gilbreath (2012)

It's no exaggeration to say that literary magazines inhabit the same outer ring of popular consciousness as lute players and the name of the man who invented Sticky Notes. When the average person dreams about being a writer, most imagine sending their stuff to a Big Publishing House, not to a literary magazine. Mention the term and you'll likely hear some variation of "What's a literary magazine?" Despite these publications' relative obscurity, the nonfiction that lingers with me years after I read it rarely comes from the big, recognizable publications such as *Time* or *GQ*. What stays with me are the essays I read in lit mags such as the *Gettysburg Review*, *Black Warrior Review*, *The Believer*, and *Oxford American*. Although I read it daily, I can barely remember what I read in *The Guardian* last month, but I'll never forget Lynne Sharon Schwartz's essay "At a Certain Age" from a 1999 issue of *The Threepenny Review*. This is less a byproduct of my fallible mind as it is of form: essays versus articles, narrative versus exposition, texts that map human thought versus texts that report facts. This is what Ezra Pound meant when he said, "Literature is news that stays news." So durable are their best contents that we might extend Pound's comment to, "Literary magazines are the magazines that stay magazines." This is one reason why they matter.

Surely the same can be said for music and movies. Our greatest songs and films are great partly because time hardly weakens their impact. The appeal of The Beatles' *Revolver*, like that of John Hughes's *Ferris Bueller's Day Off*, will barely lessen with age. The comparison to literary magazines mostly ends there. How many kids sit alone in their rooms at night running their hands over the matted cover of *The Southern Review* in the same way they do their iPods or records? The specific numbers don't matter, only the disparity.

To talk about lit mags is to talk about the issues that surround them: limited readership, niche interest, cultural importance inverse to relative obscurity.

I'm no kid anymore, but I am one of those people who run their hands over *The Southern Review*. I recite lines from *Star Wars*. I fetishize favorite albums like The Clean's *Vehicle* and The Stooges' *Raw Power*, and I love my lit mags. Just as I did with CDs and records as a teenager, I spend many quiet nights alone in my bedroom reading magazines under lamplight, as if engaged in a religious ritual or illicit affair. I appreciate these periodicals so much that I hoard them and use words like periodical to fortify the feelings they elicit. "Hoard" isn't to say I don't share my magazines—I'm always suggesting certain essays to friends—only that I rarely dispose of them. A great literary magazine is like a great book, except it's co-written by multiple authors, and if you're the sort of person who likes a record of your best reading experiences, then you might keep those mags on the shelf alongside favorite novels and memoirs. By name, lit mags constitute the realm of "little magazines," yet their visibility on my bookshelves signifies their importance. When I think about reading, I think as much about literary magazines as I do about books.

Vice magazine once began an article with,

> There are too many literary magazines in the world. "Hey, we should start a lit mag?" is one of the most common things people say in the just-fucking-around phase of life, right up there with "Hey, we should start a band?" and "Hey why don't we just start selling weed?" I suppose it's better to have too many magazines than not enough—still, it's a drag when you see the piles of journals in a bookstore (most bookstores sell lit mags, often in some out-of-the-way corner) and have no idea which, if any, you should buy.

Vice is right. Lit mags are so numerous, and many have such hideous covers and short, gnat-like lifespans that they can be difficult to distinguish and hard to take seriously. It's easier to dismiss them all as amateurish. If the writers in them were any good, goes the logic, wouldn't they be writing for something that didn't have a grainy, pastel, country-kitchen type painting on the front of it? And quality varies. Some journals are great. Some are horrific. The bulk lies somewhere between powerful and unreadable. Even my favorite magazines put out inconsistent issues. But a closer inspection—meaning a close read of what's available—reveals that, despite their often dull names (Location + Review = Title), their style and readability is wildly diverse. Which is the thing: if you write, you should be reading journals.

I started reading journals when I was twenty-seven, maybe twenty-eight. I'd seen them in bookstores for years but never paid them more than passing attention. When Powell's Books hired me in 2000, I found myself surrounded by so much mind-blowing material that I vowed to dismantle the cordons of my old reading habits. I began to read novels. I scoured the travel writing section, browsed books of journalism, photography, East Coast ecology, music writing, food writing, and biographies. I also opened the covers of the *Kenyon* and *Missouri* reviews. To spend my working days inside one of the world's largest bookstores and not explore would have been contrary to the core impulse of my reading life, especially when exploring was so easy.

On breaks and lunches, I ducked into different aisles and browsed. I did the same on the clock when I should have been working, keeping one eye on the page and another on the lookout for floor managers. I spent a lot of time in the Literature and Small Press sections, rifling through back issues of *Tin House, Paris Review* and *Open City*, as well as defunct magazines such as *Grand Street* and *Evergreen Review*. As I emerged from the Edward Abbey phase that defined my early twenties, these became two of my favorite parts of our store. Powell's employees could check out books like a library, so I started buying and renting magazines to read at home. Whichever new journals Powell's didn't carry, I bought at nearby Rich's Cigar Store, which had an expansive newsstand. The rest I ordered through the mail. It was as if I'd been bitten by a malarial bug. I couldn't get enough.

At this time, I was waking early every day before work to write, and then writing all weekend, too. I knew that improvement required practice, just as I knew that nicotine and caffeine powered me through the consequent exhaustion. Eventually, as I wrote more short fiction and nonfiction, and threw most of it in the trash, I realized that these journals with the humble names ending in "review" were the ideal outlet for my work if it ever got better, because my favorite ones published the very things I was trying to write.

Although I read tons of short stories in these magazines, what resonated most were the essays. I loved the fusion of thought and sensation, showing and telling, the way writers married scenes, dialogue, and character development with ideas, metaphors, themes, and information. With nonfiction, I liked a story, but I wanted to think and even learn something, too. As much as I tried, I couldn't seem to turn my own life into equally compelling nonfiction. I consumed published essays with the joy of a reader and the wonder of an aspirant: How to do this? I wanted nothing more than to create essays like these, and while my autobiographical fiction later proved to be my training ground, at the time I felt inept.

Until I discovered Philip Lopate's canonical *Art of the Personal Essay*, literary magazines were my primary source for this sort of nonfiction, a form that Lopate said was often at its best when it displayed the movement of an interesting mind. Had I read *The New Yorker* back then, I would have discovered great nonfiction in there, too. (Only later in life did I learn that it wasn't, in fact, a magazine dedicated to New York.) Reading helped establish my preferences, and I soon found myself with favorite journals. Those whose contents were routinely lackluster—and they were many—I abandoned after a few issues. When I started to think I was getting the hang of short stories, around 2004, I began sending them to the magazines that I read. It was premature; rejections poured in. But the routine proved useful.

One common wisdom about submitting writing to literary magazines is that you should only submit to the magazines you love. Beyond the superficial I-dig-the-font-and-layout sort of way, it seems difficult to truly love a lit mag without reading it. Ideally, they construct their identities around their written content, rather than around ads or marketable brand identities with stylistic associations. And if you're part of a journal's core audience, then you likely understand that publication's mission and aesthetic more intimately than someone who only knows its name or cachet. Intimacy generally makes you a suitable submitter, because if the magazine's contents speak to you, then maybe your writing will speak to readers with similar tastes.

The Paris Review editor Lorin Stein put it more succinctly. In response to a reader who asked where he should submit his writing, Stein said, "I could give you the names of some good journals, but—supposing they take your work—what's the point of publishing in a magazine that you don't already read?" To read one is to know one, and they aren't all created equal. Stein mentioned a related issue: "Here's the thing: no matter how many classes you take, no matter how much time you spend at the keyboard, you cannot write seriously unless you read. And that means, partly, reading your contemporaries. Their problems are your problems; you can't write—that is, you can't write for serious readers—until you know what the problems are."

While working at Powell's and writing every day, I decided to do something I never did: volunteer my time. Literary magazines helped teach me to write, but reading them also made them more mysterious. Curious about where they came from and how they worked, I volunteered to read submissions for the *Portland Review*. Housed on the Portland State University campus not far from my bookstore, the *Portland Review* was the most accessible journal for me then. It proved a relaxed affair. The editors would hand me a stack of manila envelopes. I'd read them at home and during lunch breaks, and I'd make notes: accept, reject, strong contender, and why. The experience was enlightening. Despite journals' powerful effects, production was neither supernatural nor glamorous. The proverbial wizard behind *Portland Review*'s curtain was two bright, ambitious grad students shoved in a cramped back room at the end of a basement hall.

Volunteering not only revealed the small press's spare inner workings, it put my own writing in context. Reading story after story showed me that, compared to these submissions, even my most promising stories weren't ready for circulation.

Alongside poems and fiction, author interviews are standard lit mag fair. I read so many of them that I decided to try to do one myself. I'd never interviewed anyone, but as a born talker with a Jewish mother from New York City, how hard could it be? My interview subject arrived accidentally.

Steve Almond was coming to Powell's to read. I loved both his books, *Candyfreak* and *My Life in Heavy Metal*, so I got his email address and asked to interview him. Before his event, we slipped into a meeting room on the store's third floor, and he answered my litany of questions. As embarrassingly unsophisticated as some of my questions sound now, I managed to sell the interview to the literary magazine *Glimmer Train*, another Portland publication. It was my first paid writing job.

Of all Almond's insightful answers, what struck me most was what he said about literary magazines. During grad school, Almond served as fiction editor of the *Greensboro Review*. "That was the boot camp for me as a story writer," he said:

> When you read twelve hundred stories in the space of
> a year, you see all the bad moves, all the evasions, all
> the extra words, all the bogus, you know, 'let's give this
> character a dead mother or a crippled sister, or make
> them sexually abused when they were a kid,' all the ways
> inexperienced writers try to lend their characters weight,
> meaning, as defined by tragedy. The editorial experience
> was just incredible. I learned more doing that than I did
> in any other aspect of my MFA program. The classes, the
> workshops, those were all helpful, but there was nothing
> like seeing the same mistakes over and over and over again.
> Writers who don't give the reader enough basic facts to
> figure out what's happening 'cause they think that's making
> the story 'mysterious' and it's gonna make people read on
> when it's really just confusing the fuck out of them. I mean,
> all those common mistakes, all the totally obvious similes
> and metaphors that get in the way of actually being in the
> world of the characters—I was just pounded by them day
> after day, and I think it made my prose, through that sheer
> process, at least less stupid, if not suddenly elegant and
> poetic.

I kept writing, kept dragging my tired ass out of bed every morning to write all week and weekend. And I kept reading journals, thinking often of what Almond said, and feeling a sense of relief that such a talented writer and thinker still used the word fuck so frequently.

When people find out that I'm a writer, people often nod and make kind comments like, "Sounds cool," followed by, "So who do you write for?" or "Where can I read some of your stuff?" This can go a few different ways.

I can tell them the confusing truth and say, "I mostly write for literary magazines," or I can try to simplify things by throwing in a few more recognizable mainstream publications that might counteract the effect of the obscure literary ones, such as, "I mostly write the essays for literary magazines, but I've written articles for places like *The New York Times* and *Men's Journal*." And, depending on how chatty I'm feeling, I might add, "for literary magazines like the *Paris Review* and *Kenyon Review*," though, through no fault of the listeners, such specificity doesn't always help. Those are just names to most people, the literary equivalent of a therapist expecting me to understand what she means when she says, "The patient in room two is a poor coping somatiziser with what feels like some serious Axis 2 issues." Even if I mention *The Paris Review* when describing who I've written for, it's mostly because, as one of the world's most-widely distributed literary magazines, more readers are likely to have heard of it than, say, the *Gettysburg Review*, though it's a great publication. Also, George Plimpton, one of *The Paris Review*'s longstanding founding editors, appeared on an episode of *The Simpsons*, and I hope a few people might make that connection. No one has yet.

No matter what I say, if I think too much about it, these simple exchanges can be dispiriting, because they offer proof that my life's central passion is a medium with which few readers are familiar. Essayists, like poets, have no choice but to make peace with this fact.

Because I don't write in order to pay my rent, I don't have to spend my waking life generating service pieces about the ten best hotels on the Amalfi Coast, or writing the text that ad people call "copy." I write because I'm curious about the world both inside and around me. I write because I'm simultaneously liberated and burdened by what author Jim Harrison describes as the writer's "vow of obedience to awareness," an "excessive consciousness" that drives me to record, share and make sense of things. Although I don't want to work in a fluorescent-lit cubicle for some hive-brain boss who begins sentences with clichés like "at the end of the day," I don't write just to avoid that kind of profession. I write in order to stay emotionally and intellectually engaged, and once I do, I try to find my readers, even if they're the hundred or so people who subscribe to a certain Midwestern lit mag. For those of us publishing in such places, those one hundred people are *our* people, both as readers and kindred spirits. If you put your email address in your author bio, those kindred spirits sometimes contact you. "Aaron," a young man once wrote me, "Today I was in Barnes and Noble flipping through the Spring Issue of the *New Ohio Review*, and was impressed by the poetry (being a poet myself) so I decided to buy it . . . I rarely if ever read non-fiction or short prose, but I took a chance and read your piece. It was immediately engaging, entertaining, moving, and meaningful on many levels." Kind words from a stranger.

There is an honesty in literary magazines often lacking in commercial ones, a willingness to shuck salability for the sake of whatever the less precious word for art is—beauty for beauty's sake, maybe, or just stuff no business-minded publisher would mess with. This isn't true across the board, but the overall sense of purpose is one that poet Robert Graves might have inadvertently expressed when he said, "There's no money in poetry, but then there's no poetry in money either."

As a writer, I've accepted that I may never publish a book. That's just the harsh reality of the market. As an essayist, I've made peace with the fact that I'm even less likely to publish a collection of essays. Despite the relative commercial success of essayists such as David Sedaris, Sloan Crosley, and David Rakoff, essay collections are notoriously difficult to publish with trade publishers. As an acquisitions editor at a major New York house once told me about such books: "We don't even think twice about rejecting them." Phillip Lopate captured the prevailing tone and logic in his 2010 essay "In Defense of the Essay Collection":

> In these uncertain times for the book trade, when the very
> future of the printed word seems in question, the one thing
> certain is that *no one wants to publish a collection of essays.*
> Your agent would prefer not to have to sell it, your old pub-
> lishers don't want to touch it, and even those pretty young
> editors who smile enticingly around the buffet table and
> give midlist authors such as yourself their cards don't want
> anything to do with it. Perhaps—*perhaps*—an essay collec-
> tion with a focus, a hot topic that will get an author on talk
> shows, yes, that's conceivable. But a mere compendium of
> random essays previously published in magazines, forget it.
> What could possibly be justification for such a miscellany,
> except misguided ego? A hip, briskly selling novelist one
> knows from the start is not going to give it his all, but is
> only trying his hand at this minor form—that could work,
> but a writer idiotic enough to be dedicated to essays from
> the start, no way.

I am proud to be that idiot.

We love stories; it's part of our nature. If I died tomorrow, and all I left as evidence of my existence was a bundle of essays, memories with friends, and some photos, I'd be content. And I'd have literary magazines to thank for that, all of the editors—student, faculty, volunteer and otherwise—that read my submissions, sent me encouraging notes, and suggested revisions, and who occasionally believed in these pieces enough to help me revise and publish them. And when my essays were ready to be read by others, these lit mags disseminated them. It's no exaggeration to say that, here among the lute players on the outer rings of popular consciousness, whatever I'm accomplishing as a writer, I owe to these magazines.

Lorin Stein affirms this essential relationship between reader and writer, a connection these journals foster: "Whatever its defenders say, the M.F.A. system has created a surplus of would-be writers and a deficit of habitual readers—and I'm afraid it shows in the work submitted to us here at the *Review*. This trend is easy to reverse, at least in your own life. Join the writing community for real: become a reader." It's a suggestion that I can vouch for, and which Faulkner put another way: "Read, read, read."

PUBLICATION

by Jane Armstrong (2008)

I was the least promising student ever admitted to the graduate creative writing program at Florida State University. I still don't know how I got in. I sent a term paper from a literature class as the manuscript with my application. I had never written a short story. I thought they'd teach me how to do that when I got there. And they did. More or less.

Two literary magazines were published out of Tallahassee. One, *Sun Dog* (now known less interestingly as *The Southeast Review*), was edited by second-year master's students and Ph.D. candidates. Gods. In workshop, simultaneously despised and worshipped, they coolly dispensed judgment, slashing the first-years' stories ex cathedra. At the magazine, they had the power to accept and reject. Out of their few acceptances, they made something, created a book. I devoured every issue I could find, trying to detect the specialness the editors discerned. I read the bios first. I still read the bios first. Who were these people? How could I become one of them? This became my only goal as a writer: To be published in a literary magazine like *Sun Dog*. Just one. Then I'd be a successful writer.

Apalachee Review was the other magazine. It's still called that. The editor-in-chief was a third-year Ph.D. candidate on fellowship. In the pantheon, he was Zeus. He was in the first fiction workshop I took. He said nice things about the second story I submitted to the class (the second story I had ever written). I thought he was showing pity to the nervous newbie. At the end of the semester, he asked if he could publish my story in *Apalachee Quarterly*.

When the issue came out, I couldn't stop looking at it, touching the linen textured card-stock cover, reading my bio (two lines), reading my story (four pages). That was it. Goal met. My career. *Apalachee Quarterly*, Number

22, 1985. I've taken that issue out lately, stroked it, trying to make it into a touchstone to a time when I was perfectly and completely satisfied, when one publication in one small magazine was enough. Is enough.

MEAT AND POTATOES

by T. C. Boyle (2008)

When I was a student at the Iowa Writers' Workshop in the 1970s, Ray Carver was hanging around Iowa City. He hadn't yet published his first collection, *Will You Please Be Quiet, Please?*, which came out in 1977, but we students knew his stories from the little magazines and we knew how good they were and how good he was. I was then beginning to publish my own work and I met Ray when I stopped by to see him one day and talk about editors and writing and the quality of the stories being published in the little magazines. He knew everything and everybody. No surprise. If I look now at the acknowledgments page in *Will You Please Be Quiet, Please?*, I see that Ray published in many of the magazines that would come to nurture and sustain me as I experimented with the form and collected the stories for my own first book, *Descent of Man*, which came out in 1979. My first story was published in the fall 1972 issue of the *North American Review* under the aegis of its longtime editor, Robley Wilson, Jr., and it was the imprimatur of that publication that made me feel that I was a writer after all, and it gave me the confidence (chutzpah?) to apply to Iowa, the only program I'd ever heard of.

Meat and potatoes, yes, indeed. That was what the literary magazines were to the writers of that period, as they'd been to the writers before them and as they are to the writers of today. The slicks may provide a different sort of entrée altogether, a little pricier, maybe, a little richer, and thank the gods for them, but it is, was and always will be the little magazines that give us all the chance to become writers. If I pull *Descent of Man* off the shelf today, I see that of the seventeen stories collected there, two appeared in *The Atlantic Monthly*, one each in *Harper's*, *Esquire*, and *Penthouse*, and the others in *The Paris Review*, *Epoch*, *TriQuarterly*, *The Transatlantic Review*, *Fiction*, *Quest 77* and *Quest 78*, and *South Dakota Review*. And these were only the seventeen stories I'd collected—there were as many others, all published in the quarterlies, that didn't make the cut, but that I'd nonetheless needed desperately to shake out and hold up and show to somebody.

And what about the dessert? That was the great gift and opportunity to cut my editing chops at *The Iowa Review*, where I began as assistant to one of my gods and heroes, Robert Coover, and finally graduated to the position of fiction editor. What did I think, that I was going to revolutionize publishing? Yes, I certainly did think that. The reality was a wee bit different, but I do believe we published some fine stories in that period and I was honored to have been offered the opportunity to see how things run from the editor's perspective. Speaking of which, my daughter, Kerrie Kvashay-Boyle, also got to work at *The Iowa Review* under the auspices of David Hamilton, under whom I'd joyously served during my final year at Iowa.

I remember the day that first story appeared in the *North American Review*. I hadn't yet received my copies, but I kept haunting the magazine room at the library until one day there it was, a miraculous presence laid out on the shelf for all to see. I went up the hill from the library on that wind-blown fall afternoon, feeling like a conqueror and calculating just how I might best spend the check I would soon receive, the first concrete acknowledgment that someone outside of my immediate circle felt that I had something. (God bless you, Rob.) Twenty-five dollars, that was what the pay came to. Forget the meat and potatoes. In those days, in Iowa City, twenty-five dollars bought one hell of a lot of beer.

COMMENTS

by Mary Grimm (2008)

When I worked for a college magazine that published fiction and poetry (along with articles of more general interest), I had two editors. I was reader of the slush pile and doer of other thankless jobs; my sister did PR and direct mailings. A happy little dysfunctional family, with two red-pen-slashing dads. We called them by their first names when they weren't around and mocked them unmercifully, but in some ways they were the best thing that happened to two dreamy would-be writers: they taught us to judge (and if necessary, reject), and to edit. Even better, since they were diametrically opposed in their approach to a text, they taught us that editing was nuanced, personal, and sometimes as creative as the original writer's work. Lou Milic was imperious, arbitrary: the kind of editor who brilliantly rewrites bad bits as he would write them himself. Leonard Trawick was marvelously insidious, for he got inside the text and suggested changes that the writer would have thought of, if only he had done a couple (or twenty) more drafts. One of their triumphs (fought over long and hard at staff meetings and in sniping memos) was the transformation of a monstrously unreadable article on sacred architecture into something that anyone with a college education could appreciate. When I started work for *The Gamut* (now regrettably extinct), I had written a few stories. I was waiting for my real life as a writer to begin, with no idea how that would happen. When I left six years later, I was a published writer, about to start teaching creative writing. A good part of that shift was due to working under my two beloved battling editors.

COMMENTS

by Rick Moody (2008)

Since literary magazines are incorporated to publish things that the big slick magazines don't want to publish, they should, by nature, be about range. What bugs me about literary magazines, therefore, is when they act like regional outposts for *The New Yorker* fiction department, which is to say when they act conservatively. I think the quarterly, by and large, should be a sloppy mess, full of experiments, full of heterodoxy, full of failure, even, but never ever dull. If you look at the whole field of small press publishing, it looks exactly like this: there are little stapled-together-on-newsprint publications that publish only free verse about homelessness, there are online magazines, there are rural magazines from colleges out in the corn belt that favor the rustic and unpretentious, there are heavily designed magazines with lots of art that are big enough to go on your coffee table with your art books. In short, there is every kind of literary magazine under the sun, not many of them ever worrying too much about readerships in the hundreds or low thousands. And this is as it should be. I got my start in magazines like this, magazines that favored risk (*Another Chicago Magazine* and the *Antioch Review* being two examples of places that took a chance on me). I still publish in the quarterlies regularly, and I feel, in truth, like they are my true home. I am a contributing editor to, I think, four literary magazines now, and when my time is short, I will not be thinking about the odd, uncharacteristic moments when the slicks published me; I will be thinking about how good it was to work in and to be read by the community of people who really know and understand literature. That readership exists in the quarterlies, and nowhere else.

Bottles in a Midnight Sea

by Benjamin Percy (2008)

I have slaughtered thousands of trees. Sometimes, late at night, when shadows play across the ceiling and sleep escapes me, I think about all the stories my printer has laid gently in its tray— all the manila envelopes shoved full, licked, pressed, stamped, then patted for good luck—all the rejection letters that snuck into my mailbox when my back was turned—and I feel a certain nervousness, imagining the dark forest that waits for me on the other side, eager to root through my bones and knock me about with its branches.

This dreadful nervousness—the nervousness brought on by piles of papery carcasses—assaults all writers. It is seeded in insecurity. No matter how hard we work, no matter how much or how long we write, no one will care. No one will run their eyes lovingly across the black letters we have stitched on white paper. All those hours we spent locked away—away from the zoo, the bar, the world—all for nothing. Without an audience—whether a teacher or a parent or a workshop or a magazine subscriber or a book club—a writer is impotent. Don't pretend to tell me you write purely for yourself. That's hippie talk.

Think of what we do. We close the door and sit alone, hunched over a keyboard, our fingers poised as if ready to cast some spell. Sometimes we type. More often we think—and sip from our stained coffee mug and chew our fingernails and pick at our scabs. We wear ill-fitting jeans. We need haircuts. We have squashy bellies. We talk to ourselves. It is a miserable existence, not so different than that of a gibbering lunatic who wanders his cell and fumbles vaguely with his genitals.

Alone. We are alone. And the literary journal is not only an antidote to our loneliness—it is the very reason we write.

The lunatic shakes the bars of his cell or howls from a street corner or scrawls bloody messages on a bathroom stall because he wants to be heard. I remember the rejection letters I used to receive as a grad student—the ones with some encouraging message scribbled across their bottom, advising me to shift the point of view or expand the backstory—or, or, or. To keep trying, in other words. I tacked these notes to my office door and read them count-less times—because someone had heard me, someone was out there. And when this very journal sent me my very first acceptance letter, I drank my way through a six-pack of Coors and danced to Lynyrd Skynyrd in my living room, I was so goddamned thrilled.

Because I wasn't alone after all, I realized.

Over time, now that acceptance has become the rule rather than the exception, the thrill has certainly lessened, but my objective and determina-tion remain the same: I am the lonely madman crumpling messages into bottles and sending them off into a midnight sea. Every response seems a miracle. Every publication makes me more and more gratefully aware of this community we belong to—all of us hidden away, only occasionally showing our faces, but engaged in an intimate, sacred togetherness made possible by journals whose pages serve as ink-stained harbors.

THE CHAIR OF REJECTION

by Stacey Richter (2008)

Before I published anything in a literary magazine, I was rejected by literary magazines, dozens of them, and these rejections gave birth to one of my more strange and long-lived art projects. At that time, before email, literary magazines would reject a person (me) with slips of paper inscribed with polite brush offs that usually included a combination of the words *pleased*, *quality*, *at this time*, *honored*, *we*, *the future*, and *however*. I collected these slips in a box, and when I had enough saved up I began to use them to decoupage an old wooden chair. I called this The Chair of Rejection and sat in it whenever I felt like a sucky writer and a worthless human being, which was often. This was fun because I don't like to be cheered up; I like to wallow, I find it restorative and oddly calming. However, I was pretty sure I was the only person who thought this way, so I kept quiet about the chair. But after a while, news of its existence began to leak out.

The problem was that even though I was rejected incessantly, I didn't have enough rejection slips to decoupage the entire chair from top to bottom (as my artistic vision commanded). So eventually I invited my friends to contribute their own rejection slips, and explained the idea of the chair to them, and was surprised to find that they were enthusiastic about it. I might even say that they were pleased with its quality and honored that I invited them to contribute to its future at this time. And I guess people liked the idea of having a specific place to go when they felt pathetic, because after a while my friends began to ask to come over and sit in the chair when they were rejected. The chair was hard, highbacked, and uncomfortable, which made it even better. More people began to drop by, and then a few more, until it became clear that sitting in The Chair of Rejection had become a new kind of emotional experience in my social set, a sanctioned wallowing. Everyone was into it.

Then something shifted—I think this was after a reporter I knew published a short piece about the chair in a weekly newspaper. After that, it wasn't just my friends who stopped by. Acquaintances I'd only met once or twice began to come to my house and ask for the chair; sometimes complete strangers even showed up. Every time I heard a knock on the door, I wondered if I'd open it to find an unshowered person waiting there slack-faced, maybe a little hung-over or possibly still drunk. I think the chair emitted some sort of silent whistle only the forlorn could hear, and it seemed like they were helpless to refuse the call. "Can I use your chair?" the person would ask. I'd usually let them. They'd shuffle across the room, they'd collapse in its embrace. The rejection slips were glossy with lacquer and singed around the edges (this is how I learned to decoupage in summer camp), and the dejected person would press their knees together and slump into a cloud of disheartening words: *"Despite the quality of your submission . . ."*

It took a while, but eventually everyone I knew, no matter how smart or talented or pretty or fortunate, sat in the chair. There was something mystical about this. We all sit in the chair. I knew this! But metaphors are just words that zing around in your head. Until you actually *sit* in the chair of rejection—until you actually see everyone you know sitting in the chair of rejection—you don't *really* know that someday everyone must take their seat. I was learning this. The chair was teaching me.

Though my rejection slips were from literary magazines, my friends brought over other kinds of rejections—from employers, graduate programs, foundations, ex-lovers; there was even one from the Army. It didn't take long to collect enough slips to finish decoupaging the chair. Once every surface was covered, including the bottom of the legs, I had to consider ending the project. Yet it seemed wrong to end the project. If it ended, what would people do with their rejections? It was boring to learn from them when we could make something out of them instead. So I found a little wooden table and covered that, and then a foot stool. Then someone had the idea to wrap a six pack of beer bottles with various rejections (eventually to be known as Thank You for Your Application Beer); by then it was almost starting to be fun to be a loser. Almost, but not exactly. There's no way quite to describe the feeling of sitting in The Chair of Rejection, with your feet up on The Guggenheim Foundation Hates You Footstool, drinking a bottle of Thank You for Your Application Beer. It was awful, it was wonderful, but mostly it was strange to feel how something as trivial as decoupage could change the pain of smashed hopes and shattered dreams into something different.

Then, one day, I got a letter that said I'd been accepted. And then another. And after a while I got an agent who screened things and the rejection letters didn't pour in at the same rate. Time passed and my friends began to be accepted too. They found good jobs or got into graduate programs or had wonderful babies that were better than any residency program on some stupid harbor. I moved and moved again. I still sat in the chair, but after a certain number of acceptances I didn't *need* to sit in the chair anymore. Other people stopped wanting to use it too and the chair migrated to a back room where it gathered dust. I guess I got out of the habit of sitting in the chair. When I felt like I sucked—when I feel like I suck—I'd sit by myself, in any random location, and feel bad without any special fanfare or equipment.

When I moved the last time, The Chair of Rejection wound up in storage in the shed of a pothead friend. The awful thing that's happening now, which is also kind of great, is that the bank is foreclosing on his house. This wouldn't be great except for the fact that he's started using the notices from his creditors as wallpaper. When I was over there a week ago, he'd brought the chair into the kitchen, which was already half-covered with threatening notes, and started plastering over the appliances. I sat there smoking his brain-melting indica as he went on about his grand scheme to cover every interior surface of the house with letters from creditors, rejection letters, dear John letters, divorce petitions, whatever he could get his hands on. If he had enough time before he was evicted, he said, the entire house would eventually be transformed into a giant monument to pain, failure, and disappointment. Everyone would want to see it; even winners would want to. It's human nature. He'd charge admission.

"Uh, I don't think so," I said.

"What do you mean?"

"It sounds like a stoner fantasy. I don't think it's actually feasible."

For a moment my friend stared at me with bloodshot eyes. Finally he said, "Write it down," and handed me a slip of paper.

Though we are pleased by your insane idea, I wrote, *we do not think it's actually feasible at this time.*

I handed it to my friend. He brushed some glue on the back and stuck it on the oven door.

COMMENTS

by Jim Shepard (2008)

A few years ago at Notre Dame I gave the sort of reading I often find my-self giving if I stray out of Brooklyn or lower Manhattan. In this case I was marooned in an immense hall before fifteen or so undergraduates who seemed to have been selected for their nearly completely unresponsive faces. After I'd finished, the guy who'd introduced me announced that there'd be time for a few questions. A girl in the front row raised her hand and asked, "Where do you get your *ideas?*" the way you or I might ask our mother where she found that beaver pelt.

In other words, I'm not always—or almost never—*New Yorker* mate-rial. My stuff is strange enough that it's often not mainstream, and on top of that, as everyone will tell you, the mainstream is contracting rapidly, as fewer and fewer trade magazines are willing to devote space to fiction. All of which means that smart and resourceful editors that can A) keep a literary journal going and B) keep it interesting and provocative are becoming more and more crucial when it comes to the literary landscape. Or at least when it comes to *my* literary landscape. Some of my stuff that's struck me as the most ambitious, whatever its other strengths and weaknesses, was stuff that I un-derstood immediately upon completion was going to need a non-mainstream home. And so: thank God for people like Rob Spillman, who made sure that *Tin House* found a place for an oddly modular and tonally ambiguous story narrated by John Ashcroft. Or for people like Eli Horowitz, who read a thirty page and probably excessively creepy story narrated by one of Gilles de Rais' accomplices, and responded on behalf of *McSweeney's*, "Sure. We can publish that." *Try something new. Try something weird. Try something a little disruptive to reader expectations*: the major trade magazines are less built for

that than ever. Which means that for the foreseeable future, literary magazines are going to be carrying more and more of the load, when it comes to
the production of literature in these United States. Which means, as well,
that it's up to us to spread the word about them.

COMMENTS

by Shara McCallum (2012)

So, what do I think about literary magazines? I probably engage them most, to be honest, as a writer. It's not that I don't read literary magazines at all; but I prefer reading books by a single author over the anthology approach to reading poems. I guest-edited an issue of *West Branch* a few years ago—and very much enjoyed that process—but I don't think of myself as an editor either. My interface with literary magazines as a poet who tries to get her work in print in them, then, is the best way for me to entertain your question.

To that end, I have a good deal of ambivalence toward them. I am very grateful to those editors who have published and continue to publish my poems—for the encouragement it's given me at times when I really needed it, as well as for helping to create an audience for poetry (my poems as well as those of others). But I still really don't like sending out my work to magazines, and I am not sure I'd ever do it if journal and book publications weren't in some way connected. I send to literary journals, as most every poet I know does, but I have been and remain pretty determined not to focus any large amount of time or energy on the task. I often go two or more years after a book comes out before I start sending poems to magazines again, and I love these periods in my writing life where I am *not* submitting work. It's not just the prospect or actuality of rejection that I don't like (of course, that's no fun). It's that I find the whole process of sending out work and waiting for a response (consciously or unconsciously) to be an unwelcome distraction from writing. Another reason I like to go long periods without sending my poems to editors is that I write in spurts, and I like to wait a good while to make sure I'm happy with the work I am sending.

When I do get ready to submit, for the past fifteen or so years, I've pretty much sent poems to the same journals/magazines that published me when I was first starting out and didn't yet have a book. There are exceptions—every so many years I'll try a magazine that hasn't taken my work before. But I'm not very persistent or methodical about it. I also don't simultaneously submit work in any large fashion, because it has always felt to me like I'm being inconsiderate to the editors of the magazines, as well as to other writers out there. I figure no one is getting a decent reading if an editor is screening thousands of poems a year; and, partly as a response to this, we now have more and more magazines run by students. While this is good experience for the students—and I know many of them work tirelessly on these magazines, so I am not condemning the students who work on these magazines when I say this—I think this is not a healthy practice for poetry.

I have friends who are writers (some of whom are also editors) who tell me my personal ethics concerning magazine publishing are really out-of-date and out-of-touch, and I believe they are right; but I haven't so far been able to bring myself to send work in the way I see so many other writers doing now—constantly submitting and exponentially (not multiply) submitting their work to every magazine under the sun. I recognize that I've been lucky enough to continue to have poems published despite my approach; but I've also been clear with myself that I don't care enough (not that I don't care at all—just not enough) about being in a wider selection of journals to spend more time on this aspect of publishing. As old-fashioned a notion as it may be, at the end of the day—when my work does appear in journals—I also really like the idea that I have a professional relationship with the editor and she (sometimes he—though most often it's been she, in my experience) with my work.

COMMENTS

by Andrew Foster Altschul (2012)

Boy, do I hate literary journals. Why? First of all, there's so damned many of them, crammed with work by writers from all over the literary map. I've never heard of half these people! What business do they have piling up on my nightstand, making me feel guilty? And they just keep coming.

Plus: some of this stuff is just weird. I don't know about you, but I like my literature safe and predictable. Why can't we stick to a few big, corporate publishers, putting out a limited number of books by nice, established authors—you know, the kind who always win the awards? Books about the stuff we always read: bad marriages, mother-daughter reconciliation, personal redemption. Stuff Oprah likes. Who has time for anything else?

If we keep letting these upstarts publish these "little magazines," there'll be no end to the risky, unfamiliar, even *experimental* writing that gets published. We'll have crazies from outside New York and San Francisco thinking they've got a shot at publication—nameless, faceless writers, hordes of them every year, banging at the gates, crashing our cocktail parties, distracting us from the *New York Times* Bestseller List.

So that's the other thing: How often do you see a literary journal on the *New York Times* Bestseller List? Am I right? Face it: these things don't sell. They don't make any money! How valuable can they be? Is this, or is this not, America?

No, we can't afford to let these people muddy our pristine literary waters. Let's form a committee, pass some laws, build a wall if we have to. Literary journals must be stopped.

COMMENTS

by Lucy Ives (2012)

Whenever I have not been working as an editor at a magazine I have always been a little sad. (Childhood, certainly, but also in later periods.) If you've ever tried to write something with another person, then you know how difficult this is. It's infinitely easier to edit with others.

Someone else writing here may well have quoted the André Breton line, "One publishes to find comrades!" I'm only really able to say something about the work of editing. I'm actually not even all that clear on what is so special about publication. At one time it was a necessary evil; now it is something that everyone has to do all the time.

So here is what I think: you can learn a lot from editing other people's work, from talking to them about what they're doing. That's probably selfish, but it's true. On the other side of this, an editor might hope that her aggregation, her choices and interventions, and the choices of those she works with, make sense to others, or seem new to others, or overall aren't useless, but maybe that would just be extra?

COMMENTS

by Andrew Porter (2012)

I've always felt that literary magazines play an important (even crucial) role in literary culture, but their most valuable service is perhaps to the young writer or at least to the writer who is just starting out. For those who don't yet have the confidence or life experience to write an entire novel or complete an entire short story collection, a single publication in a literary magazine can give him/her hope. That single publication says to the young writer: well, yeah, maybe you can do this. That single publication can also give the young writer a chance to begin building a readership or perhaps attract the interest of an agent or help advance his/her career in some other way. Few of us have the fortitude to simply write a big book without any small signs along the way that we might actually be skilled enough to do such a thing, and those literary magazine publications—whether they come every few months, or every few years—are one of the few important signs we rely on.

Comments

by Laura van den Berg (2012)

Over the years, I've had the good fortune of working for a number of magazines in a number of different capacities. While the editorial education has been invaluable, it has also radically changed the way I approach the submission process (if you ever have a chance to work for a lit mag, do it!). I came to understand that hundreds, sometimes thousands, of writers were vying for publication in the same journals I was sending to. I learned that rejection is hardly ever personal. I used to think "this isn't the right fit" was bullshit, but sometimes it really does come down to just that—a story, despite its obvious merits, just not striking you in the way you want to be struck. I stopped seeing editors as heartless gatekeepers, but people who were willing to work incredibly hard to find literature that resonated with them and to share that vision with others. Perhaps more than anything, working for literary magazines taught me to treat submitting like a job. Send your best work, do your research, do your best to shake off the rejection and keep submitting, and stay focused on what matters: the work. I had—and have—plenty of angst about publishing. Not even the most well-adjusted among us is immune to the difficulty of rejection and the anxiety that can accompany it, but the real angst should be saved for laboring over sentences and characters. This is our art; this is what we have the power to perfect. Much of the rest is, ultimately, in someone else's (probably very dedicated, probably very subjective) hands.

COMMENTS

by G. C. Waldrep (2012)

Literary magazines and journals have always represented, to me, the best sort of extracurricular conversation: among writers, yes, but more importantly, among works. There's an imbrication, an electricity of contact that happens when this poem is placed next to that story (or poem or essay, etc.). This human conversation is, over time, what we call literature. The value of literary magazines and journals is that each issue constitutes a quick snapshot of that conversation, that particular moment in time, who's standing next to whom, what energies are flowing back and forth among the products of our varied talents and imaginations. In art as in life, some conversations are more interesting—and more enduring—than others.

When I first started out as a writer, I had doubts—ethical, aesthetic, procedural—about publishing. What made me overcome those doubts was wanting my poems to be part of this larger conversation. As an editor, I aspire to curate that same sort of human conversation, create those same shocks of delight and terror a creative juxtaposition of works can produce.

VI. SELECTED MANIFESTOS

Perhaps more than the average magazine, literary magazines tend to have very passionate reasons for being. These were often expressed during literary Modernism as manifestos, and are documented more commonly in the more business-minded world today as mission statements. These manifestos/missions give a (hopefully) clear vision of the intent of the publication, how its editors see it fitting into and reacting against the wider literary, popular, perhaps even political, realities. Ideally, these should be read against the actual published objects with which they are aligned, which are the physical manifestations of these abstracted ideals.

THE EDITOR TO THE READER

by Ralph Waldo Emerson
(*The Dial,* Volume 1, Number 1, July 1840)

THE DIAL: 1840–1844; 1860; 1880–1929

We invite the attention of our countrymen to a new design. Probably not quite unexpected or unannounced will our Journal appear, though small pains have been taken to secure its welcome. Those, who have immediately acted in editing the present Number, cannot accuse themselves of any unbecoming forwardness in their undertaking, but rather of a backwardness, when they remember how often in many private circles the work was projected, how eagerly desired, and only postponed because no individual volunteered to combine and concentrate the free-will offerings of many co-operators. With some reluctance the present conductors of this work have yielded themselves to the wishes of their friends, finding something sacred and not to be withstood in the importunity which urged the production of a Journal in a new spirit.

As they have not proposed themselves to the work, neither can they lay any the least claim to an option or determination of the spirit in which it is conceived, or to what is peculiar in the design. In that respect, they have obeyed, though with great joy, the strong current of thought and feeling, which, for a few years past, has led many sincere persons in New England to make new demands on literature, and to reprobate that rigor of our conventions of religion and education which is turning us to stone, which renounces hope, which looks only backward, which asks only such a future as the past, which suspects improvement, and holds nothing so much in horror as new views and the dreams of youth.

With these terrors the conductors of the present Journal have nothing to do,—not even so much as a word of reproach to waste. They know that there is a portion of the youth and of the adult population of this country, who have not shared them; who have in secret or in public paid their vows to truth and freedom; who love reality too well to care for names, and who live by a faith too earnest and profound to suffer them to doubt the eternity of its object, or to shake themselves free from its authority. Under the fictions and Customs which occupied others, these have explored the Necessary, the Plain, the True, the Human,—and so gained a vantage ground which commands the history of the past and the present.

No one can converse much with different classes of society in New England, without remarking the progress of a revolution. Those who share in it have no external organization, no badge, no creed, no name. They do not vote, or print, or even meet together. They do not know each other's faces or names. They are united only in a common love of truth, and love of its work. They are of all conditions and constitutions. Of these acolytes, if some are happily born and well bred, many are no doubt ill dressed, ill placed, ill made—with as many scars of hereditary vice as other men. Without pomp, without trumpet, in lonely and obscure places, in solitude, in servitude, in compunctions and privations, trudging beside the team in the dusty road, or drudging a hireling in other men's cornfields, schoolmasters, who teach a few children rudiments for a pittance, ministers of small parishes of the obscurer sects, lone women in dependent condition, matrons and young maidens, rich and poor, beautiful and hard-favored, without concert or proclamation of any kind, they have silently given in their several adherence to a new hope, and in all companies do signify a greater trust in the nature and resources of man, than the laws or the popular opinions will well allow.

This spirit of the time is felt by every individual with some difference,—to each one casting its light upon the objects nearest to his temper and habits of thought;—to one, coming in the shape of special reforms in the state; to another, in modifications of the various callings of men, and the customs of business; to a third, opening a new scope for literature and art; to a fourth, in philosophical insight; to a fifth, in the vast solitudes of prayer. It is in every form a protest against usage, and a search for principles. In all its movements, it is peaceable, and in the very lowest marked with a triumphant success. Of course, it rouses, the opposition of all which it judges and condemns, but it is too confident in its tone to comprehend an objection, and so builds no outworks for possible defence against contingent enemies. It has the step of Fate, and goes on existing like an oak or a river, because it must.

In literature, this influence appears not yet in new books so much as in the higher tone of criticism. The antidote to all narrowness is the comparison of the record with nature, which at once shames the record and stimulates to new attempts. Whilst we look at this, we wonder how any book has been thought worthy to be preserved. There is somewhat in all life, untranslatable into language. He who keeps his eye on that will write better than others, and think less of his writing, and of all writing. Every thought has a certain imprisoning as well as uplifting quality, and, in proportion to its energy on the will, refuses to become an object of intellectual contemplation. Thus what is great usually slips through our fingers, and it seems wonderful how a lifelike word ever comes to be written. If our Journal share the impulses of the time, it cannot now proscribe its own course. It cannot foretell in orderly propositions what it shall attempt. All criticism should be poetic; unpredictable; superseding, as every new thought does, all forgone thoughts, and making a new light on the whole world. Its brow is not wrinkled with circumspection, but serene, cheerful, adoring. It has all things to say, and no less than all the world for its final audience.

Our plan embraces much more than criticism; were it not so, our criticism would be naught. Everything noble is directed on life and this is. We do not wish to say pretty or curious things, or to reiterate a few propositions in varied forms, but, if we can, to give expression to that spirit which lifts men to a higher platform, restores to them the religious sentiment, brings them worthy aims and pure pleasures, purges the inward eye, makes life less desultory, and, through raising man to the level of nature, takes away its melancholy from the landscape, and reconciles the practical with the speculative powers. But perhaps we are telling our little story too gravely. There are always great arguments at hand for a true action, even for the writing of a few pages. There is nothing but seems near it and prompts it,—the sphere in the ecliptic the sap in the apple tree,—every fact, every appearance seem to persuade to it.

Our means correspond with the ends we have indicated. As we wish not to multiply books, but to report life, our resources are therefore not so much the pens of practiced writers, as the discourse of the living, and the portfolios which friendship has opened to us. From the beautiful recesses of private thought; from the experience and hope of spirits which are withdrawing from all old forms, and seeking in all that is new somewhat to meet their inappeasable longings; from the secret confession of genius afraid to trust itself to aught but sympathy; from the conversation of fervid and mystical pietists; from tear- stained diaries of sorrow and passion; from the manuscripts of young poets; and from the records of youthful taste commenting on old works of art; we hope to draw thoughts and feelings, which being alive can impart life.

And so with diligent hands and good intent we set down our Dial on the earth. We wish it may resemble that instrument in its celebrated happiness, that of measuring no hours but those of sunshine. Let it be one cheerful rational voice amidst the din of mourners and polemics. Or to abide by our chosen image, let it be such a Dial, not as the dead face of a clock, hardly even such as the Gnomon in a garden, but rather such a Dial as is the Garden itself, in whose leaves and flowers and fruits the suddenly awakened sleeper is instantly apprised not what part of dead time, but what state of life and growth is now arrived and arriving.

The Motive of the Magazine

by Harriet Monroe (*Poetry,* Volume 1, Number 1, October 1912)

Poetry: 1912–PRESENT

In the huge democracy of our age no interest is too slight to have an organ. Every sport, every little industry requires its own corner, its own voice, that it may find its friends, greet them, welcome them.

The arts especially have need of each an entrenched place, a voice of power, if they are to do their work and be heard. For as the world grows greater day by day, as every member of it, through something he buys or knows or loves, reaches out to the ends of the earth, things precious to the race, things rare and delicate, may be overpowered, lost in the criss-cross of modern currents, the confusion of modern immensities.

Painting, sculpture, music are housed in palaces in the great cities of the world; and every week or two a new periodical is born to speak for one or the other of them, and tenderly nursed at some guardian's expense. Architecture, responding to commercial and social demands, is whipped into shape by the rough and tumble of life and fostered, willy-nilly, by men's material needs. Poetry alone, of all the fine arts, has been left to shift for herself in a world unaware of its immediate and desperate need of her, a world whose great deeds, whose triumphs over matter, over the wilderness, over racial enmities and distances, require her eve-living voice to give them glory and glamour.

Poetry has been left to herself and blamed for inefficiency, a process as unreasonable as blaming the desert for barrenness. This art, like every other, is not a miracle of direct creation, but a reciprocal relation between the artist and his public. The people must do their part if the poet is to tell their story to the future; they must cultivate and irrigate the soil if the desert is to blossom as the rose.

The present venture is a modest effort to give to poetry her own place, her own voice. The popular magazines can afford her but scant courtesy— a Cinderella corner in the ashes—because they seek a large public which is not hers, a public which buys them not for their verse but for their stories, pictures, journalism, rarely for their literature, even in prose. Most magazine editors say that there is no public for poetry in America; one of them wrote to a young poet that the verse his monthly accepted "must appeal to the barber's wife of the Middle West," and others prove their distrust by printing less verse from year to year, and that rarely beyond page-end length and importance.

We believe that there is a public for poetry, that it will grow, and that as it becomes more numerous and appreciative the work produced in this art will grow in power, in beauty, in significance. In this belief we have been encouraged by the generous enthusiasm of many subscribers to our fund, by the sympathy of other lovers of the art, and by the quick response of many prominent poets, both American and English, who have sent or promised contributions.

We hope to publish in *Poetry* some of the best work now being done in English verse. Within space limitations set at present by the small size of our monthly sheaf, we shall be able to print poems longer, and of more intimate and serious character, than the popular magazines can afford to use. The test, limited by ever—fallible human judgment, is to be quality alone; all forms, whether narrative, dramatic or lyric, will be acceptable. We hope to offer our subscribers a place of refuge, a green isle in the sea, where Beauty may plant her gardens, and Truth, austere revealer of joy and sorrow, of hidden delights and despairs, may follow her brave quest unafraid.

"As for the future, it cannot possibly shock us, since we have already done everything possible to scandalize ourselves. We have so completely debunked the old idea of the Self that we can hardly continue in the same way. Perhaps some power within us will tell us what we are, now that the old misconceptions have been laid low. Undeniably the human being is not what we commonly thought a century ago. The question nevertheless remains. He is something. What is he?"

—Saul Bellow

MINOR ASPIRATIONS AND MOCK DEBATE

by Charles Newman (*TriQuarterly,* Number 1, 1964)

TriQuarterly: 1958–1964 (STUDENT PRINT PUBLICATION); 1964–2010 (NATIONAL PRINT PUBLICATION); 2010–PRESENT (MFA-STUDENT RUN ONLINE PUBLICATION)
There are two kinds of magazines—those which fascinate with nouns, and those which delight in verbs. The former are more proper: dealing modestly with time and life, they assert rather than explain; to sell things, they *name* things. The latter, more common, more active, tend to make a statement, ask a question, give a command. Their tenses are generally more progressive and less tangible. This is a perfect situation for dialectic, but there isn't one. It is not at all as simple as that. This accounts for the ambiguity of the title—*TriQuarterly.* We read it as an adverb—a modified occurrence, in which *action* and *naming* are indivisible. It may tell place, sense, manner, frequency, degree, direction. Yes and no are also adverbs.

PLURALISM
When Dos Passos said, "All right! Now we are two nations," he was right save one particular—the number. Dualism for his generation dramatized a final disgust with oneness, the phony unities of the modern world. We have since learned that even something elemental as disgust is not easy to come by. In a society where poets use the marketing techniques of advertising, where businessmen hire poets to sensitize their images, where radicals captivate the very audience they are pledged to destroy, where the bourgeois find anarchism fashionable, where the ethics of corporations and universities appear interchangeable, it is difficult to draw that old dialectic taut again. Heaven and Hell are no longer popular concepts in an affluent democracy. The social

TriQuarterly 26
WINTER 1973 $2.95

these be

s!

r genitals!
f them,

the
n never
2!

ency,
s,

of teachers,
rsons!
. the lobster,
like
ning but copies

he atmosphere...

Ongoing American Fiction I ➤ ➤ ➤ ➤ ➤ ➤ ➤ ➤ ➤ ➤

scientists have given us another, less pejorative vocabulary to explain our-selves. What De Tocqueville noted as the tyranny of equality, what Jefferson envisioned as the chance for each talent to find its own authority, we call now Pluralism—which is both the fear and promise of unlimited possibility. Now we are x nations.

It is possible, of course, that we simply cannot calculate fast enough, that a machine will come up with that number and set us straight again. But that is to assume that mere *naming* will again suffice. It is who makes use of that pure mathematics, and how, which concerns us. Pluralism means that the number in Dos Passos' retort is an unknown integer. It does not mean that any single reply is inadmissible—but that answers are viable, dangerously so, precisely because they are mutable. Pluralism means that the stuff of each choice is a genuine confusion, and that order may be as various as the unique personalities which lay claim to it.

Order is perverse then, when a personality is absent or synthetic. Mod-ern journalism is awesomely adept in avoiding the price of order. In collec-tive editorializing, the personality is subsumed by committee for the sake of consistency. The voice must never catch or waver; that would complicate things. There are the 'Objectivists,' on the other hand, who would let the "images speak for themselves." Thus, we are treated, in successive exposures, to a president, a quadruple amputee, tomato soup, a debutante, and earth-quake—bound together simply because they are all "news." In one case, the perspective is synthetic; in the other it is non-existent. Both lack the unity of personal vision and the courage implicit. Commercialism is only one kind of cowardice, however. Who know what to make of that president, that cripple, that girlie, that soup, that disaster.

ART

Modern art is the creative personality's confrontation with pluralism—the sharing of the spectrum. There is an old and engaging ideal that art, litera-ture, particularly, might structure reality in such a way as to develop human sensitivity, and if not create values, at least indicate alternatives. A figure as recent as James Joyce is said to have thought that the worst thing about World War II is that it kept people from reading *Ulysses*. The *Sturm und Drang* literary reviews at the time of "two nations" believed that after that blasting, what floated back to earth would find new roots, grow new patterns. It is no secret that all the pieces did not fit together. The tradition that Art might affect Life, even uplift it, is now carried on, not so much by artists, but by the profession of criticism, which—whatever its merits as a discipline in itself—must be considered a rear guard action in terms of art.

A most compelling fact of modern life is that much of modern art seems to repudiate it. It is the old debate between Jefferson and De Tocqueville again; whether you choose to celebrate the dynamism or the vulgarity of a pluralistic world. The cultural elite used to allow that people get along pretty well without art. It has taken them the last half century to say that art gets along pretty well without people—since the people confuse their capacity to react with the artist's ability to explore.

It is not for us to gauge the proper relationship between art and society, or even to bring the mind and marketplace together. They are already too close for comfort. The idea that art should serve society is impractical, not because some societies, like ours, have failed at it, or others like Russia, have succeed all too well—but simply because it is impossible to harness the creative personality to a phenomenon which is more or less than himself. It takes too much out of everybody concerned.

But what if society should serve art? The artist's task, we have often been told, is to question without regard to the consequences. Society's task is less newsworthy, but no less compelling—for they must have the courage to confront questions which not only do not occur to them, but which they could not answer if they did. In that sense appreciation is a selfless act. It is the audience, themselves, who must reject the synthetic order of those who serve their needs or presume to create them. In the supermarket the consumer must provide his own synthesis.

The necessity for the artist's personal vision, the value of his partiality is clear. The creative individual has his place, such as it is. Art, and what passes for it, is surely taken seriously enough. Perhaps it is the audience in which we no longer believe.

THE UNIVERSITY

Proof of pluralism is that we can now talk of the university in the same breath with art and society. Higher education has come in for a good share of attention lately. It has been criticized both for a willful aloofness from society and its needs, and for a fatally perfect adaptation to society and its impositions. One thing is clear—its scope has been immeasurably increased—not only does everyone end up at college, but as institutions, universities have been made responsible for everything from driver training to the preservation of grand opera. Given modern military and technological goals, some have acquired a power, prestige, and concomitant awe, once reserved for nation-states. The competition between them is purer than between our oligopolies; the politics within them as proselytizing as in any of our parties. They insist upon tangible credentials from a society whose motive force has always been a pragmatic test of talent. They talk among themselves in specialized languages provocative as any underground, yet justify themselves to society in a common counter-revolutionary rhetoric. They are becoming a sub-culture unto themselves.

Most importantly, perhaps, is the number of artists who are not only educated in universities, but make their subsequent living off them. What this relocation of dissent will cost us is not yet clear. It has gone far enough, however, that the old Bohemian/Bourgeois debate has been set along new lines; the "academic" and the "beat," or in Robert Lowell's words between the "cooked" and the "uncooked." We want to elaborate that debate—make the dialectic something more than the rejection of some foul unity. We are not interested in making anybody's career, although we hope our existence may dignify many. We hope to search out new talent, and encourage the established to venture beyond their reputations.

One recalls, however, that universities, like all institutions dependent upon the good will of the community, have not always been receptive to the kind of questions good artists ask. One can tell artists to avoid such institutions, or demand that the institutions become more accountable. It may be that in the expanding university, we are witnessing an affluent democracy's oblique answer to the patronage system of the old world—although we could not afford to call it that yet. Still, leisure does strange things to people. And the university's function, most magnificently conceived, has after all been roughly akin to the artist's, in that it is pledged to the damnation of spurious order, and devoted to questions that society will not, alone, ask itself. This does not negate synthesis; it simply enhances its value. The university serves art by witnessing the pluralism of society.

All this implies the concept of limited revolution; revolution in the America tradition by chance, in that it makes use of the Establishment. We believe that to be more in accord with both the ideal and the real. This is not the time to profess loyalty to institutions, but to the discipline which keeps institutions alive.

Our task is to assemble. Literary reviews provide no more viable standards than I.Q. tests or annual income. They are simply another alternative; an attempt to bind temperament and action through language. Without resorting to epilogues or manifestoes, we want to embellish those proper nouns and common verbs which have made our culture too often a vehicle for minor aspirations and mock debate. It will be a modern enterprise, perhaps embarrassingly so, in that we are justified by little save our own potential. We're getting dressed up to celebrate the fact we're still looking.

n+1

$11.95US $13.50CAN

0 74470 58387 5

06>

Editorial Statements

by the *n+1* Founding Editors

N+1: 2004–PRESENT

The following are two drafts of the n+1 *mission—the first, "Preamble: The Infinite Series," from an* n+1 *prototype issue, and the second, "Editorial Statement," from* n+1 *issue one, the first nationally distributed issue of the journal.*

Preamble, The Infinite Series
N+1, PROTOTYPE, 2004

I.

Everywhere we see a loss of confidence. Believe in yourselves!

Somebody taught us the unsayable. It became the unthinkable. We traded our truth for a false amiability. We came to doubt our dreamed-of world because no one else dreamed of it.

We hear that society is sick. The demands on our bodies go too much against nature: sick. The hypocritical reversals of values in politics go too much against our goodwill: sick. The distribution of money goes against our unhappiness that other people suffer: sick. But too sick to speak?

The doubt we experience today is a common cold. Someone coughed on us and we got hoarse. The fever crept up, and we took to our bed. The sickbed is the right place from which to launch your attacks. Feverish, you have nothing to lose.

This is true convalescence. Let me put my ear close to your lips: "I—have—nothing—to—lose." You have nothing to lose. Take a chisel: add the unsuspected other side to one, to show what it will equal in the real world. Understand this as positive negation: an act of canceling that exposes the consequences of the terms, to clear us for something new.

Undo a piety, and you will give someone room to think. "Fresh air!" And that means mostly saying no, before anything else.

The task of the thinker now has to be to clear some room, to make an open space for thinking.

Abbie Hoffman watched television with a message taped beneath the screen: "Bullshit." Thinkers, do your duty!

Tomorrow is the first day. All our memories of the past will only make us wake up the more gladly to it. Our era is the cold you don't need to catch. But if you do: let the symptoms of this illness be your health.

II.

Our answer is in thinking.

Thought is evenly distributed, as a capability. It is the basis of democracy. It's seen as an indulgence in a time of quick reactions, thumbs up or thumbs down. Our job now, as we understand it, is to counter-think ordinary convention, so as to free others to think differently. The statements are engraved.

III.

Our answer is in politics.

From Republicans to Democrats, you go from dumber to dumb.

The "end of history" came when we were still teenagers. Know-it-alls are always ending history when someone else is just beginning it. An argument was made that this political system was final, markets embodied the principles of democracy, and time's epilogue would extend this permanent present-day to the whole globe. This was a terrible concept to us. Subsequently, its adherents admitted technology might still produce a little history yet. A false generosity: as if we should take from our machines what we can no longer shape with other men and women.

No one should pretend to speak of "what the American people want," or believe, or know any longer. The broken poll data, each fact disconnected from the rest, make everybody believe the rest of the country is against him. It's not in human nature to identify with a percentage. But oddly you do believe the percentages that are against you.

In politics, the left lacks the courage to say that the war on terror is not opposed to terror and not a war. It lacks the coherence to keep two thoughts in mind: our democracy is the best the world has known, and also unfulfilled.

We know by now the stupidity of this worship of the market. Rather than argue with the prancers around a Golden Calf, drop the tablets. Go listen to the voice for a new dispensation.

Americans, show some faith in your neighbors! Could it be possible every citizen of the United States has been counseled that no one else believes what he does?

IV.

Our answer is in art.

Hand-wringing is unnecessary, because the cardboard cut-outs of today will be pulled down tomorrow. The artists of our time, nobodies now, will warm their hands around the fires of undeserved reputations. Every age suffers its own mediocrity. History doesn't.

A new aestheticism is needed: the doctrine that the limitations of human life are justified and redeemed through art, and art has as its duty the analysis of the changing conditions of life.

Those who kicked against limits were sick. Thoreau, Flaubert, Nietzsche, Lawrence, Woolf, Foucault. The rebellion against limits starts the best love of human beings and worldly nature. It circles back, inevitably, to a discovery of the hidden aspect of what already is, a concentration on the unlimited wonders of earth.

Perfectionism is right for thought, wrong for technology. The people who want to undo human limits in our physical world, end death, medicine our bodies, swell our brains, drug our moods, escape the planet, are ones who don't know to see the excess and limitlessness that is in art.

Numb to life, they extend their numbness to immortality.

If an entirely fresh language came into being, unfamiliar in words and syntax, that was still intelligible to us—it could only be in a work of art. And if our existing language shed its dead layers, and revealed new truths to us—it could only be in a work of art.

V.

Our answer is in the thinker, the artist, the political being, who will be one and the same.

The antinomian, the nonconformist, the nihilist, the anarchist, the aesthete, will all be others' names for him or her; yet his allegiance is to the muser, the letter-writer, the saunterer, the idle gazer, the daydreamer, the reader.

The idea of progress is not uncomfortable to us. The question is who controls its direction. Who will drive progress?

To every tradition, and every art, and aspect of culture, and line of thought, a step is added. This dream of advance in every human endeavor, in line with what we need, not just what we're capable of, is futurism humanized. It is wanted in a time of repetition. It is needed whenever authorities declare an end to history. It is desperate when the future we are offered is the outcome of technology. It is called for now.

To those who insist the series is at an end, we say: **n+1.**

EDITORIAL STATEMENT
N+1, NUMBER 1, 2004

We are living in an era of demented self-censorship. The old private matters—the functions of the body, the chase after love and money, the unhappiness of the family—are now the commonest stuff of public life. We are rotten with confession. But try saying that the act we call "war" would more properly be termed a massacre, and that the state we call "occupation" would more properly be termed a war; that the conspiracy theories, here and abroad, which have not yet been proved true by Seymour Hersh or the General Accounting Office are probably, nonetheless, true; or that the political freedoms so cherished and, really, so necessary, are also the mask of a more pervasive, insidious repression—try saying all this, or any of it, and see how far you get. Then try saying it in a complex way, at some length, expressing as you do so an actual human personality.

We are living in a time when Nabokov and Henry James are read in Tehran but we have pornography and publicity at home; a time when serious writing about culture has become the exclusive province of bullies, reactionaries, and Englishmen; a time when journalists can refer to Vladimir Sorokin, a towering figure of Russian postmodernism, as a "shocking" writer who became a "best seller" after his books were trampled in public by a neofascist youth group; a time when a magazine like *Lingua Franca* can't publish, but *Zagat* prospers. In the future, it will be seen as a time when some of the best people in our intellectual class gave their "critical support" to a hubristic, suicidal adventure in Iraq.

The problem is hardly a lack of magazines, even literary magazines. Culture can expand now to fill the superstore. But civilization is the dream of advance—to find the new, or take what we know from the past and say it with the care that only the living can claim. "One must have been in exile and in the wilds to appreciate a new periodical," said Alexander Herzen, founder of the mighty *Bell*. Perhaps you live in the city or the town, and in the safety of your own country. But you have known the exile, and are acquainted with the wilds.

VII.
APPENDIX
MATERIALS

The various areas of human life literature touches can hardly be contained in the pages of one book, and this is true for the literary magazine as well. What follows then is an assortment of material—from a literary magazine timeline to guidelines for writers—that will hopefully help to cover some of this vast territory, and some magazines, underexplored in the earlier material.

FENCE

Winter
2008-09

Some Notes on the History of the Literary Magazine

These "Notes" were completed with the generous assistance of Richard Burgin, Speer Morgan, Bradford Morrow, Marco Roth, and Robley Wilson.

1684—*Nouvelles de la Republique des Lettres* is begun by Pierre Bayle in France. Though it might not be recognized as such by today's definition, the magazine is widely regarded as the first literary magazine due to its editorial focus on literature.

1711—First issue of British daily newspaper *The Spectator* is published, regarded as a literary heir to literary magazines and public interest journals. Brought out at the height of early eighteenth century coffeehouse reading culture and during the "Grub Street" surge in writing and publishing, each paper was believed by editor Joseph Addison to be read by twenty people.

1815—The oldest currently publishing American magazine, *North American Review*, begins publication in Boston under the editorship of William Tudor. The magazine ceased publishing in 1940, but was revived in 1964 by Robert Dana (at Cornell College) and later flourished for thirty years at the University of Northern Iowa.

1817—*Blackwoods* magazine is founded by William Blackwood. Originally begun as the *Edinburgh Monthly Magazine*, Blackwood soon fired the editors and renamed the publication. In its more than seventy year publication history, *Blackwoods* was a strong proponent of romanticism, fostering the

The first issue of *Big Table* reproduced the entire contents of the suppressed winter 1959 *Chicago Review* issue, which included Burroughs's excerpt.

1960—Saul Bellow, Keith Botsford, and Jack Ludwig release the first issue of *The Noble Savage*. Though, largely due to Bellow's influence and fame, the magazine publishes a good percentage of quality writing from significant authors—the first issue had work from art critic Harold Rosenberg, an excerpt from a forthcoming novel by Ralph Ellison, and poetry from John Berryman that would be included in his *Dream Songs*—the magazine's backer Meridian pulls the plug after just five issues.

1962—Edward Sanders begins anti-establishment *Fuck You, a magazine of the arts*, which claimed it was "Edited, Published & Printed by Ed Sanders at a Secret location in the Lower East Side, New York City, USA." The magazine was a seminal work of the Mimeo Revolution in American publishing—a proliferation of cheap, independent magazine and book production.

1962—Soviet literary magazine *Novy Mir* publishes Alexander Solzhenitsyn's novella O*ne Day in the Life of Ivan Denisovich*. Within a day all 95,000 copies of the issue had been purchased and Solzhenitsyn was catapulted into international fame.

1967—Theodore Solotaroff begins *New American Review* (later changes to simply *American Review* in 1973). For a decade it is one of the nation's most significant literary magazines. Its first issue had writing by Philip Roth, Grace Paley, Anne Sexton, William H. Gass, Robert Graves, and John Ashberry, among others. Roth's story "The Jewish Blues" from the first issue of the magazine became a section of his popular and controversial novel *Portnoy's Complaint*.

1972—First issue of *Yardbird Reader* is released, edited by Ishmael Reed, Al Young, Shawn Wong, Frank Chin, and William Lawson. The magazine is a prime example of the burgeoning interest in world and minority writing throughout American literary publishing. In its five volumes, *Yardbird* published the work of a wide range of cultures, such as African American, Asian American, Colombian, Puerto Rican, Filipino-American, Franco-American, Anglo- American, North African, Kenyan, and Caribbean.

1972—Mark Jay Mirsky begins *Fiction* magazine in New York (layout of the magazine is designed by Donald Barthelme). The magazine becomes a major venue for experimental fiction writing from around the world.

WINTER 1970 / NUMBER 1   TWO DOLLARS

the NEW YORK QUARTERLY

1972—Herbert Leibowitz begins *Parnassus,* which soon grows to be the premiere venue for scholarly writing on contemporary poetry.

1976—First Pushcart Prize annual published by Bill Henderson, begun in an effort to bring greater recognition to the small and independent presses.

1976—H. Rowell begins African American literary magazine *Callaloo* in Baton Rouge, LA. It quickly grows to become one of the most prominent African American literary magazines.

1978—*TriQuarterly* and Pushcart Press together publish *The Little Magazine in America: A Modern Documentary History,* edited by Elliott Anderson and Mary Kinzie. Intended as a follow-up to Princeton's study of the literary magazine thirty years earlier (see 1947 above), the book covers recent literary magazine history through essays by and interviews with a variety of editors and scholars in the field, such as George Plimpton, Robert Boyers, Gilbert Sorrentino, Leroi Jones, Karl Shapiro, and Anne Waldman.

1978—Poets Larry Levis and Marsha Southwick found *The Missouri Review,* along with first *TMR* managing editor Eric Staley. Current editor Speer Morgan takes over the following year, and in 1984 the magazine becomes a pioneer online magazine by establishing a "pre-web" internet site, which it maintains for three years.

1980—*The Threepenny Review* is begun in Berkley, California by the then twenty-seven-year-old Wendy Lesser. Though having almost no editing experience at the time, Lesser quickly turns *Threepenny* into one of the most respected literary magazines in the nation. The publication is printed in tabloid format on newsprint, allowing Lesser to keep the price low and the quality of writing high.

1980—First issue of *The Quarterly* is released. Edited by Gordon Lish, it is of no surprise that the magazine remains influential in its promotion of literary minimalism in the forms of the very short story and dirty realism (a phrase coined by *Granta* editor Bill Buford for a theme issue of his magazine in 1983).

1980—*Ontario Review* editor Raymond Smith begins Ontario Review Press, one of the first and most respected of a later widespread trend of book imprint start-ups by literary magazines. Many of these book imprints are begun in an effort to counteract diminishing literary magazine sales.

1981—Bradford Morrow founds *Conjunctions* at Bard College, soon becoming well-known for its promotion of experimental and slipstream work by

Ms 73   50c

new World Writing

An Important Cross Section of Current Literature and Criticism

First Mentor Selection
A New American Library Publication

writers such as Richard Powers, Kelly Link, and David Foster Wallace. Morrow received the PEN/Nora Magid Award for Magazine Editing in 2007.

1984—Frank Davey, Fred Wah, and David Godfrey start *Swift Current*, regarded as the first online literary magazine. Technically, the magazine was a literary database loaded onto a VAX 11-750 computer located at York University in Toronto and made accessible by subscription to personal users and institutions. More of a creative commons than an editor-run literary publication, *Swift Current* nonetheless served as a forerunner to the now popular online literary magazine.

1986—The first issue of *Boulevard* debuts, founded and published by Richard Burgin, who also helped found *Boston Review* in 1975. The magazine becomes known for its aesthetic diversity and writer symposiums on such subjects as the Internet, writers in the university, and film.

1987—*Witness* is launched in Detroit and has since received much acclaim. The magazine is best known for its special issues focusing on contemporary themes of social interest, such as writing from prison, the holocaust, ethnicity, and aging.

1992—Marc Smirnoff begins *Oxford American* five years after his car broke down in Oxford, Mississippi. Smirnoff decided that the south needed a general interest magazine of its own in the same vein as *The New Yorker*. After the magazine ran out of money two years later, popular legal thriller novelist (and Oxford resident) John Grisham picked up the tab. It bounced around from various revenue streams, eventually landing at University of Central Arkansas in 2004, becoming a non-profit soon after.

1995—*Mississippi Review* publishes its first full-content (not an advertisement for a print edition) online issue.

1998—Rebecca Wolff launches *Fence* and Dave Eggers launches *Timothy McSweeney's Quarterly Concern* (commonly called *McSweeney's*). Both magazines soon develop popular followings and become representative of new trends in literary production towards experimental and ironic work. Thanks largely to the philanthropy and success of Eggers, *McSweeney's* goes on to develop a following and influence outside the typically literary magazine audience, often cited in major national and international media.

2002—*Poetry* is given $200 million by pharmaceutical heiress Ruth Lilly. This is by far the largest endowment ever received by a literary magazine, and apparently has secured the magazine financially in perpetuity.

2002—*One Story* publishes its first issue, titled "Villanova or: How I Became a Former Professional Literary Agent," written by John Hodgman. This is the first literary magazine to devote each issue to the publication of a single piece of writing. *One Story* later becomes the first literary magazine available by subscription on Amazon's Kindle.

2003—Ted Genoways takes over as editor of the *Virginia Quarterly Review* and directs the magazine's editorial focus more towards that of a general interest publication by adding more journalism and photography. *The Paris Review* follows suit a year later, forcing out disagreeing editor Brigid Hughes and bringing in journalist Philip Gourevitch of *The New Yorker* to take her place. Circulation numbers for both magazines soon begin to increase.

2004—First issue of *n+1* is published by Keith Gessen, Benjamin Kunkel, Mark Greif, Chad Harbach, Allison Lorentzen, and Marco Roth, all becoming successful authors themselves in the first decades of the 21st century. The magazine fills the gap in literary/political magazine publishing left by the disappearance of such magazines as *Partisan Review*. Though sometimes criticized as elitist—and painted as a foil to McSweeney's publication, *The Believer*—the magazine is also applauded for publishing critical commentary of the literary and intellectual world, something many peer literary magazines shy away from.

2008—Two longstanding literary magazine institutions, *Granta* (1889) and *The Southern Review* (1935), both hire their first ever female editors, Alex Clark and Jeanne Leiby, respectively. Alex Clark steps down as editor the following year. Much more tragically, Leiby dies in a car accident just three years into the job, after making great strides with the magazine and successfully maneuvering the 2008 financial recession.

2008—Taking their lead from the trend in commercial magazines, *Opium* magazine publishes the first literary magazine eco-minded Green Issue. The issue is thematically focused on the environment and printed on wholly recycled paper, with none of the issues delivered by air.

2009—Recent Brooklyn College graduates Andy Hunter and Scott Lindenbaum launch *Electric Literature*, offering the publication on paper, as an e-book, on the iPhone, and in audio format. The publication quickly begins a trend towards multi-platform publishing in the industry. *EL* also experiments with publishing on Twitter, quickly accumulating over 150,000 followers on the social media platform.

A Quote History of Literary Magazines

"Journals are already books written with others. The art of writing with others is a strange symptom which foreshadows a great progress of literature. One day we will perhaps write, think, act collectively."
—Novalis (1772–1801), commenting on German Romantic literary magazine *Athenaeum*

"The study of American magazine history dates from 1741 when Benjamin Franklin and Andrew Bradford published the first real magazines in the country. They were called, respectively, *General Magazine* and *American Magazine*, and they appeared three days apart—Bradford's first, much to Franklin's chagrin."
—Eric Staley in *The Missouri Review*'s 1983 issue devoted to the literary magazine

"The story of the little magazine is in itself a fascinating and an important part of our history. It is a story of ideas, of experiments in style, and of personalities."
—from preface to *The Little Magazine: A History and a Bibliography*, 1947

"I consider [magazines] such easy vehicles of knowledge, more happily calculated than any other, to preserve the liberty, stimulate the industry and meliorate the morals of an enlightened and free people."
—first U.S. President George Washington

"The significance of the small magazine has, obviously, nothing to do with format. The significance of any work of art or literature is a root significance that goes down to its original motivation."
—Ezra Pound, November 1930, *The English Journal*

"The value of fugitive periodicals 'of small circulation' is ultimately measured by the work they have brought to press."
—Pound

"The work of writers who have emerged in or via such magazines outweighs in permanent value the work of the writers who have not emerged in this manner. The history of contemporary letters has, to a very manifest extent, been written in such magazines."
—Pound

"When there is not the binding force of some agreement, however vague or unanalyzed, between three or four writers, it seems improbable that the need of a periodical really exists. Everyone concerned would probably be happier in publishing individual volumes."
—Pound

"The little magazine is something I have always fostered; for without it, I myself would have been early silenced. To me it is one magazine, not several. It is a continuous magazine, the only one I know with an absolute freedom of editorial policy and a succession of proprietorships that follows a democratic rule. There is absolutely no dominating policy permitting anyone to dictate anything. When it is in any way successful, it is because it fills a need in someone's mind to keep going. When it dies, someone else takes it up in some other part of the country—quite by accident—out of a desire to get the writing down on paper. I have wanted to see established some central or sectional agency which would recognize, and where possible, support little magazines. I was wrong. It must be a person who does it, a person, a fallible person, subject to devotions and accidents."
—William Carlos Williams

"*The English Review* sets boldly upon its front the words 'No party bias.' This means to say that we are here not to cry out 'Go in this direction,' but simply to point out where we stand."
—from the editor's note in the first issue of *The English Review*

"The little magazines, of course, are absolutely indispensable. They give the beginning writer his first important step—a chance to see how the thing looks in print. And there's nothing as salutary."
—Letter from Stephen Vincent Benét to Charles Allen, September 1939

"Nothing would please me more than a quarterly such as you suggest; there is no project more difficult."
—William Carlos Williams in response to Richard Johns' request that he be on the board of Johns' new literary magazine venture, *Pagany*

"I hope (this is a personal prejudice I have had for a long time) you never go in for names. To hell with 'names.' If I were king and could run a magazine and, let's say for instance, Dreiser, Anderson, and Joyce sent me some pieces I didn't like and I thought were rotten I'd stick a one-cent stamp on each piece and shoot them back like a bad check."
—Erskine Caldwell in a 1930 letter to Richard Johns, editor of *Pagany*

"As soon as I was invited to do this little introduction to Richard Johns' memorable literary magazine I got a complete, bound file of *Pagany* from the University of California library. As I looked through it, it was just like Proust's madeleine."
—Kenneth Rexroth in his 1969 introduction to *A Return to Pagany*

"The average magazine editor's conception of good verse is verse that will fill out a page. No editor is looking for long poems; he wants something light and convenient. Consequently a Milton might be living in Chicago today and be unable to find an outlet for his verse."
—Founder and former editor of *Poetry*, Harriet Monroe, in her autobiography, *A Poet's Life*

"A review is not measured by the number of stars and scoops it gets. Good literature is produced by a few queer people in odd corners; the use of a review is not to force talent, but to create a favourable atmosphere."
—T.S. Eliot to Ford Madox Ford

"In what a high-pitched anticipatory mood we ducked into this book shop once or twice a week to see what was new on its magazine rack. Here were the publications of the new movements in American art and thought and literature. Here were the reviews that were stimulating the young. Here were the magazines we wanted to write for."
—Gorham Munson, former editor of *Secession* (1922–4)

"If I had a magazine I could spend my time filling it up with the best conversation the world has to offer."
—Margaret Anderson, founder and former editor of *The Little Review*

"I have none of the qualifications of the editor; that's why I think *The Little Review* is in good hands."
—Anderson's editorial in *The Little Review*, February 1915

"You said I was
Such a terrible poet, I'd better
Do something useful and become
A publisher, a profession which
You inferred required no talent
And only limited intelligence."
—New Directions publisher James Laughlin on Ezra Pound's influence regarding his career choice, from his verse autobiography, *Byways*

"I was an adventurer; *Hound & Horn* was my passport . . ."
—Lincoln Kirstein remembering the national literary magazine he founded as a Harvard undergraduate, *Hound & Horn* (1927–34)

"A revolutionary and not a reform magazine; a magazine with no dividends to pay; a free magazine; frank, arrogant, impertinent, searching for the true causes; a magazine directed against rigidity and dogma wherever it is found; printing what is too naked or true for a moneymaking press; a magazine whose final policy is to do as it pleases and conciliate nobody, not even its readers—there is room for this publication in America."
—Printed in the masthead of each issue of *The Masses*

"Most of all, however, the editors felt that they could best serve their region by insisting on the highest possible standards of excellence for the magazine itself. The phrase 'highest possible' is a tricky thing here. What is 'possible' for any magazine is what is actually available, from issue to issue, for its pages. And what is 'highest' is what the editors feel to be highest. So, in a fashion, a magazine is at the uncertain mercy of the morning mail delivery and the taste of its editors."
—Cleanth Brooks and Robert Penn Warren on their founding of *The Southern Review*

"Among the other points I tried to make was one which involved *The Paris Review* having no axe to grind. In this we're pretty much in agreement, I believe, although one of you mentioned the fact that in the first number of *The Exile* there were 'powerful blasts' by Pound, among others, which added considerably to the interest of the magazine. True, perhaps. But is it because we're sissies that we plan to beat no drum for anything; is it only because we're wan imitations of our predecessors—those who came out bravely for anything they felt deeply enough was worth coming out bravely for? I don't think so. I think that if we have no axes to grind, no drums to beat, it's because it seems to us—for the moment, at least—that the axes have all been ground, the drumheads burst with beating."
—William Styron in a 1953 editor's note to the first issue of *The Paris Review*

"Resembling a Rorschach test, 'literary journal' is a fuzzy little ink blob of a name. To a romantic, it might bring to mind *The Paris Review*, its very title carrying the whiff of Hemingway paring down sentences at some Left Bank cafe in the 1920s. Never mind that the journal was founded in the 1950s and has an office overlooking the East River."
—Columnist Caryn James in a 1989 article for *The New York Times*

"One proposition we all agreed on and did achieve was that we wanted to get away from the style of most of the other American literary quarterlies, with *Partisan Review* in the lead, which were steeped in literary and political theory, as were our French counterparts . . . You were not serieux unless you were politically engagé—no matter what. I, on the contrary . . . was convinced that theories, both literary and political, are the enemy of art."
—an early managing editor of *The Paris Review*, John Train, reminiscing on the magazine's early life

"A review needs a firm centre, a compact group with some similarity of viewpoint or opinion who provide the paper with character."
—Malcolm Bradbury, *The London Magazine*, August 1958

"Little magazines are 'the furnace where American literature is being forged.'"
—Peter Michelson, former editor of *Purple Sage*, quoting George Hitchcock, former editor of *Kayak* (1964–84)

"Hemingway remains the only person the Editor has ever seen buy a copy of the magazine."
—George Plimpton, co-founder and longtime editor of *The Paris Review*, reflecting on meeting Hemingway in Paris

"Every little-magazine editor who is worth his salt knows that he's creating a work of art and, in the aggregate, creating a new genre."
—Poet and curator Felix Pollack in a 1977 interview

"Yes, I believe the time of isms is over. There are no more flaming manifestos in magazines."
—Pollack

"The historical character of the literary periodical is immutable. It cannot for a moment be separated from its context in the accumulative literary record. Unlike a play by Shakespeare, and ode by Keats, a lyric by Wordsworth, a novel by Joyce, a periodical never achieves—in a single issue, in a single volume, in its whole serial run—even a quasi transcendence."
—Lewis P. Simpson, former editor of *The Southern Review*

"When John Crowe Ransom turned the *Review* over to me, he said simply, 'Now I can get a good night's sleep for the first time in years.'"
—Robie Macauley on his taking over as editor of *The Kenyon Review*

"I remember that shortly after I came to *Poetry*, *Time* magazine sent a reporter over to Erie Street, and he said, 'What is your policy?' I was sort of horrified because I never thought of a literary magazine having a policy in *Time*'s sense."
—poet Karl Shapiro on taking over as editor of *Poetry* in 1950

"If the next generation sees the present as dull and empty, I'm certain we will see the birth of another literary movement that will view the present generation of younger writers as the establishment, and launch its own rebellious magazines."
—novelist Gilbert Sorrentino on his years as book editor for *Kulchur* and editor of *Neon*

"I started *Fiction* out of desperation. One is supposed to be ashamed to admit such things."
—Mark Jay Mirsky, founder and editor of *Fiction*

"Most people have sports stars as their idols. Not me. My real heroes are the selfless editors of the hundreds of reviews published for small audiences all over America."
—literary agent Nat Sobel

"What the hell do we have to worry about that for? Half the people who read the magazine don't know what the hell we're saying. So why do we need more readers?"
—Roger Straus quoting *Partisan Review* co-founder and former editor William Phillips

"Working with younger writers, and reading magazines in which they publish such as *Tin House* and *McSweeney's*, I have noticed a coherent generational style and sensibility. Strange is the new normal, irony the new sincerity, and fragmentation the new unity."
—James Nolan in *Boulevard*

"Journals are the prime archeological dig of the American Imagination."
—J. D. McClatchy, editor at *The Yale Review*

"I suspect most of us who persist in this business, either as writers or editors, do so because we believe the connection between language and life is worth preserving. It's a deeply conservative impulse, really, though the aim is, or ought to be, toward the future."
—Christian Wiman, former editor of *Poetry* (2003–13)

"This is the dirty little secret about editors of literary magazines: not a few of them were writers who couldn't get their own work published."
—Don Lee, former editor of *Ploughshares*

"I wanted it [*McSweeney's*] to have the almost tragically personal feel of a newspaper run by a loony old man."
—Dave Eggers, founder/editor of *Timothy McSweeney's Quarterly Concern*

"Let's face it. Most literary magazines are powerfully evocative of smelly socks: the smelly socks poking out of the sandals worn by some unwashed poet standing on a street corner trying to sell you his or her (although, for some reason, invariably his) awful, earnest, tedious publication."
—Bill Buford, editor of *Granta* from 1979–95

"It's almost like you press a button for scholarly journal and they come out looking the same."
—Joshua Glenn, publisher of *Hermenaut*

"To start a little magazine, then—to commit yourself to making an immutable, finite set of perfect-bound pages that will appear, typos and all, every month or two, or six, or whenever, even if you are also, and of necessity, maintaining an affiliated Web site, to say nothing of holding down a day job or sweating over a dissertation—is, at least in part, to lodge a protest against the tyranny of timeliness. It is to opt for slowness, for rumination, for patience and for length. It is to defend the possibility of seriousness against the glibness and superficiality of the age—and also, of course, against other magazines."
—A.O. Scott article in *The New York Times*, 2005

"There will always be idealists and happy fools, so there will always be literary magazines."
—Rob Spillman of *Tin House*

"The magazine is an object filled with objects."
—Tod Lippy, editor of *Esopus*

DISCOVERIES: A LIST OF FIRST FICTION PUBLICATIONS

The following information was compiled by referencing the 1994 anthology First Fiction: An Anthology of the First Published Stories by Famous Writers *(Back Bay Books), edited by Kathy Kiernan and Michael M. Moore.*

Nelson Algren—"So Help Me," *Story*, August 1933

Margaret Atwood—"The War in the Bathroom," *Alphabet*, 1964

James Baldwin—"Previous Condition," *Commentary*, October 1948

Harold Brodkey—"The State of Grace," *The New Yorker*, November 11, 1954

Charles Bukowski—"Aftermath of a Lengthy Rejection Slip," *Story*, April 1944

Truman Capote—"My Side of the Matter," *Story*, May–June 1945 [first story *sold*]

Raymond Carver—"Furious Seasons," *Selection*, Winter 1960–61

John Cheever—"Expelled," *The New Republic*, October 1, 1930

William Faulkner—"Landing in Luck," *Mississippian*, November 26, 1919

F. Scott Fitzgerald—"Babes in the Woods," *Nassau Literary Magazine*, May 1917

E. M. Forster—"Albergo Empedocle," *Temple Bar*, December 1903

Graham Greene—"The End of the Party," *London Mercury*, January 1931

Mark Helprin—"Because of the Waters of the Flood," *The New Yorker*, September 27, 1969

Chester B. Himes—"Crazy in the Stir," *Esquire*, August 1934

Shirley Jackson—"After You, My Dear Alphonse," *The New Yorker*, January 16, 1943

David Leavitt—"Territory," *The New Yorker*, May 31, 1982

Ursula K. Le Guin—"April in Paris," *Fantastic*, 1962

Doris Lessing—"The Pig," *Trek*, April 1948

Mary McCarthy—"Cruel and Barbarous Treatment," *The Southern Review*, Spring 1939

Carson McCullers—"Wunderkind," *Story*, December 1936

Norman Mailer—"The Greatest Thing in the World," *Story*, December 1941 [College Fiction contest winner]

Bernard Malamud—"Benefit Performance," *Threshold*, February 1943

Henry Miller—"Mademoiselle Claude," *The New Review*, Fall 1931

Alice Munro—"A Basket of Strawberries," *Mayfair*, November 1953

Joyce Carol Oates—"In the Old World," *Mademoiselle*, 1959 [*Mademoiselle* College Fiction contest winner]

Flannery O'Connor—"The Geranium," *Accent*, 1946

Grace Paley—"Goodbye and Good Luck," *Accent*, 1956

Dorothy Parker—"Such a Pretty Little Picture," *The Smart Set*, December 1922

Philip Roth—"The Day It Snowed," *Chicago Review*, Fall 1954

William Saroyan—"The Daring Young Man on the Flying Trapeze," *Story*, 1934

Irwin Shaw—"Flash in the Pan," *Stage Theatre Guild Quarterly*, 1936

Isaac Bashevis Singer—"Gimpel the Fool," *Partisan Review*, 1953 [first in English-language]

Jane Smiley—"And the Baby Makes Three," *Redbook*, May 1977

Muriel Spark—"The Seraph and the Zambesi," *The Observer*, December 1951 [newspaper]

Jim Thompson—"Oil Field Vignettes: Thumbnail Biographies of Three Picturesque Characters of the Drilling Fraternity," *Texas Monthly*, February 1929

John Updike—"Friends from Philadelphia," *The New Yorker*, October 30, 1954

Kurt Vonnegut—"Report on the Barnhouse Effect," *Collier's*, February 11, 1950

Alice Walker—"To Hell with Dying," *The Best Short Stories by Black Writers*, 1967 [anthology]

Eudora Welty—"Death of a Traveling Salesman," *Manuscript*, June 1936

Tennessee Williams—"The Vengeance of Nitocris," *Weird Tales*, August 1928

40 Over 25: Honoring the Longevity of America's Literary Magazine Editors

by David Messineo (2012)

In 2011, David Messineo, Publisher and Poetry Editor of Sensations Magazine *(www.sensationsmag.com), got curious as to how many other poetry editors,
fiction editors, and literary magazine publishers in America served on literary
magazines for 25 years or more and still remained active today. His original research published in* Sensations Magazine *Issue 49 identified 37 active editors
and/or publishers, 17 past editors and/or publishers, 3 "likely to achieve 25 years
by 2015," and 12 poetry reading series operating continually in America for over
20 years. Messineo updated the article for republication in* Sensations Magazine
*in December 2013, offering a preview of the 2013 "active editor" list here be-
low, recognizing 40 individuals. In order by starting year, it includes years in
service in the field, individual's name, literary magazine(s) served, and base
of operation for current publication. The number of years in service is accurate
as of 2013; citations where starting year and years in service differ indicate a
break in service for one or more years. Finally: the timeframes include the entire
2013 year—so, for example, 1986 to 2013 would be 28 years of editing service.*

1. 1966 - 47 yrs. - Bob Hershon - *Hanging Loose* (Brooklyn, NY)

2. 1966 - 47 yrs. - Dick Lourie - *Hanging Loose* (Brooklyn, NY)

3. 1966 - 47 yrs. - Richard Mathews, Ph.D. - *Florida Quarterly, Konglom-
erati,* and *Tampa Review* (Tampa, FL)

4. 1969 - 44 yrs. - David Young - *FIELD* (Oberlin, OH)

5. 1971 - 38 yrs. - David Walker - *FIELD* (Oberlin, OH)

6. 1972 - 41 yrs. - George Core - *Sewanee Review* (Sewanee, TN)

7. 1972 - 41 yrs. - Herbert Liebowitz - *Parnassus: Poetry in Review* (New York, NY)

8. 1972 - 41 yrs. - Mark Jay Mirsky - *Fiction* (New York, NY)

9. 1973 - 40 yrs. - R.T. Smith - *Cold Mountain Review*, Southern Humanities Review, and Shenandoah (Lexington, VA)

10. 1974 - 39 yrs. - Sy Safransky - *The Sun Magazine* (Chapel Hill, NC)

11. 1976 - 32 yrs. - Richard Peabody - *Gargoyle* (Arlington, VA)

12. 1976 - 37 yrs. - John Rosenwald - *Beloit Poetry Journal* (Farmington, ME)

13. 1976 - 37 yrs. - Susan Weidman Schneider - *Lilith* (New York, NY)

14. 1977 - 36 yrs. - Robert S. Fogarty - *Antioch Review* (Yellow Springs, OH)

15. 1977 - 36 yrs. - Stephen Corey - *The Devil's Millhopper* and *The Georgia Review* (Athens, GA)

16. 1977 - 34 yrs. - Laura Boss - *Lunch* and *Lips* (Guttenberg, NJ)

17. 1978 - 35 yrs. - Speer Morgan - *The Missouri Review* (Columbia, MO)

18. 1979 - 33 yrs. - Donald Lev - *Home Planet News* (High Falls, NY)

19. 1979 - 33 yrs. - Bradley R. Strahan - Black Buzzard Press/*Visions-International* (Austin, TX)

20. 1979 - 31 yrs. - David Messineo - *Images*, *The Monthly*, *Alternative Motifs*, and *Sensations Magazine* (Lafayette, NJ)

21. 1980 - 34 yrs. - Philip Fried - *The Manhattan Review* (New York, NY)

22. 1980 - 34 yrs. - Maria Mazziotti Gillan - *The Paterson Literary Review* (Paterson, NJ)

23. 1980 - 34 yrs. - Wendy Lesser - *The Threepenny Review* (Berkeley, CA)

24. 1980 - 34 yrs. - Bradford Murrow - *Conjunctions* (Annandale-on-Hudson, NY)

25. 1980 - 34 yrs. - Mark Pawlak - *Hanging Loose* (Brooklyn, NY)

26. 1982 - 31 yrs. - Robert W. Lewis - *North Dakota Quarterly* (Grand Forks, ND)

27. 1983 - 25 yrs. - Walter Cummins - *The Literary Review* (Madison, NJ)

28. 1983 - 31 yrs. - Frank Finale - *Without Halos* and *the new renaissance (tnr)* - NJ editor serving Arlington, MA publication

29. 1983 - 31 yrs. - Jill Hoffman - *Mudfish* (New York, NY)

30. 1985 - 29 yrs. - Richard Burgin - *Boulevard* (Richmond Heights, MO)

31. 1986 - 28 yrs. - Rodger Martin - *The Worcester Review* (Worcester, MA)

32. 1987 - 27 yrs. - Lee Sharkey - *Beloit Poetry Journal* (Farmington, ME)

33. 1988 - 26 yrs. - John Daniel - *Wilderness Magazine* – (OR editor serving Washington, DC publication)

34. 1988 - 26 yrs. - Virginia Howard - *Thema* (Metairie, LA)

35. 1988 - 26 yrs. - Marilyn Hartl - *Sensations Magazine* – (NY editor serving Lafayette, NJ publication)

36. 1988 - 26 yrs. - Timothy Monaghan - *The Ledge Poetry & Fiction Magazine* (Bellport, NY)

37. 1988 - 25 yrs. - Tom Plante - *Exit 13* (Fanwood, NJ)

38. 1989 - 25 yrs. - Michael Koch - *Epoch Literary Magazine* (Ithaca, NY)

39. 1989 - 25 yrs. - Frank Stewart - *MANOA* (Honolulu, HI)

40. 1989 - 25 yrs. - Sander Zulauf - *Journal of New Jersey Poets* (Randolph, NJ). Mr. Zulauf also founded and published the annual Index of American Periodical Verse from 1971 to 1980.

Submitting to Literary Magazines

by Katie Chase (2008; with minor updates for 2012)

This piece was originally composed for University of Iowa undergraduate students.

Nothing makes you feel like a "real writer" like sending out that first piece to a journal in hopes of publication. Even if you figure that in return you'll only receive a slip of paper rejecting it—you're still on your way. But how does all this work? Here are some questions you might consider during the process:

Is the Piece Ready?

Send your best revised work. This means, if you feel half-heartedly about a piece, chances are others will feel the same and probably it's not worth sending out. This also means, don't send out the first draft of a new work the day after you've finished it. Let a piece sit for a time (months, at least), find other critical readers for it: revise until it's stood the test of time and in your mind is the very best you can make it, representing the best of what you can do creatively.

Where to Send?

Research your mags. Don't send blindly. Take the time to research what mags are out there, what kind of work they typically publish, what they're looking for currently. The best way to research them is by reading them—most will have info on their web site on how to order a sample copy. You can also peruse the excellent collection at Prairie Lights [an Iowa City bookstore] or the university or city library; keep up with blogs on books and writing for what's new and hot; scan the pages of magazines like *Poets and Writers* for ads and calls for manuscripts.

In your research, what you're looking for is an idea of the magazine's style and needs. Start a list of mags that interest you, mags where you think your work would fit and be presented to your liking. You might order the list from your highest hope to your next best bets and start from the top. Always check the publication's web site before sending to make sure they're currently reading manuscripts and if they're looking for anything in particular. (Sometimes a journal will be reading for a special issue on a particular theme.)

ONLINE RESOURCES.

Newpages.com – they not only list what may be every single one currently in print, but they also review monthly a selection of journals, giving you a good idea of what each one publishes.

Webdelsol.com – promotes and provides links to several independent journals.

PRINT RESOURCES.

Writer's Market (comes out annually) – your bible; includes such valuable information as how often publications select new writers and if they pay. Worth buying one and double-checking its information in following years. Also available for your perusal at the library.

Poets and Writers Magazine (bimonthly) – each issue lists upcoming deadlines for contests.

MAGAZINES.

Your general tiers (for fiction) are National Magazines (such as *The New Yorker*, *Harper's*, *The Atlantic Monthly*); Top Independents (*Tin House*, *McSweeney's*, *Zoetrope*, *Granta*, *Glimmer Train*); College and University-Supported Reviews (*Ploughshares*, *Missouri Review*, *Black Warrior Review*); Other Independents (*One Story*, *Burnside Review*); Zines. Online publications are being read more and more (*Joyland* and *FiveChapters* are a couple of my faves).

HOW TO SEND?

Many publications these days allow you to submit online; simply follow the instructions for uploading your file that they provide on their site. For those that request hard copy submissions, present your work simply and professionally. No need for pink, scented paper or a special protective folder. Always check each magazine's personal preferences, but in general:

1) double space (unless poetry) and print your work on standard weight paper

2) use a standard font such as Times New Roman, Courier, or Garamond

3) number your pages

4) include on the first page a heading of your name and contact info; you may also wish to include your last name along with the page number in the footer of each subsequent page

5) paperclip pages or staple

6) include a SASE—if they can't respond to your work, they may not even read it. A business-sized envelope is fine, as these days most publications will just recycle your manuscript; but if you wish to receive it back, make sure you include an envelope large enough with adequate postage.

What about the Cover Letter?

In general, keep it simple with something like *I've enclosed this piece for your consideration. Thank you for reading.* If you've been published elsewhere, you can mention it. If you've received other writing-related honors, you might mention those. But all that will matter in the end is whether the reader is impressed by and drawn to your work. I don't recommend trying to be cute in your letter (unless you're submitting to something like *McSweeney's*) or using big writerly-sounding words in efforts to come off serious or smart—this will likely only annoy the reader who's sitting down to read dozens of manuscripts. As with the manuscript itself, no need for special paper.

What's All This about Simultaneous Submissions?

Often a magazine will ask that you do not submit your work simultaneously to other publications—they wish to be the sole publication considering your work at the time. Others say they don't mind receiving simultaneous submissions, so long as you mention in your cover letter that it's under consideration elsewhere.

Of course, they ask these things as a courtesy to them and there's no one who will hunt you down if you disregard such requests. You might wonder how you'll ever get anything published if you're sending to one magazine at a time and waiting up to six months to hear back from each. In truth, the only thing you *must* do is immediately notify the magazines your work is sitting with if and when it is accepted elsewhere.

How Many Should I Send to at a Time?

This is up to you and may depend on how new the draft is or how long your list of magazines is. I usually send to three or four magazines at a time, wait until I've been rejected to all but one, then send to the next batch, possibly giving the work another read and revising first.

What about Contests?

You can try those too. Most of the time they require a submission fee, but you might also receive a one-year subscription in return. Your money helps support the magazine and keeps it alive so that it can publish people like you. You might win the grand prize, often monetary and substantial. Often famous writers are the judges; this can be exciting. Then again, maybe you are poor and would rather just send during open reading periods.

Should I Be Keeping Track of All This?

Yes, I think so. Lately I've been keeping a list of which stories I've sent where and when and the date I receive a response. Patterns will emerge and mistakes won't be made. This is especially handy if you're sending out more than one piece.

If I Am Published, Will I Get Paid Big Bucks and Become Famous?

Probably not, sadly. Unless you make the big splash (your outstanding debut piece in *The New Yorker* that has agents and publishers scrambling, say).

Is it Better to Hold Out for a Big Splash or to Build a Publishing History with Smaller Mags?

Either would be pretty good, I think. Agents seem to say a history is nice but I think they'd also love to land you in *The New Yorker* for your debut.

Some Last Words of Advice:

Expect Rejection—You Won't be Disappointed! (and Possibly Pleasantly Surprised)
It's very difficult to get published, especially as an untested (unpublished) new writer. Just because a magazine isn't *The New Yorker*, for instance, doesn't mean it's necessarily any easier to get into. Journals receive hundreds, even thousands of submissions, and publish the tiniest handful. Famous writers and the editor's friends are submitting too. So make a game of it. Collect your rejection slips with pride, plastering them to the wall or slipping them into an album. Every rejection means you're one step closer to an acceptance,

or so I put it to myself. Don't be disheartened, because your work can't be published if you're not sending it out. And trying makes you feel a part of the game—you're a "real writer," going for it.

Don't Write to Publish, Write to Write.

Succeeding in getting your work accepted is fun, but you'll be surprised how little it changes. Your validation should come from the work of writing itself. Publishing shouldn't be your goal; writing good work you're proud of, should be.

Support the Literary World.

Magazines that can afford to pay you are either supported by wealthy donors or have a large circulation. Magazines get large circulations from having people like you subscribed to them and people like your rich uncle donating. Magazines without much money at all will die and can't publish you. Subscribe to (and read!) a couple of lit journals each year; support these publications and your fellow writers.

CREATIVE

TRUE STORIES,
WELL TOLD.

TIVE

NON

FICTION

ISSUE
38

SPRING 2010 $10.00

PLUS: a history of creative
nonfiction, 1993 to the
present; tiny truths; the future
of the literary magazine; stunt
writing; the art of the start;
and more

Teachers: Use Literary Magazines

by Nicholas Ripatrazone (2009)

Can secondary school teachers save literary magazines? "Save" might not the best choice of words: it presupposes both power in the savior and tremendous need in the recipient. Perhaps help would work better: yes, secondary school teachers can greatly help literary magazines by inculcating excerpts or whole issues into their curriculum. The same dictum applies for university professors, of course, but the consideration must be made that secondary school instructors have a wider breadth of influence, as not every student who graduates high school attends college.

I teach public high-school English full-time. My schedule includes advanced and introductory creative writing courses, as well as a course called Advanced Placement Literature and Composition. I use contemporary literary magazines in all of my courses as often as possible, and—at least based on my perception of student performance and the feedback from alumni—to a fair amount of pedagogical success. Sure, it's important for students to read Thomas Pynchon's *The Crying of Lot 49* and Flannery O'Connor's "Parker's Back," but it's also important for them to know that both writers had published work in *The Kenyon Review*, among other literary magazines. The Pynchons and O'Connors of the present are doing the same—and it would be a short-sighted injustice to avoid the good work accumulating in these "little magazines" and instead pining for and discussing in classrooms the latest novel release.

Before I go any further, I should admit that I could be doing a much better job in my financial support of literary magazines. I wish I could get classroom subscriptions to the *New England Review*, *The Southern Review*, *AGNI*, and other wonderful journals, but those who have worked in public

THE
LITTLE
MAGAZINE

A History and a
Bibliography

education know the difficulties of working within community-voted budgets. Literary magazine subscriptions at the classroom level are an educational luxury, not a need. But that's not a sufficient excuse. I should push for some measure of subscription at the classroom level, and this is certainly a goal for upcoming years.

Here's a sampling of how I've used literary magazines in the classroom. Although Advanced Placement Literature and Composition is geared toward critical rather than creative output, it would be unrealistic to only analyze dated texts. For example, *A Portrait of the Artist as a Young Man* should be taught alongside contemporary work that hopes to fragment narrative; the enigmatic work of Gerard Manley Hopkins would benefit from juxtaposition with new poets. Our most recent critical analysis essay focused on three poems culled from *Verse* (Volume 23, Numbers 1–3). A classroom set of this issue of *Verse* was kindly donated to us by the journal's editor, Brian Henry, and we've since put the texts to good use. Students completed their analyses on G.C. Waldrep's "What Lived in Our Mouths," Emily Wilson's "Micrographia," and James Galvin's "Girl Without Her Nightgown." All three are strong, recent poems that demand rereading and are open to healthy analysis. And, when I returned these graded essays to students, I chose Aimee Nezhukumatathil's wonderfully palpable "Baked Goods" to review salient elements of analysis observed in their written work. I could have chosen work from Sylvia Plath or Theodore Roethke, but "Baked Goods," published in the Summer 2009 issue of *The Indiana Review*, was the perfect complement to the linguistic moves in the three assigned poems. This is not to claim that teachers should ignore the canon, rather that they should recognize the canon is organic, provincial, and born from bias, positive and negative alike. Teachers should certainly choose wisely when they choose from literary magazines, in the same way that they might avoid the "lesser" poems of W. B. Yeats in deference to "The Second Coming."

While some could posit the argument that time-proven texts might be the best reading fodder for literature courses, it is perplexing that teachers of creative writing might not provide work from contemporary literary magazines for their aspiring writers. Besides being essential examples of contemporary applications of the elements of prose and poetry, exposing students to the current trends in literary culture will aid them as they prepare their own manuscripts for submission. (Should a creative writing student know which market is best suited for her work? No. Even MFA students need to research appropriate placement. But a creative writing student, after reading some stories from *Hobart*, should be able to decide whether her work fits that magazine's observed aesthetic, and so begin also to understand where *Hobart* fits into the publishing landscape.)

At the introductory creative writing level, I provide students with sample flash fictions from *Quick Fiction* and *The Indiana Review*. Although I begin with "Cheers" by Jayne Anne Phillips, students truly learn the pivotal elements of flash fiction—situation, characterization, and completion—from the more contemporary samples. From *Quick Fiction*: "Hunger" by Anthony Varallo, "Open" by Mary Miller, and "Tether" by Susannah Felts. Then, from *The Indiana Review*: "New Grocery Strategy" by Mark Leidner and "Fat Children" by Natalie Day. We read these flash fictions and define the genre from the inside; we define by observation, not prescription. And then, of course, students write their own flash fictions, and I even encourage them to submit that work to representative markets after a class period of instruction on preparing work for submission.

The students in my advanced fiction courses are strong, well-read writers, many of whom major in creative writing or a related discipline, and student exposure to the world of literary magazines is essential in this course. Anything less would be a disservice to them. We begin with Blake Butler's powerful "The Disappeared," from the *New Ohio Review*, then move into Benjamin Percy's timely "Refresh, Refresh," originally published in *The Paris Review*. Both allow me to create a critical foundation for advanced storytelling. Since the advanced fiction course is a year-long endeavor, we read far too many pieces to mention here, but two notables are "We Make Mud" by Peter Markus, also from the donated edition of *Verse*, and Megan Mayhew Bergman's recent non-fiction piece, "How to Make Collard Greens," from *Mississippi Review*. "We Make Mud" is a model of the rhetorical impact of recursivity; Bergman's essay is a wonder at the sentence-level, an example of how a work can accumulate through feeling rather than plot (and how creative nonfiction can help fiction writers).

Next semester I'll begin teaching contemporary literature courses at Rutgers University, and I intend to continue the trend of integrating literary magazines into the classroom. Whether the pedagogical goal is analysis, comparison, or simply exposure, literary magazines are the literature of the moment, and students benefit from such contemporary reading.

RANDOM ANNOTATED BIBLIOGRAPHY ON AMERICAN LITERARY MAGAZINES

Anderson, Elliott and Mary Kinzie. *The Little Magazine in America: A Modern Documentary History*. Pushcart Press: Yonkers, 1978. Written as a companion to Princeton Press's 1947 history of the little magazines, this *Modern Documentary* compiled by *TriQuarterly* and published in conjunction with Pushcart Press is a very different beast than the Princeton edition (see below). Where the Princeton book liked to wax philosophical about the meaning of the magazines and the writing published within them—to discuss them in a more ephemeral, theoretical manner—this book goes straight to the heart of the matter of literary magazines, asking editors of these magazines how it all happened, how it works, what they did (do) and why. Though an uneven book again, this one is much more satisfactorily uneven than the Princeton. As its text comes from editorials by literary magazine editors or interviews with them, the book seems to grow right out of the essential diversity of the literary magazine genre in America, and in this way the book not only forms a documentary of literary magazines, but it is an event in the world of literary magazines, adding and increasing to their diversity. Again, like the Princeton, this text comes with a thorough bibliography of past and current literary magazines.

Hoffman, Frederick J., Charles Allen, and Carolyn P. Ulrich. *The Little Magazine: A History and a Bibliography*. 2nd edition. Princeton University Press: Princeton, 1947. This is the seminal work of study on the literary magazine in the United States, cited in nearly all lengthy studies on the little magazine. Hoffman and Co. cover the literary magazine from its beginnings with *The Dial*—though they do not spend much time with the early *Dial*. Most of their attentions are focused on modernist and regional literary magazines, taking a side road every once in a while into the university literary magazine. The work is thorough enough for an introduction, but the authors soon get bogged down in literary analysis of the journals, at times going for pages on end without mentioning a literary journal by name while at the same time mentioning Freud perhaps two dozen times. Work includes bibliography of literary magazines from 1891's *The Mirror* to 1946's *The New York Quarterly of Poetry*.

Joost, Nicholas. *Ernest Hemingway and the Little Magazines: The Paris Years.* Barre Publishers: Barre, 1968. Joost gives a (sometimes overly dramatic) narrative history of Hemingway being first published and rejected between the years 1921 and 1935 in the little magazines *The Dial*, *The Double-Dealer* (where Hemingway published his first story and poems), *The Little Review*, Ezra Pound's short-lived *Exile*, *Broom*, *Poetry*, *The Transatlantic Review*, *Transition*, *The Yellow Book*, and *This Quarter*, which, in 1931, was Hemingway's final appearance in any of these or other little magazines. What is most interesting in Joost's book for literary magazine scholars is his nit-picking attention to the primary texts of the literary magazines he refers to, isolating dates of and persons behind specific editorial decisions—this is a precision unseen in the majority of literary magazine studies.

Kenner, Hugh. *The Pound Era.* University of California Press: Berkeley, 1971. Kenner's descriptions of Pound's influence on the early twentieth century literary magazines are relayed in a very broad, sporadic, and energetic manner, so, though we get the gist of, say, the compilation of the first imagist issue of a literary magazine in *The Glebe* (as well as engaging writing on Pound's influence on *Blast*), what we get this gist from is largely narrative, which, though making Kenner's book highly engaging and literary, is not the perfect reference one would want to check when ascertaining specific names, dates, or events. Sadly, Kenner seems to leave out Pound's own literary magazine creation, the prophetically named *Exile*.

Marek, Jayne E. *Women Editing Modernism: "Little" Magazines and Literary History*. University of Kentucky Press: Lexington, 1995. An exhilarating read about the major role of women editors in the making of not only the modern literary journal, but also the making of early twentieth century literary modernism. Too often modernist literary magazines are interpreted by critics as though having emerged from Ezra Pound's forehead fully born. This book illuminates not only that the literary magazine world is hardly a man's world but that—at least in regards to the early twentieth century, modernist texts, and some women named Marianne Moore (*The Dial*), Margaret Anderson (*The Little Review*), Jane Heap (*The Little Review*), Harriet Monroe (*Poetry*), Alice Corbin Henderson (*Poetry*), H.D. (*The Egoist*), and Bryer (*The Egoist*)—this world was in many ways shaped by the influences of talented female editors. Not only does Marek dim Pound's historical luminesence by devoting space to these women editors working alongside him, she goes one further, devoting her final chapter to showing that, though Pound was undoubtedly influential in the literary magazine world, he "attempt[ed] to control the editorial directions of little magazines headed by women, and his statements about such magazines in articles and correspondence form an extreme expression of a male-oriented viewpoint through which modernist women's editorial and critical activities have often been viewed—or ignored."

Morrison, Mark S. *The Public Face of Modernism: Little Magazines, Audiences, and Reception, 1905–1920*. University of Wisconsin Press: Madison, 2001. Morrison's book convincingly argues how early twentieth century literary magazine editors such as Ezra Pound (in *Blast*, *Exile*, and others), Ford Madox Ford (in *The English Review*), Dora Marsden (in *The Freewoman*), Margaret Anderson (in *The Little Review*), and Max Eastman (in *The Masses*) were essential participants in the modernist movement. Though this is not a significantly new reading of these magazines or their editors, Morrison's analysis is more thorough than any before and engages the subject in a broader, more expansive way than others have (something roundly asserted when one stumbles upon Morrison's substantial seventeen page, single-spaced works cited list). What is engagingly new here is Morrison's assertion that these modernist editors did not view the new magazine technology and commercial viability in the early twentieth century with disdain, as many literary magazine editors did, but instead "saw the new commercial magazine genres and the advertising that supported them as providing opportunities for modernism."

Peterson, Theodore. *Magazines in the Twentieth Century.* 2ⁿᵈ edition. University of IllinoisPress: Urbana, 1964. Peterson (sadly) isolates the beginning of modern magazine publishing to a broad span of two decades: from March 3, 1879 to a day in 1899—or, from the instigation of a new postal act in 1879, giving greatly reduced mailing rates to periodicals, up until "George Horace Lorimer slid into the editor's chair of the Saturday Evening Post and set about attuning it to popular tastes." Though this edition of Peterson's survey of the American magazine in the twentieth century is overbearingly commercial in its focus, it does, in a small section of the appallingly titled chapter "Magazines for Cultural Minorities," discuss the literary magazine for about fifteen pages, focusing largely on their lack of funds and devoting much more time in the same chapter to magazines like *The Nation* and *Harper's*. Still, Peterson's dissection and elucidation of the financial and circulative aspects of the national magazine industry (at least up until the mid 1970s) is top notch.

Scholes, Robert and Clifford Wulfman. *Modernism in the Magazines: An Introduction.* Yale University Press: New Haven, 2010. Modernist Journals Project (www.modjourn.org) co-editors Scholes and Wulfman give the first thorough overview of specifically how and why to study literary magazines. This is a fantastic resource for beginning scholars and educators looking towards literary magazines—especially modernist ones—as a subject of study. Finally, the book offers an interesting (and refreshingly critical) argument that all of this study of literary magazines began, as with so many things regarding the subject, with Ezra Pound.

"The Literary Magazine in America." *The Missouri Review.* Volume 7, number 1. 1986. Pages 175–259. If only more literary magazines devoted such focus and insight to themselves. From Eric Staley's insightful analysis of the birth of the literary magazine alongside the invention of the short story and nationwide saturation of magazine advertising [included in this book] to Reginald Gibbons's criticism of the hegemony of the literary magazine world and its lack of aesthetic focus, the issue contrasts the theoretical backgrounds of literary magazines with their actualities in the world.

Wood, James. *Magazines in the United States*. The Ronald Press Company: New York, 1956.

The most impressive thing about this dated but informative text is its detailed description of the beginning of the United States' oldest extant literary magazine, *The North American Review*—a description made fascinating by its connection to the lives of John Quincy Adams's son and grandson, Henry Adams. Little magazines as a group, though, are all but left out of this book, given only three pages in the book's final chapter. Even then Wood brings the focus away from the accomplishments of literary magazines in order to lament the fact that commercial magazines don't publish good fiction—though he seems to reassure himself again with the realization, "That they publish light fiction which millions enjoy is a fact." Well, perhaps.

CONTRIBUTOR BIOS

Gwen Allen is Assistant Professor of Art History at San Francisco State University and the author of *Artists' Magazines: An Alternative Space for Art* (MIT Press, 2011).

Andrew Foster Altschul is the author of the novels *Lady Lazarus* and *Deus Ex Machina*, and the founding Books Editor of *The Rumpus*.

Jane Armstrong's stories and essays have appeared in *Newsweek*, *North American Review*, *Mississippi Review*, *Beloit Fiction Journal*, *New Orleans Review*, *River Teeth*, *Brevity* and elsewhere. Her commentaries have aired on National Public Radio's All Things Considered. She teaches at Northern Arizona University in Flagstaff.

David Barringer is a writer, designer, and teacher. He teaches at MICA and Winthrop University. His books on design include *There's Nothing Funny About Design* (Princeton Architectural Press, 2009) and *American Mutt Barks in the Yard* (Emigre 68, 2005). He has written novels and fiction collections. Barringer is currently working on a couple design books, several screenplays, and a big novel that combines conversation with graphic design. www.davidbarringer.com

Frederick Barthelme is the author of 14 works of fiction, most recently the novel *Waveland* (Doubleday, 2009). He is also author of the memoir *Double Down: Reflections on Gambling and Loss* (Houghton Mifflin, 1999), co-written with his brother, Steven Barthelme. He was director of The Center For

Writers at The University of Southern Mississippi and editor of *Mississippi Review* for over three decades, and is currently the editor of *Blip Magazine*.

Pierre Bayle (1647–1706) was a French philosopher and writer best known for his biographical dictionary *Historical and Critical Dictionary*, published beginning in 1695. Bayle founded the periodical *Nouvelles de la république des lettres*—considered by some as the first literary magazine—in 1684, editing and largely writing it until 1687.

Laura van den Berg's stories have or will soon appear in *One Story, Conjunctions, American Short Fiction, Ploughshares, Glimmer Train, Best American Nonrequired Reading 2008, Best New American Voices 2010*, and *The Pushcart Prize XXIV*. Her debut collection of stories, *What the World Will Look Like When All the Water Leaves Us* (Dzanc Books, 2009), was a Barnes & Noble "Discover Great New Writers" selection, longlisted for The Story Prize, and shortlisted for the Frank O'Connor International Award. She is also the author of the chapbook *There Will Be No More Good Nights Without Good Nights* (Origami Zoo Press, 2012). She lives in Baltimore.

Paul Bixler was a founding editor of *Antioch Review* and his essays appeared in the journal from March 1941 until the summer of 1979. He served on the *Antioch Review* board for many years. He died in 1991.

T. C. Boyle is the author of twenty-three books of fiction, most recently *San Miguel* (2012). His stories have appeared in most of the major American magazines, including *The New Yorker, Harper's*, and *The Atlantic Monthly*, and he has been the recipient of a number of literary awards, including the PEN/Faulkner Prize, the PEN/Malamud Prize, and the Prix Médicis Étranger. He has been a member of the English Department at the University of Southern California since 1978, where he is Distinguished Professor of English. He currently lives near Santa Barbara with his wife and three children.

Aaron Burch has had stories appear in *New York Tyrant, Barrelhouse, Another Chicago Magazine*, and *Quick Fiction*, among other publications. He is the author of the chapbook *How to Take Yourself Apart, How to Make Yourself Anew* (PANK Books, 2010) and the novella *How to Predict the Weather* (Keyhole Press, 2010). He is the editor of the literary journal *Hobart*.

Katie Chase's stories have appeared in *Five Chapters, ZYZZYVA, The Missouri Review, Prairie Schooner*, and elsewhere. Her work has been honored with inclusion in the Best American Short Stories series, a Pushcart Prize, and third place in *Narrative*'s Winter 2010 Story Contest. She received an

MFA from the Iowa Writers' Workshop, where she was a Teaching-Writing Fellow and a Provost's Post-Graduate Writing Fellow.

Billy Collins is a former U.S. Poet Laureate (2001–2003) who has published eight collections of poetry and two anthologies. Billy Collins is a Distinguished Professor of English at Lehman College of the City University of New York, as well as a Senior Distinguished Fellow of the Winter Park Institute at Rollins College. His next book, *Aimless Love: Poems 2003–2013*, will be released in October 2013.

Ralph Waldo Emerson (1803–1882) was the well-known American author largely remembered for his essays and prominence in the counter-culture transcendentalist movement.

Len Fulton (1934–2011) was the publisher of Dustbooks and the *Small Press Review*, one of the most comprehensive indexes of literary magazines and small presses.

Megan M. Garr is the author of *The Preservationist Documents* (Pilot Books, 2012) and the editor of the literary & arts journal *Versal*, which she founded in 2002. Originally from Nashville, Megan lives in Amsterdam, the Netherlands with her wife, artist Shayna Schapp. www.meganmgarr.com

Roxane Gay's writing has appeared in *Best American Short Stories 2012*, *Oxford American*, the *Rumpus*, the *Wall Street Journal*, and many other publications. She co-edits *PANK*, is publisher of Tiny Hardcore Press, and serves as a regular contributor to *HTMLGIANT*. Her multi-genre collection, *Ayiti*, was published by Artistically Declined Press in 2011.

Aaron Gilbreath has written essays and articles, some forthcoming, for *The New York Times*, *Paris Review*, *Kenyon Review*, *Tin House*, *The Threepenny Review*, *Oxford American*, *The Awl* and others. Future Tense Publishing put out his chapbook *A Secondary Landscape*, and his essay "Dreams of the Atomic Era," from *Cincinnati Review*, was a notable mention in *The Best American Essays 2011*. He writes about food, music and miscellany at http://aarongilbreath.wordpress.com

Peter Gizzi is the author of several collections of poetry, including *The Outernationale* (Wesleyan, 2007), *Some Values of Landscape and Weather* (2003), and *Artificial Heart* (1998). Gizzi has been poetry editor for *The Nation* as well as founding co-editor, with Connell McGrath, of *o•blék: a journal of language arts*. He has also published several magazines, limited-edition chapbooks, folios, and artist books. His work has been widely anthologized and translated into numerous languages. He is a professor at University of Massachusetts Amherst.

Mary Grimm is the author of the novel *Left to Themselves* and the short story collection *Stealing Time*, both from Random House. Her short stories have appeared in *The New Yorker*, *Redbook*, *Antioch Review*, and elsewhere. She teaches fiction writing at Case Western Reserve University.

Raymond Hammond is the editor of *New York Quarterly*.

Marcelle Heath is Editor-at-Large for *Luna Park Review*. She is a contributing editor for Fictionaut and a fiction writer. Her stories have appeared in *Wigleaf*, *PANK*, *Snake Nation Review*, *Necessary Fiction*, *Matchbook*, and other journals. She works as a freelance editor and lives in Portland, Oregon. www.marcelleheath.com

Eli Horowitz was the managing editor and then publisher of McSweeney's for eight years, working closely with authors including Chris Adrian, Salvador Plascencia, Deb Olin Unferth, Michael Chabon, Adam Levin, Joyce Carol Oates, and William Vollmann. He is the coauthor of *The Clock Without a Face*, a treasure-hunt mystery, and *Everything You Know Is Pong*, an illustrated cultural history of ping pong, and his design work has been honored by *I.D.*, *Print* and the American Institute of Graphic Arts. Before McSweeney's, he was employed as a carpenter and wrote science trivia questions tenuously linked to popular films. He was born in Virginia and now lives in San Francisco.

Lucy Ives is the author of a long poem, *Anamnesis*, and the forthcoming *Early Poems*. She is a contributing editor at *Triple Canopy*.

Abby Ann Arthur Johnson was a prominent scholar of African American literature and faculty member at Howard University.

Richard Kostelanetz is the author of numerous books as both writer and editor—such as the recent *SoHo: The Rise and Fall of an Artists' Colony* (Routledge, 2003) and *Recircuits* (New York Quarterly Books, 2009)—the creator of artworks in a variety of media, and has been awarded a number of prizes and grants. Kostelanetz began his literary career writing critical pieces for magazines such as *Partisan Review* and *The Hudson Review*, and he remains one of the most prodigious documentarians of small press publishing in the late 20th century. www.richardkostelanetz.com

Travis Kurowski's writing has appeared in *Hobart*, *Ninth Letter*, *TriQuarterly*, *Creative Nonfiction*, and elsewhere, and he writes the "Literary MagNet"

column for *Poets & Writers*. In 2008 he co-guest edited with Gary Percesepe an issue of *Mississippi Review* on literary magazines, which was developed into this book. He teaches creative writing and literature at York College of Pennsylvania.

Linda Lappin is the author of *The Etruscan*, a novel set in Italy in 1922.

Herbert Leibowitz has been the editor of the literary magazine *Parnassus* since he helped found it in 1973. Leibowitz is the author of *Fabricating Lives: Explorations in American Autobiography* (New Directions, 1991) and *Something Urgent I Have to Say to You: The Life and Works of William Carlos Williams* (Farrar, Straus and Giroux, 2011). He lives in New York City.

Ben Leubner teaches literature at Montana State University.

Ralph Lombreglia is the author of the short story collections *Men Under Water* and *Make Me Work*, and has been the recipient of support from the Guggenheim and Whiting foundations as well as the National Endowment for the Arts. He is now working on a novel.

Jayne Marek is the author of *Women Editing Modernism: "Little" Magazines & Literary History* (University Press of Kentucky, 1995). She is a professor of English at Franklin College.

Shara McCallum is the author of four books of poetry, *This Strange Land, Song of Thieves, The Water Between Us*, and *The Face of Water: New & Selected Poems*. Her poems and personal essays have appeared in numerous literary journals and been reprinted in over twenty anthologies of American, African American, Caribbean, and World poetry. McCallum is a professor of English at Bucknell University and the director of the Stadler Center for Poetry.

David Messineo is publisher and poetry editor of *Sensations Magazine*, a three-time winner in the national American Literary Magazine Awards. The author of eight books of poetry, his poetry has been published on four continents.

Harriet Monroe (1860–1936) was a poet and the founding editor of *Poetry*, the nation's longest running literary magazine devoted to poetry, and one of the most influential literary magazines in history.

Speer Morgan is a professor of English at University of Missouri in Columbia and has been editor of *The Missouri Review* since 1980. Morgan won

Best Story of the Year from *Prairie Schooner*, an American Book Award in 1999, and a Lawrence Foundation Prize in 2000. His story "The Big Bang" received the Goodheart Prize for *Shenandoah*'s best story of 2008. Morgan has contributed short stories to several other magazines and journals, including *Harper's*, the *Atlantic Monthly*, *Northwest Review*, *New Letters*, *River Styx*, and *Iowa Review*.

Ian Morris is co-founder and editor of Fifth Star Press and a former associate editor for *TriQuarterly*.

Rick Moody is the author of five novels, three collections of stories, a memoir, and, most recently, a collection of essays, *On Celestial Music*. He also sings and plays in The Wingdale Community Singers.

Gorham Munson (1896–1969) was a literary critic and teacher. In 1922 he founded *Secession*, a foundational avant garde New York literary magazine, which ran for eight issues.

n+1 was founded by Keith Gessen, Mark Greif, Chad Harbach, Benjamin Kunkel, Allison Lorentzen, and Marco Roth.

Jay Neugeboren is the author of eighteen books, including two prize-winning novels (*The Stolen Jew, Before My Life Began*), two award-winning books of non-fiction (*Imagining Robert, Transforming Madness*), and three collections of award-winning stories. His stories have appeared in *The Atlantic, Esquire, Virginia Quarterly Review, Best American Short Stories, The O. Henry Prize Stories*, and *Penguin Modern Stories*. He is the only author to have won six consecutive Syndicated Fiction Prizes. He lives in New York City.

Charles Newman (1938–2006) was a novelist, literary critic, and founding editor of the nationally acclaimed *TriQuarterly* from Northwestern University, in many ways forming the model for future literary magazines in the United States. His posthumous novel, *In Partial Disgrace*, is to be released from Dalkey Archive Press in February 2013.

Gary Percesepe is Associate Editor at *BLIP Magazine* and a contributor to *The Nervous Breakdown*. A former assistant fiction editor at *Antioch Review*, his fiction, poetry, essays, and interviews have been published at *Story Quarterly, n+1, Salon, Mississippi Review, The Millions, PANK*, and other places. He is the author of four books in philosophy, including *Future(s) of Philosophy: The Marginal Thinking of Jacques Derrida*. He just completed his second novel, *Leaving Telluride*, set in Telluride, Colorado.

Benjamin Percy is the author of two novels, *Red Moon* (Grand Central/Hachette, 2013) and *The Wilding*, as well as two books of short stories, *Refresh, Refresh* and *The Language of Elk*. His fiction and nonfiction have been published in *Esquire* (where he is a contributing editor), *GQ*, *Time*, *Men's Journal*, *Outside*, the *Wall Street Journal*, *Tin House* and the *Paris Review*. His honors include an NEA fellowship, the Whiting Writer's Award, the Plimpton Prize, the Pushcart Prize and inclusion in Best American Short Stories and Best American Comics. He is the writer-in-residence at St. Olaf College and teaches at the low-residency MFA program at Pacific University.

Felix Pollak (1909–1987) was an American poet and librarian. During his tenure at University of Wisconsin from 1959 until 1974, he developed the Sukov collection of literary magazines—now called the Little Magazine Collection—one of the world's finest collections of literary magazines.

Andrew Porter is the author of the story collection *The Theory of Light and Matter*, which won the Flannery O'Connor Award for Short Fiction, and the novel *In Between Days*, which was a Barnes & Noble "Discover Great New Writers" selection. A graduate of the Iowa Writers' Workshop, he has received a Pushcart Prize, a James Michener/Copernicus Fellowship, and the W.K. Rose Fellowship in the Creative Arts. His work has appeared in *One Story*, *The Threepenny Review*, and on public radio's Selected Shorts. Currently, he teaches fiction writing and directs the creative writing program at Trinity University in San Antonio, Texas.

Ezra Pound (1885–1972) was a major poet and critic of literary modernism, most remembered for his epic poem *The Cantos*. Pound was inarguably the most persuasive single voice in early 20th century American literary magazines, influencing to various degrees the directions of such canonical publications as *Little Review* and *Poetry*.

Hilda Raz is Luschei Professor of English and Gender Studies, emerita, at the University of Nebraska. She was the editor of *Prairie Schooner* and the founding director of the *Prairie Schooner* Book Prizes. Now she is the editor of the Mary Burritt Christiansen Poetry Series, University of New Mexico Press, and the poetry editor for *Bosque*. She has published twelve books including a memoir with Aaron Raz Link, *What Becomes You*, and *Trans* and *All Odd and Splendid* (poetry). She lives in Placitas, New Mexico.

Stacey Richter is the author of two short story collections, *My Date with Satan* and *Twin Study*. She lives in Tucson, Arizona.

Nicholas Ripatrazone is the author of two books of poetry, *Oblations* and *This Is Not About Birds* (Gold Wake Press 2012) and a forthcoming book of non-fiction, *The Fine Delight* (Cascade Books 2013). His fiction has appeared in *Esquire* and *The Kenyon Review*, and has received honors from *ESPN: The Magazine*.

Jill Allyn Rosser has published three books of poetry: *Bright Moves*, winner of the Morse Poetry Prize; *Misery Prefigured*, winner of the Crab Orchard Award; and, most recently, *Foiled Again*, winner of the New Criterion Poetry Prize. She has received the Lavan Award for younger poets from the Academy of American Poets, and fellowships from the National Endowment for the Arts, the Ohio State Arts Council, and the New Jersey State Council on the Arts. She teaches at Ohio University, where she is the editor of the *New Ohio Review*.

Marco Roth (b. 1974) is a co-founding editor of *n+1* magazine, and the author, most recently, of *The Scientists: A Family Romance* (FSG, 2012).

Benjamin Samuel is an editor at *Electric Literature*. He has an MFA in Fiction from Brooklyn College, and lives in Brooklyn with his dog, Bela Lugosi.

Kyle Schlesinger is a poet who writes and lectures on the art of the book. His recent books of poetry include: *Parts of Speech* (Chax Press, 2013), *Picture Day* (Electio Editions, 2012); *Bad Words to the Radio and Other Poems* (Least Weasel, 2011); and *What You Will* (NewLights Press, 2011). In 2010 he curated Poems & Pictures: A Renaissance in the Art of the Book at the Center for Book Arts in New York City. He is proprietor of Cuneiform Press and co-director of the Graduate Program in Publishing at UHV.

Jim Shepard is the author of eleven books of fiction, including 2007 Story Prize winner, *Like You'd Understand Anyway* (Knopf, 2008), and the short story collection, *You Think That's Bad* (Knopf, 2011). He teaches fiction and film at Williams College.

Eric Staley was a co-founder of *The Missouri Review* as a graduate student, it's first managing editor, its first designer (creating a design for the magazine that lasted until recent history), and former Executive Director of AWP.

Jodee Stanley is the editor of *Ninth Letter*, the award-winning literary/arts journal published by UIUC's MFA in Creative Writing Program in collaboration with the School of Art and Design. She has worked in literary publishing for twenty years and has been a speaker and panelist at various conferences and festivals, including Bread Loaf, AWP, MLA, and the

Kenyon Review Literary Festival. In 2009, she was awarded an Academic Professional Award from the College of Liberal Arts and Sciences at UIUC, and she received a 2007 Faculty Fellowship from the University of Illinois Academy for Entrepreneurial Leadership. Her fiction, essays, and book reviews have appeared in several publications including *Crab Orchard Review*, *Mississippi Review*, *Hobart*, *Cincinnati Review*, *Future Fire*, *BkMk Quarterly*, *The Smoking Poet*, *580 Split*, and *Electric Velocipede*, and have received special mention in the 2004 Year's Best Fantasy and Horror and the 2001 Pushcart Prize. She is currently co-editing an anthology of Midwest Gothic fiction.

Algernon de Vivier Tassin was a playwright, author, and early early scholar of periodical studies, with his seminal 1916 study, *The Magazine in America*.

G. C. Waldrep's most recent books are *Your Father on the Train of Ghosts* (BOA Editions, 2011), a collaboration with John Gallaher, and *The Arcadia Project: North American Postmodern Pastoral* (Ahsahta, 2012), co-edited with Joshua Corey. He teaches at Bucknell University, edits the journal *West Branch*, and serves as Editor-at-Large for *The Kenyon Review*.

Adrian Todd Zuniga is the host/creator/CCO of Literary Death Match (a literary event now featured in 43 cities worldwide), and the founding editor of *Opium Magazine*. His fiction has recently been featured in *Gopher Illustrated* and *Stymie*, and online at *Lost Magazine* and *McSweeney's*. He lives between Los Angeles and guest rooms all over Europe. He longs for a Chicago Cubs World Series and an EU passport.